Arc of Power

Arc of Power

INSIDE NANCY PELOSI'S SPEAKERSHIP, 2005–2010

JOHN A. LAWRENCE

UNIVERSITY PRESS OF KANSAS

Published by the University Press of Kansas (Lawrence, Kansas 66045), which was
organized by the Kansas Board of Regents and is operated and funded by Emporia
State University, Fort Hays State University, Kansas State University, Pittsburg
State University, the University of Kansas, and Wichita State University.

Library of Congress Cataloging-in-Publication Data

Names: Lawrence, John A., 1949– author.
Title: Arc of power : inside Nancy Pelosi's speakership, 2005–2010 /
John A. Lawrence.
Description: Lawrence, Kansas : University Press of Kansas, 2022. |
Includes bibliographical references and index.
Identifiers: LCCN 2022007577
ISBN 9780700633791 (cloth)
ISBN 9780700633814 (ebook)
Subjects: LCSH: Pelosi, Nancy, 1940– | United States. Congress.
House—Speakers. | Political culture—United States. | United
States—Politics and government—2001–2009. | United States—Politics
and government—2009–2017. | BISAC: BIOGRAPHY & AUTOBIOGRAPHY /
Political | POLITICAL SCIENCE / American Government / Legislative Branch
Classification: LCC E840.8.P37 L39 2022 | DDC 328.73/092
[B]—dc23/eng/20220719
LC record available at https://lccn.loc.gov/2022007577.

British Library Cataloguing-in-Publication Data is available.

Printed in the United States of America
10 9 8 7 6 5 4 3 2 1

The paper used in this publication is acid free and meets the minimum
requirements of the American National Standard for Permanence
of Paper for Printed Library Materials Z39.48–1992.

Contents

Dedication and Acknowledgments   vii

Introduction   ix

Prologue: Discouraged, Disorganized, Defeated   xiii

1 The New Direction: "6 for '06"   1

2 "I Had to Win the House First"   12

3 Madam Speaker   23

4 "Everything Becomes Urgent"   31

5 "The Slowest Ship"   38

6 The Economy Wobbles   50

7 "The Flagship"   60

8 "You Can't Have It the Way You Want to Have It"   72

9 "The Prospects Don't Look Good"   87

10 Yes, We Can!   96

11 The Abyss   108

12 "We Have to Look Out for Ourselves"   123

13 "The Country Is Falling Apart!"   131

14 "Like Swans Going across the Lake"   139

15 The Firehose   155

16 Short-Circuited   165

17 "Number One among Equals"   177

18 The Summer of Hate   192

19 "The Most Important Bill You Will Ever Vote For"   199

20 "Let's Go for It!"   211

21 The Unwinnable War   227

22 "Keep Steering the Ship"   239

23 The Unfinished Agenda   255

24 The "Shellacking"   261

25 Their Last Bow   277

Conclusion: The Perishability of Power   287

Notes   297

Bibliographical Guide to the John A. Lawrence Papers   345

Selected Bibliography   349

Index   353

Dedication and Acknowledgments

This book is dedicated to the men and women who serve as staff in the House and Senate.

Intelligent, committed, anonymous, loyal, driven, underpaid, and perennially exhausted, they play an invaluable role in the operation of our Congress and the preservation of our government. The best representative or senator would be hard-pressed to function without them and disingenuous to minimize their dedication, skill, and contributions. Throughout this book, I generally avoid referencing their names out of consideration for their privacy and confidentiality, but their expertise is found in every policy and strategy described in this account.

I also dedicate this book to my wife, Deborah Phillips, professor of psychology at Georgetown University, whose many sacrifices that allowed me to pursue a career in the House of Representatives are matched only by her encouragement of my subsequent academic endeavors, including the writing of this book.

I would like to acknowledge David Congdon of the University Press of Kansas for his steady support for this project and my agent, Lauren Sharp of Aevitas Creative Management, for her valued assistance with my publishing efforts. I am grateful to faculty colleagues at the University of California Washington Center, fellow scholars and other students of the Congress, the staff of the Library of Congress Manuscript Division, and colleagues from my years on Capitol Hill—members and staff alike—whose insights, recollections, and encouragement have contributed greatly to the production of this book.

Introduction

"Winning is good," Speaker of the House Nancy Pelosi has observed. "Are you talking about the [San Francisco] Warriors or politics?" a reporter followed up. "Anywhere," she responded. "It's always preferable."[1]

This book is a unique examination of the winning, the exercise, and the loss of political power by congressional Democrats in a crisis-ridden but highly productive period: the last two years of the Bush presidency and the first two of the Obama era. In a nation as large, complex, and divided along partisan lines as the contemporary United States, the struggle to secure a congressional majority requires a deft combination of strategic planning, party discipline, and luck provided by uncontrollable events.

Utilizing that power is just as complicated, whether during periods of divided government as in 2007–8 or, as was the case in 2009–10, with one party comfortably in control of the legislative and executive branches. As the history of this period demonstrates, the successful exercise of power often results in political decisions that can destabilize that very power and or destroy it altogether. Majorities, alliances, and agreements are ephemeral and can change after a protracted election campaign or a day of unanticipated events. It is why Washington, DC, is "a perishable city," as Nancy Pelosi is fond of observing.

This "arc of power"—the gaining, exercise, and loss of political power—is the subject this book documents: the issues, institutions, and personalities that clash and collaborate in the wielding of power during a turbulent five-year period. The major actors are the key political leaders in the House, Senate, and White House. The issues that consume their energies range from matters of war to health care, from economic crisis to political corruption.

This book admits the reader to a unique degree into the conversations,

friendships, animosities, rivalries, and confrontations: the meetings and negotiations that produce the policies that are the focus of most political histories.
Readers will come to appreciate the sheer number and miscellany of issues that
demand the attention of political leaders and underlay the unrelenting pressures
that are ever present in the policy-making process.

As a trained historian and Capitol Hill veteran of over thirty years, I was
uniquely situated for eight years as the chief of staff to Nancy Pelosi both as
Speaker and minority leader, a participant in hundreds of conversations that
would otherwise be undocumented or only recalled days or years after they
occurred. Serving as a major source for this account are nearly nine thousand
pages of contemporaneous handwritten notes I took during my eight years as
Pelosi's chief of staff. These notes, together with other papers, are deposited in
the Manuscript Division of the Library of Congress. Along with my transcrip-
tions of much of this material, these notes will be available in the future to
researchers. It is important to note that these accounts were not recalled after
the fact but recorded in real time, as participants were speaking, and thus reflect
the most accurate version of these interactions ever likely to become available.

All of the quotations attributed to individuals are derived from my notes,
and most are referenced here in footnotes. On occasion, I have not attributed
quotations to a specific person due to considerations of anonymity. And while
some of the language quoted might strike some readers as unusually frank, I
have declined to use many quotations that would have marketability only for
their shock value. My goal is not to produce ephemeral headlines of who said
what to whom, but rather to help readers understand the complex personal,
institutional, and political relationships among the men and women who determine the political course of this nation.

This book is not intended to serve as a complete history of the Pelosi speakership (which resumed in 2019) nor as a biography of the first woman to lead
the legislative branch of the government. It is rather a history of this time during
which she, among others included in this story, played a determinative role by
their actions involving both foreign and domestic issues of the highest magni-
tude. Despite my best efforts to maintain the dispassionate distance from my
subject that historians strive to achieve, this work inevitably reflects perspec-
tives attributable to my years on Capitol Hill and my perspective in experienc-
ing these events from the viewpoint of the House of Representatives. Other
accounts will analyze these events from alternative viewpoints and may draw
different conclusions. Similarly, while I admit my admiration for Mrs. Pelosi's
devotion to the Congress and her consummate parliamentary skills, this book is

not intended to serve as an homage or an apologia. Where I believe her decisions merit critical evaluation, I have not hesitated to offer it.

While I have striven to remove myself largely from much of this account, occasionally I have incorporated personal experiences and observations when an event or conversation would be instructive for the reader. Such material is clearly set off from the other text.

While this book is very much the product of my records and research, I do want to extend my deepest appreciation to the members of Congress, my fellow staff, White House personnel, and others whose diligent efforts on behalf of our government are recorded in these pages. I am hopeful that they will recognize the frenetic, exhilarating, infuriating, and satisfying whirlwind that is congressional politics at its highest and most rewarding levels.

For those with less experience in the mosh pit of Capitol Hill, I am confident this account can help explain why it is so challenging to formulate complex national policies, even when the political stars have seemingly aligned to provide large congressional majorities and a president of one's own party in the White House. This history also offers hopes for a restoration of a less divided, or at least more functional, Washington, DC, as illustrated by moments that display the ability of political competitors during periods of divided government to put aside at least temporarily the ideological beliefs that divide them and collaborate on behalf of the country.

"Nobody ever gives away power," Pelosi has said. "When you get it, you must use it."[2] Rarely is it used as unilaterally or decisively as the most partisan and expectant of activists hope. "I am a master legislator," Pelosi boasts. "I know the budget to the nth degree. I know the motivation of people and I respect the people who are in Congress."[3] But knowledge of the policy and the formal process is not enough to be a successful leader on Capitol Hill, and Pelosi as Speaker demonstrated a unique set of wide-ranging skills needed to produce legislation in her often fractious chamber and to defend that work product, with varying degree of success, in clashes with other individual and institutional interests.

"We campaign in poetry," the saying goes, "but we govern in prose." Inevitably, this is a book about the often-frustrating struggle to reconcile the promises of a campaign with the realities of governing amid conflicting personalities, parties, institutions, factions, and ambitions. Resolving that incongruity, while retaining the integrity of what you initially came to Washington to accomplish, is what successful political leadership is all about and, ultimately, a lesson everyone engaged in politics must learn.

Prologue: Discouraged, Disorganized, Defeated

"I can do better than these guys," Nancy Pelosi (D-CA) decided after the 2000 congressional election. For the fourth time since losing their forty-year hold on the House of Representatives in 1994, the party's leaders had again fallen short. "Don't agonize," she declared, "organize!"

Democrats had plummeted into a deep chasm following the Supreme Court's *Bush v. Gore* decision on December 12, 2000. Not only had a few hundred mangled ballots cost Al Gore the presidency despite winning the popular vote, but congressional Democrats again had failed to win back the majority. In Congress, many Democrats unused to serving in the minority had initially rationalized the 1994 reversal as an aberration and believed voters would restore Democrats to the majority they had held for all but four of the sixty-two preceding years.

Yet as the 1990s became the 2000s, Republicans remained in power, albeit narrowly: a majority of just nine in 1996 and four in 1998, which perpetually raised expectations of a Democratic restoration. But after the 2000 setback, it seemed evident that Democratic messaging, fundraising, and field operations were woefully impotent. The leaders "were all going through the motions, but they weren't kicking it into gear," recalled George Miller (CA), one of the caucus's senior liberals. "Everybody was smarting about the fact that Democrats had no message. [We had] lost a sense of purpose. A sense of direction and commitment had to be restored and rebuilt."[1]

Only a few years earlier, it seemed unlikely the party's revival would center around Pelosi. But she made a bargain with the leadership in 2000; she would flip at least four Republican seats in California. If they could pick up as many in the other forty-nine states, Democrats would return to the majority.[2] Pelosi delivered her victories, but elsewhere the party lost seats and the majority again slipped from the Democrats' fingers. Without a change in leadership in the incoming 107th Congress, it seemed to many, why would anyone believe Democratic prospects could improve anytime soon?

Pelosi was a relative newcomer, first elected in 1987 to a seat held for nearly a quarter century by the legendary Phil and Sala Burton, pillars of San Francisco's liberal Democratic establishment. Pelosi was part of her own political dynasty, the youngest of six children (and the only daughter) of "Big Tommy" D'Alesandro, a former Baltimore congressman and mayor from whom she learned the mechanics of campaigning, constituent services, and coalition building. As an adult in San Francisco, while raising five children (born in six years) of her own, Pelosi segued into politics through an appointment to the Library Commission, then won Democratic Party positions before rising to state chair in 1981. Along the way, she built key alliances with influential San Franciscans, including the Burtons, Mayor Joseph Alioto, and Assembly Speaker Leo McCarthy.[3]

In her first race for public office at the age of forty-seven, Pelosi was pegged "the establishment candidate" by pollster Mervin Field.[4] Many of the city's progressive and LGBTQ leaders lined up behind more activist and liberal candidates, chastising Pelosi as the product of "a political machine," something she dismissed—although crucial momentum for her election was provided by Sala Burton's deathbed endorsement.[5] With aggressive fundraising and a strong ground operation (learned from her father and executed by labor organizers Fred Ross and Larry Tramutola), she narrowly won.

Once in office, Pelosi quickly disproved allegations she was an affluent dilettante, earning respect as a tenacious liberal. She espoused support for HIV-AIDS research in her inaugural speech on the House floor, to the surprise of many colleagues. Her eponymous amendment imposing environmental conditions on beneficiaries of foreign aid won her plaudits on the Left, and she became a human rights hero for defiantly unfurling a banner in Tiananmen Square in support of Chinese dissidents.

Pelosi soon landed plum assignments on the Intelligence and Appropriations Committees. She paid her dues serving on the thankless Ethics Committee that investigated allegations of member misbehavior. In that role, she gained notoriety after spending a year "locked in a room in an undisclosed location" reviewing corruption allegations against Speaker Newt Gingrich, which resulted in an unprecedented $300,000 fine and bipartisan House reprimand that diminished his standing and helped set the stage for his resignation as Speaker in 1998.[6]

Three months into the new Congress in 2001, Democratic whip Dave Bonior (MI), facing a difficult reapportionment, announced his resignation from his leadership position and his decision not to seek reelection to the House. Senior allies like Miller and Jack Murtha (PA), reflecting a wide ideological swath of the caucus, encouraged Pelosi to announce her candidacy. "She looked around and said, 'I didn't come here to hang out,'" recalled Miller, who had introduced the freshman as a future Speaker back in 1987.[7] Although she had served in none of the lower rungs on the leadership ladder that typically vaulted members into top positions, Pelosi's decision to enter the race reflected a long-standing interest in joining the leadership. "She has always wanted to be speaker," former representative Tony Coelho (D-CA) would recall.[8]

Her chief opponent's biography differed from hers in almost every respect. Steny Hoyer (MD) was a business-oriented, southern-twanged moderate whose easy laugh and backslapping bonhomie made him popular among his colleagues on both sides of the aisle. Hoyer had a gregariously charming style that won friendships across the ideological and party spectrum. "If Steny Hoyer were dropped buck naked into the Kremlin," Ohio's Charlie Wilson once told a reporter, "in twenty years, he'd be head of the Politburo."[9] He and Pelosi had met in the 1960s while serving as staff to Maryland's senator Daniel Brewster. While Pelosi only contemplated law school before marrying and beginning a family, Hoyer became an attorney and entered politics, winning election to the Maryland state senate in 1967. By 1975, the youngest Senate president in history, he was widely viewed as a prospective governor or senator before unexpectedly losing a 1978 race for lieutenant governor. He took an appointment to the Maryland Board of Higher Education and waited to run for office again.

That opportunity was not long in coming. Late in 1980, the occupant of Maryland's Fifth District House seat, Gladys Noon Spellman, was left comatose after a stroke, and the House declared the seat vacant. The next May, Hoyer defeated over thirty other candidates to fill the remainder of her term. Back on track, in just seven years Hoyer had a foot on the leadership ladder as vice chair of the Democratic Caucus. When the caucus chair, Bill Gray (PA), was elevated to whip in May 1989, Hoyer won the race to replace him and was seemingly on a trajectory to the speakership. But that ascent was blocked as the top leadership team of Dick Gephardt (MO) and Bonior remained in place for years, and after completing his time-limited term as chair in 1995, Hoyer had nowhere to go until the latter's unanticipated retirement.

Ideologically, the caucus would seem to favor the more liberal Pelosi, but

Hoyer was popular and his experience on the leadership ladder, in a tradition-rich institution, was on his side; moreover, no woman had ever held such a powerful position on Capitol Hill. But Pelosi had her own assets, including prodigious fundraising abilities, a growing number of women in the caucus, and loyalty from most (though not all) of California's huge thirty-two-member Democratic delegation. Electing a woman, many thought, would "promote diversity in the caucus."[10]

The race was a mini-test of the whip job itself, necessitating proficiency in counting votes, a skill on which Pelosi prided herself. On October 10, 2001, Pelosi's calculations proved nearly flawless as she received 118 votes (two less than she had projected) to Hoyer's 95.[11] Hoyer marked the bitter defeat as had no other defeated leadership candidate: kissing his victorious rival on the cheek. But despite the public display of unity, members would perennially be classified as "Hoyer people" or "Pelosi people," and the rivalry endured in both political and policy battles for years.

"She's going to be a giant," predicted minority leader Gephardt, the only person standing between Pelosi and the leadership of House Democrats. When the party fell short yet again in the 2002 midterms, the members did little to hide their displeasure. Two days later, Gephardt announced his retirement to devote himself to his second presidential campaign.

There was little doubt Pelosi would waltz into the leader's office. Her main opposition consisted of the lightly regarded Harold Ford Jr. (TN), a moderate member of the Congressional Black Caucus. The vote demonstrated Pelosi's formidable organization. Less than two years after edging Hoyer for whip, she was elected party leader by a decisive 177–29 margin.

"I didn't run as a woman," she insisted in her victory speech. "I ran as a seasoned politician and experienced legislator." But she could not help but concede the historic nature of her achievement. "It just so happens that I am a woman, and we have been waiting a long time for this moment."[12] The Republican conference was uniformly overjoyed that Democrats had selected a "San Francisco liberal," the epitome of the culturally elitist liberals who purportedly oozed contempt for noncoastal, traditional values.

Democrats began the 2004 political season determined to reclaim the House majority and oust George W. Bush from the office he had dubiously won in 2000's disputed election. Pelosi envisioned a national messaging strategy that unified the party and identified Democrats as a clear policy alternative to the GOP. The idea for such a nationalized House campaign had originated in 1976 with minority leader John Rhodes's "Program for Progress."[13] Eighteen years later, Gingrich unified House Republicans behind his "Contract with America," which unified his conference in the election that secured the majority for the first time in four decades.

Pelosi distrusted much of the Washington-based political consulting establishment that regularly but ineffectually vacuumed up vast campaign resources without producing victories. She turned instead to marketing experts from the private sector who recommended that the party rely on the monotonous repetition of a simple message. "When you are so sick of it that you'll throw up if you say it again," they advised, "the public is just beginning to hear you." Pelosi admired John Cullinane, a software pioneer who insisted that an "effective sales message" required that you "take down the leader," and in 2004, that meant President George Bush.[14]

Democrats needed to avoid the common mistake of offering voters too much information, Cullinane believed, because peoples' working memory was limited. "Five [ideas] were too few, and seven were too many," Cullinane advised. "After six, prospects start to lose interest." Candidates lose races by making three correctable mistakes, he insisted: verbosity, failure to read the audience, and allowing opponents to put them on the defensive. Pelosi embraced the strategy. "We must keep the competition on the defensive," she argued. "We must draw clear distinctions between our vision of the future and the extreme vision put forward by the Republicans [and not] allow the Republicans to pretend they share our values."

Ultimately, the messaging project produced "The New Partnership for America's Future," which, like Gingrich's Contract with America ten years earlier, was unveiled on the steps of the Capitol. On September 22, 2004, 150 members surrounded by red, white, and blue banners and waving small American flags sang "God Bless America" before describing the package of homilies Hoyer described as "the roadmap that we will use to lead and make our country stronger." The proposals marked a departure from the lack of clarity in recent elections when, as Miller said, "there was no 'there' there for House Democrats."[15] In actuality, the Partnership was a collection of traditional party nostrums. "There's nothing new in here," Pelosi candidly admitted, "but ours is a pledge to keep this promise."[16]

Members and Cullinane loved the event, but it was "too little too late."[17] Despite recruiting more than three dozen candidates and raising tens of millions of dollars, the momentum created by Bush's hard-edged reelection campaign against Senator John Kerry proved impossible to overcome. Democrats lost House seats, including five in Texas where House Majority Leader Tom DeLay had engineered a radical reapportionment to favor Republicans. Senate Democrats also lost seats, leaving the chamber divided 55–45. In both houses, the climb to a majority in the off year 2006 seemed formidable, but Pelosi vowed to try again. "This is a long-term fight for us," she pledged. "This is about who we are and the values we represent."

Arc of Power

CHAPTER I

THE NEW DIRECTION: "6 FOR '06"

Congressional Democrats enjoyed two electoral advantages in 2006. The election would occur in the sixth year of a lame duck presidency, traditionally a weak midterm for the party of an incumbent president. In addition, House Democrats had gained discipline in developing a coordinated campaign message that unified the diverse party, however briefly.

Pelosi knew her own credibility at winning elections was on the line, and she agreed to develop the 2006 message jointly with the Senate, a challenge because each chamber had its own idiosyncrasies and harbored doubts about the other's trustworthiness. Over a year before the election, her top staff and that of Senate Democratic leader Harry Reid (NV) initiated regular meetings with Democratic strategists, including Stan Greenberg, James Carville, and John Podesta.[1] Democrats had failed, Greenberg argued, because they were perceived as being on the wrong side of cultural values and national security issues. But now, voters had grown weary of George W. Bush and his policies, especially regarding the war in Iraq. By July 2005, Democrats enjoyed a solid seven-point lead in generic polling on the question of which party should control Congress.[2]

Bush had provided an opening for Democrats by proposing that Americans have the option of diverting to private savings some of their Social Security contributions, a revolutionary change that could leave retirees vulnerable to the vicissitudes of the stock market.[3] Democrats launched a withering assault, accusing Bush of plotting to "privatize" the sacrosanct retirement program. Within a few months, voter disapproval of Bush's handling of Social Security skyrocketed from 48 to 64 percent.[4]

Some Democrats, fearful Bush's plan would gain traction or that the party would appear obstructionist, argued for offering a counterproposal. Pelosi's refusal was unequivocal. "Never!" she responded when asked about when she might unveil a response to the Bush plan. "Does never work for you?"[5] Seniors made up a disproportionately high percentage of the off-year electorate, she noted, and the party must avoid any appearance that Democrats would tamper with the retirement guarantee.[6] For years afterward, Pelosi cited this unqualified rejection of Bush's plan as a major factor in the party's success in 2006.[7]

The pool of messaging strategists again included experts from academia, business, and politics.[8] Pelosi's new favorite was marketing innovator Jack Trout, who had coined the concept of "repositioning" for private companies seeking to retool their image, which sounded a lot like what Hill Democrats needed.[9] His key idea was "taking positions against the leaders" by highlighting their failings and differentiating from their positions.[10] Not until voters had embraced skepticism about the existing brand—Bush and Republicans—would they entertain support for the alternative "product."

In January 2005, she had selected second-term dynamo Rahm Emanuel (IL) to run the Democratic Congressional Campaign Committee (DCCC). The Chicago congressman, a one-time DCCC staffer, was irrepressibly competitive but initially skeptical that Democrats could win the majority in 2006.[11] A short, wiry, onetime ballet dancer, the intense Emanuel had sharp elbows and a half-amputated middle finger that colleagues teased left him digitally handicapped in his frequent use of profanity. DNC chairman Howard Dean worried that Emanuel's "negative image" as a political bruiser would undermine fundraising.[12]

Democrats unveiled a withering assault on what they termed the Republican "culture of corruption," which could only be cleansed by new congressional leadership, a theme reminiscent of Gingrich's own accusations a dozen years earlier.[13] They were able to point to a litany of embarrassing scandals involving Republican officeholders, including the resignation of "Duke" Cunningham (CA), who once had recommended that the Democratic leadership be "lined up and shot."[14] Another dishonest poster child was lobbyist Jack Abramoff, who would be jailed for bribery, including lavish foreign travel, involving numerous members including former majority leader Tom DeLay (who resigned his leadership post after being indicted in September) and House Administration Committee chairman Bob Ney (R-OH) (indicted in August 2005). Democrats exploited each new scandal, excoriating the "cover-up Congress" and demanding floor votes on ethics issues.[15] It was a simple message to sell, free from the complexities of legislation and confirmed by independent judicial sanctions. By mid-December, voters by a margin of 65 to 35 percent believed the 109th was "the most corrupt Congress in history."[16]

As the 2006 election neared, the last thing Republicans needed was another ethics scandal, but late in August, a devastating accusation surfaced against Mark Foley (R-FL), a relentless critic of child pornography who chaired the House Caucus on Missing and Exploited Children.[17] On September 28, ABC News reported Foley had sent sexually explicit emails to a male, teenage House page, one of dozens of high school students who for generations had served as message runners and performed other tasks in Congress. The charge was affirmed by other pages who also revealed the congressman's efforts to enter the page dormitory without authorization. Democrats went ballistic. "It is time to inflame [this story] as an issue," George Miller demanded, "not to investigate it."[18]

The scandal's broader dimensions became clear when reporters' calls to Foley were returned by the staff of Tom Reynolds (NY), the chairman of the Republican Campaign Committee. Speaker Dennis Hastert, who later would be imprisoned for "transgressions involving children" committed before entering politics, initially disclaimed knowledge of the provocative emails, claiming "Foley had deceived people around the country." But the *Washington Post* reported that at least three Republican members had alerted Hastert in late 2005 of Foley's "inappropriate and 'overly-friendly' e-mails." The chairman of the Page Board that supervised the program, John Shimkus (R-IL), had ordered Foley to end his periodic night visits to the pages' dorm and to stop inviting them out to dinner.[19]

"The Republican Leadership knew about it for six months to a year," Pelosi charged, declaring "abhorrent" the concealment of Foley's transgressions. "There should be an investigation [about] who knew or had possession of these messages but did not report them," Hastert agreed, "and why they were not given to prosecutors before now."[20] He also asked Attorney General Alberto Gonzales to extend the inquiry beyond Foley.

The beleaguered Foley quit on September 29, but the House still unanimously passed a resolution launching an investigation into the scandal. Two weeks later, Ney pleaded guilty to bribery and "accept[ed] responsibility for [his] actions" but refused to resign his seat.[21] To protect themselves from criticism, Republicans implicated their own leaders in the cover-up. Rodney Alexander (LA), whose page had reportedly been the object of Foley's interest, claimed he had passed complaints from the boy's family to leadership; Reynolds told the Ethics Committee he had spoken with Hastert months before the scandal broke. With the intraparty finger-pointing expanding, a Zogby poll warned that the GOP could be in free fall. After the election, the House Ethics Committee would conclude that Hastert and other leaders were "willfully ignorant" in how they responded to the Foley revelations.[22] Another report found that Hastert's staff had been told of Foley's misbehavior as early as 2002.[23]

Hastert tried to cleanse Republicans by bringing a Republican ethics reform package to the floor, where the weak measure barely passed 217–213 and received ridicule from Pelosi. "When lobbyists write the lobbying reform bill," she asserted, "we end up with a ruse that winks at reform and does nothing to curtail the culture of corruption."[24] Hastert also called for the reform of earmarks, the long-honored practice by which members targeted spending to their districts and favored beneficiaries. Many viewed the initiative cynically because under Hastert, the number of earmarks had quintupled. The 2005 highway bill alone contained 6,300 earmarks valued at $23 billion, including the "Prairie Parkway" that critics charged would inflate the value of property Hastert owned.

Democrats were convinced they had found a winning issue. The messaging, one senator suggested, was succinct: "We're honest, they're corrupt." Rosa DeLauro (CT) and Miller, the House policy cochairs, endorsed a sweeping campaign against corruption even if that required Democrats to "call in the artillery on our own position," Miller declared. Predictably, the enhanced scrutiny did result in several Democrats becoming embroiled in scandal, including the senior member of the Ethics Committee, Alan Mollohan (WV), for allegedly steering millions of dollars to nonprofit organizations run by supporters and contributors. Unsurprisingly, Reynolds accused Democrats of a "culture of hypocrisy," and Mollohan took a leave from Ethics to "ease the political burden" on his colleagues.[25]

However, another ethics blowup united Hastert and Pelosi against the Department of Justice for encroaching on the legislative branch. During a raid on the home of Bill Jefferson (LA) in early August 2005, FBI agents found $90,000 wrapped in aluminum foil in his freezer, part of a bribe paid him in an FBI sting. "Tired of waiting" for Jefferson to produce documents, the FBI raided his Rayburn Building office, an unprecedented intrusion that was quickly condemned by Capitol Hill attorneys as violating the Constitution's "speech and debate" clause protecting the official records of members.[26]

"The speaker is willing to stick his neck out" to challenge Attorney General Alberto Gonzales, Hastert's chief of staff Scott Palmer advised. Gonzales had tried to call the Speaker after the raid, but an incensed Hastert would not even speak to him.[27] Pelosi was similarly outraged by the "blatant political move [that] broke a 219-year tradition."

Pelosi and I met with Hastert in the speaker's ornate office, a warren of rooms just off the Capitol Rotunda that had remained in the hands of the Republican leadership since the early 1950s. Few Democrats had ever seen the suite, replete with cornices, columns, and chandeliers and a wide balcony offering a spectacular view of the Mall. "If we win in November," I whispered to Pelosi, eyeing the sumptuous rooms, "we're throwing these guys out of here!"

The two leaders convened the Bipartisan Legal Action Group to defend the House's interests, and an appeals court found that the FBI must accommodate congressional prerogatives. Pelosi moved swiftly to sanction the unrepentant Jefferson. "I want him off" the Ways and Means committee, she declared. "He should take one for the team. We took one for him."[28] Pelosi insisted she would have removed Jefferson "months ago" but for his membership in the Congressional Black Caucus (CBC), many of whose members believed they were disproportionately targeted for ethics probes. Unconvinced, CBC chair Mel Watt (NC) demanded to know Pelosi's criteria for punishing a member. "The criteria," Pelosi tartly responded, "is $90,000 in your freezer."

The anger spilled out at a Steering and Policy Committee meeting. Jefferson insisted he was being sacrificed because his case ran counter to the Democrats' "culture of corruption" story line, while Watt dismissed calls for the Louisianan to resign from Ways and Means or even the House itself.[29] But influential CBC members including John Lewis (GA) and Charlie Rangel (NY) defended Pelosi, and a divided caucus voted 99 to 58 to remove Jefferson from the committee.[30] The Republicans "were elated" with the Democratic infighting, and Bush's political director, Karl Rove, met with six CBC members to encourage them to pour fuel on the fire.[31]

Adding to the Republicans' troubles was the devastation caused by Hurricane Katrina, a category 5 hurricane that tore into the Gulf Coast on August 29, killing over 1,800 and costing over $160 billion in losses. The Bush administration was caught flat-footed. Instead of touring the damage and consoling victims in relocation centers, the president inspected the ravaged region from the air on Air Force One. He also lavished praise on Michael Brown, the director of the Federal Emergency Management Agency (FEMA) who was widely criticized for bungling the response. "Brownie," Bush gushed, "you're doing a heck of a job!"

Hastert exacerbated the Republicans' apparent indifference to the widespread suffering by resisting Pelosi's request that the House be recalled from its summer break to take "extraordinary action." The Speaker belatedly signed off on $10.5 billion in emergency aid, but Democrats kept up the condemnation, blasting Bush's refusal to apply the Davis-Bacon prevailing wage mandate to apply to federally financed reconstruction work, which outraged even Republican-leaning unionists, forcing the president to reverse his position.[32] Even that concession did little to calm the partisan blowback. When Hastert created a select committee to conduct "a full and complete investigation," Democrats declined to appoint members, insisting on an independent review.[33]

Meanwhile, Pelosi's staff developed a template for members' town hall meetings focusing on the alliterative "cronyism, corruption, and incompetence," drawing a parallel between the bumbling Katrina response and the unpopular Iraq War that pollster Cornell Belcher argued was "the primary positive driver" favoring Democrats. "The mood for change is overwhelming," Greenberg told members, blaming the Iraq War and Katrina for a precipitous drop in Bush's support.[34]

The war had not always been a partisan issue. The vote to authorize Bush to send US forces to Iraq in 2002 had divided Democrats with 61 percent in the House and 40 percent in the Senate opposed. After becoming Democratic leader, Pelosi, an opponent, had convened regular meetings and demanded hearings examining the conduct of the war. To widespread ridicule from Bush officials who predicted that Iraq would reimburse the United States from its oil revenues, she warned that the war costs would exceed $1 trillion. A decade and a half later, the cost of the Iraq and Afghanistan wars, the longest in US history, exceeded seven times Pelosi's original prediction.[35]

With the evidence against Bush's Iraq strategy mounting, Democrats largely closed ranks. In the House, that shift was exemplified by Vietnam veteran, reliable Pentagon supporter, and Defense Appropriations ranking member Jack Murtha (PA), a close committee ally of Pelosi. In September 2006, the hulking, taciturn Murtha concluded that the war could not be won militarily.[36] Pelosi quickly elevated the former marine to serve as the conscience of the caucus on Iraq and veterans' issues, regularly calling on him to present his assessment of the war and joining him in visits to Walter Reed Army Hospital. During one memorable caucus meeting, he recalled having asked one wounded soldier why he lacked a Purple Heart. (Murtha himself had earned two in Vietnam.) The soldier explained that although his injury had occurred in a combat zone, the Pentagon had determined he did not merit the medal. Incensed, Murtha fumed to an officer at the hospital, "If you don't give this man a Purple Heart, I will give him *one* of mine!"[37]

By 57 to 40 percent, Americans believed Bush had deceived the country by intentionally exaggerating the likelihood that Iraq's Saddam Hussein possessed weapons of mass destruction. With rising costs and heavy casualties, 61 percent of Americans wanted the Iraq policy to move in a different direction. The issue was especially important to the activist Democratic base, many of whom insisted on imposing restrictions on any further money appropriated for the war.[38] Pelosi felt herself uniquely suited to address the issue given her lengthy service on the Intelligence Committee. "Nobody has ever served in leadership who had [as much] intelligence experience and exposure," she reminded her colleagues.[39] The election might well turn, she argued, on which party could be trusted to "keep Americans safe at home."[40]

But despite the demands of anti-war groups for an immediate withdrawal, Pelosi was intent on avoiding that trip wire. "I won't allow anyone to define us as favoring a speedy, hasty retreat," she told a leaders' breakfast early in December.[41] Such pragmatism disappointed anti-war activists in the caucus and the Code Pink demonstrators who regularly picketed outside Pelosi's San Francisco home. For his part, Bush remained resolute, echoing his 2003 assertion of "Mission Accomplished" in Iraq and hailing the "swiftest rise in democracy in history" two and a half years later. "We will never back down, never give in, and never accept anything less than complete victory," he insisted.

As the election neared, Greenberg reported a "sweeping . . . crash of Republican identity."[42] Bush's approval, which had exceeded 90 percent after the September 11 attacks, had plummeted to 42 percent, a grim omen for his party. By a two-to-one margin (60–34), voters believed the country was on the "wrong track," and 55 percent of voters wanted to go in a different direction. Generic preference for Democratic control of Congress was +12 points, an 11-point uptick from the preceding year, exceeding even the Republicans' 1994 victorious margin.

Still, only 59 percent of voters said they knew what Democrats stood for. If anything, Democrats had too many targets—Social Security, Iraq, Katrina, corruption. The party still needed a differentiating, unifying central theme. Several ideas were developed in conjunction with the messaging team but were quickly rejected: "A stronger America begins at home,"[43] "Together, America can do better,"[44] "Restoring the American Promise," and "Commitment to Change." "A New Direction" polled the strongest, and Reid and Pelosi signed off on the slogan.

Democrats also needed to agree on policy goals, an excruciatingly difficult task for policy-prolific progressives. Emanuel expressed frustration with the lengthy process Pelosi and other leaders undertook to refine a distinct set of issues that unified the party, preferring "more aggressive solutions" that would "throw the furniture around here," he suggested. "We've got a lot of people who like the furniture just as it is."[45]

"Laundry lists bore people" and strained their cognitive capabilities, counseled George Lakoff, a Berkeley linguistics professor. The tight criteria favored by Pelosi and Reid would rule out many issues embraced by the party's base in favor of a more centrist agenda that would unite Democrats, differentiate them from Republicans, and secure bipartisan support to demonstrate that Republican control alone was the impediment to enactment. A key overarching theme was denunciation of Republican policies that favored the wealthy while ignoring the worsening "middle class squeeze."

Pelosi insisted on reaffirming Democratic support for the budgetary Pay As You Go (Paygo) rule to insulate the party from perennial charges of indifference to the deficit. Embraced by the Democrats in 1982 and implemented in the 1990s, Paygo required corresponding tax increases or spending cuts to ensure that new spending did not contribute to the deficit. Emanuel wanted to go even further, endorsing a freeze on federal employee health benefits until all children had insurance, but others argued doing so would leave Democrats vulnerable to a charge of slashing health benefits for the heavily minority government workforce.

Pelosi favored tough ethics reform, and other members also offered their own initiatives. Zoe Lofgren (CA) advocated sweeping health care, Barney Frank (MA) spoke up for housing, and Jan Schakowsky (IL) for small business. Miller insisted on including a boost in the decade-old minimum wage (although Reid's staff thought it a throwback issue), which Emanuel insisted precede any congressional pay raise, a condition Pelosi heartily endorsed.[46] Others proposed immigration reform and energy efficiency.

In mid-June, Pelosi directed Emanuel to begin purchasing $2 million in TV time to promote the "New Direction" theme. "We need to explain how we will govern," Pelosi declared, pledging to pass the key bills during the first hundred *hours* in January, an unprecedented timetable. Immediately after the July 4th break, the "6 for '06" agenda was rolled out in a twenty-five-page booklet—"A New Direction for America"—designed with daily input from Pelosi on its text, shape, design, and even its patriotic color scheme.[47] Peppered with inspirational quotes from John F. Kennedy, Thomas Jefferson, and Abraham Lincoln, the pamphlet proclaimed, "Democrats believe that America needs—and Americans deserve—a New Direction that provides security, prosperity, and opportunity for all."

Elect Democrats, the manifesto promised, and these bills would become laws—with significant bipartisan support.

Real Security—at Home and Overseas: Implementation of the 9/11 Commission; "transition to full Iraqi sovereignty [and] finish the job in Afghanistan"; a "GI Bill of Rights for the 21st Century"; eliminate Osama bin Laden and al Qaeda; inspect all cargo bound for the United States; and improve interconnectivity among first responders.

Prosperity—Better American Jobs, Better Pay: "expand markets for American products"; "twenty-first century jobs."

Opportunity—College Access for All: deductibility of college tuition; cut loan interest rates; expand Pell Grants.

Energy Independence—Lower Gas Prices: end "tax giveaways to Big Oil"; end price gouging; promote renewable alternatives; energy independence in ten years.

Affordable Health Care—Life Saving Science: negotiation of lower prescription drug prices; promote stem cell research.

Retirement Security and Dignity: end plans to privatize Social Security; expand personal savings.

Despite Cullinane's admonition, the drafters added a seventh plank:

"Honest Leadership and Open Government": end the "culture of corruption" and "restore accountability, honesty and openness at all levels of government."

Other policy initiatives were put on hold while members echoed the "6 for '06" package. "This isn't a freelance operation," Pelosi admonished. Cheered by a fifteen-point margin among likely voters, Pelosi pressured her members to "own August [by using] the 'New Direction' in all your communications with constituents, town halls and press releases to sustain the message effort." If candidates could not hold a town hall on August 5, she demanded to know their alternative date.

A "totally committed" Reid promised to convene a Senate caucus to familiarize his members with the platform. Support groups agreed to launch outreach efforts to college students, rural areas, veterans, seniors, faith-based voters,

and internet users. Americans United (AU), closely affiliated with congressional Democrats, designated September 22 as "Donut Hole Day" to highlight a
loophole in Bush's prescription law that led to huge out-of-pocket expenses to
seniors. AU also pressed members to sign the "Golden Promise Pledge" not to
reduce Social Security benefits.

Republican leaders did not remain passive under the Democratic onslaught,
announcing initiatives designed to rile up their base like curtailing undocumented immigrants. But Democrats fought back aggressively when the Republican attacks misrepresented their views as when majority leader John Boehner
(OH) charged they were more interested in supporting terrorists than in standing up for the country. Pelosi demanded that Republicans repudiate the attack.
"Democrats will not be swift boated" like John Kerry in 2004, referring to the
Bush campaign's highly successful effort to impugn the Vietnam War record of
the decorated Democratic nominee. Democrats issued broadsides of their own,
castigating Republicans for a "Rubber Stamp Congress" that deferred to the
unpopular Bush. Talking points provided by Pelosi's office documented GOP
failures on sensitive issues like health care, the deficit, immigration, the middle-
class economic squeeze, and corruption. "You have to own October!" Pelosi
inveighed in meeting after meeting.

Despite the effort to focus on "6 for '06," it was clear that Iraq was "eclipsing
everything" else on the agenda. A "devastating" National Intelligence Estimate
(NIE) faulted the Pentagon for sending inexperienced, undertrained, and ill-
equipped troops into combat. The legendary pollster Lou Harris recommended
Democrats hit the beleaguered Bush for allowing terrorism to grow in the af-
termath of 9/11. "The bad guys," he said, "are winning!"[48] Democrats eagerly
complied, assailing Bush and his party for failing to capture bin Laden or solve
domestic anthrax terror plots.

As the campaign appeared increasingly likely to result in a new Democratic
majority, the contributions poured in, allowing the DCCC to spend $10 million
on field operations and recruit dozens of lawyers to challenge potential voting
irregularities.[49] On the eve of the election, CNN reported, Democrats enjoyed
an eleven-point generic advantage, prompting growing press speculation about
the likely first woman Speaker of the House, and Pelosi moved to ensure that
the right image was created. The staff was instructed to highlight her commitment to "honesty, civility, bipartisanship and integrity," to children, the environment, and the role of women in government. Validators were enlisted to laud
her leadership skills with the press.[50] Soon, favorable stories began to appear,
with Newsweek describing her "driven, effective" management style. Republicans

countered with a caricature alternative, the extreme San Francisco liberal who embraced culturally extreme issues, an accusation that drew guffaws in her district where Pelosi was considered a moderate.

Conservatives also raised alarms over who would serve as prospective committee chairs in a Democratic House. Rush Limbaugh attacked John Dingell, likely chair of the powerful Commerce Committee, as sympathetic to Hezbollah because of the large Muslim population in his Michigan district. Dingell responded with a guest article in the *Washington Post* touting his long-standing support for Israel. Others drew attention to liberal minorities like John Conyers (MI) who were poised to wield committee gavels.

Amid the optimism, some Democrats quietly raised questions about the wisdom of elevating Pelosi to the speakership. There were "real legs to anti-Pelosi sentiment," one campaign staffer warned. Some blamed Hoyer for fueling anger within the Congressional Black Caucus over her treatment of Jefferson. Even at Emanuel's DCCC, critics viewed her as "radioactive" in many House districts where candidates did "not want to be seen with her." In one survey, over half of the likely Democratic freshmen were concerned about casting their first vote for "Speaker" Pelosi.[51]

But such disquiet was far from most minds a week before Election Day. The generic lead was up to 52–34 percent according to one poll; even the conservative Fox News gave Democrats an eleven-point lead, enough to boost even long shots like John Hall (NY), a guitarist with the 1970s band Orleans.

On the eve of the election, the caucus mood was jubilant, and Hoyer lauded Pelosi for her constant travel and fundraising. A confident Pelosi predicted a Democratic gain of twenty-two to twenty-five seats, more than enough to make the Democrats the majority and her Speaker. For once in her career as a master counter, she was off the mark.

CHAPTER 2

"I HAD TO WIN THE
HOUSE FIRST"

In the warren of offices at the Democratic Congressional Campaign Committee (DCCC) on the evening of November 7, 2006, party leaders and senior advisors watched as computers relentlessly churned out the latest returns. Strewn on the tables and desktops were cups of cold coffee, flat sodas, and half-eaten pizzas. Nancy Pelosi sat on a sofa, methodically assessing numbers as they filtered in. As the blue districts spread across the TV screens, easily surpassing the 218 needed for the House majority, someone exultantly called out "Madam Speaker!" Dozens of voices echoed the historic call.

At the Capitol Hill Hyatt, a victory celebration was already in full swing. Late in the evening, as the Rolling Stones' "Start Me Up" deafeningly blared and confetti rained down on the jubilant crowd, Harry Reid, Pelosi and their key lieutenants strode onto the stage before the large "A New Direction for America" poster, their clasped hands raised in triumph. After a lengthy introduction by Emanuel, the chant began, a few at first, then becoming deafening: "Nancy, Nancy, Nancy" and then "Speaker! Speaker! Speaker!"

The confetti was not even swept up before Pelosi began plotting the hundred-hour race to pass the "6 for '06" agenda. With 233 seats, the presumptive Speaker presumably could find a majority of votes for any legislation she favored, although knowledgeable House hands knew the majority was riven with factions that would complicate the task. Reid faced a more formidable challenge because he lacked the sixty votes needed to break a Senate filibuster, necessitating the support of some Republicans to pass almost any legislation.

The reaction from 1600 Pennsylvania Avenue was gracious. President Bush called Pelosi the morning after the "thumpin,'" greeting her as "Madam Speaker." Earlier in the day, he had fired his controversial Defense secretary, Donald Rumsfeld, indicating a potential rethinking of Middle East policy. He pledged to work collaboratively with Democrats on a variety of issues, provided Pelosi his social secretary's direct line, and invited her and her husband Paul to a private White House dinner.

Pelosi echoed the conciliatory tone, rejecting a staff draft of a radio address as "too partisan," preferring to "go to a higher level." Abandoning the campaign's combative tone was the exact approach favored by messaging consultants like Celinda Lake, who urged the incoming Speaker to "extend the olive branch" because "people want to hear about civility."[1] "The overall theme," former Clinton advisor Mike McCurry counseled, "should be 'come together.'"

Although the 110th Congress would not be sworn in for two months, the incoming leadership wasted little time preparing for a high-pressure session. Meeting the hundred-hour pledge was essential to winning voter trust but could present dangers for freshmen—the so-called majority makers—who would be confronted with casting controversial votes even before they understood the issues or quirky floor procedures.

The Associated Press's exit polls confirmed that substantial public support existed for the agenda. Over 40 percent of respondents embraced stronger ethics rules; fighting terrorism and improving the economy enjoyed similar support. Six in ten voters opposed US involvement in the Iraq War, including nearly 90 percent of those who had voted for Democrats. Among the third who identified Iraq as their top concern, 62 percent rejected the record of the Republican Congress.

Despite the positive ratings, the consultants warned about setting unrealistic expectations. "Be careful about overselling," warned McCurry. The activist groups would expect a quick withdrawal from Iraq, for example, but a precipitous departure could undermine the al-Maliki government in Baghdad and lead to a return to militia warfare, intervention by Iran, and perhaps the reintroduction of US forces.

Pelosi would enter the Speaker's office in an atypical fashion. Unlike a half century of Democratic speakers—McCormack, Albert, O'Neill, Wright, and Foley—Pelosi had not merely inherited the title from a Democratic predecessor. "I had to win the House first," she would remind people. And having secured the office in a combative way those precursors had not, she intended to exercise the power that came with the gavel.

It was crucial that Republicans, who would remain in the majority for two months, not destroy or abscond with official documents. She reminded each outgoing chair and staff director that everything on committee servers and computers belonged to the House and must be sent to the National Archives' Center for Legislative Archives at the end of each Congress. In addition, there were endless organizational issues to resolve: allocation of rooms, leadership budgets, committee assignments, and appointment of chairs for leadership committees.[2] Pelosi's own staff would expand from about fifty to nearly seventy-five with special attention to the communications team that would cultivate and protect her image.

Quick changes were also forthcoming concerning her personal security. The morning after the election, Sergeant at Arms Bill Livingood upgraded her detail of plainclothes agents to round-the-clock protection. Since she would be second in line to the presidency, a dedicated cell phone and landline would assure 24/7 secure communications with the White House. All incoming mail to her offices and her homes in California and Washington, DC, would be screened for biohazards and other threats.[3] Pelosi protested the beefed-up measures despite mounting threats to her safety, but Livingood, while deferential, reminded her that "security [decisions] were not up to her, they are up to the Capitol Hill police."

Each new Congress has the authority to rewrite the House rules, and in cases of party changes, the revisions offer an opportunity to reallocate power in the House by altering committees and jurisdiction. In 1994, Newt Gingrich had used his newfound power to eliminate three permanent committees and numerous select committees and to slash staffs. Now, incoming chairs like Miller and Dingell sought to expand their jurisdiction at the expense of weaker committees, but Pelosi was reluctant to sanction such raids that could divide her members.[4]

Unlike Republicans, who had given the power to name chairs to the Speaker in 1994, Democrats reverted to the traditional seniority system that presumed the longest-serving majority member of a committee would be chair, if confirmed by the caucus.[5] Abandoning the seniority system would have been highly unpopular with minority member caucuses who argued that absent seniority, which benefited those representing safely Democratic districts, their members were unlikely to win chairmanships, in part due to their limited ability to raise campaign money to lavish on colleagues.

One particular chairmanship presented a challenge to Pelosi. Under the seniority rules, Ed Markey (MA) could claim the gavel of the Natural Resources Committee but only if he first forfeited his position as chair of the Energy Subcommittee on Commerce.[6] Markey had passed on serving as ranking Democrat on Resources when the position opened up in 2001, allowing Nick Joe Rahall (WV) to occupy that slot during the years in the minority. But pushing aside

Rahall might appear to be favoring a safe liberal over the more vulnerable moderates whose victories had made a discussion of chairmanships germane in the first place.

Pelosi suggested that Markey defer to Rahall during the 110th Congress and claim the chairmanship in 2009, when Rahall could switch to a powerful subcommittee chairmanship on Transportation, his other committee. Markey agreed but insisted Rahall put the agreement in writing. He then asked Pelosi for several favors, including a shift of several high-profile issues to Commerce from Natural Resources, reappointment to the Commission on Security and Cooperation in Europe, and the chairmanship of a new select committee on global warming the Speaker was considering.[7]

Markey was far from the only member driven by personal ambition to seek waivers from House rules limiting the accumulation of power. Carolyn Maloney (NY) and Juanita Millender-McDonald (CA) wanted to serve as chair of the Joint Tax and the House Administration Committees, respectively, while also chairing a subcommittee on another committee. Mike Doyle (PA), a Pelosi favorite, needed a waiver to serve on the Transportation Committee despite serving on another exclusive committee that barred such appointments.[8]

The improved House ratios meant more seats for Democrats on key committees, and many sought to upgrade to more prestigious assignments. Often members would no sooner be given such a choice assignment than they would double back for more. Betty Sutton (OH) won appointment to the highly desirable Rules and Budget Committees and immediately enlisted the Trial Lawyers Association to lobby for a Judiciary seat. Ellen Tauscher (CA) wanted a seat on the Intelligence Committee and a waiver to let her remain on Transportation, which provided her "political cover" against her neighbor, freshman Jerry McNerney, who aspired to replace her as the "'go-to' person for California" on transportation issues.[9]

There were also requests to conform archaic House rules to contemporary legal and cultural standards. Some unmarried members wanted fiancées and domestic partners to be able to participate in foreign travel like spouses, but Pelosi was wary, recalling that many "fiancées" had a way of losing that status shortly after trips. But pressed by Tammy Baldwin (WI) to change rules on unmarried partners accompanying members (prior to legalization of same-sex unions), Pelosi signed off on the change, a modernization DoD opposed strongly. She also eliminated the antiquated requirement that an adult child companion be of the "opposite sex" from the traveling member.[10]

At one point, an exasperated Pelosi called me into her office, wondering if the demands would ever abate. "When one of your Bay Area friends asks you to get them a better seat on the 5:30 United flight to San Francisco," I replied, "you'll know you've hit rock bottom." A few minutes later, a member solicited her help in securing better seats at the upcoming Kennedy Center Honors.

Not all requests were granted, and none was more controversial than denying the chairmanship of the Intelligence Committee to its senior Democrat, Jane Harman (CA). Convinced the decision was retribution for supporting the Iraq War, Harman unleashed a fierce lobbying effort including Gen. Joseph Hoar, the former chief of the US Central Command, and members of the moderate New Democrats caucus. Others weighed in against Harman, including former representative Porter Goss (R-IL), the Intel chairman before his appointment as Central Intelligence Agency director, who warned that Harman had avoided a Justice Department inquiry over contact with an Israeli intelligence operative only because Attorney General Alberto Gonzales viewed her as "a valuable ally" on eavesdropping policy.[11]

Pelosi remained unmovable, insisting she was simply following the caucus rules that limited the top slot on Intelligence to a four-year term whether in the minority or majority. "When she leapfrogged over the others," Pelosi noted, "I said, 'That's just for two terms.' So, when we took the majority, [I rejected] the idea that Jane would have three terms." She insisted the decision to replace Harman "had nothing to do with her position on Iraq. It only had to do with the fact that this extraordinarily talented member of Congress had served her two terms."[12] Instead, she appointed Sylvestre Reyes (TX), a twenty-six-year veteran of the Border Patrol. Emanuel viewed the appointment as "big trouble," predicting the leadership would "need to . . . run his shop and hire his staff."[13]

Pelosi was less willing to bypass the ailing Millender-McDonald for chair of the House Administration Committee.[14] Despite her serious health problems, Pelosi was determined to appoint the fellow California woman and CBC member. When Millender-McDonald died early in 2007, Pelosi replaced her with the Philadelphia party kingpin Bob Brady.

The most significant challenge came from a crucial Pelosi ally who targeted a long-standing Pelosi rival. Earlier in 2006, Murtha had vowed to challenge Hoyer for majority leader if Democrats regained the majority. Although both were moderates and, like Pelosi and Clyburn, veterans of the Appropriations Committee, they could not have been less similar. Murtha, the first Vietnam veteran elected to Congress, was a brooding and hulking presence who spoke in a grave and humorless manner. By lending his military credibility to the anti-war effort, Pelosi believed, Murtha had "saved our butt on Iraq."[15]

Where Murtha was taciturn and indifferent to fundraising or campaigning for colleagues, Hoyer was a glad-handing, personable caucus veteran. He had spent years crisscrossing the country campaigning for colleagues, solidifying a strong network as caucus chair and whip among moderates and liberals alike who were willing to overlook his close ties to lobbyists and the business community.

Despite his apostasy on Iraq, many liberals viewed Murtha with skepticism. On defining issues like deficits, guns, and abortion, he aligned with the party's conservative wing. His general enthusiasm for military spending alienated many in the Out of Iraq Caucus, while his lavish earmarking on behalf of his beleaguered Pennsylvania district drew disapproval from deficit hawks. He also had a tarnished image on ethics, having been swept up—though not indicted—in the Abscam bribery scandal of the late 1970s during which he had testified against several colleagues who were later convicted.[16] Years afterward, a member of the prosecution team confided that by telling the agents he was open to taking bribes in the future, Murtha had demonstrated that he was "very, very guilty." That record outraged some reform advocates who assumed Pelosi had encouraged Murtha to enter the race. "She was interested in the culture of corruption only as a campaign issue and has no real interest in true reform," charged Melanie Sloan, the executive director of Citizens for Responsibility and Ethics in Washington (CREW). "It is shocking to me that someone with [Murtha's] ethics problems could be number two in the House leadership."[17]

Pelosi insisted that she played no part in encouraging a "fratricidal challenge" sure to divide the caucus at its moment of triumph, but few in Washington believed her protestations of neutrality.[18] "If John Murtha was running for dog-catcher or President of the United States, Nancy Pelosi would support him," insisted one Pelosi supporter.[19] For a week after the election, Pelosi remained silent, but then, the weekend before the caucus vote, she instructed me to draft an endorsement letter accentuating Murtha's leadership on Iraq and Appropriations but without challenging Hoyer's record. "I salute your courageous leadership that changed the national debate and helped make Iraq the central issue of this historic election," the draft read. "Your strong voice for national security, the war on terror and Iraq provides genuine leadership for our party, and I count on you to lead on these vital issues." On Monday morning, November 13, the letter was emailed to all Democratic members of the incoming 110th Congress.

Reporters believed that "Pelosi's decision could be a significant blow to Hoyer," but not everyone agreed.[20] One Hoyer supporter dismissed the letter as "egotistical hubris" by the incoming Speaker. Others disagreed. "I can't imagine that the caucus will not give her the first big request she makes," one supporter said.[21] But tellingly, the moderate Blue Dog Dennis Cardoza, a Californian who might have been expected to support Pelosi's recommendation, did not. "Everyone already knew she was supporting Murtha," he said, but "Steny's going to win this fight."[22] Hoyer claimed the votes of twenty-one of the roughly forty incoming freshmen, even though many of them owed their election to money and campaign support provided by Pelosi and the DCCC. They believed, said John Sarbanes (MD), that the Democrats should stick with the team that won them to the majority. For his part, Hoyer refused to cast the disagreement as a dispute with the incoming Speaker. "Nancy told me some time ago that she would personally support Jack," he wrote. "I respect her decisions as the two are very close [and] I look forward to working with Speaker Pelosi as Majority Leader."

Most close observers believed that Pelosi had little alternative given the enormous value she placed on personal loyalty. She reminded critics that she lingered until the last minute to issue her letter, telling Murtha (as she told aspirants regularly) it was his job, not hers, to find his votes. Two days before the caucus, Murtha claimed 105 hard "yes" votes and another nineteen leaning his way, enough for victory. "We've got the votes, and we are going to win it," Murtha's staff confidently predicted, dismissing rumors he had conceded to Hoyer as "total crap."[23]

At the November 15 caucus, Pelosi loyalist Henry Waxman (CA) nominated Hoyer, a signal of the deep divide even among California liberals. "It is a great leadership team," Waxman declared of the Pelosi-Hoyer coalition. "Let's keep it in place." When the secret ballots were counted, Hoyer had decisively crushed Murtha 149 to 86. It was entirely possible, a *Washington Post* story concluded, that "Pelosi and her allies may not have swayed a single vote for Murtha." Instead, the outcome likely reflected "a repudiation of Pelosi's strong-arm tactics and a recognition of Hoyer's tireless work to elect a Democratic majority."[24]

Barney Frank (MA) declared Pelosi's attempt to undercut Hoyer "a mistake in judgment [by] a very smart woman." Years later, he asserted that the decision to endorse Murtha "wrongfooted her speakership from Day One, to no apparent avail."[25] "She violated every conceivable rule of Boss-like behavior," *Newsweek's*

Howard Fineman wrote. "She lost, she lost publicly, she lost after issuing useless and unenforceable threats to people she barely had met, knowing . . . they would tell the world about her unsuccessful arm-twisting."[26]

In a photo of the victorious leadership team, a glum Murtha dutifully applauds as the awkward team of Pelosi and Hoyer flashes wide if forced smiles. "Let the healing begin," Pelosi proclaimed. But resentments lingered; months later, Hoyer complained about Murtha holding press conferences on issues beyond his role as an Appropriations Subcommittee chair while the majority leader was excluded from national security discussions. For years, long after the rivalry had been decisively settled, Pelosi loyalists would still scrutinize Hoyer's remarks for efforts to undercut the Speaker, often finding evidence of subtle criticisms. Even Hoyer would wonder whether the Democratic leadership was "falling into what Boehner had predicted"—an ongoing, testy rivalry between the Speaker and majority leader.[27]

The third rung on the leadership ladder—whip—was expected to be filled by the outgoing caucus chair, Jim Clyburn (SC). A stickler for diversity, Pelosi was enthusiastic that Clyburn would become only the second African American to occupy so high a position in the House leadership.[28] But Emanuel, who often was accused of having a tin ear when dealing with minorities, was unhappy about anyone insinuating their way onto the leadership ladder ahead of him, complicating his rise to what he—and many others—believed was his destiny: Speaker. Emanuel's carefully honed persona as the hard-nosed realist, disdainful of gauzy, idealistic liberals, alienated many of his colleagues not accustomed to such aggressiveness from a relatively junior—if highly talented—colleague. Many Black members, in particular, were suspicious of Emanuel's predilection for prematurely embracing partial victories in order to move on to the next challenge. His deference to the Speaker was also doubted by some. Pelosi acolytes recalled that during the majority leader contest, Emanuel had reminded members that Murtha had derided the speaker's ethics reform bill as "crap."[29]

Challenging the popular Clyburn, Emanuel recognized, would damage his caucus appeal over the long term. A battle between an African American and a Jewish member, following the Murtha challenge, was a guaranteed public relations disaster. He pulled back from the confrontation and instead announced he would run for caucus chair, asking Pelosi to allow him to retain some of his DCCC responsibilities in that new role, including the supervision of freshmen members, which would enable him to cultivate support for his ambitions.

One last distraction marred the transition to the majority. Shortly after the election, Livingood recommended that for security reasons, Pelosi should request regular use of an air force plane for official domestic travel (standard practice for official international trips by members).[30] Hastert had used such military aircraft on 118 occasions, often with other members and his staff, to fly between Washington and his district in Illinois and occasionally to other domestic locations.[31]

The military planes provided improved security and communication in the wake of the 9/11 terrorist attacks and allowed the Speaker to bypass crowded airports. The availability of such aircraft came as news to Pelosi, but she insisted she be accorded the same security protocols as her male predecessors.[32] However, flying nonstop to San Francisco required a larger (and costlier) plane than the twelve-seat C-20 Gulfstream Hastert typically was given. Tipped off by someone in the Pentagon, Republicans pounced on the plane request, deriding it as "Pelosi One" and falsely accusing her of demanding a forty-five-seat jet that cost $22,000 an hour to operate. Republican Conference chair Adam Putnam lambasted Pelosi's "arrogance of office," erroneously alleging she had insisted on a "jumbo jet" that was the equivalent of "Air Force Three."[33] Republican whip Roy Blunt described the plane as "a kind of a flying Lincoln bedroom," and conservative news anchor Lou Dobbs joked, "She could take a circus with her, for crying out loud!" With no evidence at all, both Putnam and Blunt accused Pelosi of wanting to fly "supporters" for free. (In fact, even House colleagues had to reimburse the military when they accompanied her.) One critic even asserted she wanted to install a hot tub.

Angered by the allegations, Pelosi insisted that Livingood publicly acknowledge it was his "strong preference, for security reasons" that the highly visible Pelosi, already the object of an increased number of threats, use a military plane. The air force agreed to "do the best we can" in accommodating her requests, and Assistant Defense Secretary Robert Wilkie signed off on the plane arrangements.[34]

With the House leadership team set, members quickly filed requests for rooms, staff, and money from the Speaker for their personal empire building. Clyburn announced a plan to designate nine deputy whips compared to the lone deputy in the Republicans' organization and asked Pelosi to allocate him resources from her own budget to fund his growing official infrastructure.[35] Even bigger demands came from Hoyer, who had raised objections in 2005 about the "growing financial disparity" between their offices. A fairer allocation, he insisted, would increase his whip budget by $300,000.[36] Now, he insisted, his share of leadership resources should match the elevated levels enjoyed by former majority leader Tom DeLay, who, under the low-key Hastert, had played an unusually prominent role in running the House. Hoyer insisted he needed the resources to build legislative, press, and member service operations, many of which would parallel (and potentially work at cross purposes with) the Speaker's own staff. Within a few months, Hoyer was insisting he was entitled to even more while the Speaker worried that her own funds were becoming constrained.

Members of the caucus also issued demands, and one of them, launching impeachment proceedings against Bush, met with vigorous disapproval from Pelosi, who shared the disdain for the president's apparent distortion of the intelligence about the threat posed by Iraq. "What could be worse than the misrepresentations that were made to the American people about Saddam Hussein's WMDs?" Pelosi asked. Invading Iraq had been "one of the worst mistakes in our country['s history]."[37] But she wanted to keep attention and energy focused on fulfilling the tight "6 for '06" timetable, and initiating an impeachment inquiry would surely stagnate the legislative agenda and extinguish any hope for cooperation with Republicans. Besides, there was no chance the Senate would produce anything approaching the two-thirds needed for conviction. "I have said it before and I will say it again: Impeachment is off the table," Pelosi declared. "We are not going down that path."[38]

The new Speaker's public message was to "pledge partnerships not partisanship with the Republicans in Congress and the president," as her message advisors encouraged.[39] "We can pass those bills without Republicans, but I want Republican votes" on issues like the minimum wage, prescription drug price control, and stem cell research to demonstrate they were mainstream issues, not a radical Democratic platform. She also thought many Republicans who had campaigned against deficits might agree to restore the Paygo budgeting mandate.[40]

But her willingness to embrace bipartisanship had its limits, as when she rejected my advice to speak to the Republican conference. She was not ready to take the chance of going before a hostile audience that blamed her for losing its majority. Still, a few weeks later, she offered to hold regular joint meetings to discuss the floor schedule with the new Republican leader. Boehner waved his hand dismissively. "I already have too many meetings," he responded as he walked out the door. Later, she invited him to collaborate on jobs legislation, but again Boehner demurred. "Why would I do that?" he asked, preferring to let Democrats legislate alone, leaving his members free to criticize the new spending.

Pelosi implored committee chairs to "own January," enunciating a clear message of reform, competency, transparency, and legislative productivity. Committees had to come out of the gates in the first two weeks of the new Congress demonstrating an end to gridlock. The benefits of the change in congressional control must also be demonstrated with vigorous oversight of the Bush record, including the bungled response to Hurricane Katrina. These were not requests but instructions from the incoming Speaker, Pelosi reminded the chairs, noting they held the gavel at the sufferance of the caucus and warning that discipline would be reinforced in weekly leadership meetings to "validate the playbook."[41]

The 2008 election would be upon them with unexpected swiftness, and Pelosi instructed every vulnerable Democrat to schedule a hundred district coffee klatches and to implement a diligent casework and outreach capability. Freshmen were encouraged to join some of the unofficial issue caucuses to demonstrate their commitment to constituent priorities. To solidify an ongoing relationship with the freshmen, Pelosi initiated 8:00 a.m. Wednesday breakfasts in her conference room that gave novice lawmakers unprecedented access to engage with leadership members and committee chairs.[42]

On December 8, Pelosi held a rare meeting with Hastert in the elaborate offices that soon would become her own rooms. Hastert disclosed he would soon resign from Congress and offered his successor advice after his decade in the speakership. "Listen, keep an open door," he counseled. "Don't be a second guesser" like Newt Gingrich.[43] He admitted frustration with some of his hard-nosed chairs but also complained that few Democrats had been willing to "meet or work with the Republicans." Yielding so much of his power to the disgraced DeLay had been a mistake, and he cautioned her to closely monitor the Rules Committee, which, at the Speaker's direction, sets the parameters for the debate of legislation to ensure members didn't slip embarrassing amendments into bills heading to the floor. Despite his own use of earmarks, he warned about the abuse of the practice, especially by the Senate, citing the example of Arlen Specter (R-PA), who had once deleted all House earmarks while inserting one naming a National Institutes of Health building for himself.

With many of the initial decisions made and organization well underway, Democrats prepared to move into the majority. Their priorities were clear, and they would have to pass bills quickly because, as Emanuel reminded his colleagues, the party would only "get one shot" at establishing its credibility. The last few years had been "a scrimmage," he informed his colleagues. "The real game is now."[44]

CHAPTER 3

MADAM SPEAKER

Nancy Pelosi was very focused on planning the day when she would stand before her colleagues, hand on the Bible, to be sworn in as Speaker of the House of Representatives. The festivities would begin in Baltimore where she and her brother Tommy, like her father a former mayor, would visit their childhood home on Albemarle Street. Swearing-in day itself would begin with a Mass at her alma mater, Trinity College in Washington, officiated by former Massachusetts congressman Rev. Robert Drinan.

Before she could take up the gavel, however, the 109th Congress's Republican majority maneuvered to pass bills unlikely to fare well under the new Democratic majority. In the House, outgoing Ways and Means chair Bill Thomas (CA) sought unsuccessfully to extend the Bush tax cuts beyond their 2010 expiration. There was better chance for a bipartisan agreement on a continuing resolution (CR) to avoid a government shutdown, necessitated by the failure to approve individual appropriations bills before the beginning of the fiscal year on October 1. Few had the patience for protracted negotiations even though a CR meant freezing most spending at levels favored by Bush and the Republicans. "Let's just take the pain and move on," Reid suggested, so the incoming Democrats could focus on the next budget and the "6 for '06" agenda.

Pelosi instructed her chairs to put everything but the "6 for '06" issues on hold until after January 18, the target date for passing the "New Direction" package through the House.[1] That meant deferring a long list of bills, including facilitating union organizing and energy independence, disincentives for outsourcing jobs, student loan reform, and pension modernization. Each had powerful advocates within the caucus and among outside advocacy groups, and Pelosi knew she would have to pace the members. "We can't run out of steam," she insisted.[2]

In addition to legislating, the chairs were anxious to launch sweeping investigations of Bush's executive branch after six years of lax scrutiny by Republicans. The focus would be on waste, corruption, and failure to implement policies approved by prior Democratic Congresses. The oversight should be aggressive but not gratuitously confrontational, Pelosi advised, warning against issuing subpoenas unless the chair could make "the best possible case" the administration was stonewalling requests for documents.[3] Anticipating just such inquisitive activities, the Bush administration hired Washington powerhouse Fred Fielding to coordinate its oversight pushback.

Enormous challenges awaited the "6 for '06" agenda, especially in the Senate. Reid faced painful negotiations to attract the Republicans he required to reach sixty votes to invoke cloture against threatened filibusters, assuming he could even unite his own ideologically fractious caucus. Even more ominous for House Democrats, senators would almost certainly entreat them to accept whatever version of legislation they crafted that could squeeze through the sixty-vote keyhole. Such legislation was certain to reflect the demands and priorities of the Senate, often at the expense of policies favored by minorities who are far more equitably represented in the House. This fundamental imbalance of power reflected the reality of the allocation of power on Capitol Hill and would impact the ability of House Democrats to deliver many political victories despite their large margins.

Even if they could thread that needle, the incoming Democrats still were confronted with a lame-duck president wielding a veto pen. The situation was reminiscent of the 94th Congress following the post-Watergate wave election when dozens of new Democratic members provided large majorities to pass their legislative priorities but not the margins needed to override President Gerald Ford's aggressive use of the veto. Surveying the Senate filibuster, the Bush veto, and the prohibitive chances of overriding it, it was not surprising some top Democrats were "very skeptical" of their ability to pass the promised agenda.[4]

After working without a break over the holidays, Pelosi and members of her staff gathered on New Year's Day. She planned quick action on reforms to mark the demise of the "culture of corruption" against which Democrats had railed. None was more contentious than her plan to create an independent ethics office to supplement the House's formal Committee on Standards of Official Conduct (informally known as the Ethics Committee), which critics asserted routinely ignored allegations of improper behavior. The new entity could receive complaints from any source in or outside the Congress, which it would evaluate and pass along to the formal committee with recommendations for further action. The two-step process was "designed to protect members from irresponsible charges" by political adversaries while still "rais[ing] a high ethical standard."[5] When members responded negatively to the plan, she proclaimed herself "agnostic" on the best approach for toughening ethics enforcement. In reality, she had no intention of backing down, although it took months before the new committee was in place.[6]

Another controversial innovation was creation of a Select Committee on Energy Independence and Global Warming to highlight the dangers of climate change, an issue of such importance to the Speaker that she briefly contemplated chairing the panel herself.[7] The initiative put her on a collision course with John Dingell, whose Commerce panel had legislative jurisdiction over most of the Select Committee's issues. A feared investigator and skilled legislator, the chair was determined not to yield a scintilla of control over high-profile issues.

Dingell had a rocky relationship with the new Speaker and some of her key allies. He had strongly supported Hoyer in the 2001 whip contest, but even so, many were surprised when Pelosi endorsed a junior member, Lynn Rivers, who had been thrown into the same district as Dingell by the 2000 reapportionment process. Dingell emerged from the primary victorious and without much affection for Pelosi, with whom he disagreed on many policy matters, including gun control. Dingell was an unabashed supporter of the National Rifle Association, lending a powerful Democratic voice to conservative arguments over the Second Amendment. Even more significant was his long-standing resistance to rigorous clean air and auto safety laws he believed would damage Michigan's industrial base. Although eighty years old and with infirmities sometimes requiring the use of crutches or a wheelchair, he remained a formidable adversary even for the strong-willed Pelosi. His brusque, old-school manner offended many of his colleagues, particularly women like Anna Eshoo, a close Bay Area colleague of Pelosi's. Early in her House career, Dingell had dangled an appointment to a conference committee before Eshoo, who had assumed her assignment was a forgone conclusion. "After all," she asserted, "it *is* my bill." The chair's only condition was that she pledge to vote with him on unrelated legislation, which Eshoo refused. "Well, my dear," Dingell had responded, before abruptly hanging up, "you will not be a conferee."[8]

The Select Committee would function as "an extension of the office of the Speaker," Pelosi informed Dingell, promising the skeptical chair it would only conduct hearings to establish a record for legislation that would then be written in Commerce and other standing committees. None of this made Dingell feel any better. The Select Committee, he believed, was a "glorified task force" and a direct assault on his committee and on him personally, demonstrating the Speaker's lack of confidence. He became apoplectic when Pelosi disclosed that her choice for chair was Markey, a voluble climate advocate who had been an irritant to Dingell since the 1970s. Markey was savvy about "technologically advanced way[s]" to reach out to younger voters who viewed global climate change as a cutting-edge issue. His chairmanship assured the panel would operate "in cyberspace," using online avatars, and perhaps even holding a hearing in Antarctica.[9] When he learned the Select Committee would be given a $2 million budget, Dingell threatened to withhold funding for Markey's Energy subcommittee.

Although Dingell dismissed the panel as nothing but "showboating," the intended insult had no effect on the message-focused Speaker. "I *want* responsible showboating," Pelosi responded, rather than the plodding, old-school incrementalism Dingell represented.[10] She was similarly unimpressed when the chair warned that he alone possessed the unique skills to legislate on complex energy issues. The last revision of the Clean Air Act, he reminded her, had taken thirteen years, which only confirmed Pelosi's fear he would try to slow-walk climate legislation.

When the Speaker refused to abandon her proposal, Dingell hinted he might join with Commerce's top Republican, Joe Barton (TX), to kill the Select Committee on a floor vote. "That would be a mistake," she advised. "You need to be a part of it." The incoming members "are excited about doing something" on climate, and it was important to demonstrate to the "next generation of voters that we can communicate where they live" on such issues. Besides, the panel would last just two years and have no legislative jurisdiction, she reminded him.[11] Dingell asked her to put that promise in writing, which she agreed to do.[12]

Dingell was not alone in attempting to foil the creation of the Select Committee. Alan Reuther, the legislative representative of the United Auto Workers, feared Markey would press for tougher regulation of the already beleaguered car manufacturers. That argument was unlikely to persuade Pelosi, who had long criticized domestic manufacturers' failure to innovate. But even Henry Waxman, the House's most skilled supporter of clean air legislation, was unenthusiastic about a panel that could diminish the authority of Commerce, which he was next in line to chair. Since no climate bill stood a chance of enactment with Bush in the White House, he suggested Markey use his Energy subcommittee to position the issue for a receptive Democratic administration. Pelosi knew she had to assuage Waxman's misgivings. "He's the key" to selling the Select

Committee, she concluded.[13] At the same time, she warned, "Whoever votes against the Speaker will pay a price."[14]

At the end of January, Pelosi spoke with Dingell in an effort to resolve the lingering animosities. "I give you my word," she pledged, the Select Committee was "designed to complement, not to be a challenge to, your committee. It is not there to cause trouble." But she also reminded Dingell her ultimate goal was a tough climate bill that he would be expected to develop, hopefully by June. "I'm a very strong person," she advised, "and I am not going through all this to produce a weak product." Dingell realized the fight was hopeless, but he predicted, "Markey and I won't be friends."[15]

In early March, Pelosi announced the new committee.[16] Dingell seemed to be less agitated in subsequent weeks, content to display Pelosi's letter time-limiting the panel and assuring it had no law-writing authority. But late in June, he flared again, complaining that the Speaker had discouraged former vice president Al Gore, the leading advocate on climate policy, from testifying before Commerce. That report was untrue, I informed Dingell, after Gore's chief of staff, Roy Neel, affirmed he had told Dingell the exact opposite.[17]

Other innovations by the Speaker were less contentious. Pelosi had a special interest in expanding the diversity of appointed House officials, and she had the authority to achieve that goal. She decided to retain the neutral parliamentarians "for now," avoiding the 1995 contretemps that flared when Gingrich had threatened to dismiss them. She also reappointed the chaplain and sergeant at arms named by Hastert, both white men. As clerk of the House, she named Lorraine Miller, her director of outreach services, as the first African American to hold that position, and she appointed women to other key jobs for the first time, including legislative counsel and the House inspector general. Later, Pelosi would name the first openly gay and Hispanic reading clerks. She also ordered the conversion of closets and public restrooms into spaces dedicated to the needs of nursing mothers and announced her intention to conclude House business at the family-friendly goal of 9:00 p.m., although few believed it feasible. But she declined requests to convert an office just off the House floor into a women's restroom like the one available for men out of concern that the expense of the modification would be ridiculed as self-serving profligacy.

Pelosi unilaterally imposed a ban on smoking on the House side of the Capitol complex except in personal offices where some, like Boehner, continued to do so. Within the House chamber, the Speaker directed the architect of the Capitol to modify the three-tiered podium so that members in wheelchairs could have access to the top level when presiding over the House. A series of ingenious lifts was designed, and on July 26, 2010, the twentieth anniversary of the Americans with Disabilities Act, Jim Langevin (RI) became the first member in a wheelchair to preside from the Speaker's chair.

Pelosi also wanted to demonstrate that Democrats embraced the veterans of the Iraq and Afghan wars even if they disapproved of the war policy, in contrast to the widespread shunning of returning Vietnam veterans in the 1970s. The Speaker created a Wounded Warriors program to encourage House members to recruit veterans injured in battle; by January 2010, nearly thirty had been hired.[18] Pelosi also began hosting wounded vets and their families at the Speaker's Balcony during concerts and fireworks. Celebrities and members often attended the celebrations, and on one occasion, actors Tom Cruise and Katie Holmes spent hours with the soldiers, posing for photographs and calling absent parents and children on the veterans' cell phones.

One decision was specifically intended to symbolically reassert the role of the Congress as a coequal branch of government. Instead of privately signing the original parchment copy before sending a bill to the president, the Speaker orchestrated well-attended press events in the Capitol's Rayburn Room where, surrounded by flags, posters, and legislative heavyweights, she would leave no doubt about the primacy of Congress in crafting the new law. Then, using specially designed black pens—with a gold facsimile of her signature above the words "Speaker of the House" and a miniature Speaker's seal on the pocket clip—she would sign her name and distribute the pens to the bill's authors and other guests.

Meticulous planning went into the swearing-in ceremony in the House chamber on January 6. Protocol called for Dingell as dean of the House to administer the oath to the new Speaker and for Boehner, the defeated candidate, to hand her the gavel. On opening day, members were allowed to bring their young children to the floor, and Pelosi was determined to invite them all —including her own grandchildren—to join her on the podium as she dedicated her speakership to the next generation. When informed of the plan, however, the parliamentarian demurred, citing rules restricting those permitted on the three-tiered podium.

One group Pelosi did not want on the floor during the ceremony were former members employed as lobbyists. Although banned from lobbying in the chamber, they were permitted floor access during "ceremonial or educational" events, which included the ceremonial first day of the new Congress, according to the parliamentarian. In the ethics-conscious era, however, their presence struck many as an Abramoff-type scandal waiting to explode. "She was furious at the parliamentarians for saying it is OK," Miller recalled.[19]

For her "gavel speech," Pelosi focused on themes of deep personal significance: family, faith, and unity, with a special deference to the teachings of Saint Francis. "My parents didn't raise me to be the Speaker," she said. "They raised me to be holy, to have faith and to act upon it in the public arena." She called on Democrats and Republicans to close ranks in the wake of the election. She aspired to be "the Speaker of the *whole* House," pledging to preside over "a Congress that works for everyone," one marked by "civility, integrity, [by providing a] fresh start on the twenty-first century."[20]

Then, defying the parliamentarian, she summoned to the podium all the children in the chamber and banged the gavel for the first time as Speaker, accepting the responsibility "on behalf of America's children."[21] The historic event was marked at celebrations across Washington, including a tea at the Commerce Department's massive ballroom and an evening concert at the National Building Museum that included Pelosi favorites Carole King, Tony Bennett, and surviving members of San Francisco's Grateful Dead.

Pelosi's willingness to engage in high-stakes confrontations with formidable institutionalists like Dingell illustrated the self-confidence that fueled her swift rise to power and her determination to use her authority to reshape the House. Some observers speculated whether she relished challenging powerful men to demonstrate her superior authority, and certainly, there were times when a private comment about the "mansplaining" and arrogance of male leadership hinted that some decisions were motivated, at least in part, by an assertive feminist perspective. In years to come, when asked whether she was considering retirement given her age and unfavorable election outcomes, she would demand to know why similar questions were not asked of male leaders like Mitch McConnell who were close to her age.

But those closest to Pelosi generally downplay any gender motivations, instead interpreting her decisions as indistinguishable from those of male leaders who had secured the reins of power. Her actions demonstrated a willingness to trust her own political instincts when challenging institutional barriers including domineering chairs. "Power is perishable," she would often say, and she intended to employ it aggressively while she held the gavel, even if doing so occasionally meant getting out in front of her caucus and her chairs. Knowing when, how far, and how often to do so was the hallmark of a savvy leader. She was "a troublemaker with a gavel," she would say. "Nobody ever gives away power. When you get it, you must use it."[22]

A rare moment of unity occurred on January 23 when President Bush arrived on Capitol Hill for his first State of the Union to a Democratic Congress. Although his policy agenda was severely at odds with the "6 for '06" priorities, on this evening, the differences were largely papered over. After joining Pelosi and Vice President Dick Cheney on the House podium, Bush turned to shake hands with the Speaker and handed her a copy of the speech. "You're going to be surprised," he told her. "I wondered what that surprise might be," Pelosi wondered. "A veto? A signature on a bill? That would be a surprise!"

Instead, following the Speaker's traditional declaration of having the "high privilege and distinct honor" of introducing the president, Bush returned the sentiment. "I have the high privilege and distinct honor of my own," he declared, "as the first president to begin his State of the Union with these words: 'Madam Speaker.'" The House floor erupted with a prolonged standing ovation, and Bush could not repress a slight smirk. Nancy Pelosi, who as a young girl had first visited the floor with her congressman father decades earlier, beamed from the highest chair in the House chamber.[23]

CHAPTER 4

"EVERYTHING BECOMES URGENT"

Bush's gracious tribute did not diminish the deep partisan divide coursing through the Congress or the Hill's sharp criticisms of his administration. The dramatic change of party control raised expectations of swift approval of Democratic legislation but also exposed the conflicting priorities and ideological fissures running through the Democratic caucus that would complicate efforts to move speedily.

Agriculture Committee chair Collin Peterson (MN), one of the most conservative members of the caucus, wanted to solidify rural support crucial to moderate and conservative Democrats by passing a major agriculture bill. But Xavier Becerra and liberals in the Hispanic Caucus insisted that any bill delivering billions of dollars in aid to farmers also provide legal protections against arrest and deportation for hundreds of thousands of undocumented agricultural workers. Rural and conservative members felt such questions should be addressed through comprehensive immigration reform, which would be a difficult bill to enact.

Other issues were just as divisive. Andy Stern, the president of the Service Employees Union, pressed for universal health care, while Tom Matzzie, the leader of the anti-war group Move On, organized hundreds of events around the country demanding a swift exit from Iraq.[1] By early March, Matzzie and activist veterans were insisting on a statutory timetable for the withdrawal of all US forces from the war zone.[2]

Many of these demands were fanciful, especially with Bush in the White House for two more years. Reid and Pelosi remained focused on the "6 for '06" items, strategizing during their weekly one-on-one meetings attended only by their chiefs of staff, Gary Myrick and me. They also scheduled regular bicameral leadership meetings to nail down timing and messaging strategies. But despite such coordination, the different constituencies, procedural rules, electoral time-tables, and personalities distinguishing the two chambers assured there would be unavoidable conflicts and delays.

The most serious impediment to the Senate's matching the swift action planned in the House was the cloture rule requiring sixty votes to curtail any filibuster so that a bill could be considered. Reid began the 110th Congress with just fifty-one senators, so even with unanimous Democratic support, which was far from guaranteed on divisive issues like Iraq or immigration, he needed nine Republican crossovers to reach sixty, a tall order in a heavily partisan Senate. Any concessions made to secure Republican votes would invariably enrage other senators and many in the House. Beset by such complications, Reid could not hope to match Pelosi's deadline of a hundred legislative hours. When the Speaker pressed him for a definitive timetable, Reid glumly removed his rimless glasses and slowly shook his head. "Sometimes I wish I were back in the House," he softly mused, where the Speaker drove the schedule with a simple majority, although as a House veteran himself, Reid knew the caucus's factions made success a far more challenging proposition than many presumed. Over the years, this internal caucus division often would prove almost as vexing as disagreements with Republicans. "Politics is tough," Pelosi would observe, "but intraparty? Oh, brother!"[3]

While Reid and other senators bemoaned the filibuster as an immutable constraint on their actions, in fact it could be changed at any time by a majority vote of senators (as would occur in 2013 and 2017). But senators of both parties safeguarded their supermajoritarian rules as a time-tested means for extracting concessions from their colleagues, the House, and the president, regardless of which party was in control.[4] Tamper with a carefully crafted Senate product that satisfied the sixty senators' parochial demands, House colleagues were warned, and the likely result would be no bill at all.

Undeterred, the House moved swiftly, addressing concern for the deficit by reinstating the Paygo budget rules. Self-proclaimed anti-deficit Republicans who had ignored the rising deficit during Bush's presidency had little choice but to vote to embrace the restriction they had regularly circumvented, and the Paygo restoration passed 430–1. The massive vote was an early confirmation of the central theorem behind the "6 for '06" agenda: only the GOP majority's opposition to bringing the measure to a vote had obstructed passage of consensus legislation.

Another quick victory was the "Honest Leadership—Open Government" (HLOG) bill tightening congressional ethics rules in response to the "culture of corruption" allegations. The new law prohibited members and staff from accepting gifts from lobbyists, including meals, flights, sporting tickets, and trips with few exceptions. Another transparency reform required disclosure of the authors and beneficiaries of earmarks. Again, dozens of Republicans joined in passing the reforms.

The House also approved HR 1 to implement the recommendations of the 9/11 Commission by an overwhelming 299–128 vote, winning support from all Democrats and over one-third of the Republican conference. Later in the first week, the House approved the first increase in the minimum wage in a decade by a bipartisan 315–116 vote.[5]

So it went for an exhausting week of legislating in the House: reversing Bush's ban on stem cell research, allowing the government to negotiate lower drug prices for Medicare recipients, cutting the cost of student loans—all securing strong bipartisan support. Even a conceptual version of an energy conservation bill, which will be discussed in chapter 7, was approved 264–163, with thirty-six Republicans defecting to support the measure.[6]

By January 19, the "6 for '06" promise had been fulfilled by a bleary-eyed and exhausted House. "Hickory, dickory dock, the Democrats beat the clock," the Associated Press confirmed, in just eighty-seven hours of legislative business.[7] Despite bipartisan public support for most of the bills, Republicans did not join in the acclaim. "Many of the flawed 100-hours bills either face an uphill battle in the Senate or are destined for a veto pen," Boehner predicted with some accuracy, but Pelosi dismissed the dire projections. "It was about keeping our promise," she said, "not about adhering to some process."[8] The remedy, Democrats argued, was not to abandon their priorities in the face of Senate resistance but to add to Reid's majority and elect a Democratic president in 2008 to diminish the Republicans' ability to obstruct.

The campaign agenda was not the only legislation demanding Congress's immediate attention. The short-term CR needed renewal and Reid had limited Republican opportunities for reaching sixty votes—Maine's Olympia Snowe and Susan Collins and Arlen Specter of Pennsylvania—and they were far from reliable. Nor could Reid be confident of conservative Democrats like Blanche Lincoln (AR), Kent Conrad (ND), Mary Landrieu (LA), and Evan Bayh (IN) or the prickly Russ Feingold (WI), Joe Lieberman (CT), and Bernie Sanders (VT).

On the first major spending decision of the 110th Congress, Reid entreated the House to accept whatever version could squeak past sixty senators. Only after closing the book on the prior year's spending, Reid explained, could he address the "6 for '06" measures piling up at the Senate's threshold. But Pelosi and the House majority viewed the request as establishing a poor precedent. If the Senate could not pass a long-term CR covering the rest of the year, the House would pass only short-term extensions, forcing the Senate to revisit the time-consuming issue again and again.

The CR was not the only early issue where senators sought House concessions. To pass the promised minimum wage increase, Reid hinted he might need to add billions of dollars in tax breaks for small businesses. Otherwise, Republican leader Mitch McConnell (KY) would likely block efforts to go to a conference committee with the House to negotiate the final version of the bill. Moreover, the moderate Finance chair Max Baucus (MT) was sympathetic to McConnell and controlled the committee that could produce the tax cuts. Lacking the votes to proceed without the business cuts, the liberal Senate whip Chuck Schumer (NY) urged his House colleagues to accept the tax cuts, which he promised to delete in the conference.[9]

"We're set up *again!*" Pelosi complained, refusing to accept the Senate tax cut number.[10] The squabble was not the kind of unity message the Democratic leadership had hoped to project. But the Senate could take weeks to find the sixty votes to pass a minimum wage increase, Myrick warned, even with the tax breaks. Pelosi dismissed the probability of senators mounting the threatened delays for a bill benefiting their constituents. "Make them vote," Pelosi demanded.[11] Early in March, the Senate agreed to pare down business tax cuts by 84 percent, a major concession to the House. "Fantastic!" Ways and Means chair Charlie Rangel (NY) exulted. The Speaker's success in extracting the concession from the Senate won plaudits in and outside Congress. "She stuck it up the Republicans' ass," San Francisco's former representative John Burton gloated. "She let the . . . senators know who's doing the people's work!"[12]

Despite the early skirmishes, Bush saw the possibility of collaborating with Democrats on several issues including a renewable energy bill and revisions to his signature "No Child Left Behind" education law, negotiated in 2002 with Ted Kennedy, George Miller, and John Boehner. On immigration reform, he urged Senate Republicans to "get their act together," and he expressed gratification at receiving a letter from ten senators endorsing a bipartisan health initiative.[13]

Democrats liked the policy agenda Bush described but were more skeptical about his newfound emphasis on deficit reduction. Since inheriting four years of balanced budgets from the Clinton administration, annual deficits had risen by close to $600 billion in each of the last four years, primarily attributable to the wars in Iraq and Afghanistan, a massive military buildup, two rounds of tax cuts, and the new Medicare prescription drug benefit—none of them paid for. Now, many Democrats believed, Republicans were resurrecting the deficit issue to justify massive spending cuts in the relatively small portion of the budget— non-defense discretionary spending—that included Democratic priorities but bore little responsibility for the burgeoning deficits. "Everything becomes ur- gent" in the minds of members, Bush declared, noting the long list of Demo- cratic priorities, and he promised to veto spending he considered excessive.[14]

As a former campaign chairman, Emanuel wanted to get past the deficit and spending countercharges and make a "hard turn" toward issues that would en- hance the reelectability of the freshmen. "No one wants to talk about the past," he insisted.[15] He felt the party should emphasize ideas that won strong public support like rooting out government waste and fraud and drug reimportation, stopping online identity theft, and ensuring child safety on the internet.

But such advice did not sit well with activists who expected the leadership to press ahead with progressive objectives like facilitating union organizing. Find- ing the balance was Pelosi's responsibility. "My job," the Speaker explained, was not to intimidate people but to be "an orchestrator, a maestro," helping resolve disputes within the caucus, including battles between competing chairmen.[16]

One hope for bipartisan action was immigration reform, and the Speaker credited Bush for having "provided leadership" on the issue. "Energy and climate change are my flagship issues," Pelosi said. "But if we can only do that or im- migration, we should do immigration."[17] However, she was hesitant to ask her members to cast a politically charged vote on issues like the future status of twelve million undocumented residents without an assurance the Senate could pass a bill. Deporting that many people was impractical, Blunt agreed, but con- servatives strongly opposed the path to citizenship many Democrats favored. Bush also ruled out citizenship, but he was open to discussing a path to legaliza- tion for undocumented entrants, an option Pelosi did not rule out. As a result, hopes rose among Democrats for a deal before the political jostling began for the 2008 election. "If it doesn't happen by August," Pelosi predicted, "it won't happen this Congress."[18]

An upbeat Hoyer predicted a bipartisan bill would pass both houses by the summer, and early in March, even McConnell thought a bipartisan agreement was "likely." But Reid remained doubtful because of the opposition of several key Republicans like Chuck Hagel (NE), and Myrick grew increasingly pessi- mistic, accusing Bush and Republicans of squandering a historic opportunity.[19]

House Democrats had their own disagreements as reflected in a whip count hovering around 150, nearly seventy votes short of the number needed for

passage. Several unions voiced the century-old concern about cheap labor flood-
ing US job markets and undercutting high-wage union jobs. The threat of job
competition was shared by the Black Caucus, which demanded a jobs program
to soften the impact.[20] Other unions favored action, especially unions representing a significant number of lower-income Hispanic members that saw an
opportunity to boost their memberships with hundreds of thousands of green
card holders.

Distrust between the houses also represented an obstacle to moving ahead.
Several conservative senators worried that their bill would invariably become
more pro-immigrant in a conference committee dominated by Democrats.
Many House Democrats, including the Hispanic Caucus, worried they would
be pressured to acquiesce in a Senate bill designed to win Republican votes to
secure the sixty-vote margin needed to avoid a filibuster. The CHC pointed, for
example, to a proposal for a lengthy border fence advocated by Hagel (NE) and
Mel Martinez (FL), an idea Pelosi dismissed as "the most ridiculous, with strong
competition." Nevertheless, she agreed to keep an open mind. "If [a fence] was
needed to get a bill," she reluctantly agreed, "then OK."[21]

Even with an agreement among Bush, Kennedy, and Specter to grant 12
million undocumented residents green cards, the pace remained slow and the
infighting grew. By late March, the White House and John McCain (AZ), a
key vote and presidential contender, told Reid they were no longer interested
in actively pursuing the legislation.[22] On June 7, a cloture effort to take up the
bill garnered just thirty-four votes, signaling a probable dead end for the issue
in the 110th Congress.

The early public enthusiasm for the new Congress began to wither as the
pace of legislating on issues like lobbying reform, the 9/11 Commission bill, and
gas price gouging slowed in the Senate. "McConnell is tying things up," Reid
told Pelosi, in part in retribution for his slow-walking a Bush judicial nominee
accused of using racially derogatory language. "It's hard to pass *anything* in the
Senate," Reid lamented.[23] "Do the best the Senate can," Pelosi counseled, "then
we can negotiate in a conference with the White House."

The new polling certainly indicated Democrats were "taking a bit of a hit"
just weeks into the new session, evidence that the party's messaging was "not
breaking through."[24] Voters were "very cynical," Emanuel worried, especially
about the Republican-hyped issues of spending and deficits. By nearly a four-
to-one margin (68 to 18 percent), voters said "government consistently wastes
money." Even among Democrats, the inability to pass many of the big initiatives swiftly was dissipating enthusiasm; just months after the swearing in, the

progressive grassroots group Move On was preparing a report castigating the "do-nothing" Congress.

The schedule of the "New Direction" Congress was punishing, the achievements limited; some wondered how long the pace could be sustained. The short time frame of House terms meant attention would invariably soon turn to re-election planning and the willingness of many members to tackle controversial issues would diminish. After five exhausting months, "everyone is tired," Miller counseled Pelosi. "*You* are tired." The Speaker dismissed his assessment. "*I'm* not tired," she rebuked Miller. Indeed, that same day, she sent the leadership a lengthy schedule outlining her expectations during the coming months. "These are our priorities," her note declared. She was open to discussing how they were handled, but not the issues themselves. "Let me know if you have anything to add."[25]

CHAPTER 5

"THE SLOWEST SHIP"

As the Memorial Day break approached, Pelosi armed her members with laminated pocket cards detailing the achievements of the "New Direction" Congress. The House had approved deficit control, lobbying reform, job creation, a minimum wage increase, removing energy company subsidies, open and ethical government, and veterans' benefits. Congress also had incorporated provisions into war spending bills to hold the Iraqi government accountable for progress both on the battlefield and in building a democratic government in Baghdad.[1] But the Senate had still to act on many of the initiatives, and the agenda for the rest of the year remained daunting.

"We lose control of our destiny by Thanksgiving," Emanuel pronounced, when attention would invariably pivot to the 2008 election.[2] The survival of some Democratic freshmen depended on retaining the support of independent voters who had swung behind Democrats in 2006 expecting they could deliver on their promises. "Independents want to get things done!" Emanuel reminded the leadership. Since portions of the Democratic "base [were] dejected" that more had not been accomplished, keeping those independents content was crucial to maintaining the majority.

An important issue to independent voters was reducing or eliminating earmarks, legislative provisions that directed government largesse to specific districts or states. The new GOP leader, Boehner, was the atypical Republican who had battled earmarks throughout his career, and he raised vigorous objections when a large number appeared in two appropriations bills, Energy and Water, and Interior.

Members unsurprisingly loved having the ability to direct spending to their constituents and contributors, often without full public review and sometimes dropped into bills when no one was looking. Leaders of both parties, in both the

House and the Senate, had long employed earmarks to encourage recalcitrant members with a reason to support a bill they otherwise might oppose. But the practice smacked of sleaze and secrecy, and Pelosi had instructed Obey to impose transparency reforms on future appropriations bills. The chair endorsed a 50 percent reduction as well as requiring the author of any earmarks to assure there was no conflict of interest. But Obey's proposal was unwelcome in the Senate where Reid said it "put pressure on senators" he needed for key votes. He offered a 30 percent cut instead.[3]

The intense scrutiny around ethics complicated the effort to resolve the "Honest Leadership and Open Government" bill. The bill included a ban on member use of private aircraft intended to discourage members from taking favors from corporate or affluent interests. But private planes often were the only practical means of traveling through vast western and rural districts, and the proposed provisions were loosened to allow some travel. Another disagreement involved the House's restriction on bundling campaign contributions, the practice of a donor gathering donations from multiple sources. The Senate's rejection of the House's ban elicited opprobrium from the Speaker. "You screwed us on bundling!" she scolded Reid, an atypically strong accusation from someone who scrupulously avoided off-color language. Reid promptly blamed Pelosi's California colleague Sen. Dianne Feinstein and Republican leader Mitch McConnell, a longtime opponent of campaign finance restrictions whom Reid termed "gutless." Exasperated, Pelosi agreed to drop the bundling provision if necessary to pass the bill, and Reid leapt at the offer.[4]

The houses also disagreed on how long to bar former members and staff from going through a "revolving door" to become lobbyists trying to influence their former colleagues. The practice had become toxic as a result of former House majority leader Tom DeLay's notorious K Street Project, which installed large numbers of former staff into corporate lobbying jobs. On this issue, the two houses agreed to disagree. The House's one-year ban was half that favored by the Senate.

Even these restrictions did not satisfy the most ardent of reformers who insisted on bans on gifts and parties at national conventions; some demanded that every member or staff encounter with a lobbyist, however incidental, be reported. Most of the leadership recoiled from overly onerous regulations and wanted to focus on the worst practices so Republicans could not "turn the tables on us on corruption and ethics" by inflating petty violations into major accusations of wrongdoing. These and other disagreements delayed finalization of the broadly favored ethics law for months.[5]

Senate leaders offered gloomy assessments about the prospects for taking up other House-passed bills.[6] There was "no chance" for repealing Bush's tax cuts for the affluent or for passing labor's card check bill to facilitate unionization drives, Reid bluntly reported. The resistance came not only from Republicans but also from several moderate Democrats like Baucus. With spending cuts and tax increases encountering opposition from disparate wings of the party, there was little new money available for Democratic initiatives the base demanded without adding to the deficit, and that was opposed by the Blue Dog caucus.

Democrats also faced internal dissent on emotionally charged cultural issues favored by the party's base. Obey, one of the rare liberals who opposed abortion, angered pro-abortion groups by approving $28 million to support abstinence programs to reduce pregnancy rates. The Speaker, a devout but pro-choice Catholic, was no fan of that form of birth control. "I had five kids" in six years, she told a Whip meeting. "I *know* God's a man." Democrats faced similar disagreements over stem cell research, as illustrated by the thirty-one Democrats who joined in the 213–204 defeat of a bill to reverse Bush's ban. Pelosi regrouped and brought a Senate-passed version to the floor, and this time it passed 247–176, with just sixteen Democrats voting "no" and thirty-seven Republicans voting in favor. But when Bush vetoed the bill, there were insufficient votes to override, leading some to question the wisdom of having picked the fight. Reid called the battle a "disaster" for exposing marginal members to criticism.[7]

Internal caucus disagreement also broke out over the farm bill that combined aid to farmers for the rural, moderate faction crucial to maintaining the majority with nutrition programs vitally important to liberals representing urban centers. For the most part, this dichotomy cleaved along racial and ethnic lines that made the debate even more delicate. In addition, CBC members insisted on adding $5 billion ordered by the courts to compensate Black farmers for decades of exclusion from federal farm supports. Because the bill modernized archaic but munificent payments to farmers, rural Democrats like Marion Berry (AR) described it as "a political disaster," insisting the farmer safety net was being undercut by urban liberals "pandering to the environmental community."[8] A failure to unite the factions could mean no farm bill in 2007, a severe blow to the agriculture economy, rural voters, and moderate Democrats.

Yet another wedge issue involved whether employees of the Transportation Security Administration (TSA), created after the 9/11 terrorist attacks, should be granted collective bargaining rights. The Bush administration adamantly opposed unionization and threatened a veto if it was included in the bill implementing the 9/11 recommendations. Democrats were divided when McConnell hinted he would drop his opposition to the bill if the labor provision were de-leted. The offer had some appeal since the 9/11 families were "getting impatient" with the congressional delays and some threatened a negative ad campaign against Pelosi for defending the unionization provision.[9]

The AFL-CIO leadership was willing to call Bush's bluff on the veto, but most legislators were not. The responsibility of calling the avuncular AFL presi-dent, John Sweeney, fell to the Speaker, who explained the bill would simply die if the organizing provision were not deleted. Even if Reid could find the votes in the Senate to pass it, he would never be able to override a veto. "We promised to pass this bill, and I don't have much choice," she explained, promising to try to add the organizing language to another bill, which Sweeney surely recognized as an empty promise.[10]

The inability to produce legislation on immigration, State Children's Health Insurance Program, lobbying, earmarks, the farm bill, and more was quickly tarnishing the Democrats' promises of delivering for the base.[11] Party strategists worried that the mushrooming list of contentious bills undercut party discipline and devalued the tightly crafted "6 for '06" package. Even a resolution honoring women compelled to serve as World War II sex slaves for Japanese troops be-came bogged down when the US ambassador warned that passage could bring down the teetering Tokyo government. "The Republicans are saying we are get-ting nothing done!" warned Emanuel.[12] Still, the legislative logjams did not seem to be hurting members in battleground districts, who continued to poll around 60 percent approval, and overall, Democrats retained a fifteen-point advantage. Even so, warned former White House aide Doug Sosnick, "The window is clos-ing for this cycle" to pass key legislation.

Public opinion was so favorable to Democrats that they were even tied with Republicans on the crucial issue of safeguarding the country, a typical party weakness. "If the Republicans don't have [the] terrorism [issue]," pollster Geoff Garin advised, "they have nothing."[13] But one security issue prompted bitter internal Democratic battles: use of special Foreign Intelligence Service Act (FISA) courts to authorize domestic surveillance. Civil libertarians feared intrusiveness by law enforcement while conservatives viewed the FISA process as unnecessarily cumbersome. Bush was demanding swift action on a FISA ex-tension, warning in a message to the Hill that "under the current statute, we are missing a significant amount of foreign intelligence that we should be col-lecting to protect our country. Every day that Congress puts off these reforms," he ominously warned, left the intelligence agencies hamstrung and Americans vulnerable to terrorism.

The Senate swiftly approved the bill 60–28 and recessed, hoping the House would simply ratify the same language.[14] And in fact, a formidable group including Hoyer and Intelligence chair Reyes warned about the risk from a protracted confrontation if a terrorist attack was linked to the FISA delay. "The Senate won't move and we can't win," frustrated Judiciary chair John Conyers (MI) told Pelosi.[15] Although the Speaker vehemently opposed the Senate bill, she bowed to reality and the House passed it 227–183, primarily with Republican votes.[16] Pelosi herself voted no.

The experience flared the tension between the Hill allies. "I'm very annoyed at Harry for allowing the Senate to leave us with a bad bill," she said. "I've had it with the Senate!" The pattern of the Senate expecting the House to concede was a deep worry. "We need to look out for us" in dealing with the Senate, Pelosi counseled. As to the Bush administration, she was even more blunt. "Forget negotiations with the White House," she advised. "It just takes up time."[17]

But the House sometimes put itself in a disadvantageous position by passing measures that gratified the liberal wing of the caucus but faced insuperable odds in the Senate. "We must operate from a position of strength," Emanuel declared, and "not look like we are suing for peace." It was important to show voters that Democrats appear to be "willing to meet [Republicans] halfway and find common ground" and let the minority be the ones to appear obstructionist. He suggested the Speaker send Bush a public letter declaring "we are ready to deal, here are our offers." One issue that fit Emanuel's description was an infrastructure initiative that would "identify a bridge in every district" that needed replacing or repairing; Republicans would be hard-pressed to refuse to collaborate on such an issue.[18]

A revised set of talking points and plasticized pocket cards for Democratic members was distributed as the House left town for August. Also included at the Speaker's direction was a column she had written identifying an end to the Iraq War as her "highest priority as speaker" even though Congress had appropriated funds for the troops in the battle zone.[19] Days before the break, Pelosi huddled with her messaging and polling experts and tested out a new theme—"Restoring the American Dream"—claiming credit for legislation benefiting middle-income Americans. Just before the meeting broke up, campaign strategist Howard Wolfson drew the participants' attention to an emerging problem. The subprime real estate market, which provided millions of Americans with affordable mortgages, was showing signs of weakness after years of fast profits and vigorous housing sales. Don't ignore the danger signs, Wolfson advised, warning the weak market could escalate into a major financial crisis.[20] Pelosi agreed to raise the topic on an upcoming leadership call.

The messaging challenge led to indifferent efforts during the district work period. Concerned that many members failed to understand the growing influence of the internet, Pelosi designated a "hit team" of members and staff to train offices to plan electronic town hall meetings and utilize social media platforms to reach new voters. "We need to infuse our message with youth," she insisted.

One issue that enjoyed strong support among younger voters but had not been on the "6 for '06" list was the Employment Non-Discrimination Act (ENDA) to bar workplace bias. Even within the LGBTQ community, there were divisions over whether the bill's provisions should extend to transgender people. Barney Frank (MA), the openly gay liberal and a vigorous proponent of the measure, worried that insisting on covering transgender people could jeopardize the entire bill. He recommended deleting the provision, a view shared by many in the Black and Hispanic Caucuses, who were concerned about offending their culturally conservative constituencies.

Frank's assessment that most in the LGBTQ community would accept dropping the transgender provision was refuted by Tammy Baldwin (WI), the only openly lesbian House member. She produced a letter from the Human Rights Coalition (HRC) challenging Frank and counseling that Baldwin was "much closer to the trenches." Yet while the HRC publicly vowed to oppose the legislation if transgender coverage was removed, one leader privately admitted the group could not oppose a truncated bill. At a meeting of three thousand ENDA activists, he reported, 2,500 were "thrilled" with the bill in either form.

Although Pelosi wanted ENDA on the floor by late September, Miller predicted the bill faced "a huge problem" on the House floor, where it could fail by forty votes or more. That dire prediction led several prominent members of the Washington LGBTQ elite to urge abandonment of the bill.[21] There would be "a lot of noise" if they did so, some activists admitted, but "most people in the community are likely to support" whatever strategic decision the Speaker made. In San Francisco, however, one activist predicted a "firestorm" if the bill were pulled and warned Pelosi "would be the fall guy."[22]

When the White House declared that Bush would veto any version of ENDA, vulnerable Democrats pleaded against scheduling a vote. With a whip count showing just 209 commitments, Pelosi pulled the plug, informing Baldwin the bill would only move when there were 218 hard commitments. It's "ridiculous," Pelosi concluded, to put the bill on the floor given the caucus divisions, the inflammatory amendments that might be hard to defeat, Senate indifference, and a certain veto. "If the community can't get its act together," she told one civil rights leader, "I'm not putting members at risk."[23] Like Iraq, choice, stem cells, and other issues, ENDA illustrated the Democrats' internal conundrum: after a decade in the minority, those from safe districts, encouraged by an energized base, insisted on pressing legislative action regardless of the risk to vulnerable members responsible for maintaining the majority.

Other issues could not be deferred as easily. The looming September 30 fiscal year deadline necessitated another CR to avert a government shutdown. Tucked into the must-pass bill was over $10 billion for military activities in Afghanistan and another $7 billion for domestic military bases as well as Democratic priorities like the Women, Infants and Children (WIC) nutrition program, Low-Income Home Energy Assistance Program (LIHEAP), and an extension of the Trade Adjustment Act (TAA) assisting workers impacted by trade policy. Democrats hoped to add additional provisions like applying the wage-boosting Davis Bacon requirements to homeland security construction programs and repealing the Reagan-era Mexico City restrictions barring non-US groups that perform or actively promote abortion from receiving financial aid. House progressives insisted on passing the divisive policies, but a forlorn Myrick, while promising to "tell the Republicans we want it," predicted, "I know they will reject it."[24]

House appropriators were loath to add such controversial provisions to a must-pass CR even if doing so was likely the only way to leverage them onto the Senate floor. Democrats had to pass the CR to avoid a government shutdown and "show that we can govern," Obey insisted, and Hoyer believed Bush was happy to battle with Democrats over the divisive hot-button issues. Reid warned that acquiescing to the House demands could complicate his efforts to pass a CR, which could be a challenge even without adding the divisive provocations.[25] Once again, he raised with the Speaker the possibility of accepting whatever the Senate could pass, which inevitably would entail accepting dozens of Senate earmarks needed to secure the necessary sixty votes.

"Don't back us up to a wall," Pelosi warned. She countered with her own proposal to remove all of the Iraq money from the CR, pass only domestic funding, and then force the Senate to approve war funds including conditions to "chang[e] the course in Iraq this year." When she heard that Hoyer was predicting Democrats would ultimately fold on the Iraq money, an angry Pelosi warned him Reid was "too angry to talk" to her second-in-command. "We need to end the fight," she advised, accept a cut in overall spending, and slash earmarks.[26] "I'm deadly serious," she said. "The members just want to go home."

But the Senate remained defiant, with McConnell insisting on retaining all of the Senate's earmarks and imposing a 2 percent across-the-board cut, which Pelosi rejected as "indefensible." Even so, Myrick warned, any House changes to the Senate version would doom the measure and likely shut down the government on the Democrats' watch. "We need to set priorities," Myrick explained, but Pelosi dismissed the idea if it meant dropping House priorities like climate change.

The two houses were on a collision course on earmarks. "Why are you so afraid of earmarks?" Reid pressed Obey. "The Senate can't agree to a 50 percent cut." Hoyer was sympathetic to Reid's situation, noting the designated spending was "the only way to pass the bills because Republicans get earmarks."[27] But Pelosi was infuriated with the Senate's intransigence. "Nobody's walking out of here saying anything if they want to keep an intact neck," she warned negotiators as they wrestled with the earmark issue. "The House will stick to our guns," she declared. "We will not acquiesce in the Senate's inaction."[28]

The weeks continued to drag as Congress approved a number of short-term CRs to avert shutdowns. Finally, exhausted and angry, the members and the administration cut a deal that produced what conservatives denounced as "the biggest spending bill of all time," funding eleven of the twelve regular appropriations measures at a cost of nearly a half trillion dollars, $20 billion above Bush's red line veto threat. The final measure (which was opposed by a majority of House Democrats) imposed cuts on six of the eleven sections of the budget and included more than nine thousand earmarks costing over $23 billion, some of which Bush vowed to pare back administratively. No one could claim the bill achieved much in terms of advancing policy goals. It was "loaded with pork, gimmicks, excessive spending, and bad policy," the conservative Heritage Foundation concluded, and the budget battles of 2007 ended because there was no consensus to fight on.[29]

The protracted budget confrontation left little time or energy for anything else. "I'm very negative on virtually everything" in the Senate, Myrick admitted. FISA was likely to expire, leaving Democrats vulnerable to a charge of undercutting national security efforts; inaction on tax policy meant the alternative minimum tax that affected upper-income Americans would expire, which left Republicans pleased. "It's a win for the Republicans either way," Myrick explained. Nor could Reid find sixty votes to take up the House's energy package.[30]

"I'm pissed off at Reid," the Speaker declared, for "not putting up a better fight" on a litany of bills left "undone or incomplete" in Reid's chamber.[31] Nor were House members sympathetic to the explanation of senators that the supermajority cloture requirement was to blame, pointing out senators had not been compelled to occupy the floor in all-night talkathons but simply registered an intention to delay a bill brought to the floor. "If there's going to be a filibuster, let's *hear* the damned filibuster," complained Rangel. "Let's fight this damned thing out." Instead, House legislation "died quietly . . . before the first vote was cast." Reid finally filled several rooms off the Senate floor with cots, warning he might force senators to debate around the clock, but the tactic only inflamed additional resentment.

The frustration ran in both directions down the Capitol's long north-south transept. Reid's colleagues complained about Pelosi's "style of governance" and her enthusiasm for sending bills to the Senate that had no chance of passage, making them look ineffectual. "Holding a bunch of Kabuki theater doesn't get anything done," groused Evan Bayh (IN), a conservative Democrat, but Reid brushed off admonitions to keep Pelosi from passing hopeless bills. "I can't control Speaker Pelosi," he explained. "I hope everybody understands that. She is a strong, independent woman. She runs the House with an iron hand."[32] But neither did he appreciate her criticisms when he failed to pass bills he had promised to try to approve. "No one needs to come and tell me I didn't keep my word," he declared.

The disagreements with Bush were even more serious. On three occasions, he chose to use his veto power to stymie bipartisan bills. An extension of the SCHIP bill increasing health coverage from 6.6 million children to 10 million passed the House in the fall by 265 to 159 (with 45 Republicans in support). In the Senate, the vote was 67–29 (with 18 Republicans). "I have all these children gathering in my office," Pelosi told Bush. "I am praying you will sign SCHIP." But the president doubted the program was needed. "After all," he said, "you just go to an emergency room."[33] "I'm still praying," Pelosi reported. Bush gave her credit for persistence. "I like a person who doesn't give up!" he observed. "You can identify with that," she responded.[34]

Angry the bill cost $30 billion above his proposed level, Bush vetoed the SCHIP bill, warning that it "moves our health care system in the wrong direction [toward the] federalization of health care." His action prompted a bipartisan cacophony of opposition, including from Orrin Hatch (R-UT), who charged that "some have given the president bad advice," and Gordon Smith, (R-OR), who criticized "an irresponsible use of the veto pen."[35] The Democratic response was even more vituperative, with Reid denouncing Bush's "heartless veto."

After the House failed to override the veto, a new version was quickly cobbled together, approved, and again vetoed after Bush blamed the congressional leadership for having "refused" to negotiate. The impasse was "a major disappointment" to the Speaker, but Congress could not risk the program lapsing. An agreement was reached on a bill cutting out 75 percent of the expansion Congress wanted, extending the program until a new Congress and administration could address it in March 2009.[36]

Congress was more successful in overriding Bush's veto of a major water resources development bill that showered benefits on members of both parties. "If you throw pork in front of a congressman," Rep. Richard Baker (R-LA) observed, consensus was possible notwithstanding the cost. The $13 billion bill, which passed the House 394–25 and the Senate 91–4, contained a familiar grab bag of nine hundred projects as well as millions for Hurricane Katrina reconstruction. With those margins of approval, Bush's action was "irresponsible," Reid declared, and both houses easily overrode the veto. "Perhaps the president will finally recognize that Congress is an equal branch of government," Reid said, "and reconsider his many other reckless veto threats."[37]

Yet another disagreement involved a defense bill both houses approved by veto-proof margins. Bush objected to a provision freezing Iraqi assets in US banks so that American citizens, including former American prisoners of war tortured during the 1991 Gulf War, could seek $94 million in damages a court had awarded them from the Iraqi government. The Bush administration argued that al-Maliki's shaky government, which had not been in power at the time of the torturing of Americans, "cannot afford to have its funds entangled in such lawsuits." Democratic leaders accused Bush of "bowing to the demands of the Iraqi government," which threatened to withdraw $25 billion in assets from US banks if the provision was not deleted.[38]

The disagreement escalated into a constitutional confrontation when Bush announced he would use a pocket veto to kill the bill once Congress left Washington for the Christmas holiday. The Speaker was incredulous. "How can the president cave in" to a threat from the Iraqi government that, Pelosi quoted US generals, was "the biggest impediment to peace" and whose actions "have not met the sacrifice of US troops"?[39] The "intransigence" of the al-Maliki government and "the Bush reaction are not worthy" of US troops, whose 3.5 percent pay raise would also be voided by the veto, as would increases in veteran health care.

The day after Christmas, House parliamentarian John Sullivan, House counsel Irv Nathan, and Pelosi's staff huddled with White House and Justice Department officials. Nathan dismissed the constitutionality of Bush's action, noting the Senate was technically in session throughout the holiday and the

House could easily reconvene to address a veto. Pocket vetoes were appropriate only when Congress had adjourned and could not reconvene.[40] Although Dan Meyer thought the House was winning the argument, Steve Bradbury of the Justice Department insisted that "only the pocket veto is available to the president now," and he promised, "the bill is going to be vetoed." On December 28, in an action Reid and Pelosi called "unfortunate," Bush issued what he called a "memorandum of disapproval" asserting that a pocket veto blocked any override attempt.

The staff of the House Armed Services Committee was annoyed that the Iraqi assets section, which the Speaker had insisted be included, was responsible for the crisis. The chair, Ike Skelton (MO), "doesn't want to risk the entire bill" over it, they complained, and he wasn't convinced GOP supporters of the bill would join in an override.[41] Skelton became so overwrought by the pressure that he was hospitalized for dehydration.

As Americans hung their Christmas decorations, the atmosphere between House and Senate Democrats was as chilly as the winter weather outside. According to the *Washington Post*, "Democrats in each chamber are now blaming their colleagues in the other for the mess in which they find themselves."[42] Although the House had successfully moved the "6 for '06" agenda in record time, overall there was thin evidence of having moved the country in a "New Direction." The challenge of moving from the minority to the majority and from critics to effective legislators was a complex one, especially without a filibuster-proof majority in the Senate and with a president willing to wield the veto pen.

The internecine Democratic jostling surprised observers who had presumed the greatest challenge would be confronting the Bush administration. And the limited record of achievement denied Democrats the ability to claim credit for much of anything, the messaging team advised. "Whatever we've done is not good enough," Celinda Lake counseled them to say in district events. Culpability for blocking the agenda needed to be placed squarely on Bush, Republicans, and special interests.[43]

Although McCurry remained wedded to a message of bipartisanship, others questioned its validity after a year of interparty battling.[44] At least voters still viewed Democrats very favorably—+14 points in the *Washington Post* poll, +20 according to NBC—even in swing districts. In fact, congressional Republicans had the highest unfavorability of any group polled. On major issues like Iraq withdrawal and energy independence, voters embraced Democrats; only on immigration were Democrats polling negatively.[45]

Pelosi won plaudits for maintaining discipline among the famously fractious

Democrats even though few major bills had been finalized. "Despite her revolutionary, smash-the-china image," noted Michelle Cottlec in the *New Republic*, "Pelosi is a savvy institutionalist who amassed power in part because of her intimate understanding of the House's rules, quirks, and morés." Her deft handling of her legislative issues pleased the party's progressive faction while "propelling [Bush's] slide into political oblivion—blocking his bills, stiff-arming his congressional compatriots, and reminding everyone of how lame the duck has become."[46]

In that *New Republic* profile, I observed Pelosi's embrace of the philosophy of Rolling Stones front man Mick Jagger. "She knows what the members want [and] what the members need," I remarked. "And she knows the difference between the two." My evaluation was graphically confirmed by a top Senate staffer who "works closely with her." The Speaker, the staffer admiringly declared, "has brass balls."

Yet the first year also illustrated the limitations of the majority: caucus factionalism, House and Senate tensions, and the challenge of translating slogans into policy. Despite her insistence she would not be constrained by the "slowest ship," the Democrats' momentum had been checked. But there was also a bright possibility for 2008: an election that could produce a Democrat in the White House and larger congressional majorities, especially in the Senate, that would diminish the obstructive power of McConnell's Republicans. What they did not see coming, however, was a shaking, then a rumbling, and then a near catastrophic collapse of the economy that altered the legislative agenda and forced House and Senate, Republican and Democrat, and the lame-duck president to find untapped reservoirs of trust and collaboration.

CHAPTER 6

THE ECONOMY WOBBLES

The new year began much as the old year ended: with policy and constitutional confrontations between the Democratic Congress and the Republican White House.[1]

Everyone agreed the dispute over the defense bill needed to be solved since a standoff delayed veterans' benefits and a pay raise for active-duty troops. Both the House and Senate Armed Services chairs signaled they could live with the administration's position, and Pelosi and Reid were wary of pressing a battle they could not win.

"There are no votes for that," she told liberals itching for an override fight.[2] Shortly after reconvening in January, the House cleared a revised DoD bill 369-46, including a milquetoast provision granting the president power to waive the provision on Iraqi assets and exhorting Bush to negotiate with the Iraqis "to satisfy the legitimate claims [of] American citizens." A few days later, the Senate followed with a 91–3 vote.

The parties segued into another confrontation over a Bush "signing statement" declaring he would disregard certain provisions of the new law. He had applied such qualifications, used previously by many presidents, to 10 percent of all the laws he had signed. The procedure lacks a clear basis in the Constitution, which does not permit a president to veto a portion of a bill he or she signs.[3] "I reject the notion . . . that he can pick and choose which provisions of this law to execute," the Speaker declared. "His job, under the Constitution, is to faithfully execute the law—every part of it."

The parties also remained enmeshed in an extended disagreement over the December 2006 firing of nine US attorneys (USAs) Bush had appointed; a tenth had been reassigned to make room for a friend of Karl Rove. The firings, insisted David Iglesias, one of the fired USAs, were "a political fragging, pure and simple."[4]

Culpability for the action focused on the White House, including chief of staff Josh Bolten and counsel Harriet Miers "acting at the direction of the President of the United States," according to House counsel Irvin Nathan.[5] Early in 2007, a House subcommittee demanded an explanation for the terminations from Attorney General Alberto Gonzalez, who criticized the USAs as "poor performers," although former deputy attorney general James Comey called Iglesias "one of our finest." Nathan was convinced that Gonzalez's testimony was "false and misleading testimony" and that the firings were attributable to the White House opinion that the USAs focused excessively on GOP misdeeds instead of investigating Democratic legislators.[6] The USAs had reported substantial political interference, including "complaints, improper telephone calls and thinly veiled threats from a high-ranking Justice Department official or members of Congress."[7]

Bolten and Miers declined to provide direct testimony about the firings, asserting that as employees of the executive branch at the time, they were immune from congressional subpoenas. Democrats had few options since any contempt prosecution they might demand would invariably be ignored by Bush's own Justice Department. Nor was Pelosi inclined to use her authority to order the House sergeant at arms to arrest the offending parties.

The administration offered to let the aides be questioned privately, without swearing an oath to tell the truth with no transcript of the interrogation. "This is beyond arrogance," the exasperated Speaker said. "It's hubris taken to the ultimate degree."[8] Bowing to the White House's claim of immunity would render the House a "paper tiger," unable to enforce its edicts. At Pelosi's direction, Nathan proposed bipartisan legal action as Hastert and Pelosi had undertaken in the Jefferson case to "preserve the institutional integrity and powers" of the House. "The White House is thumbing its nose at us," Nathan told the GOP leader. "Next time, it could be a Democratic president and a Republican Congress."[9] But Boehner turned him down cold. The GOP leader "wanted Congress to do nothing" with the matter so he could "blame the Democrats" for conducting a partisan witch hunt, Nathan believed.[10] With negotiations at a standstill, the House voted 223–32 early in 2008 to hold Bolten and Miers in contempt of Congress. Boehner had dismissed the inquiry as "a politically charged fishing expedition," and when the Speaker called for a vote, he suggested, "Let's just get up and leave the floor." Most Republicans followed him out.

Months later, district judge John Bates rejected the White House's separa-
tion of powers assertion and ruled for the House on every point.[11] The ruling
was a "ringing reaffirmation of the fundamental principle of checks and balances
and the basic American idea that no person is above the law," Judiciary chair
John Conyers exulted. Asked for a comment, Democratic presidential candidate
Barack Obama promised, "You won't see that [kind of obstruction] if we are
in the White House!" But when he and the Speaker discussed the case shortly
after the 2008 election, Obama responded like the incoming head of the executive branch. His staff asked Nathan to agree to set aside the judgment to avoid
creating an unfavorable precedent that could leave a president subject to congressional investigators.[12] "Nancy, this is the best you'll get," the president-elect
insisted. "Take it." But Pelosi was no less resistant to a Democratic president's
effort to diminish congressional power. "For the purpose of this discussion, it's
not Nancy," she corrected Obama. "It's Madam Speaker."[13]

The interbranch dispute, while significant, was less consequential for the nation than the wobbling of the economy, which Democrats were anxious to blame
on Bush.[14] Emanuel's former Wall Street colleagues were becoming "hysterical"
about the indicators, especially the plummeting of home sales and prices and a
57 percent increase in foreclosures over the prior January.[15] "No one wants to say
'recession,'" the Speaker told her informal finance brain trust, which included
Alan Sinai, Felix Rohatyn, and Bill Hambrecht. But House members were frustrated that the Senate had taken up none of the nine bills they had already
approved to aid vulnerable mortgage holders, and Barney Frank, the Financial
Services chair, had enlisted Treasury secretary Hank Paulson, a former Goldman Sachs chairman, to press Reid.[16]

Something much broader than mortgage aid was clearly required, and the
economic advisors recommended a collaboration with Bush on a stimulus that
would also help Democrats burnish a bipartisan image. Pelosi took the advice to
heart, asking Bush to convene the joint leadership to work on a plan to stimulate
consumer spending and instructing her staff to "work in a bipartisan way to
avert a downturn."[17]

Such legislation was easier said than done. A stimulus bill of tens of billions
of dollars was a hard sell for Republicans and conservative Democrats, especially if it added to the deficit by waving the Paygo requirement, as was common
for recovery measures. In the early discussions, each party took some ideas off
the table. Republicans refused to consider raising taxes on affluent or large cor-
porations, and Democrats rejected a Bush plan to increase Medicare costs for

seniors or cut payments for health providers. House and Senate Democratic staffs quickly produced a laundry list of provisions: a tax rebate of $500 per household, expansion of the child tax credit (CTC), aid to states encountering rising Medicaid and unemployment insurance (UI) costs, expanded food stamp eligibility, low-income energy assistance, increased housing loans, and mortgage relief. A priority was an infrastructure jobs initiative funding "shovel ready" transportation improvements whose "blueprints are ready to go." The administration pushed to include a stalled trade pact with Peru; Democrats countered with expanding Trade Adjustment Assistance (TAA) to assist workers displaced by such trade agreements. As senators exerted "tremendous pressure" to incorporate provisions that threatened to spin the cost of the bill out of control, Reid had to push back.[18] "I need to rein them in," Reid sighed. Only spending conforming to the speaker's alliterative criteria—"timely, targeted, and temporary"—would be permitted because "we need the president's signature," she reminded Reid.

The parties' conflicting ideologies quickly became evident. Boehner favored $50 billion in business investment deductions and rebates for upper-income earners since "they pay the taxes." But rebates that excluded non–tax-paying lower-income families were a nonstarter for Democrats, who rejected Republican initiatives like accelerated business deduction of investments. There was greater consensus around policies aiding banks and other lenders impacted by the housing crisis.

In a mid-January discussion with Bush and Paulson, congressional leaders agreed to move, and "the quicker the better" in Boehner's words. Bush, who had been "absent from the scene" overseas, wanted to "tell the American people we are feeling their pain" and suggested it "might look more bipartisan" if he presented Congress with "broad principles [that] could be a starting point" for the legislation.[19] Democrats suspected Bush would propose popular but costly tax cuts that Congress would be criticized for paring back to make room for Democratic priorities. "If the president alone drafts and releases a bill," the atmosphere would be combative rather than collaborative, Pelosi cautioned. Putting Congress in the position of responding to a Bush plan would squander an important "opportunity to send a message of common ground to the American people."

But Bush ignored her concern and revealed his own plan while welcoming congressional modifications to make it "look more bipartisan." As Democrats had feared, the centerpiece was a tax rebate aimed "at putting money in peoples' pockets," said Paulson, as well as business tax cuts.[20] "Let's keep it simple and macro, and get the money out quickly," he suggested. How much money was the president prepared to spend? asked Reid. "I haven't made up my mind," Bush answered ambiguously.

The administration plan was "more like a notification than a consultation," Reid complained, and that made it "real difficult" to round up Democratic votes. Pelosi summarily rejected Bush's tax cut–friendly plan but promised to work with Republicans to produce "a better plan," including the infrastructure jobs component missing in Bush's proposal. Only with such a provision, Reid advised, would a bill "move very fast."[21] That optimism was immediately countered by McConnell, who expressed astonishment at the Democrats' spending plans and predicted Republicans would not support it. Paulson also rejected the call for large outlays. "I was expecting that," he told Pelosi in a follow-up call. "We can't have big spending. We're trying to keep the conservatives quiet."[22]

Pelosi was more concerned about keeping her caucus unified, but she chose to focus on the good news. "The president acknowledged the need for a stimulus package," and they would write one that steered the benefits toward middle-income families and small businesses. Without informing Reid, Pelosi proposed a House–White House alliance that would "put big pressure on the Senate" not to bid up the cost with earmarks. "Don't give a rebate to everyone," she suggested; target those who would spend the rebate quickly for stimulative effect. Off the record, Paulson agreed to limit the scope of the tax cut and pledged to "keep the conservatives quiet." "We'll celebrate in a week," she assured Paulson.[23]

But House conservatives were unhappy with the drift of the legislation. Most Republicans—Boehner was an exception—opposed temporarily expanding food stamp eligibility, pointing to past emergency expansions that proved difficult to roll back after the crisis passed. Republicans also drew the line at Democrats' insistence that tax rebates be "refundable"—available to those who did not pay enough taxes to qualify for them—which progressive economists argued drove money to the people certain to spend it immediately.[24]

"I can't sell rebates to non-income taxpayers," Boehner insisted. But under the GOP plan, I noted, a twenty-eight-year-old single worker earning $28,000 would receive no relief while high-income earners would. Boehner backed off, offering to cap eligibility for the rebates to those earning $75,000 (or $150,000 for a couple).[25]

Discussions were less cordial with the intractable administration that Pelosi blamed for running the economy into the ground. "I don't want anything to do with your potential recession!" she lectured Paulson. "If we are going to reach an agreement, we need to have more than just agreeing with what *you* want! We need some agreement on *our* package." Pelosi refused to delete any of the Democrats' priorities, insisting the bill "need[ed] to be more robust" than Bush and the Republicans favored.[26] And she warned her negotiating partners she would abide by the old deal-cutters' adage: "Nothing is agreed to until *everything* is agreed to."

Privately, Pelosi offered Paulson a trade: a smaller infrastructure jobs program in return for dropping nonstimulative provisions like the upper-income tax cuts. "It will be a great signal for the whole country if we move together," the secretary agreed, and he would try to sell McConnell on the trade-off. Pelosi disabused him of any suggestion the House would simply accept whatever he could sell to the senators. "The Senate can either come to agreement with the House," she declared, "or pass our bill."[27] The secretary assured her he was prepared to move forward only with the House if the Senate proved too contentious.

Two days later, plans were underway for what Paulson described as a "touch the gloves" session to finalize a plan. The spreading crises in the credit markets had growing international implications, Paulson warned, especially in Asia, and could prompt an imminent drop in housing prices and large insurance losses, all of which could precipitate a worldwide slowdown. The stimulus bill needed to be bigger than initially planned—about $150 billion—but no larger, to avoid inflaming deficit concerns.

In the interest of speed, Reid proposed the House begin by sending a bill to the Senate. House negotiators became immediately suspicious that once the House revealed its cards, the Senate would load on trinkets for senators to discourage a filibuster and then dare the House to jeopardize finalization of the bill. Privately Boehner was "hopeful, optimistic, and realistic" despite the intra-House belly-bumping disagreements, but Pelosi cautioned the anti-earmark GOP leader they would have to bite their tongues about "overreaching" by senators. "We do not have the luxury of getting everything we want," she warned, "and then we fail."[28]

As reporters blanketed the Capitol seeking leaks on the design of the recovery package, Pelosi was closeted with Paulson and Boehner in the Speaker's "Board of Education" room on the Capitol's first floor, safely sheltered from prying journalists. Paulson, exasperated by the unfamiliar congressional machinations and nursing a bad cold, was nearing his wit's end. "The Senate Republicans make me feel like taking a shower," he admitted.[29]

Anxious to reach a deal with the House, he offered a $200 child tax credit at a cost of $12 billion (less than one-third the Democrats' version) and suggested the administration might be willing to eliminate the income eligibility requirement, but Boehner quickly objected. "No reimbursement unless the parents pay taxes," he insisted, which would disqualify millions of families. Expanded food stamps and unemployment insurance also had to go, demands Pelosi abruptly dismissed, and it seemed the impasse would drag on. But a combination of fatigue and urgency finally intruded, and in quick order, the negotiators reached compromises that channeled over a third of the benefits to low-income Americans who paid no taxes.

My long-standing relationship with Boehner, stretching back to the Education and Workforce Committee, proved beneficial in closing the deal. Boehner remained intransigent against dropping the CTC's minimum parental earnings level from its $10,000 level. "Let's go to $3,000," I floated, but he shook his head. That was the highest level the Speaker could accept, I pressed, with Pelosi and Paulson looking on. He looked at me for a long moment and said, "OK." It was a textbook example of how personal relationships—along with fatigue—influence the lawmaking process.

Pelosi insisted the bill pass quickly to prevent its unraveling in "the perishable city," and the blowback did not take long to begin. Rangel objected to absence of a UI extension, especially given the inclusion of business tax breaks. "We thought we had the Republicans' backs against the wall," he complained. Bush's initial plan was terrible, and "our improvement on it isn't great." But Pelosi didn't have time for the second-guessing, and Emanuel pointed out that unlike earlier Bush tax policies, most benefits would not flow to the wealthy. "We need to move fast to seal the deal," she insisted, promising to revisit UI. Conservative Democrats expressed concern about the Paygo waiver that could invite the Senate to load up the bill with spending.

But the bipartisan leaders rallied their forces behind the agreement as "the best option at this time," in Hoyer's words. Bill and David Harris, Democratic activists who had devoted years promoting the CTC, called the expanded eligibility "fantastic," and Pelosi urged the caucus to embrace the bill before Bush seized full credit. "Tell the Senate not to mess with the rebate package," Pelosi warned Paulson. "You need to tell them what cannot happen." Paulson reported he was working to keep Republicans in line.

Still, Pelosi was worried about Reid's ability to control senators. "The Senate is a mess," she told Paulson, "but they can't hurt our plan." It was up to the White House to present a "definite view of what was acceptable," she informed Boehner, but the word from the White House was anything but definitive. The Senate Finance alternative bill was "not the end of the world," Meyer reported, even though "the president prefers the House bill."

Reid counseled the nervous Paulson that the Senate would make "only small changes" to the House's bill, but the Treasury secretary had learned enough about Capitol Hill to know what that meant. "The bazaar is open," Paulson glumly told the Speaker. Baucus and Grassley were contemplating tax revisions that would blow open the cost of the bill. "They're joined at the hip," a disapproving Pelosi told Boehner, who agreed, "They're closer than Siamese twins."[30] Paulson pressed back against the senators. "Baucus was begging, 'Where can we make changes?'" but the secretary told the Montanan, "None."

But Reid could not simply tell his members what they could not have. "I know what we need to do," Reid explained, and that included securing Republican votes by steering additional benefits to the affluent. Doing so "causes a gag reflex," Reid agreed, and he would seek to compensate by expanding rebates for seniors with little or no income, extending UI, and funding a host of Democratic priorities from low-income energy aid to food stamps, increases that Hoyer warned might complicate keeping the Blue Dogs in line. Pelosi was furious with the tax changes, charging senators with "tak[ing] money from pockets of working-class people," and Paulson shared her concerns. Raising the bill's cost by $7 billion risked a veto he desperately wanted to avoid. He pledged Bush would honor the Pelosi-Paulson agreement and veto any bill that made extensive changes, but Pelosi explained that if the Senate added a UI extension, "we'd have to accept it."

As McConnell employed procedural delays to stall Senate action, Pelosi warned that "undermining our package is not an act of friendship. Time is passing," she warned Paulson, and the Senate's additions would necessitate further delays while a conference committee sorted out the discrepancies. Indifferently, senators did exactly as the House had feared, loading the bill with rebates to coal companies, clean energy bonds, home construction incentives, and tax benefits for oil wells, which a disgusted Paulson termed "my favorite so far."[31]

"They have to pack everything with pork" to get cloture, Pelosi told her own leadership. "It's not about the sixty votes. They don't *want* to move fast." She promised to scrutinize the Senate bill and "throw down the gauntlet" on issues important to her caucus members. Boehner shared the Speaker's frustration, speculating about uniting with her to jam the Senate. "It would be a courageous act," he told Pelosi.[32]

The tension between the houses spiked when Myrick privately accused the Speaker of colluding with McConnell to delete provisions added by Democratic senators.[33] Pelosi was incensed by the accusation, let alone by the effrontery of a staffer leveling such an allegation. "That's not true!" she rebuked him. "Where did you hear that?" Reid quickly tried to patch things up, proclaiming his support for the Speaker, but the hatchet was not yet buried.[34] No sooner had Pelosi shaken hands with a chastened Myrick than she tore into Reid for reducing benefits to women and children. "This is supposed to be a *stimulus*," she reminded Reid, "not a stimulus and *pork* package." Both she and Paulson condemned Baucus for "always loading up Finance Committee bills" with provisions that constituted a "big bonanza," especially for energy producers.[35]

The stringent blowback worked, and on February 7, word circulated that senators would abandon their sweeping rewrite of the House bill, although they still increased the size of the tax rebates before passing it 81–16. The urgency of the moment overcame the institutional annoyance at being pressed again to accept the Senate's changes, and the House voted 380–34 for the revised version. A week later, Bush signed the stimulus, calling it a "booster shot" for the American economy.

The plan had gone from proposal to law in "relative breakneck speed," CNN noted, even if few believed its modest provisions represented "the key to ending or preventing a recession."[36] The final cost was $152 billion, remarkably close to the original estimate considering the ballooning floated during Senate consideration. As Democrats had insisted, the $300 to $600 tax rebates were targeted to lower- and middle-income Americans, and the bill also included the Republicans' tax breaks to boost business investment. Barney Frank called the bill "the most progressive piece of tax policy in American history" because of both the billions of dollars it steered to lower-income Americans and the mortgage refinancing option he and Senate chair Chris Dodd had included.[37]

In a celebratory phone call, the president confidently asserted that the "country will be pleased we came together." "We both gave a little," agreed Boehner. "Harry Reid is singing your praises," she told a pleased Bush. "It's a good deal," the president responded, commending Pelosi for persuading a "raucous caucus" to support a bill many still regarded as inadequate. And while much of the

$96 billion in tax rebates ultimately was saved rather than spent by nervous Americans fearing a worsening of the economy, a Federal Reserve study concluded the rebates "had a non-trivial effect on aggregate spending."[38]

"We will praise you," Bush assured the Speaker, for having "hammered it out," but Pelosi glumly replied, "Now *we're* going to get hammered!" Pelosi knew her constituency. AFL-CIO president John Sweeney blasted the bill as a "Goddamned disgrace" for failing to include the UI extension, and Paulson sheepishly acknowledged that even his eighty-five-year old mother, a liberal Republican, complained that extended jobless aid was not included.

Yet the approval of the stimulus was a rare example of divided government acting in a swift manner despite deep ideological disagreement, deep partisan contentiousness over issues like the Iraq War, and in the midst of a quickening electoral season. Arguably, that consensus was achieved because the economic risks of inaction were even greater than the risks of collaboration, a not uncommon precondition for bold action. But the success did little to calm the roiling anger between the branches and the parties on other matters.[39]

Still, the high-pressure and conciliatory deliberations surrounding the Bush stimulus turned out to be a fortuitous dry run for a far graver crisis that emerged later in the year, necessitating even greater levels of trust, risk-taking, and collaboration under deeply unfavorable political circumstances.

CHAPTER 7

"THE FLAGSHIP"

One bright spot in the early tumult of the "New Direction" Congress was the legislation promoting energy renewability and efficiency.[1] For Pelosi, climate change constituted the most urgent challenge confronting humanity, and she pledged sweeping legislation would be "the flagship" of her speakership. An ally in the effort was former vice president Al Gore, who in March discussed with the Speaker the issue for which he would be awarded the Nobel Peace Prize six months later.[2]

Energy policy always proved difficult for Congress, in part because defenders of the status quo were found in both parties. Dozens of the Democrats' most powerful and most marginal members represented districts where fossil fuels provided thousands of jobs sensitive to the impact of environmental regulations and fuel prices; unions, a traditional component of the Democratic base, were often at odds with the youthful green faction. Many of these Democrats joined with pro-industry Republicans to resist emission and efficiency controls and promote aggressive fuel production. Waxman's own staff acknowledged it would be "very hard to prevail" on imposing rigorous standards given energy-oriented districts, including many represented by some CBC members who worried tough environmental protections cost minorities jobs.[3]

The Corporate Average Fuel Economy (CAFE) standard was created by the Energy Policy and Conservation Act two years after the 1973 embargo that had quadrupled gasoline prices and left millions of Americans on long refueling lines. Under the law, automotive manufacturers had been required to meet higher mileage standards, but in the ensuing thirty years, vigorous industry lobbying had prevented an upgrading of the standards.

Pelosi and a clique of energy reformers were adamant the New Direction Congress would end that lethargic response. Introduced on January 12, 2007, with 199 sponsors, the Clean Energy Act was approved by the House just six days later with only four Democrats opposed and thirty-four Republicans voting in favor, an unusually strong bipartisan vote on a volatile issue. The legislation was not a detailed blueprint for ending dependence on carbon-based fuels but served as a fourteen-page aspirational placeholder to put the House on record early in the session in favor of a smorgasbord of initiatives for promoting clean, renewable, domestic sources of energy: solar, wind, and biofuels, efficiency in motor vehicles and buildings, and the capture of greenhouse gases. It also set ambitious goals for a renewable fuels standard (RFS) and a renewable electricity standard (RES) to replace fossil fuels with nonpolluting sources. Far from damaging the American economy, as critics alleged, energy activists insisted a conversion to renewable sources would yield millions of new jobs. To help pay for the program, the bill slashed billions of dollars in long-standing subsidies underwriting the oil and gas industry.

The job of writing the detailed bill fell to the Commerce Committee chaired by Dingell, long a thorn in the side of proponents for tougher auto safety and clean air rules. He prided himself on moving cautiously and assembling bipartisan coalitions, but his bills often shortchanged environmental concerns and took years to negotiate, neither acceptable to the activists. He had spent decades clashing with reformers; now, with the influx of dozens of new members influenced by the environmental movement, his grasp on power was far more tenuous.

He remained undeterred, however. He warned the reformers' plan—a cap-and-trade policy for regulating carbon production—would devastate coal producing areas in twenty-seven states, many represented by vulnerable Democrats. Already furious about the creation of the Select Committee on Climate Change, he bristled at Pelosi's insistence he move expeditiously. "You don't have any choice in what the committees do!" Dingell flared at a chairs' meeting. "What bill" are you telling Commerce to move, he testily demanded, "and when?"[4] The other chairs sharing the energy portfolio, Rangel and Peterson, were Pelosi loyalists far more enthusiastic about producing bills with incentives for renewable energy, including cellulosics produced from agricultural products.

Dingell's irritation was fueled in part by a cornerstone of the initiative, the significant upgrading of CAFE standards to 35 mpg or even higher. He had long viewed tougher standards as inimical to tens of thousands of his constituents who worked for Detroit's Big Three—General Motors, Ford, and Chrysler. Reformers including the Speaker blamed such resistance for the collapse of US manufacturers' market share from 84 percent in 1971 to 63 percent in 2001 as consumers embraced more innovative foreign models. The shrinking market share undercut the power of the industry's unions because the foreign manufacturers invariably operated nonunion shops overseas, in border states, and in the South. In Pelosi's mind, the companies had no one to blame but themselves. "The auto industry has undermined the industrial base in this country," Pelosi insisted.[5]

Developing the details of an energy bill proved far more vexing than writing the initial placeholder bill. A draft by Dingell and Rick Boucher (VA), a coal proponent, drew sharp rebukes for its weak efficiency standards. Releasing the proposal was "a mistake," Hoyer told his longtime ally. "Your time has run out" on resisting CAFE increases. Dingell needed "to minimize the war" within the committee.[6]

But Dingell had a strategy, many believed, based on an alliance of moderate Democrats and Republicans, which he defiantly declared was the only roadmap for success. The leadership recoiled from the possibility. "A bad bill can't go to the floor," Emanuel declared, although open warfare between Dingell and the Speaker was also undesirable. "That's a bridge too far," Emanuel agreed. "We have to avoid that fight."[7]

Waxman, a foot shorter than Dingell but just as tenacious, had been battling "Big John" over energy and air quality since the 1970s. Although Peterson's overall voting record was much more conservative than Dingell's, he saw great opportunities for rural communities in an energy policy that emphasized renewability.[8] He demanded investments of at least $3.5 billion to promote plant-based fuels that he insisted qualify as "renewable," although growing and burning those products also exacerbated climate change. Pelosi, herself an enthusiastic supporter of biofuels, supported his request, which she considered far preferable to fossil-based innovations like coal-to-liquids (CTL), which several coal-state senators, including Barack Obama, favored.

Dingell scoffed at the notion biofuels could replace a major portion of imported energy. He also lashed out at Waxman and other reformers who insisted that states be permitted to impose rigorous mileage and emission standards that preempted those set in federal law. He shared that viewpoint with the Bush administration, which was already battling California's tougher regulations, a decision Waxman termed "completely unacceptable."

Dingell was a skilled political operator with powerful connections. He enlisted influential union leaders like Ron Gettlefinger of the United Auto Workers (UAW) and Richard Trumka of the United Mine Workers of America (UMWA) to lobby for his moderate approach. "The AFL has to back the autoworkers," confided Bill Samuel, the federation's chief lobbyist.[9] But the unions did not want to rebuff the Speaker completely, and the UAW's lobbyist, Alan Reuther, proposed putting several of the contentious issues like CAFE and state preemption into a second bill that would also provide billions of dollars to help companies adapt to the tougher standards. Pelosi rejected the two-bill strategy, speculating that Bush would veto the bill containing the new standards.

Pelosi turned to Gore, who maintained a relationship with his one-time Commerce Committee colleagues, including Dingell. She invited the former vice president to show his climate change film, *An Inconvenient Truth*, to the annual caucus issues conference, where it received an enthusiastic reception. Even so, Waxman's version of the bill lost badly in the Energy subcommittee. Undeterred, he knew he faced better odds in the full committee, which approved the bill after lobbying by FedEx's Fred Smith and former Marine commandant P. X. Kelly.

Robert Redford, the actor and environmental activist who had lobbied several committee members, declared the "shift in energy policy" reflected in the new bill nothing short of "miraculous."[10] Waxman's strategy-savvy staff was so upbeat they considered bypassing the floor, where a Dingell-Republican alliance might pare back the committee's product, and instead take the bill straight to a conference with the Senate. But there were problems getting a strong CAFE bill out of the Senate, thanks in part to determined opposition from Dingell's Democratic Michigan colleagues, Debbie Stabenow and Carl Levin. The Speaker was appalled. "Without CAFE," she told Reid, "we're dead on energy."[11]

To rally wary moderates behind the CAFE standard in the Commerce bill, the Speaker was willing to oppose efforts to make it tougher. "Some may wish to improve CAFE, but I hope not," said Pelosi, advising that a defeat for a higher standard would undermine any prospect for increasing the number in conference. She acknowledged that "if the word got out that I blocked a vote on CAFE, it would cause divisions and a firestorm." Her recommendation was to "work together" within the caucus and defer a final decision until the fall. She pledged to Dingell that she would try to protect the bill from being toughened further by reformers who pressed for an aggressive renewable electricity standard of at least 20 percent within a decade as well as a higher CAFE level.[12]

"This issue could divide the caucus," Dingell ominously warned, adding, "*and* you and me!"[13] Privately, his staff director sought assurances the Speaker would stand by the Commerce bill. "Can we say that they've discussed it and she understands the logic of proceeding in this way," I was asked, "without implying she has endorsed it?" I did not have to check with the Speaker to know that she would strongly disapprove of anyone, let alone Dingell, characterizing her opinion. Instead, she would wait to see what, if anything, Reid could move in the Senate.

Pelosi also faced pushbacks from her energy state moderates fearful the legislation could cost the industry $25 billion. "The bill is just too oriented toward the environment," Chet Edwards (TX) complained. Gene Green (TX) proposed compensating the oil industry by reviving the Clinton program royalty holiday. Jim Matheson (UT) insisted that his home state be completely exempted from efficiency standards. "The special interests are never satisfied," she complained.[14]

Early in June, Reid reached an agreement to allow the Senate to begin debate on a bill that included appliance standards and a 35 mpg CAFE standard. The bill that passed on June 21 by a 65–27 margin represented a high-water mark for Senate energy legislation, with nearly half of the chamber's Republicans and 90 percent of the Democrats supporting the measure. Even so, the rough road forward was illustrated by the opposition of Levin and Stabenow, which led Pelosi to lament the auto industry's leaders were "not thinking of the future of the planet."[15]

Yet the wide margin in the Senate unsurprisingly led some to propose acceptance of the Senate bill. Maria Cantwell (WA) urged San Franciscan Carl Pope, the influential president of the Sierra Club, to approach Pelosi with the strategy. Pelosi resented the interference. She also told Myrick to stop Senate Democrats from "lobby[ing] against us."[16] "Don't feed the flames," she instructed Dingell, who despite pledging to move "with vigor" was warning that disagreements over CAFE and other contentious items would slow a resolution of the differences between the bills. Meanwhile, she advised Reid, there should be "no negotiations with Dingell."[17]

The House also moved forward with legislation setting a "carbon neutral" goal for 2050 and requiring investor-owned utilities to meet a 15 percent RES using solar, wind, geothermal, water, and other non–fossil fuel sources, as well as conservation.[18] One change that would impact every American required the phase-out of the 100-watt incandescent light bulb by 2012 and the tripling of bulb efficiency by 2020. The 241–172 vote was bipartisan—twenty-six Republicans favored it while nine Democrats opposed. "It's a big, big deal," exulted Markey, one of the coauthors. "There has been no legislation like this for a generation." Public enthusiasm for the legislation was high among Democratic activists, as demonstrated by a thousand universities and over six hundred high schools scheduling teach-ins on global warming.

But the bipartisan support behind the CAFE bill was not extended to cap and trade. Republicans ridiculed the bill as "going nowhere," and Barton dismissed it as "an exercise in sterile futility." In fact, Bush immediately threatened a veto in part because the bill repealed $16 billion in tax breaks for the oil industry. Utility companies also opposed the bill, predicting the mandate for renewable electricity would drive up rates for consumers. In mid-September, the chief Republican climate negotiator, Pete Domenici (NM), abandoned the bipartisan talks, and McConnell asked the White House to abandon discussions with Democrats. Dingell also informed Pelosi that while he was "anxious to cooperate, and I will cooperate," there was insufficient time to negotiate on climate. Key staff for Senate Resources chair Jeff Bingaman (NM) were understandably deflated.[19]

But Bingaman was not prepared to throw in the towel on energy altogether and remained committed to finalizing a CAFE bill in 2007. He reinforced his commitment to tough standards, rejecting as "totally unacceptable" an industry-supported, bipartisan alternative proposed by Reps. Baron Hill (D-IN) and Lee Terry (R-IN).[20] In return, Pelosi reiterated that the House would stick by its pledge not to ratchet up the standards even higher. "This isn't a turf battle," she said, "it is the future."

Negotiators were cheered to hear the White House would sign off on the Senate's CAFE version and RFS provision. But Bush remained dubious on the RES and also wanted the mileage requirements for auto and truck fleets to be separated and greater flexibility if the standards proved infeasible.[21] Wary of deals being cut without her input, the Speaker insisted that all future negotiations be managed through her office, not the committees or their chairs. Nor, she insisted, would there be a formal conference committee; revisions would be sent back and forth between the House and Senate in a parliamentary procedure called "ping pong" to avert the obstructionism enabled by the conference process. With senators warning there would have to be a trade-off between two House priorities—CAFE and RES—and demands from Baucus for billions in aid to the Montana coal industry, Reid sent a warning to environmentalists.[22] He could "make a run at passing a bill this year," although finding sixty votes to take up the House bill would be very difficult. But "if the bill does not pass this year," he warned "it will be #4 or #5 on the list of priorities for 2008."[23]

With the path to completion convoluted and deadlines fast approaching, Durbin, at Reid's request, raised the prospect of the House accepting the Senate's bill. "No," a displeased Speaker responded. "I have ten committees that have worked for months."[24] Some Senate provisions, like underwriting new nuclear energy construction, were nonnegotiable. Nor could she wait indefinitely. "I must have the proposal tomorrow," she told the Senate on November 6.

The next day did not begin optimistically. The Senate schedule could force a delay until December, Reid's office warned. That grim news prompted some in the House to suggest weakening the CAFE language, but Emanuel warned Dingell that doing so meant Pelosi would "teach him a lesson" about resisting her. The House revolt quickly disintegrated with Pelosi challenging the manufacturers' assertions that consumers would not buy alternative fuel vehicles. "What were you thinking to fight CAFE for thirty years?" she demanded, reasserting her support to help the industry modernize. "We can't end up where we have been for twenty-five years."[25]

Although the UAW backed down, Sen. Dan Inouye (D-HI), a vigorous defender of Nissan Motors, still wanted "flexibility" for the Japanese car builder. Moreover, he advised Pelosi, "Dingell needs some face-saving." But the Speaker was defiant, calling the argument for looser standards "the worst idea I have heard yet," adding, "with substantial competition." And Dingell had assured her the remaining problems were "solvable," she advised. He claimed to have warned the industry against crossing Pelosi. "You hate this bill but you can live with it if you work with me," he reported telling car executives. "Otherwise, you'll get a bill you *can't* live with." He assured Pelosi he wanted to "stuff [it] down the throats of industry," but he begged for more lead time to implement the reforms. "You can't order change too fast," he pleaded.[26]

For the impatient Speaker who accepted incrementalism grudgingly, Dingell could not have pressed a less effective button. "We're going to freeze the design" and go to the Rules Committee before the Thanksgiving recess, she vowed. "This bill is going to be a Christmas present to the American people," she predicted. "We will be burned at the stake if we don't do this bill. It just has to happen."[27]

When she learned that Dingell was attempting to renegotiate the fuel standard, Pelosi lost patience, instructing Hoyer to tell the chair to "stop moving the goalpost." Staff negotiators blamed his committee aides for "trying to kill the energy bill" altogether, and Dingell promptly threw them under the bus. "The staff hasn't done what is needed," the chair complained, "and hasn't served me well." Dingell also blamed Pelosi's aides for spreading rumors he intended to vote against the bill even though he termed it "a tremendous achievement." But Pelosi had reached the end of her rope. "We are going forward," she declared, with or without Dingell. She was unamused when reports leaked from a closed Commerce meeting that Dingell had lauded dissenters who wanted to weaken CAFE and other provisions. "You people make me proud," he reportedly said, promising not to "criticize anyone for voting 'no'" because "I share the unhappiness" of those displeased with the bill. "The process [was] worse than anything we saw under Hastert or Gingrich," he asserted, adding that "the Speaker made poor judgments" in setting the policy.[28]

Yet despite the threats, Dingell and several critics including Stupak, Rahall, and Matheson (who was called the night before by Redford) voted for the bill on December 6, when the House passed its bill 235–181, sending it across the Capitol.[29] As predicted, Reid could not sell all three standards: fuel (RFS), electricity (RES), and CAFE. Reluctantly, Pelosi signaled she would accept deleting the electricity standard and limiting the scope of the Davis-Bacon prevailing wage provision as Bush demanded, saving $5 billion in costs but disappointing organized labor. But she warned Reid not to go too far to attract Republicans or tax provisions Baucus was promoting, which the White House called "delusional."[30]

The approach of the Christmas holiday did not seem to promote much good cheer. Myrick reported that the indefatigable Dingell was still stirring up Senate Republicans over CAFE. Nevertheless, the Senate approved the renegotiated version 86–8 with Debbie Stabenow (MI) the only dissenting Democrat to join with most of the Senate's most conservative Republicans.[31] Five days later, the House gave final approval to the Senate's amended version, fulfilling one of Pelosi's top goals: improving energy efficiency and moving the country more aggressively toward renewable energy. The final vote in the House was 314–100, and all but four Democrats—including the original sponsor, Nick Joe Rahall—joined in support.

The final bill set the CAFE standard at 35 mpg for a company's fleet as of 2020. The RFS set a goal of 9 billion gallons of renewable product in 2009, increasing to 36 billion gallons by 2022, including 5.5 billion gallons of biofuel by 2017, which pleased the farming community.[32] New appliance efficiency requirements affected appliances and buildings. While deferring action on carbon reduction, federal research into the causes of climate change was significantly increased.

"You are present at a moment of change, of real change," Pelosi praised her members, but some energy activists were dejected. "We lost . . . some of the best aspects of the bill," Energy Justice told its members, including the RES and the repeal of tax subsidies for the energy industry.[33] The group declared the emphasis on "insane biofuel schemes [a] major tragedy" by effectively creating "biorefineries" in hundreds of communities. Having argued for an unrealistic 60 mpg CAFE standard, the group dismissed the 35 mpg provision as "a joke," arguing rising gasoline prices would have forced car manufacturers to exceed that goal anyway. "Zero miles per gallon would have been more appropriate," the advocates insisted.[34]

Most reviewers hailed the bill as "one of the largest steps on energy the nation has taken since the oil crises of the 1970s."[35] True, some key climate provisions had been deleted, but "we'll fight for those another day," climate activist Sen. Barbara Boxer (CA) promised.[36] On the other side, a spokesman for the Organization of Petroleum Exporting Countries warned the increased use of biofuels could lead OPEC to cut oil production, damaging the US economy.

Only a few weeks later, discussions began about reviving the climate bill despite the inevitable resistance from Democrats on the Commerce committee, including Dingell. He was in the midst of a bitter battle with liberals over tightening regulations applying to chemical products that went into the manufacture of toys. "Get off my back," he told DeLauro when she pressed for speedier action. He didn't "give a rat's ass" about the delays.[37] Pelosi called Dingell's antics "unacceptable and dysfunctional," helping convince the Speaker more progressive voices were needed on the committee. When a vacancy appeared early in 2008, Dingell pressed for the appointment for Zack Space (OH), a moderate likely to support his cautious approach. Pelosi dismissed the idea with an uncharacteristic vulgarity and appointed the reliably liberal John Sarbanes (MD).[38]

Nor was there much chance of a climate initiative moving through the Senate, although a bipartisan team of Joe Lieberman (CT) and John Warner (VA) was fashioning one. A Heritage Foundation publication alarmingly asserted the plan would "cost Americans hundreds of thousands of jobs annually and could double the price of electricity, natural gas and gasoline by 2030." Other conservatives labeled it an "anti-stimulus bill" that would damage the economy.[39] With Byrd's incapacitation, West Virginia's governor, Joe Manchin, was increasingly regarded as a potential replacement in the Senate, and he told the Speaker, "I've got real problems" with cap and trade. Manchin believed too many national Democrats "look down on us [in coal country] and don't treat governors with equal respect."[40] Other moderates including Peterson viewed portions of the bill as "foolish."

Pelosi continued pressing committees to study innovative energy proposals. "The days are limited for the status quo," she advised. "We need to be visionary." Congress could not "trade in the future of our grandchildren" by sidestepping climate change.[41] But circumstances were pushing the debate in a very different direction. As Congress prepared to recess for the summer and the 2008 political conventions, oil prices ballooned to $140 a barrel, and the debate over energy production became a central feature in the 2008 campaign. Warnings about the threat of climate change clashed with those demanding that producers "drill now, drill everywhere."[42] Bush responded on the side of his industry, endorsing a major expansion of off- and onshore energy production, including in the Alaska Refuge, and pledging to speed approval of new oil refineries.

Critics responded rapidly, noting Bush's proposals would take years to implement and even if successful would compound the climate crisis. Pelosi pressed members from energy-producing states not to "buy into Bush's failed policy" on offshore leasing.[43] Republican California governor Arnold Schwarzenegger pledged to fight any proposed offshore development, while several Democrats demanded current leases be drilled before granting the owners new ones. "Don't let the oil companies tie up more of the public land," pleaded Blumenauer. Even moderates like Stupak pointed to a suspicious rise in oil futures, and Dingell suggested a bill cracking down on oil price speculation. Cardoza, despite being a Blue Dog leader, proposed attacking "two oilmen in the White House" for their lax regulation of the industry.[44]

Reid cautioned Pelosi "not to go beyond Obama," now the presidential nominee who remained vague on drilling, promising to "look at anything as president" to expand supplies.[45] That language worried Gore. "The oil companies have silenced Obama," he concluded.[46] Meanwhile, GOP nominee John McCain rejected calls for alternative fuels and conservation, cheering on the pro-oil demonstrators besieging the Democrats in Denver and selecting Alaska governor Sarah Palin as his running mate.

Reid would not rule out reasonable development of domestic sources, and he would not consider a major climate bill before the election. Instead, he was willing to assemble a "passable bill" including withdrawals from the petroleum reserve and anti-speculation provisions, but he advised reformers, "Don't bet on the Republicans accepting it." Pelosi didn't challenge his assessment and did not want to press her own frontline candidates—those judged to be at the highest risk of a serious electoral challenge—to vote on a strong House bill that would die in the Senate. "If you pass a bill," she assured Reid uncharacteristically, "we'll take it." In actuality, she was exasperated with her colleagues across the Capitol. "I'm sick and tired of the Senate," she told her leadership team; climate would be a topic of discussion after the next election.[47]

Environmental activists refused to accept the idea of delay and prepared a national "Pain in the Gas" anti-leasing campaign complete with dozens of field organizers and television ads. Miller encouraged them, advising Pope, "You need to make more noise."[48] But the Speaker was irritated with impatient energy activists who seemed oblivious to her difficulties in passing a bill through the fractious House. "I can only lose twelve to fourteen votes," she told Gore. "The enviros are always tone deaf on this stuff!" The former VP understood her challenge. "Herding cats doesn't do justice to what you have to do," Gore marveled.[49]

The Speaker felt out members one last time in September about taking up a climate package before the election, asking Hoyer to reach out to the Blue Dogs even though she predicted most "would never vote against the oil and gas industry." Still, she was determined to "poke [the Republicans] in the eye every day" of the campaign for their subservience to the oil industry.[50] She was convinced that Republicans had "painted themselves into a corner," obsessed with accelerating production regardless of the environmental cost.[51]

Democrats had reason to press the issue. They enjoyed a healthy 41 to 29 percent polling advantage on energy and a massive 52-point advantage (64–12) on climate change.[52] If Democrats could avoid sounding gratuitously partisan and focus on innovation, technology, and global leadership on climate and energy, many believed the party would have a winning issue that would propel a new Congress to address climate change in the new year with a larger Democratic caucus on Capitol Hill and a sympathetic Democrat in the White House.

Pelosi had more success with her "Green the Capitol" (GTC) initiative to convert the eighteenth-century Capitol building into a model of twenty-first-century efficiency. Nothing sent a worse message than the Congress's own coal-burning power plant situated just two blocks from the Capitol's iconic dome. Efforts to convert the plant to natural gas had been blocked by Senate leaders Byrd and McConnell.[53] Both represented coal states whose producers helped supply the Capitol's annual requirement of 40,000 tons of coal, and both also enjoyed strong campaign support from the coal industry.

Pelosi professed sympathy for coal miners who stood to lose their jobs as the industry phased down, describing them as "dying for a bad fuel source."[54] In her office, she displayed a statuette of a miner carved from coal that had been presented to her congressman father decades earlier by Sen. Jennings Randolph (WV). But times had changed, and "with all due respect to West Virginia," she said, "we're not gonna have a coal power plant floating around" Capitol Hill.[55] Nick Joe Rahall, whose claim to the chairmanship of Natural Resources she had protected, notably supported her decision.[56]

Under the direction of her new chief administrative officer, Dan Beard, a former staff director of the House Natural Resources Committee, the House replaced over 13,000 incandescent light bulbs with compact fluorescent bulbs and added energy-conserving floodlights to illuminate the iconic Capitol dome.[57]

Beard banished nonrecyclable plastic utensils and Styrofoam from the House's cafeterias, substituting cardboard food boxes and plant-based utensils (which drew ridicule from some critics for sometimes wilting in hot food).[58]

Over the next three years, the GTC initiative cut carbon emissions by 200 tons, reducing energy consumption by 23 percent and water consumption by 32 percent. Nevertheless, Republicans scorned the changes as ideological and frivolous. Boehner condemned the $475,000 annual cost of trucking waste to a recycling facility, but Beard sloughed off the criticism. "I've been instructed to do things differently," he insisted.[59] When the Republicans regained the majority in 2010, they quickly reversed the cafeteria changes. "Plasticware is back!" exulted Boehner, the new Speaker.

CHAPTER 8

"YOU CAN'T HAVE IT THE WAY
YOU WANT TO HAVE IT"

Opposition to the Iraq War was, for many Democrats, the singular issue that explained the success of the 2006 campaign. For anti-war activists, immediate withdrawal was a top priority, but translating campaign rhetoric into actual policy proved far more complex a challenge. Terminating funding for troops already deployed in the field was an impossibility, and even limiting the use of funds for redeployment would have been vetoed by Bush. As weeks went by without any appreciable progress on bringing the troops home, activists like the Code Pink demonstrators massing daily in front of Pelosi's San Francisco home increasingly felt betrayed by the Democratic majority they had helped elect.

Many in Congress were frustrated as well. War critics believed they had been steamrolled following the September 11, 2001, terrorist attacks to granting the president broad retaliatory powers. While no evidence connected Iraqi leader Saddam Hussein to those attacks, Bush claimed evidence that the Iraqi strongman possessed weapons of mass destruction (WMDs) that he could use to intimidate the United States' regional allies or potentially give to terrorists. Based largely on those reports, Congress approved an Authorization for Use of Military Force (AUMF) in October 2002 empowering Bush to use US forces "as he determines to be necessary and appropriate . . . [to] defend US national security against the continuing threat posed by Iraq."

Unlike the initial AUMF passed with nearly unanimous support after 9/11, the second divided congressional Democrats. Over 60 percent of House Democrats, including Pelosi, broke with other members of the Democratic leadership.[1] "I was a member of the Gang of Four" privy to the most classified information, she recalled. "I knew that there was no intelligence to support the threat that the administration was putting forth."[2] In the Senate, Democrats split 26–21 in favor while Republicans voted 48–1 in support. There would be long-term political ramifications from this vote for supporters like Hillary Clinton and Joe Biden. Meanwhile, in Illinois, a junior state senator named Barack Obama criticized the vote, although no one on Capitol Hill noticed.

By the 2006 election, opinion on the war had soured significantly. Many Democrats who had initially given a green light to Bush agreed that "everyone in America believes we must extricate ourselves from Iraq," as Hoyer said, although not in a "precipitous withdrawal" that could endanger US forces and leave the region seriously destabilized. Pelosi viewed opposition to the war as a rallying point for her party and spoke often about the need to "end the war in Iraq, bring the troops home, and honor the sacrifice of our troops."[3] She won external support by recruiting prestigious validators to endorse ending America's involvement, including retired generals Barry McCaffrey and John Shinseki.

On June 13, 2006, Bush briefed the Hill leadership on his recent meeting with the new Iraqi prime minister, "an interesting cat" who had been condemned to death by Saddam Hussein.[4] Bush had "take[n] the measure" of Nouri al-Maliki and was impressed with some of his recent efforts at national reconciliation. "I can't rule if I am bitter," al-Maliki had said. He also hoped to involve regional neighbors to help end the civil war, and he wanted the United Nations to enforce the peace. Until then, he urged Bush to resist rising congressional demands for the withdrawal of US troops. "Give us time," he pleaded, to develop a strategy for success.

Six months later, Bush was planning not a withdrawal but a significant increase in US forces. Coming so soon after an election defeat in which criticism of the war was a prominent issue, Bush's plan smacked of open defiance. The incoming Speaker, who cited ending the war as the "highest priority," and the new Senate majority leader sent Bush a letter warning that an increase in US forces would be a "serious mistake" reminiscent of "a strategy that you have already tried and that has already failed."[5]

On January 9, newly powerful Democratic committee chairs, most of them longtime Pentagon supporters, met with the House leadership to discuss Bush's plan. Defense Appropriations chair Jack Murtha reminded his colleagues that the recent addition of ten thousand forces had produced no benefits. Armed Services chair Ike Skelton was deeply worried about the impact of extended deployments on troops and their families. Were there even enough adequately trained and outfitted soldiers to send into battle, he wondered? Bush "is aiming for history," Skelton told the Speaker. "He wants to be vindicated."[6] But prematurely withdrawing didn't make sense either, he thought, and would allow billions of dollars in tanks, armored vehicles, and other materiel to fall into enemy hands.

Two days later, the new leadership traveled to the White House to meet with Bush. Sitting at the Cabinet table as Speaker, Pelosi realized that this "was unlike any other meeting I, or any woman, had ever been to at the White House." As the president spoke, Pelosi experienced an odd sensation. "My chair was getting crowded in and I couldn't figure out what it was," she recalled. "I swear it never happened before, it never happened since. And then I realized Susan B. Anthony, Elizabeth Cady Stanton, Lucretia Mott, Alice Paul, Sojourner Truth. They were all in that chair, they were, more than I named, and I could hear them say, 'At last we have a seat at the table.' And then they were gone."[7] In years to come, during victories and defeats, Pelosi would often recollect this epiphany as a compelling motivation to remain the party leader, even when she questioned her own desire to continue.

"That's good!" Bush said in response to the hundred-hour marathon to pass the "6 for '06" bills, pleased that most of the bills enjoyed bipartisan support. But he grew grave describing the worsening sectarian violence al-Maliki seemed unable to control. "Now's the time, brother," he had told the Iraqi president. The United States "expects you to get the job done [so] get movin.'" If al-Maliki couldn't "get hold of the situation, he's through." To assist him, Bush announced he would send a twenty-thousand-person surge force to the region. "I understand the criticism," he assured the congressional critics. "But give this surge a chance to succeed. We can't afford to fail." He encouraged his critics to temper their public statements. "There are lots of audiences" listening to what the new Congress would be saying, he advised. "Use your best judgment."

Pelosi was having none of it, and her colleagues piled on. "The public has lost confidence in the execution of the war," she frankly told Bush. "We want to hear the voice of democracy" in Baghdad. Reid reported that only 26 percent of the public favored the current policy, which made it a "very uphill fight for" the president.[8] "I am deeply skeptical and concerned," admitted Hoyer, who reminded Bush of his vote to authorize the war. "I'm not a happy camper." Senate whip Dick Durbin (IL) warned that the number of troops was too small to achieve the president's goal, if it was achievable at all. Moreover, the leadership distrusted al-Maliki to improve the situation. "Don't trust them," Clyburn scoffed.

Bush was unfazed by the electoral repudiation or the criticism. "I also don't approve of [the conditions in] Iraq," Bush insisted. But political stability was impossible to achieve so long as violence continued. "If Malaki has the will, Iraqi forces will be in the lead, with US forces in support—so long as politicians don't get in the way," he argued. But at the moment, there weren't enough trained Iraqi troops.

The Republicans rushed to support Bush. The president "deserved a chance to put the pieces together," and the surge was the "last best chance to win," Boehner argued. "Victory is our only option! What's the alternative? Turn tail and embolden the terrorists?" McConnell called Bush's plan "courageous and correct," and Trent Lott (MS) endorsed even more aggressive intervention. "Bring in helicopter gunships," he advised, "not marines who are knocking on the doors" in house-to-house searches. Glumly, Pelosi determined, "It looks like we are there for a long time."

Bush's "New Way Forward" surge seemed to ignore the December 2006 recommendations of the bipartisan Iraq Study Group, which had warned against both "sustained increases" in US troop levels and precipitous withdrawal. Should al-Maliki fail to implement major political, diplomatic, and policy reforms, the authors had recommended, the United States might well need to implement "planned redeployments" to avoid being held hostage "to the actions or inactions of the Iraqi government."

Pelosi was enthused by the agreement of her chairs, many of whom had spent careers boosting the Pentagon, and charged them with finding "a face-saving way for the president to change course." Although unsympathetic to cutting off funds for troops in the field, she was intrigued with the idea of re-creating the Truman Commission, which had investigated waste and abuse in the military during World War II. In the Senate, Reid reported no support for Bush's surge. Like Pelosi, he wanted Democrats to "move slowly but not precipitously to the Left."[9]

Insisting on the right of Congress to play a significant role in foreign affairs, members proposed adding conditions to war appropriations. That was the proverbial line in the sand for the White House and Republicans on the Hill. Such restrictions, Boehner warned, would be "handicapping the generals or the troops," a view shared by hard-liners like Sam Johnson (TX), a former Vietnam POW who charged that imposing time lines for withdrawal "literally hands the enemy our war plan.... What world superpower would do such a thing?"[10] Indeed, far from setting a schedule for withdrawal, Bush predicted it would take three months just for the surge troops to arrive!

Emanuel, worried about appearing weak on defense, had been reluctant to confront Bush over Iraq, but increasingly he sensed the political advantages of doing so. He proposed Democrats endorse expanded diplomatic initiatives and call for withdrawing 50,000 of the 162,000 US forces by March 2008. Others in leadership offered their own proposals, including DeLauro, who recommended appointment of a "war czar" to oversee operations. Pelosi remained cool to such suggestions, preferring the views of experienced military experts.[11] But since it now seemed the chances of collaborating with Bush were slim, Democrats must be prepared to "hit the Republicans weekly" and schedule tough votes like barring permanent bases in Iraq and closing the detainee prison in Guantánamo, Cuba.

The chairs used their new oversight powers to summon the architects and critics of the Iraq policy before House committees. Skelton called in Reagan secretary of state James Baker and former House Foreign Affairs chair Lee Hamilton (IN), cochairs of the Iraq Study Group, while Foreign Affairs chair Tom Lantos (CA) summoned Secretary of State Condoleezza Rice, former Carter national security advisor Zbigniew Brzezinski, and Colin Powell, Rice's predecessor who had defended Bush's WMD findings before the United Nations in 2003.

Anti-war activists ramped up pressure. The newly formed Americans Against Escalation announced hundreds of protest events around the country and set a goal of raising $7 million to build field organizations in the districts of twenty-five Republican members who had opposed the surge but still voted to fund it. By early March, Move On's Tom Matzzie, former representative Tom Andrews (ME), and activist veterans were pressing for a statutory timetable for the withdrawal of all US forces from the war zone.[12]

With no clear consensus emerging in her caucus, Pelosi told her members the performance of the Iraqi military and government should serve as the basis for future US aid. "The best move," she said, "is to hold Bush accountable; set a timetable for ending the war."[13] Those criteria were insufficient for the strongest critics who opposed funding even if benchmarks and timetables were included. If a forthcoming analysis of progress by the Iraqi government was negative, Lloyd Doggett (TX) insisted, Democrats should only vote to fund an immediate withdrawal. At a Pelosi meeting with Out of Iraq hard-liners, the anger boiled over as some ignored the Speaker's entreaties to support funding the troops, and Miller worried the opposition inside the caucus "could get out of hand."[14] "Congress has the power to stop funding the war," Dennis Kucinich (OH) insisted. "That's what we should do." Even within the normally dependable California delegation, Maxine Waters was "actively whipping" against the emergency troop funding bill. Some faulted the Speaker's hesitance to act more aggressively. "I feel the [restraining] hook in my back," said Jim McDermott (WA), while Neil Abercrombie (HI) seethed about "she who must be obeyed."[15] So high were the stakes on this early test of Pelosi's leadership that several newspapers hypothesized that those abandoning the Speaker could face retribution, including the loss of committee assignments.[16]

Still, Pelosi's rhetoric with the president remained confrontational, criticizing the administration for sending inadequately trained forces into battle with improper equipment. The readiness numbers were "disgraceful," Pelosi declared. "The president is weakening our military strength." The war was "producing more casualties than the system can absorb," and yet Bush was threatening "to veto any law holding the Iraqis to his own standards." She insisted that Congress would not be pressured to diminish its constitutional right to influence the direction of the war. "This is the fight," she told the joint Democratic Leadership.[17]

At the end of March, a $124 billion supplemental including an August 31, 2008, deadline for the removal of US forces squeaked by in the House by a narrow vote of 218–212. The objective of the deadline was "holding the Iraqi government accountable and enabling us to bring our troops home," she explained. "The American people do not support a war without end, and neither should this Congress." She professed to be unfazed by the narrow victory, which "crystalized" her feelings about the war. "I am surprised at my own serenity," she insisted.[18] Because Congress had imposed its will, "this is an historic day," realigning the balance of power through institutional defiance of Bush.

But the bill encountered immediate trouble in the Senate, where Reid and Durbin reported difficulty in passing any bill despite support for timetables from Republicans Chuck Hagel (NB) and Gordon Smith (OR). Reid's task was complicated by senators insisting on adding their favorite riders to the must-pass bill. "I don't know how we get through the next few days," an exasperated Reid confided, frustrated by the "dirty, fat, and slow" process.

As March stretched into April, an agreement between the two Democratic-controlled houses remained elusive. The Senate could agree to a date for beginning, but not for concluding, redeployment (although Reid personally favored a hard 120-day cutoff after which money could be used only for training, embassy protection, and anti-terrorism activities).[19] The best he could do was "softer dates," general benchmarks for evaluating "success," and a "goal" of ending US involvement by March 2008. Myrick implored the House to accept the Senate's version of the overall bill that had been sweetened with Democratic riders like a minimum wage increase, since there was no chance the House's tougher proscriptions could become law. Indeed, even Reid's anemic language would prompt a defiant Bush veto of any bill containing conditions "micromanaging" the war policy. As House Democrats had predicted, Bush also lambasted Senate riders that went "beyond the war on terror" to include relief for domestic peanut and spinach producers. Pelosi needed to get the anti-war groups to face up and consider the unpleasant options because, she told Reid, "we need as many hands on the bloody knife as possible."[20]

The hopelessness of securing a cutoff of funding needed to be demonstrated to the obstinate hard-line opponents. The bill that went to the White House included a deadline for initiating withdrawals of October 1; Bush promptly vetoed it. "It makes no sense to tell the enemy when you plan to start withdrawing," Bush insisted. "All the terrorists would have to do is mark their calendars and gather their strength." He refused to force "American commanders in the middle of a combat zone to take fighting directions from politicians 6,000 miles away," which he ridiculed as "a prescription for chaos and confusion."[21]

Faced with being blamed for cutting off funding for troops in harm's way, Pelosi and Reid agreed to drop the firm timetables, substituting eighteen benchmarks by which to measure Iraqi progress toward peace and stability. But Pelosi refused to support what she termed the "baby steps" compromise, calling it "an ink blot" test that enabled everyone to see whatever they wanted. "The base thinks of us as an unfaithful husband," she bemoaned.[22] Other war opponents were more vocal in their opposition. "We have failed the very same people that placed us in the majority," Lynn Woolsey (CA) insisted. Even Ted Kennedy rejected the compromise that "doesn't do nearly enough to end the war." The bill's benchmarks, added Russ Feingold (WI), were "toothless."

The war's opponents were encouraged by retired three-star general William Odom, Reagan's intelligence chief, who argued in mid-2007 that the United States was "paralyzed" in Iraq. "Don't worry about [a loss of] US credibility," he counseled. "We're a superpower."[23] Even with such endorsements, moderates like John Spratt (SC) remained nervous about curtailing presidential options, and Skelton voiced his dislike for specific timetables, questioning if withdrawal was even feasible. Pragmatists in the caucus like John Larson (CT), the vice chair, cautioned against forcing multiple pointless votes in the House because timetables would never become law due to the Senate filibuster and the presidential veto.

As the internal dispute intensified, Pelosi undertook her first congressional delegation (CODEL) international trip as Speaker, flying to Syria to meet with that country's pariah president, Bashar al-Assad.[24] The United States had imposed economic and diplomatic measures to isolate Assad's repressive government, and Bush expressed concern the visit could be misconstrued by Assad as "a strong signal of reengagement" with the United States. "Sending delegations hasn't worked," Bush said. "It's just simply been counterproductive."[25]

Pelosi brushed off the criticism, arguing she was interested only "in promoting peace between Israel and Syria" by encouraging discussions to pacify the troubled region. She reportedly carried a message from Israeli prime minister Ehud Olmert stating that he "sought peace with Syria" while also "express[ing] concern about Syria's support for Hezbollah and Hamas," terrorist organizations sworn to the destruction of Israel.

Pelosi returned home to strong partisan criticism not just for making the trip but for wearing a headscarf when entering Damascus's Umayyad Mosque. Conservatives accused her of violating tradition (and perhaps even the Logan Act) by negotiating with a foreign government and ridiculed as naive her declaration that "the road to Damascus is a road to peace." Sen. John Cornyn (TX) called on the Senate to admonish her for consorting with Assad, and the conservative *National Review* accused her of actively supporting terrorists by "propagandizing for a dictator who was killing Americans."[26]

Pelosi countered there was nothing surreptitious about her trip. Bush's State Department had briefed CODEL participants, and she, in turn, kept State fully informed about her discussions. Clearly a novel standard was being applied to the Speaker. Three Republican congressmen recently had met with Assad in Damascus without provoking similar critiques, and First Lady Laura Bush and Secretary of State Condoleezza Rice had also worn scarves when visiting mosques. The lone Republican member of the CODEL defended the Speaker's efforts. "I think we actually helped the administration's position by showing there's no dissension" over Syria, explained David Hobson (OH).[27]

The Syria skirmish did little to reduce tensions over the stalled supplemental. Still vowing to veto any efforts at "micromanaging" war policy, Bush expected Congress would quickly back down.[28] Pelosi saw the confrontation as a "historic opportunity" to assert congressional prerogatives. "This bill sends a message to the Iraqis," she insisted, while also appropriating more money than Bush had requested. Even Robert Gates, Bush's defense secretary, believed the benchmark for transforming the US mission from combat to training "gives the administration leverage" with the Iraqis, she pointed out.

For Pelosi, the dispute raised a basic issue of comity between the branches of government. "I respect the dynamic of the veto," she told Bush, "but *you* should respect the majorities in Congress." Both branches shared a "responsibility to the American people to work together," but that did not translate into total capitulation by Congress. "You can't have it the way you want to have it," she rebuked Bush, by "extending a hand of friendship without winding down the war."[29] Reid agreed, reminding Bush of the rosy predictions before Lyndon Johnson's failed surge in Vietnam. "The war cannot be won militarily," the Senate leader declared, a view he believed was shared by "a significant percentage of the military." The president needed to "reduce the rhetoric and partisanship, pull something together [and] get a compromise" that would allow the United States to "leav[e] Iraq in the near future in a dignified way" while honoring "those who lost their lives in vain. . . . Name someone to negotiate with us," Hoyer urged the president.

Unexpectedly, cracks appeared in the once unconditional Republican leadership. Complaints from constituents about repeated deployments led Lott to express concern for the "impacts on the military." Blunt, while assuring Bush that Republicans were "dug in against micromanaging," declared he could live with setting benchmarks for Iraqi performance.

Bush seemed stunned. "We could have a good discussion on benchmarks," he acknowledged, but right now, amid rising violence, the surge would provide valuable "breathing space" for the Iraqi government. "I respect [the right of] the legislature to appropriate money," but the surge was essential "so the whole thing doesn't fall apart." Like past presidents, he rejected assertions of equivalence between the branches of government on matters of national security. As commander in chief, he insisted he possessed unilateral power to undertake the surge and that Congress was obliged to fund the troops.

"Why not take 'yes' for an answer?" Pelosi asked, emphasizing the bipartisan concern about "the [war's] strain on the military." Congress was merely establishing a timetable for achieving benchmarks proposed by Bush himself. "Our patience is wearing out," she warned. "How can we hold Iraq accountable without timetables?" If Bush stood by his insistence that Congress must defer to the president, she warned, the House would exercise its constitutional power and refuse to pass a bill containing only war money.

Convinced further negotiations would yield no better result, the conferees agreed on $100 billion for the war and $24 billion for Democratic domestic priorities. The bill also set a July 2007 date for beginning the redeployment if benchmarks were not achieved by the Iraqis, just three months away, or October 1 if they were, with total withdrawal completed by March 2008. The timetable failed to assuage hard-line war opponents who dismissed the conference agreement as "the worst of both bills." Matzzie declared Democrats were "caving" to Bush and warned that members of the Out of Iraq Caucus who supported the agreement would be "sellouts."[30]

As promised, Bush vetoed the supplemental, just his second veto in over six years; in Iraq, US forces reportedly booed on hearing the news. In a nationally broadcast speech, Bush ridiculed the withdrawal timetables as "irresponsible . . . substitut[ing] the opinions of politicians for the judgment of our military commanders." Thanks to the surge, he insisted, death squads were being broken up, and sectarian violence was dropping. He urged Congress to "put politics behind us and support the troops" as recommended by the respected Gen. David Petraeus, whom Bush had just promoted to commander in Iraq.[31] War supporters on the Hill rallied to endorse Bush's optimism. "We cannot give up," said McCain, "just as we are starting to turn things around."[32]

The response from Democrats was swift and confrontational. Reid declared the veto would not dissuade him from "working to change the direction of this war." Pelosi was even more defiant. "The president wants a blank check," she charged, and "the Congress is not going to give it to him." To force Republicans on the record, she scheduled a futile override vote the next day, which predictably failed 222–203 along mostly partisan lines.

Bush followed up the veto by declaring a "a day for common ground" to find a way to fund the troops without "artificial timetables [and] withdrawals," promising to do his "best to set the right tenor."[33] Pelosi was irritated by his underlying intransigence. "We did a bill, now, what's your idea?" she asked. "You can have input, but we'll write the bill!" Within the leadership, Hoyer suggested a thirty-day reporting requirement on Iraqi progress combined with an unspecified penalty if the deadline went unheeded, but Pelosi dismissed the flaccid proposal. "We will get clobbered by the Left," she cautioned.[34]

In the Senate, McConnell rebuked Reid for being too partisan and insisted everything but the Iraq funding be removed from the supplemental. Democrats dismissed his comment as showing indifference to the "real emergencies" the domestic spending addressed, particularly the economic crises in minority communities, Clyburn noted.[35]

Huddling with the leadership, Bush agreed he could tolerate "reasonable benchmarks" for measuring al-Maliki's progress but not specific timetables for withdrawal. "But is there a point at which Americans can leave if the Iraqis can't produce," pressed Durbin. "Yes," Bush conceded, but such an outcome would be "a catastrophe." "We've put a bill on the table," Pelosi responded, but she bowed to the realities. Perhaps the timetables were not so crucial, she conceded, since

the war would likely be over by the fall anyway. "Democrats take the responsibility to end the war in Iraq," she said after the negotiating session. "We owe it to
the American people to find common ground," but if Bush proved intractable,
"we will stand our ground."[36] Reid echoed the Speaker's positive spin, reporting
the meeting had demonstrated that "the president understands he must deal
with the Congress."

But such a diluted phasedown was not going to be an easy sell to the Left.
Move On was already preparing a report castigating the "do nothing" Congress
for its failure to end the war.[37] Warning that "the Speaker will have egg on her
face" if she made any further concessions, Matzzie counseled, "Don't meet with
[Josh] Bolten," Bush's chief of staff.

A break came in mid-May when Bolten told the Speaker the White House
could live with new benchmarks crafted by the highly respected Republican
senator John Warner (VA), but there would also have to be steep reductions
in the bill's nonmilitary spending. While dissatisfied, Pelosi told Obey that the
Iraq limitations were more important because there would be additional opportunities to supplement domestic programs. Reid advised Pelosi to accept
Bush's offer to end the standoff. "Blame the Senate," he proposed. "Look where
we've come."[38]

The compromise would include eighteen benchmarks, two additional reports on progress toward military success, a ban on torture, and a potential ter-
mination of foreign aid for Iraq if its leaders failed to meet the success criteria.[39]
Moreover, the White House relented on some of the domestic spending. "I got
my ass eaten out" for agreeing to $20 billion in domestic spending, Bolten com-
plained, although he drew the line at the "flashing lights" of a peanut farmer
bailout.

The agreement was packaged under an unwieldy, message-heavy name: the
US Troop Readiness, Veterans' Care, Katrina Recovery and Iraq Accountability
Act. Anti-war hard-liners like DNC chairman Howard Dean quickly criticized
Pelosi for failing to challenge Bush more aggressively. The reaction among the
base was so heated that Chris Van Hollen (MD) curtailed DCCC phone solici-
tations because of the negative reactions. But privately, one prominent anti-war
leader signaled satisfaction that Democrats had "forced the president to backpedal." Ultimately, "the only [thing] that matters," he said, "is ending the war."[40]

Passing the agreement in the House required deft parliamentary maneuvering because most Republicans opposed the bill's domestic funding while most
Democrats opposed the $99.5 billion in war money. Leadership floor strategists

devised an unconventional solution. The House would vote separately on each section, after which the two parts would automatically be joined together in a parliamentary immaculate conception and deemed approved. The domestic funding received a bipartisan 348–73 vote while the Iraq money was approved 280–142, mostly with Republican support. Republicans excoriated the majority for stuffing domestic spending into the bill, overlooking the 120 of their own members who voted for it. Once the Senate approved the bill later that day, 80–14, Bush signed it into law.

In the first major showdown on the war, the constraints on Democrats' ability to deliver on their campaign promises was painfully clear. As liberal reformers had found in 1975 and Republicans in 1995, despite a large congressional victory, a president of the opposite party retained decisive power in negotiations thanks to the veto. Still, many Democrats felt an important corner had been turned. "The days of six supplementals passing off of this floor, half a trillion dollars spent and no strings attached . . . are over," declared Kendrick Meek (FL).[41]

The limited success did nothing to lessen the Democrats' fervor for more aggressive steps to limit funds to redeploying US forces out of Iraq. In mid-July, the House passed the Responsible Redeployment from Iraq Act mandating that repositioning begin 120 days after enactment with a withdrawal deadline of April 1, 2008. The bill was "nothing more than a partisan political stunt," Boehner charged, since it stood no chance of consideration in the Senate. But Pelosi had to schedule such votes to keep the anti-war faction content, and she warned senators, "Don't defang the base's efforts."[42] Reid could pass nothing beyond a date for beginning redeployment. Fortunately, Move On and other war opponents were willing to temper their criticism of members whose opposition to the war was less emphatic than they would have liked, although Matzzie admitted that it "hurts us to give the Republicans cover." Pelosi was grateful, lauding the groups as "very responsible" for holding their fire, but she was less forgiving of the uncompromising "nutball cases" besieging her home.[43]

During the summer, US ambassador Ryan Crocker implored al-Malaki to demonstrate his ability to govern if US troops were removed. But al-Maliki's weakness was exposed in late August when minority parties withdrew from the Cabinet, forcing the beleaguered prime minister to seek support from minority Kurds to keep his government from collapsing altogether. The setbacks encouraged Murtha to include several caucus-inspired mandates in his next defense appropriation bill, including a 180-day closure plan for Guantánamo and a requirement that all troops sent to Iraq be "fully equipped." Most important,

Murtha wanted Bush to submit a confidential report within sixty days detailing a "reasonable" date for initiating withdrawal. By being silent on an end date,
Murtha hoped to attract Republican support. If that did not work, he was inclined to add a hard end date even if doing so split the Democratic caucus.

Bush's hard line concealed a growing division within the administration itself, Murtha reported. "Gates wants out," he said of the defense secretary. "The
White House is the sticking point." Secretary of State Rice was also concerned
the United States would be stuck in Iraq "in perpetuity." The anti-war effort received an unexpected boost late in August when John Warner endorsed a phas-
ing down of US military operations. But Pelosi predicted little aid from other
Republicans who were "guarding the gate for Bush."[44]

The Speaker could agree to remaining silent on an end date in the next Iraq
supplemental if new money was directed to initiating redeployment.[45] "We need
to put together the toughest [Iraq] issue we can send a message on," she declared. "We can't be distracted by the bedwetters" who cringed at taking on Bush
over deadlines.[46] There was no reason to oppose deadlines, assured former defense secretary Bill Perry. Iraq "will be a mess whenever we leave," he predicted,
because of the corruption and incompetence of the al-Maliki government.

With the issuance of a new National Intelligence Estimate that concluded
"no political progress," "uneven" military progress, and Al-Qaeda's strength at
higher levels than on 9/11, the Speaker instructed the chairs to gear up for tough
oversight hearings that Lantos predicted would "pull the rug out from under
Bush."[47] "We can't wait for the Senate," she insisted. "How long can United
States troops be in civil wars where the [local] government is unwilling to make
reforms?" Skelton backed her up, noting the al-Maliki government was "not doing anything" well. Moreover, his investigations had documented the serious
"overextension of US military," and a three-star general had confided to Skelton
that "the army is broken." The conservative chair had concluded that withdrawal
was necessary to protect the beleaguered military.[48] Across the Capitol, Reid's
anti-war contingent wanted a "full-fledged" fight on the Senate floor. Although
Reid feared alienating allies like Warner, he planned to take up the Iraq benchmarks in mid-September.

One day before the sixth anniversary of September 11, Petraeus and Crocker
presented their long-anticipated report, but it did not contain the endorsement
of disengagement war critics had sought. In fact, the report cautioned against
a premature drawdown of forces that would damage progress on political reform. "The military objectives of the surge are, in large measure, being met," it
found, with the number of violent incidents dropping to the lowest level since

mid-2006. And while sectarian rivalries continued, the Iraqi military was assuming more of the fighting and incurring a larger proportion of the casualties. Still, the authors admitted, the overall situation was "complex, difficult, and
sometimes downright frustrating." The United States could still "achieve our
objectives in Iraq over time," Petraeus insisted, "though doing so will be neither
quick nor easy."

"Over time" sounded ominously open-ended to war critics, and Democrats
were furious with the proposed ten-month schedule for removing surge forces.
They roundly dismissed Crocker's Pollyannaish prediction that "a secure, stable,
democratic Iraq at peace with its neighbors" was foreseeable. Even Warner believed al-Malaki "had let our troops down" and hinted he might support proposals to force withdrawal of some US forces to pressure the Iraqi leader to quit.
"In my humble judgment," Warner declared, "that is an option we all have to
consider."[49] Warner's displeasure was so strong that when Armed Services chair
Carl Levin suggested the Iraqi parliament throw al-Maliki out of office, Warner
admitted, "In no way do I criticize it." Even McConnell, who reflexively deferred
to Bush, admitted that "by any objective standard," the al-Maliki government
"deserve[s] to be criticized."

The response of the anti-war community to the report was incendiary.
Move On purchased a full-page ad in the New York Times mocking Petraeus as
"General Betray Us," prompting the House and Senate leadership to schedule
votes to condemn the "impugning [of] the integrity and professionalism" of the
general.[50] But al-Maliki stepped on a possible opportunity to rally support for
his government by condemning the bipartisan "ugly interference" in Iraq's internal affairs, impolitically insisting that US lawmakers "come to their senses" and
chastising American soldiers for killing Iraqi civilians.

The next day, congressional leaders gathered at the White House for a frank
discussion of what Pelosi called "the biggest ethical issue facing our country."[51]
"I want the views of the leadership before making up my mind," the president
assured. "I want to see if you can find common ground." Pelosi enumerated the
enormous human and financial costs of the extended surge. "Our grandchildren
could serve in Iraq ten years from now," she presciently declared. They all confronted a stark choice: "a responsible redeployment or that long-term commitment," and if the latter, "the American people need an explanation."[52] So did our
allies, who were increasingly reluctant to participate in the joint force effort, a
fact Bush admitted was "frustrating as heck." Bush dismissed Lott's dismissal of
NATO—"a debate association"—as being "full of bull," but he agreed that "no
one else wants to fight."

The president urged congressional leaders to hold their fire for six months while Petraeus updated his report, but Reid rejected the additional delay. "Focus on the *war*, not on Petraeus," he counseled. "The American people don't accept" the administration's scenario. "The surge is not working, and the war is not worth it." He was astonished by Bush's request for *another* $200 billion. "We need to avoid a train wreck," he warned. "It's not your way or the highway!" Moreover, McConnell reported that while he accepted a "long-term deployment in that area of the world," some Republican senators were "heading in a different direction," and others, Blunt said, were "holding their fire."[53]

"When *do* we find common ground?" Pelosi questioned. "Not in this meeting!" Bush replied exasperated. Nothing he or Petraeus could do would transition the mission fast enough for war critics, he complained, which was certainly true. The war had to end, the Speaker confided to Bush, and not just because of the cost and the loss of life. "I have people [demonstrating] in front of my house every day," draping anti-war banners and wet laundry on her neighbors' bushes, Pelosi lamented. Bush pointed in the direction of the permanent encampment of anti-war protestors across Pennsylvania Avenue in Lafayette Park. "Me, too!" the president responded dejectedly.

CHAPTER 9

"THE PROSPECTS DON'T LOOK GOOD"

With the enactment of energy legislation and the stimulus, the 110th Congress seemed to have found its groove. Although relationships between the House, Senate, and White House were not entirely convivial, a working level of trust had been established, particularly in addressing the worsening economic indicators. But a long list of items still awaited action during the spring of 2008 that would be marked by primaries, caucuses, and debates across the nation.

Democrats believed the weakening economy would enable them to construct a narrative allowing them to "own the future" by focusing on "jobs, jobs, jobs," including another stimulus so large they would dare Bush to veto it. Based on her conversations with Paulson, the Speaker was hopeful she also could also secure another key anti-recessionary initiative, trade adjustment assistance (TAA) for dislocated workers, as her price for the trade agreements Bush thought would promote economic activity.

Many in the House caucus wanted to revive the infrastructure component dropped from the January stimulus, but deficit hawks remained hostile to the price tag and the specific ways to offset the cost, shorthanded as "payfors." Meanwhile, the weakening housing sector pressed members to identify ways to assist homeowners, but these policies also carried big price tags. Home affordability "hits home for voters," the Speaker believed, warning that the growing number of foreclosures was "only the tip of the iceberg."[1]

Many of the House-passed bills remained stuck in the Senate. One option for running the filibuster blockade was employing the budget reconciliation procedure, which permits passage of certain legislation by a simple Senate majority exempt from normal filibuster rules. Employing that tactic required House and Senate Democrats to first approve a budget resolution, and achieving that agreement inflamed the same party fissures between liberals and moderates as much of the controversial legislation itself.[2] "We've got no margin of error" in the Senate, Reid warned.[3] "The Republicans are hitting us on terror, taxes, and spending."

Moving to a reconciliation strategy also meant securing the agreement of Kent Conrad (ND), the prickly fiscal hawk often willing to skewer colleagues over deficits. "We must do a budget," he insisted, a procedure that would inflate his role as Senate Budget Committee chair. "We are vulnerable on fiscal irresponsibility, and we cannot manage our spending without a resolution." Finance chair Max Baucus, another bête noire to many progressives, shared Conrad's enthusiasm over using the procedure, although he cringed at the Paygo rules that would require him to pay for expanded business tax credits he favored.

House liberals had long resented the preachy Conrad and pro-business Baucus as much as they bristled at the fiscal conservatism of House Blue Dogs. "Senators are always stuffing pork down their throats as fast as they can," Pelosi angrily complained to Reid. How could she be expected to convince House Democrats to back legislation loaded with provisions benefiting senators who refused to take the tough votes cast by the House? She pointed to Baucus's refusal even to pare back a tax loophole benefiting a handful of mega-wealthy hedge fund managers. "You *did* have the votes," she noted. "What *can* the Senate pass? I can't even imagine!"[4]

Another challenge was the annual appropriations bills that had to be enacted by September 30 each year. Failure to enact the bills forced reliance on must-pass continuing resolutions (CRs) to avoid government shutdowns, a scenario that gave enormous leverage to senators to insert earmarks. "We aren't going to pass any appropriations bills this year," Reid told Pelosi privately. "We're just playing with ourselves."[5] The House Appropriations chair, Obey, blamed White House "obstructionism" for confounding the complicated negotiations on spending, effectively "ripping up the Constitution [and] taking the system down." Relying on CRs largely froze spending at current levels, blocking new initiatives and delivering a victory to conservatives who opposed expanded spending in response to the deepening economic woes.

The release of April's economic numbers did little to calm anxieties. A quarter million jobs were lost during the month, including a hundred thousand in the construction industry, leading a disconcerted Frank to schedule additional hearings on the housing crisis. Over 80 percent of Americans believed the country was heading down the wrong track, a disastrous trajectory for Republicans and a wake-up call to Democrats to behave like they were solving problems and not just fighting among themselves.

While "the public sees us working together on the economy," Pelosi told the president in April, much more was needed.[6] The chairman of the Federal Reserve, Ben Bernanke, was warning that indicators like the rising cost of food and gas were signs of a burgeoning economic crisis. Again, she and Reid suggested a second stimulus including summer jobs, extended UI, and a new $60 billion GI Bill of Rights; Pelosi also wanted $15 billion to stave off mortgage foreclosures (four times the amount the Senate was considering), a bump-up in food stamps, and relief for exhausted state Medicaid programs. "I hope you are open to suggestions," she pressed, but Bush believed it was premature to discuss another bill. "Let's let the first [stimulus] work," he advised. This fight with Bush was good politics, Emanuel believed, because a battle would demonstrate the need for Democratic leadership across the board.[7]

With another Iraq supplemental soon needed, many members vowed to oppose any bill that also failed to address anti-recessionary priorities. The threat did not just come from liberals. Artur Davis (AL), a conservative African American, and a hundred others insisted on $14 billion to help states meet rising Medicaid demand, while others demanded a litany of priorities from asbestos removal to funding the Census. Without addressing these priorities, Pelosi warned, "It's not happening." Even she would vote against more war money.

But a policy-heavy bill had no chance of beginning in the Senate, Reid informed the Speaker, because of procedural rules. He encouraged the House to send a bill to the Senate. However, House leaders knew it was guaranteed to morph into a Christmas tree laden with Senate ornaments that the House would either have to accept or risk a government shutdown. In hopes of avoiding such a clash, Reid suggested Obey meet with the staff of Senate Appropriations chair Robert Byrd, who was so ill he "can't carry on a conversation." Pelosi disliked the idea of negotiating with staff, and when Baucus insisted on including billions in business tax cuts, Pelosi vowed she would no longer even meet with him.[8] "He misrepresents information," she complained to Rangel, Baucus's counterpart. Later she told Reid that Baucus "has messed up every bill! I don't think he's stable!" Within a week, she was outraged to hear Baucus was demanding over $200 million for a Montana company.[9]

Reid was in a morose mood when the Speaker met with him. "I'm not crying on your shoulder," he insisted, but with Byrd "useless," he was having trouble dealing with a dozen appropriations subcommittee chairs and Byrd's staff. "I want to live up to what I agree to," he pledged to Pelosi, who was appreciative but restated her terms. "You can't load the bill up" with Senate riders, she cautioned. "Our members are frustrated and I never want to ask [them] for Iraq money again!"[10]

Bush was prepared to sign off on a limited number of domestic provisions like emergency food assistance and a limited program to refinance mortgages, but he drew the line at "bail[ing] out the speculators" in the housing industry. His price was approval of the controversial trade agreement with Colombia, a nation where widespread violence against union officials infuriated US union leaders and pro-labor members of Congress. The Speaker was wary of the linkage and warned Paulson against an "ill-advised" effort to press the Colombia agreement, especially without also addressing the broader "needs of American families." Her warning was echoed by Obey, who predicted that abandoning Democratic priorities ensured "a blowback" from members. "What's the goal, a signature or a veto?" Obey inquired. "Either way," Pelosi optimistically replied, "we win."[11]

Bush remained unmoved on a new anti-recessionary bill, arguing the initial stimulus's benefits were taking longer to kick in than anticipated. Paulson was still struggling to issue the rebate checks approved in January. Some of the problem was just the typical business cycle, which was heading for a dip, the president said. "Don't impede the market correction," Bush warned Democrats, even if that meant additional hardship. Boehner also dismissed the grim forecasts, observing that "92 percent of homeowners are making their payments" while many of those losing their homes were speculators undeserving of assistance. An angry Clyburn dismissed those remarks as "flippant" and insensitive to the disproportionately affected, heavily minority low-income homeowners.[12]

As weeks passed, the predictable grab bag of add-ons grew: a multi-million-dollar tax benefit for McConnell's Kentucky horse farmers; a food stamp increase for Rangel; a timber relief measure; disaster relief for Haiti. Heeding Bush's admonition to keep the price tag under control, Pelosi told Paulson, depended on the administration's ability to resist outrageous Senate demands, although she also put in a plug for a $70 billion infrastructure package. Paulson was doubtful he could sell that to administration leaders. "It's a tough situation," he admitted. Perhaps the bill could not be as big as Democrats hoped, Pelosi advised, but it was going to have to be big. Privately, Reid and Pelosi were confident they could thread the needle. "It's not easy to be you and me," said Reid one afternoon, promising to pass whatever the House sent over. "It's a good thing we have one another," she replied.[13]

The House bill included $5.8 billion for repairing Louisiana's levees, a veterans' education package, and a $650 million boost for international food aid. But those provisions were dwarfed by nearly $100 billion for the Defense Department (only a half billion less than Bush sought) and an additional $63 billion "bridge fund" for the war linked to restrictions on torture. The Democratic caucus erupted into bitter divisions as members argued passionately over the bill.[14] Blue Dogs castigated the negotiators for piling new, unpaid spending on an emergency supplemental, even the popular veterans benefits. The short-tempered Obey exploded at the "economically illiterate" Blue Dogs. "We would be idiots not to support" the veterans, he insisted, since the Senate would add it back and claim the credit themselves. He castigated the Blue Dogs for protesting unpaid domestic initiatives while supporting hundreds of billions spent on the war. That went too far for John Tanner (TN), who indignantly reminded the chair that it was the election of many moderates that was responsible for Democrats being in the majority in the first place.[15]

Pelosi allowed the countercharges to fly back and forth before making her plea. "I need you to do me a favor," she explained. "Who can vote for this bill?" To the Blue Dogs, she implored, "Let it pass," before pledging, "then we will work with you." The often taciturn Alan Boyd (FL) weakened slightly. "I want to help constructively," he offered, "but I'm making no commitment," castigating Emanuel for "threatening new members" who were wavering.

On May 15, the House passed its supplemental by a 227–196 vote that included just eight moderate Republicans (and lost thirteen Democrats). But Pelosi was furious the bill failed to include a jobs initiative, admonishing Paulson that the administration was obliged to find money for jobs. The secretary was personally sympathetic. "We are woefully underinvested in infrastructure," he agreed, but "there's little likelihood this administration will do it," he confessed. "I'll be cheering you on [but] I can't deliver."[16] A week later, the Senate passed its version with seventy-five votes.

Even without a new stimulus, Democrats remained optimistic about the political fallout from the recession. Mid-May polling gave the party a twenty-one-point lead over Republicans on managing the economy, which would almost certainly translate into major victories at the presidential and congressional levels. But the exhilaration was soon tempered by a grim piece of news. Former representative Joe Kennedy called Pelosi to report that his uncle, Ted Kennedy, had suffered a seizure at the family's Hyannisport compound.[17] For Pelosi, who held a profound reverence for the family of the first Catholic president, the news was especially distressing. Although the initial reports described his condition as "serious but not life-threatening," subsequent medical tests revealed glioblastoma, a largely untreatable brain cancer that would likely kill the "Lion of the Senate" within a year.[18]

A week later, a frustrated Paulson called Pelosi to commiserate about the difficulty of working with House Republicans. "They don't care what the administration thinks," he reported. "I'm saddened the prospects don't look good" for an infrastructure initiative.[19] "I haven't given up," Pelosi responded, piquing his interest with a promise that she "want[ed] to find a way to do" the Colombia trade agreement if the "essential" assistance to impacted US workers was included. He acknowledged that winning approval would be much tougher unless Democrats also saw progress on their own priorities. "I don't want to lose on the floor," she reminded Paulson, recalling that a majority of her members had opposed a Peru agreement the prior November.[20]

As negotiators worked on the final version of the supplemental, Pelosi declared her disappointment with the White House's veto threat against the House's earmark-free version that "only included what the administration requested." By contrast, the Senate's version was loaded up with billions of dollars in earmarks reflecting "the same old cultural habits," she complained. "I'm very disappointed in the Senate." She would appreciate "some points from the White House" for sticking with "a lean bill that included payfors." The "lean" House bill was not without provisions for House members, of course, and Pelosi reminded the Treasury secretary of a wine-labeling provision important to California vintners. "I'm on it," Paulson assured.[21]

With negotiations dragging and the money for the troops running out, Reid proposed stripping out all the domestic spending except veterans' education funds and unemployment aid. Obey refused, warning there were "many surprises" lurking in the Senate bill that House members would find objectionable. "I'm fed up with the Blue Dogs *and* the House and Senate leadership!" he fumed. "The Senate can't be relied on. If the Senate can't take what we send them, we'll put everything back in and get a lot of votes in the House." A glum Reid told Pelosi the next day he was resigned to a presidential veto of even a scaled-back bill. "Let Bush be the bad guy," he recommended.[22]

"Whatever you send us, we'll try to do," Myrick glumly pledged, "but no guarantees. We might add more spending, or we might just pass it." OMB director Jim Nussell was less conciliatory. If the extension of unemployed aid did not come "off the table," he declared, all negotiations would end; Bolten agreed "it must be out." Losing UI was a particularly bitter pill for Reid, who disclosed that his own brother was exhausting his benefits. As the clock ticked closer to the funding deadline, a worried Hoyer said, "We're in real trouble. It's very late."[23]

Day after day, the Senate leaders reiterated the impossibility of securing the sixty votes for cloture, which probably necessitated sending various iterations of the bill back and forth across the Capitol to avoid a time-delaying conference committee and more cloture votes. It was a terrible way to legislate, they agreed, and Pelosi vented her exasperation to Reid. After the election, Senate Democrats would have to "address the filibuster issue" that undermined the party's ability to enact its policy goals.

At last, with the unemployment rate rising to 5.5 percent, the White House blinked on the UI benefits, signing off on a thirteen-week extension in high unemployment states, less than Democrats had wanted but enough to claim victory. The House's new version also included education scholarships for Iraq and Afghanistan veterans who could transfer benefits to other family members.[24] States were allotted $2 billion in response to recent floods, but there still was no help for the housing crisis. Most controversially, the bill included $165 billion to continue military action in Iraq and Afghanistan past the fall election.

Resistance arose from Byrd's unsupervised staffer—Obey angrily dismissed him as "a lamebrain"—who goaded Reid to make further changes but Pelosi warned the clock had run out. "The Senate always wants to add," she complained. The message was received. The next day, Myrick said that if Bush agreed to sign it, the Senate might accept the House's version.[25]

The bill reached the floor of the House on June 19, five hundred days after Bush had first requested the supplemental funding for the war. Pelosi explained she had no choice but to bring the bill to the floor even though it lacked most of the House's Iraq timetables. "I'm glad that we have something about no permanent bases," she noted, but she left no ambiguity about who bore responsibility for the bill's deficiencies. "This is not about a failure of this House of Representatives; it's about what we cannot get past the [Senate] and onto the President's desk." Under another bifurcated rule, the war funding, supported by all but four Republicans, passed 268–155 as Democrats voted two to one in opposition. The domestic portion passed almost unanimously, 406–12, and the magically unified provisions were sent to the Senate, which approved it 92–6.

The yearlong battle for the supplemental arrayed the parties and the two houses of Congress into familiar adversarial stances. With troops in harm's way and a president unwilling to extricate them, Democrats who had run in 2006 promising to end the war found themselves backed into a corner, approving billions for another six months of war while securing only weak and unenforceable conditions on redeploying troops. Anti-war activists in and out of Congress found it difficult to comprehend why majorities in Congress remained incapable of changing the war policy, but on Capitol Hill, it was understood that a new president, with a different strategy for the region, was a prerequisite to effectuate any significant change.

The divisions within the majority itself were especially vexing. The Blue Dogs claimed to be angered by the abandonment of Paygo, although virtually all of them voted for the domestic spending their districts needed. The Dogs were torn "between reality and their principles," Cardoza explained, but Pelosi offered little comfort. "You seem to have gotten over your deficit concerns about the war," she reminded him. Nor was she consoling when Tanner complained the sub-caucus was due more respect. "Only the Blue Dogs can win swing districts," he insisted, "but the liberals attack our motives." She heard the same from her progressives, who felt assaulted by the Blue Dog anti-deficit rhetoric. "Welcome to the club!" she cracked.[26]

Yet it would be inaccurate to ignore the achievement that the supplemental represented. Despite the battle over the war, the parties were able to fashion compromises on military and domestic priorities. "It's not often that on a major bill [with so] much controversy . . . we can come together and work as a Congress on both sides of the aisle and come to a compromise," Boehner noted on the floor in a foreshadowing of the outlook that would cause him grief with ideological party members in years to come. True, the bill had taken far longer and included more debt that he preferred. "There's no reason to get into that," he counseled his members. "It's a compromise. . . . At the end of the day, I think there was cooperation on both sides to come to this agreement. It's a victory for our troops, it's a victory for American families, it's a victory for our veterans, and for those in need who are unemployed." Hoyer agreed, adding that while the bill was not "perfect, [critics] can apply that to any piece of legislation that we consider." Such expressions of bipartisan collaboration were increasingly rare and, following the 2008 election, would become nearly extinct.

A few days later, Bush signed the bill he described as "a result of close collaboration between my administration and members of both parties on Capitol Hill," he declared. "This bill shows the American people that even in an election year, Republicans and Democrats can come together to stand behind our troops and their families."

Certainly, the worsening economy was heavily responsible for driving all sides to reach an agreement. As the parties gathered for their conventions in August, economic anxiety had surpassed national security as the top issue, especially among Democrats.[27] That worry grew with reports in August of over eighty thousand jobs lost, inflating pressure for the delayed second stimulus when Congress returned in September.

Congress returned after the Labor Day holiday expecting little would be accomplished before the postelection lame duck. With polls suggesting Democrats were favored, Bush sent signals he was prepared to negotiate on the Colombia trade deal, his top priority. "Let's keep it in play," Dan Meyer pleaded on Bush's behalf. "I assume we can work it out; no firm lines in the sand."[28]

But trouble was looming. The failure of the giant Wall Street investment firm Lehman Brothers the day before had shaken the White House and the Hill, and Meyer warned more bad news could be coming. Insurance giant AIG was in danger of collapse, and if that happened, "there could be a market meltdown" just weeks before the election.[29] The chair of the Securities and Exchange Commission, Chris Cox, was considering a request for an "informal" meeting of the joint congressional leadership to explain possible administration's actions. "If the companies are getting too big to fail," Meyer said, "something's wrong."

John McCain, the GOP presidential candidate, was on record as being in favor of letting those failures occur, but Bush and Paulson clearly were worried. On September 16, Myrick called me with an ominous message. The Senate's bipartisan leadership had met without staff to review confidential news about Wall Street instability. Afterward, Myrick reported, "It looked like they saw a fucking ghost."[30]

CHAPTER 10

YES, WE CAN!

One thing was indisputable: the 2008 Democratic presidential nomination battle was going to make history. Either the first woman, Hillary Clinton, or the first African American, Barack Obama, would be the nominee. Unsurprisingly, press and public attention focused on who might receive the endorsement of the first woman Speaker of the House. Both in public and private discussions, however, Pelosi avoided indicating any preference because as chair of the convention, she would make crucial rulings on delegate credentials, platform disputes, and other matters. Neutrality was therefore imperative.

Despite having endured bad press during her eight years in the White House—often due to unsubstantiated, exaggerated, and preposterous gossip—Clinton entered the race the prohibitive favorite. Yet on a key issue, Iraq, many on the party's Left remained uncomfortable with her centrist inclinations and alienated by her 2002 vote approving the war. Younger voters, minorities, and many liberals were intrigued by the largely unknown Obama, who offered slight Washington experience or legislative achievement but whose youth, eloquence, and optimism were exhilarating. A US senator for just two years when declaring his candidacy, he was largely without the greatest liability most legislators bring to a campaign: a voting record. In 2004, his stunning keynote address had convinced many delegates they were watching a future president, although he had not even been elected to the Senate. Young (just forty-five), smart (editor of the *Harvard Law Review*), and Black, with a convivial personality, compelling life story, and soaring delivery, Obama ignited crowds like a rock star, leaving supporters swooning.

Obama did little to discourage comparison to another lightly regarded senator with whom he shared a youthful family, Harvard roots, and acclaim as a best-selling author. Obama's connection to the iconic Kennedys was cemented early in the election year when Ted Kennedy endorsed him, as did JFK's only living child, Caroline, who called Obama the "one candidate who offers the same sense of hope and inspiration" as the mythologized, assassinated president. Few endorsements conferred such instant credibility, and the Clintons were mightily resentful. "I have done so much for them," Bill Clinton complained, "and they turned their backs on Hillary."[1]

Obama relentlessly reminded voters of his opposition to beginning the Iraq War, which differentiated him from Clinton, Joe Biden, and other rivals. Of course, in 2002, Obama was an obscure state senator whose views on Iraq were irrelevant to Congress's decision. At the same time, he carefully insulated himself from allegations that he was anti-military or even a pacifist, explaining he did not oppose all conflict, only a "dumb, rash war" concocted by "armchair, weekend warriors" like Vice President Dick Cheney.

Obama's stance on Iraq was close to that of the Speaker, but they barely knew each other. Indeed, the few times their paths had crossed were during informal dinners with a group of legislators including George Miller, Chuck Schumer, and Dick Durbin, who had promoted his Illinois colleague to run for the White House. For most Democrats in the House, and even quite a few in the Senate, Obama remained an enigma.

Obama's swift rise to prominence raised concerns about his security, leading the Secret Service (which guards front-running presidential candidates) to confer with the congressional leadership that reviewed requests for coverage. (Clinton, as a former first lady, already had a security detail.) Pelosi was worried the formal criteria for qualifying for a detail—a mixture of fundraising and polling strength—were too stringent for little-known candidates like Obama. On April 25, 2007, months ahead of the normal timetable, Secret Service director Mark Sullivan and Department of Homeland Security secretary Michael Chertoff described a pattern of "unusual threats" against Obama containing racist overtones and predictions of physical violence. Reid insisted on erring on the side of caution. Should Obama be injured or worse, it would "set race relations back for decades," he predicted. "It would be worse than awful." McConnell granted Obama presented a "special situation" and should be accorded coverage immediately. Although Chertoff expressed concern about starting down an expensive "slippery slope," he agreed. "Let's not roll the dice, given the amount of exposure" of the candidates, Pelosi warned, suggesting other candidates also be given "the benefit of the doubt."[2]

The prescience of Pelosi's decision to remain neutral quickly became apparent as Florida and Michigan defied party rules by scheduling primaries ahead of the formal schedule even though the Democratic National Committee (DNC) had warned such violations risked disqualification of a state's delegates at the convention. Early voting was presumed to benefit Clinton's efforts to secure a delegate lead before the lesser-known Obama could gain traction. Despite the warning, the Michigan primary was held on January 15, 2008, with Clinton winning nearly 55 percent of the vote. Obama, Biden, and John Edwards (SC) did not bother to actively campaign. Two weeks later, Florida held its unauthorized primary, and Clinton came very close to winning 50 percent of the votes.[3]

Soon afterward, Pelosi declared the convention could not seat the disputed delegations, particularly if doing so could affect the outcome in what was becoming a close race.[4] That decision could prove critical since it affected members who were superdelegates, many of whom, according to former representative Tim Roemer (IN), an early Obama supporter, were under pressure from Clinton's camp but "wary of offending voters in their districts" by appearing to bend the rules to favor her. Pelosi waved off pressure tactics by Clinton operatives. "I draw the line at threats," she advised. Later, she told George Miller, who had just endorsed Obama, "I don't join negotiations that begin with a threat. I'm the chair and I am stuck with the rules."[5]

Pelosi insisted she had a more urgent goal than trying to influence the outcome of the nomination battle: growing her House majority so a Democratic president could pass his or her legislative agenda. By late February, many observers sensed Obama's electric appeal might propel more youth and minority Democrats to the polls. The increasing turnout of absentee voters seemed attributable to Obama. In fifteen Texas cities, for example, the absentee turnout of 169,000 in 2004 exploded to 805,000 in 2008. A similar increase was noted in Ohio.[6] If Obama could duplicate this turnout in November, many House districts held by Republicans would be in play.

Worried Clinton supporters appealed to the Speaker to bolster their candidate. In early March, Democratic fundraiser and 1992 Clinton campaign manager Mickey Kantor admitted concern about the New York senator's prospects, even predicting she would drop out if she lost either the upcoming Texas or Ohio primary. If she won, it would be "a new ballgame," although even then, he admitted, Obama would likely prevail.[7] Kantor was alarmed by rumors, originating with other California mega-donors, that Pelosi was orchestrating a hundred superdelegates to endorse Obama. Pelosi dismissed the report, explaining she had only suggested that superdelegates "keep their powder dry" and consider the *timing* of any endorsement. "It would cause greater harm to the party," she reasoned, if it appeared superdelegates were acting to "overturn the will of the people" as expressed in caucuses and primaries. "I was saying the same when Hillary was ahead," she assured Kantor.

Reid was also being pressured by the Clinton campaign, reporting a "soft sell" visit by the hard-charging Harold Ickes Jr. and Maggie Williams, two top advisors. "I just want it over," Reid said, uncomfortable with the battle embroiling several members of his caucus. "I don't want people to get beat up" because he would need the losers in upcoming Senate battles. In April, Bill Clinton called Reid to pressure him to endorse Hillary and exert his influence with superdelegates to throw in with Clinton.[8]

The next day, sixty-five superdelegates announced their support for Obama even as Clinton won Ohio and Texas, prompting a conversation between the Speaker and the Illinois senator. She congratulated him on running a great race against the "Clinton machine." The former president had promised he "would do whatever it took . . . pull out all the stops" to ensure his wife's nomination.

"We made great progress," Obama confidently reported, citing delegate gains in states like Wyoming and Michigan where he had not been on the ballot. "I would have liked to put it away. But the [ultimate] math won't change." Working off a groundbreaking strategic plan devised largely by campaign manager David Plouffe, Obama had vacuumed up large numbers of delegates from state caucuses that Clinton had neglected, believing her appeal in primary states would render the caucuses inconsequential. Obama anticipated "fierce pressure" on the Speaker to seat the disputed delegations. "All I ask," said Obama, "is [for you] to be consistent. The party can't win if I've won more popular votes and two times as many states" but was still denied the nomination, even though many of his victories were in states Democrats would surely lose in November. That outcome, he warned, would "hurt the down-ballot" congressional candidates.

"From the House's self-interest, Clinton on the ticket is a problem," he warned, "because of African American and young voters who will be angry if the nomination slips away" from him. Pelosi did not dispute his assessment. "The party would pay a big price," she confirmed. "There will be a lot of resentment if the local party [activists], who have more of a grassroots connection, feel the Washington superdelegates decide the nomination." Such anger was contrary to the Speaker's self-interest. "I have a Congress to win!" she insisted.[9] She hinted that a substantial number of the superdelegates would soon be coming out for the Illinois senator, which Obama said might hopefully "staunch the losses in Ohio and Texas."[10]

Pelosi offered some advice for the unruffled candidate. "You've been gracious," she noted, "but you need to throw a punch. You can't be a *piñata*."[11]

Despite her professed neutrality, she promised to talk to Durbin about some ideas for the campaign that would serve all Democrats. "The next few weeks are competitive, but they shouldn't be about increasing [party] division" that would complicate governing. She also told Obama that Ickes and Williams had already met with Reid and had requested a meeting with her as well. "If you want to send people in, too," she proffered, "that would be OK."

Pelosi's own meeting with Ickes and Williams did nothing to persuade her to abandon her neutrality. Assured the Speaker would not weigh in on either the Michigan or Florida results, they conceded that Clinton could not secure a majority at the convention unless the disputed delegates were allowed to cast their votes for her. "Obama needs 330 superdelegates," Ickes predicted, while Clinton "needs a few more." With several hundred delegates still uncommitted, it seemed certain the race would remain tight, and Clinton would press the contest right up to the convention.

The Speaker reiterated she would not attempt to influence the superdelegates, but she believed they "cannot overturn the public will" as expressed in primaries and caucuses. "I have friends on both sides," she insisted. "My responsibility is to strengthen the Democratic Party. We *must* win the White House. No one can undermine the chances for a victory in November."

That wasn't enough for Ickes, who warned that voters did not know enough about the Illinois wunderkind. He pointed to the recent corruption trial of Chicago real estate developer and Obama booster Tony Rezko, who had sold the Obamas their upscale Chicago home and then moved in next door. Although there were no allegations of wrongdoing on the senator's part, Ickes argued Obama needed "more vetting" before the party conferred its nomination on him. "Further vetting is important for *both* candidates," she corrected. She also brushed off Ickes's argument that Clinton would run more competitively in swing states like Florida, Iowa, Nevada, and New Mexico. "Swing states are not so important to House candidates" who ran in their individual districts, she replied blithely.

The Speaker also dialed in on Clinton's gravest weakness with the Left, her vote on Iraq, which Pelosi remained convinced hobbled her campaign. "That's why she's not president," the Speaker later observed.[12] It was not enough to promise to *begin* US troop redeployment in Iraq within weeks of entering the White House. "That sounds like Bush," she scolded. "She needs to say she will get the troops *out*."

As they prepared to leave, Pelosi offered the same observation she had made to Obama. "The nomination is the property of the Democratic Party," she reminded them. "We must all invest in whoever wins the nomination. It is not about personal ambition." After Ickes and Williams were escorted out, there was an astonished look on the Speaker's face. The strong-arm tactics were reminiscent of Clinton's mocking Obama's message as "Let's just get everybody together, let's get unified, the sky will open, the light will come down, celestial choirs will be singing, and everyone will know we should do the right thing and the world will be perfect." That "appalling" mischaracterization had left Pelosi "very disappointed" and would "hurt the party and hurt members," an unpardonable offense to the Speaker. The presidential contest, she thought, was "awful [and] really deteriorating."[13]

The following week, she told Plouffe that Clinton's attacks were "putting at risk [my ability] to pull in lower officeholders," she assessed. "My role is to elect Democrats from the White House to state legislatures" but Clinton "hurts us badly in [some] districts." In her own mind, she had no doubt that "Obama, without question," would help produce a larger House majority, "but I don't say" that publicly. The Speaker also worried that if elected, Clinton "won't treat Congress well," an ominous prediction by a Speaker protective of her caucus and the House.[14]

Plouffe promised an Obama candidacy would boost House races by running active campaigns in states Clinton would overlook, recruiting two million registrars and implementing massive "get out the vote" (GOTV) efforts. That was the kind of grassroots vision that appealed to Pelosi, but she advised the Obama team to also do more work on the Hill. "House members don't care who's president," she had told Reid. "They care who's chairman" of their committees. "They don't care *what* mammal wins, as long as it's a Democrat." But, she told Plouffe, "they have no reason to be for Obama, and there is little opposition to the Clintons," she counseled. "They know who *they* are."[15] She suggested Obama follow Clinton's lead, "meet with the members, hear from them, make personal calls and hold meetings." He was going to need their assistance in the near future.[16] The advice failed to penetrate the Obama inner circle. Throughout his presidency, many House members felt cold-shouldered by Obama to the exasperation of his staff, who diligently documented the members invited to a White House dinner or to watch a basketball game in the private quarters.

As indicated from their Ickes-Williams meetings, both Pelosi and Reid were increasingly annoyed with the Clinton campaign's tactics (which soon included floating a rumor that she would offer Obama the vice presidential nomination). Pelosi resented the Clintons' "different standard for winning" that often appeared particularly ruthless.[17] She worried, for example, about Clinton's allegation that Obama was unfit to serve as commander in chief providing fodder for Republicans in the fall campaign.

Quietly, she cautioned House members about enlisting to help Clinton. In a March conversation, Pelosi had advised Murtha to delay any endorsement because Obama was improving in Pennsylvania and other members were "telling [her] they could switch from Clinton to Obama."[18] Murtha admitted he was feeling less enamored of Clinton after her recent attacks on Obama. "I don't like her tactics," he said, deciding to hold off on making any statement, depriving the New York senator of important validation from an anti-war leader.

Pelosi herself was "offended" by Clinton's statements critical not only of Obama but also the party's two previous nominees, Al Gore and John Kerry. She was also tired of Clinton's "heavy-handed tactics" in trying to pressure superdelegates, which she found "just appalling." The Clintons were "losing their credibility," she said.[19] Comments like that, and the Speaker's insistence that superdelegates not reverse voters' decisions, increasingly convinced some Democratic funders that the Speaker was leaning toward Obama. Rahm Emanuel, whose links to the Clintons went back years, told Pelosi even he was increasingly frustrated with their complaints. "They think everything happens *to* them," he said dismissively. "They need to get past it."[20]

The New York senator pushed back. A group of "unhappy, very strong supporters" was preparing a letter "straight from the Clinton campaign" reminding the Speaker of their contributions to the DCCC, a Pelosi operative reported.[21] The Speaker also received a call from Hollywood producer Harvey Weinstein threatening to raise $15 million for McCain if primary do-overs were scheduled in Michigan and Florida. Obama, Weinstein insisted, could not win the general election. As with other arrogant funders, Pelosi dismissed the threat, noting that Weinstein had never raised money for House Democrats. "This could push me some place," Pelosi told Reid. When the story of the threat leaked a few days later, Weinstein contacted Pelosi's office to suggest they issue a joint denial, but Pelosi refused to do so.[22]

"The rich guys are destroying the party!" she bemoaned. The race was becoming "awful" and "crude" because the wealthy donors were "throwing their weight around." Reid offered to help battle the heavy hitters, telling Pelosi, "If you are pushed too hard, tell me" so they could jointly respond. But the pressure wasn't affecting her impartiality, she insisted. "I've acted neutrally [and] I'll never get into the presidential," Pelosi insisted. "If I had my thumb on the scale, they'd know it. But I don't care who wins."[23]

Reid's own professions of neutrality were even less convincing. "I have tried to be neutral, but every day I am more pissed off at what the Clinton people are doing," he declared. "That's who they are." A few weeks later he admitted, "I'm bitter. The Clintons are mean people." Even Bill Clinton's former vice president, Al Gore, "can't stand the Clintons," one leader noted, reporting that the 2000 nominee would probably stay out of the primary contest. "He likes Hillary less than he likes Bill."[24]

By early May, Clinton's campaign was $20 million in debt, and even the former president conceded that the path to victory was "very tough." A group of her mega-fundraisers was preparing to shift to Obama, exacerbating money worries that Emanuel believed would drive Clinton from the race.[25] Seeking out every possible source for money, Clinton materialized one day at the DCCC dialing-for-dollars office to solicit member support as they sought funds for their own campaigns.

Although Clinton won by ten points in Pennsylvania on April 22, the allocation of delegates was so even the victory failed to slow Obama's momentum. By late May, the Clintons had fatalistically accepted defeat. "No one thinks she's the nominee," confided Carl Wagner, who had cochaired Bill Clinton's 1992 campaign. "She wants to get out with dignity. They're making it up as they go along." The former president promised, "We won't do anything to hurt" Obama, even though they believed his nomination "unbelievably risky." Several insiders believed Bill already was maneuvering to make his wife the vice presidential nominee.[26]

The inevitability of Obama's victory began to shift Pelosi's stance. "Nancy is inclined to get involved," a top fundraiser said in early May. A few days later, the Speaker and I held a clandestine meeting with Obama. He sat informally at a conference table, casually dressed and with one leg informally draped over a chair as the three of us talked for more than an hour. He showed surprisingly little strain or fatigue from the brutal year of campaigning. He wondered why "so many members are slow to endorse," he admitted. "They're chicken," Pelosi bluntly responded before correcting herself. "Well, not *chicken*, but thinking of themselves." "No, you were right," Obama agreed, "they're chicken."

Acting as though the nomination and general election were a fait accompli, she recited her stock speech about reviving Jefferson's Gallatin Project and infrastructure investment under Theodore Roosevelt, effusing about market-based, public-private, and scientifically sound approaches to climate change, energy, economic innovation, science, health care, universal broadband, and more. His campaign, she counseled, should focus on a "big vision of the agenda," sweeping themes like "Rebuild the American Economy, Protect the American

People, Rebuild the Military." "Forget incrementalism," she importuned. "Think entrepreneurially."[27]

"Those are good policy and good politics at the same time," he politely agreed, but his focus remained on more immediate challenges. He would concede a favorable distribution of the disputed state delegations to Clinton, knowing he would still prevail, and he was willing to make more deals so long as Clinton agreed to exit the race gracefully. "The question is the tone," he said.

Finally, Obama got around to the point of the meeting. "Can you help move the superdelegates?" he asked. Pelosi's reply was noncommittal. "I will encourage *all* of them to move sooner" without embracing one candidate or the other, but she advised him to push harder. There were, she advised, several Clinton supporters preparing to switch allegiances after the primaries. "You need to be scrupulous," she told him. "Tell people it's time to make a decision. The party is subject to ridicule if people are hiding. If I thought it necessary, I would push; but it's not necessary."

Obama responded with the cool analysis that would earn him the sobriquet "No Drama." "I'm trying to show restraint, not trying to gin up a big brawl. But if we need to have a big brawl," he assured, "I will." The Clintons were "trying to be the victims," Obama asserted, "but it will be OK" once the remaining votes and the Michigan and Florida disputes were resolved. "If that's so, then it's over," she responded, and then added, "It's over anyway."[28]

A statement from the Speaker declaring she would be "happy with either candidate" was interpreted by the Clinton forces as transparently pro-Obama. A top Pelosi political operative reported that Clinton, in a "mode of desperation," wanted to make the Speaker "radioactive" to blunt her role at the convention, and several Clinton loyalists, intent on "getting the Speaker to back off helping Obama," were "dragging Nancy through the mud," insinuating the Speaker was merely trying to preserve her status as the most powerful woman in politics. That, one Pelosi lieutenant declared, could be the "nail in the coffin" of Pelosi's neutrality.[29]

The tension built to a fever pitch on the eve of the decisive California primary vote. Certain "Obama has it in the bag," Reid wanted to issue a joint statement with Pelosi declaring "the elections are complete" and undecided delegates should "come forward . . . so we have a candidate." Such a statement could be interpreted only as an endorsement of Obama's inevitability. "Obama is fine," Reid told Pelosi after learning that Gov. Joe Manchin (WV) would endorse him. "He has more than enough." The next day, Reid urged a Nevada House member to endorse Obama and told Pelosi he would do so as well later in the week. Pelosi confirmed she would, too. "I told the press, 'He's the nominee,'" she confided.[30]

That night, a man who could not secure a floor pass for the Democratic convention just eight years earlier, a self-proclaimed "skinny kid with big ears and a funny name," told supporters in a Saint Paul arena, "I can stand here and say that I will be the Democratic nominee for president of the United States of America." Still, Clinton refused to formally withdraw from the race, asserting she had received more popular votes than Obama. "She wants to play hardball on vice president or she'll hurt him," Emanuel said, but Obama would not even consider her. "Absolutely no, she's a third wheel," he reported Obama as saying. Emanuel endorsed Obama on June 4, and Clinton followed suit three days later.[31]

The Speaker moved to patch things up with Clinton a few weeks later. "You've made us so proud," she declared, suggesting that gender discrimination was partly to blame for her loss. Clinton agreed her campaign had been impacted by "the rearing of sexism" and said that the media sometimes took on the appearance of "a boys' locker room."[32] The next generation would be different, Pelosi assured, but Clinton seemed less convinced. "Sexism is universal," the senator responded, "even where there is no racism."

A few days after the California primary, longtime Democratic Party official Jim Johnson and Washington attorney Eric Holder visited Pelosi to discuss potential vice presidential choices. Pelosi advised against selecting a woman like Gov. Kathy Sebelius (KS), which would be interpreted as an insult by the New York senator's loyalists. As with the top of the ticket, Pelosi insisted one criterion guided her preference: securing "stronger margins in the House of Representatives."[33]

Pelosi floated the name of Rep. Chet Edwards (TX) who had strong credentials on military and veterans' issues. "Chet votes with us more than he should," Barney Frank told Holder, given his Republican-leaning district. Pelosi enlisted Bernard Rapoport, an influential Texas fundraiser, to put in a good word with the campaign. The rumors drew attention to the unassuming Texan whom Carolyn Maloney (NY) greeted one morning with a jovial "Hello, Mr. Vice President!" Obama confirmed he liked the Texan and was "going to look it over." Although she heard that Edwards's star "had definitely risen," she soon learned that Joe Biden had gotten the call in part because the ticket needed someone of greater national stature.[34]

In the days before the convention, Democratic spirits were high, fueled by the candidate's magnetic appeal and the pure symbolism of his improbable victory over one of the best-known Democrats in history. One evening before heading to Denver, Pelosi took her young grandson to a dinner at the Italian embassy. He playfully ducked under the table only to emerge face to face with the putative nominee. "Barack Obama!" he cried out. "I must be dreaming!" Indeed, Democrats could have been forgiven if they imagined they were dreaming: they would enter the fall campaign with an appealing nominee, a largely unified party, and polling detailing effusive support for Obama among women, four times the margin among male voters, among whom Obama also led by five points.

Republicans were determined not to allow Democrats a week of undiluted, positive coverage during the nominating convention in Denver. Oil-drilling activists swarmed outside the hotels and convention hall chanting, "Drill everywhere," castigating Democrats for opposing the opening of more public lands to oil and gas development. In Washington, Republicans commandeered the vacant House chamber to conduct ersatz sessions on the energy issue, hoping to pit two strong Democratic constituencies—organized labor and environmentalists—against each other.[35] In violation of House rules banning filming on the House floor, the fantastical floor "debates" were recorded on cell phones and disseminated on social media platforms.

The morning after Obama's acceptance speech, I was in a hotel lobby in Denver when I heard that McCain had chosen Alaska's inexperienced, pro-oil governor, Sarah Palin, as his running mate. I took the elevator back upstairs to the Speaker's room. "Well, Obama just won the election," I confidently predicted. McCain, a seventy-two-year old with a history of cancer, barely knew the person he had impetuously selected to be one heartbeat away from the Oval Office. Within days, Palin's extreme views and quirky personality became electoral liabilities.[36] Her peculiarities contributed to a precipitous drop in support for the GOP ticket among white women from +19 points to -2. A study by researchers at Stanford in 2016 concluded that Palin's presence on the ticket cost the Republicans 1.6 percentage points or over two million votes.[37]

Not every Democrat was as confident about their neophyte nominee. Obey worried Obama had "no real appeal to the average worker on economic issues" and his economic plan was "anemic." Obama's oratory was too eloquent. "He sounds like Martin Luther King," he complained, "but what we need is Bobby

Kennedy or Hubert Humphrey." On foreign policy, Obey said, the war hero McCain sounded knowledgeable while Obama was "just shooting blanks."[38]

But the nominee remained unfazed by the doubters and was already focusing on the lame-duck period leading up to January 20. "By the time I'm inaugurated," Obama said, "the public [will believe we've] already been in control for three months. If [Bush's people] do something half-assed in that period, we get the blame!" He cautioned cutting major deals with the outgoing president. "You, Reid, and I agree we should do the minimum in the lame duck," he told Pelosi. "Don't negotiate when the Republicans have a strong hand."[39] He promised to schedule meetings with the House chairs, but he assured the Speaker, "Those guys are OK, but you are my favorite." And while he would arrange to speak with Reid, he insisted on a meeting with her first since she could set the agenda by pushing strong legislation through the House quickly. He wanted to assure that legislation reflected his ideas and could pass the Senate.

Obama also wanted an early meeting with Republicans. Pelosi called Boehner "a decent fellow" with whom she had developed a working relationship. But the Republicans were roiling and the two leaders agreed he might not survive. If not, his replacement could come from the "whack pack" who would be even less inclined to be cooperative.[40]

Overall, Pelosi shared his upbeat assessment. "I want to see you have the biggest number, govern down the middle, and then figure where to go," she declared. Obama's response was calm and confident. "Let's get together soon."

CHAPTER II

THE ABYSS

"A very serious situation is developing, very troublesome," Henry Paulson tersely warned Speaker Pelosi on Thursday afternoon, September 18, 2008. "We might not be able to prevent impending crisis." Lehman Brothers, the fourth largest financial company in the country, had just filed for Chapter 11 bankruptcy protection after Treasury officials rejected pleas for a multi-billion-dollar bailout. "Nothing we can say will calm the situation until we come up with a policy that is overwhelming force!"[1]

Pelosi suggested a meeting the next morning.[2] "Tomorrow will be too late," Paulson cautioned. "If we don't act now, we won't have an economy by Monday." Pelosi was alarmed. "If things are this bad, why aren't *you* calling *me?*" she asked Paulson. "The White House wouldn't let us," he admitted. "They were saving the problem for the next president."[3]

After hearing rumors of a possible run on the San Francisco Federal Reserve Bank, Pelosi had spoken with her own economic advisors that morning.[4] "The markets are frozen up," explained Alan Sinai, whom the *Wall Street Journal* had named the nation's top forecaster. "No one wants to lend money to anyone." Sinai blamed the Bush administration's lackadaisical regulatory enforcement. "There's no time to breathe," he told the Speaker. "All that can happen now is an implosion."

The deteriorating condition of the financial markets was not a complete surprise. A year earlier, France's largest bank had frozen funds that held securities backed by US subprime mortgages.[5] By late December 2007, a Morgan Stanley executive reported the company was "losing its shirt" because of subprime overexposure, and it was not alone.[6] Barney Frank and Christopher

Dodd, the House and Senate financial services chairs, had conducted hearings on the worsening mortgage crisis, and Frank was already writing legislation to allow states to buy up foreclosed property for use as low-income housing. But the administration and most Republicans in Congress remained uninterested in aiding "speculators" who, they believed, ought not to have purchased homes in the first place.[7] In January 2008, Sen. John Kerry (MA) unsuccessfully proposed the Bush stimulus bill address the mortgage crisis. In the House, Jim Clyburn had been denouncing predatory lenders for ensnaring minorities with mortgages they could ill afford, and Chaka Fattah (PA), the chair of the Urban Caucus, had pressed Bush for a mortgage relief plan.[8]

The banking industry and regulators had long ignored the gathering storm. In the thirty years before the crisis, the debt held by the financial sector skyrocketed from $3 trillion to more than $36 trillion, "more than doubling as a share of gross domestic product."[9] Since the 1999 repeal of the New Deal–era Glass-Steagall Act, wealth had become hyperconcentrated in "too big to fail" firms whose collapse would jeopardize the nation's economy. By 2005, the country's ten largest commercial banks held 55 percent of the nation's assets, more than twice the concentration in 1990.

Underneath the booming profits, however, was dangerous rot. In the decade after 1996, mortgage-related fraud multiplied twenty times and then doubled again from 2005 to 2009.[10] Five of the largest firms were dangerously overleveraged.[11] Bear Stearns held just $1 for every $38 in debt with more than $380 billion in liabilities before its collapse in March 2008. The quasi-public Fannie Mae and Freddie Mac had a leveraged ratio of 75 to 1.[12] By mid-September, many of the nation's largest financial houses were saddled with hundreds of billions of dollars in toxic paper and were frantically borrowing billions in the overnight markets.

Despite the mounting evidence, the Bush administration had done little because, as Paulson and Bernanke explained, "it's hard to fix something *before* it breaks," and some officials continued to deny there was a serious problem at all. Three days before Bear Stearns collapsed, Securities and Exchange Commission chairman Christopher Cox expressed "comfort about the capital cushions" of the major investment banks. Others knew better. When John McCain declared insurance giant AIG should be allowed to fail, an anxious Paulson told him, "Don't say that!" warning such a statement "could have very negative reactions." Paulson was so anxious that he advised Bush to delete a sentence from an upcoming speech declaring there would be no need for federal intervention. "We aren't going to do a bailout, are we?" the worried president asked.[13]

Top economists, although they feared a "downward spiral within a year" that would plunge millions of Americans into bankruptcy and jeopardize their homes, also were cautious about the federal government diving into the convoluted mess. "You need to minimize the appearance of a bailout," Alan Blinder of Princeton advised.[14] Within weeks, however, another economist warned there would be a brutal recession by the end of 2008, even raising the specter of food riots. It would be, he warned, "worse than the Great Depression."[15]

In late May 2008, Paulson believed housing legislation was still unnecessary, warning that much of what was under discussion might even be "modestly harmful." If action was required, he assured Pelosi, the good relationship they had fostered during January's stimulus negotiations would prove helpful. "We are very fortunate that you are the Speaker and that Barney is chairman," Paulson confided. On the other hand, he admitted, he "couldn't have a lower opinion of anyone than Spencer Bachus," the top Republican on Financial Services.[16]

Pelosi resisted calls to attack Bush's policies because she didn't want to "spook the markets and make matters worse." By mid-September, Paulson had let valuable weeks slip by without alerting key congressional players, and weeks before the election, there was no "big appetite for bailing out" financial institutions.[17] The problem, the secretary insisted, was "a huge loophole in regulatory structure," and he predicted that when the dust settled, "we will find plenty of fraud." In the meantime, he wanted to be free to solve the problem, not spend "three months testifying before Waxman" and his rigorous Oversight Committee.

The Speaker was unsympathetic. "*I'm* not taking the heat," she told him. "I won't pass a bill and then have Republicans criticize us for bailing out Wall Street and selling consumers down the river!" she warned. The administration's record was "a complete failure," she charged. "Imagine if Social Security [had been] privatized" as Bush had proposed and the stock market collapsed, wiping out the retirement savings of tens of millions of Americans.

When the bipartisan leadership gathered in Pelosi's second-floor conference room on September 18, Bernanke described a "very severe financial crisis, predicting "hundreds of billions in losses." While the "fire [had] burned for more than a year," they now faced "the nightmare we had been trying to prevent."[18] "It is a matter of days," he warned, before "a major meltdown in the United States and globally." Paulson morosely agreed. "I've never seen anything like it," he ruminated. "Once in a hundred years."[19]

Congress needed to pass legislation authorizing the Treasury to purchase toxic assets to prevent further disintegration on Wall Street, Paulson insisted. There was no good outcome, only hopes of limiting the damage. "If we don't deal with it by next week, the country could collapse." The best scenario, Bernanke predicted, was a "deep, long recession."

The congressional leaders sat speechless. Finally, Reid asked how much the legislation would cost. "You're getting warm at $500 billion," Paulson estimated, and even then, millions of Americans would lose their homes. A bailout to aid the very financiers and bankers blamed for the crisis would be a very tough lift politically, Frank declared. Bachus blanched at the price tag and began suggesting alternative strategies but Paulson waved him off. "If you want something to work quickly," he advised, "use our plan."

Democrats immediately demanded that the legislation also address the long-ignored concerns of "Main Street," which would reduce the "perception the bill is a [corporate] bailout." That meant including initiatives Bush had been opposing, like job creation, UI extension, and foreclosure assistance, although Pelosi agreed not to "protect people who shouldn't have been in homes" in the first place.[20] Republicans immediately pushed back. "Isn't it sufficient for Democrats to know they were voting to save the American economy" by saving the financial institutions? Sen. Judd Gregg (NH) asked. "It's political reality," Reid responded.

Democrats also demanded the bill freeze bonuses and "golden parachute" retirement packages for executives whose companies received federal assistance. "No one gets out alive without dealing with compensation," Pelosi vowed. "It's the only issue the American people understand. Democrats can't hear you until you talk about it."[21] Even the normally cautious Baucus believed the bill "was going nowhere" without the provision. Paulson's response was glum. "We won't get there if you take that approach," he admonished, predicting such restrictions would discourage business leaders from accepting aid and undermine the rescue effort. "We can't accept it."[22]

"You mean to tell me that they would rather see their banks and the economy go down the drain rather than limit their compensation?" an incredulous Frank asked. "That makes me more worried about capitalism than anything else that's happened." Without the restrictions, he warned, "I can't tell you the bill will pass."[23] After a tense moment, Paulson glumly responded, "Then God help us."

The administration's time line presented another serious challenge for Reid. "If you think the US Senate will give you $500 billion next week," he predicted, "that's not happening!" Securing a sixty-vote, bipartisan supermajority on a massive bill was a tall order just weeks before a third of the Senate would face voters at the polls. "We can't just take your word. We need hearings. It takes two weeks to pass a bill to flush a toilet" in the Senate, Reid warned. "Well, if we don't do this," Paulson testily responded, "we are flushing the toilet on the American people."[24]

Pelosi called President Bush the next day, their first conversation in months, to argue for including "homeowners [and] working families." She demanded a $50 to $70 billion jobs package, health assistance to states, expanded food stamps, low-income energy aid, and extended UI to help with "selling [the bill] to the American people" and her own members. "Let's get it done" as soon as possible, Bush noncommittally responded, but Pelosi refused to backpedal. "We need to get as much as we can," she insisted.[25]

Pelosi knew she could not win liberal votes if she were perceived as caving in to Bush and the culpable financial interests; indeed, the affluent Speaker was rankled that she, like Bush, endured castigation for sanctioning a bailout "for our Wall Street friends." For months afterward, she complained that "everyone thinks Democrats are in cahoots with Wall Street."[26] The real blame rested, she inveighed, on collusion between "cowboy capitalism [by] dangerous people" and indifferent regulators. "We are in this situation because of 'anything goes,' a failed economy [and] because no one has been watching the store."

Pelosi bluntly told Boehner he would have to contribute a hundred Republican votes to pass the legislation and agreed she would wrangle the remainder. He was not optimistic. "My people are looking for a reason not to support" the bill, he protested, and his leadership colleagues were "in hiding." Like Democrats who cited Bush's exaggerated WMD threats from Saddam Hussein, many in his party doubted the administration's assessment of the crisis. Adding an anti-recessionary wish list guaranteed that "my people will run away," he warned. Perhaps, he advised Paulson, it was better to "cool your jets" and "hit the reset button" before legislating by creating a committee to study the crisis.[27]

Paulson dismissed the plea for a delay and sent a three-page bailout bill to the Hill requesting "prompt, bipartisan action," but Democrats dismissed the superficial draft as "outrageous."[28] On the north side of the Capitol, Paulson was "laying an egg" with the Senate Finance Committee. The administration's leaders were aggravated with the unanticipated resistance they encountered on the Hill, especially from their own party. An exasperated Bush complained, "My problem is House Republicans!" whom Bolten described as "horrid."[29] Paulson viewed Spencer Bachus as "disgraceful," and the feeling was mutual; Republicans felt they had been "sold out by Paulson" and blamed the administration for "getting them into this" mess.[30]

Reid insisted "we can't pass a bill unless 80 percent of Republicans vote for it."[31] He was especially flabbergasted that McCain, who had offered little "except for an occasional, unhelpful statement," was leaning against supporting the bailout. Pelosi dismissed McCain's waffling as "just pathetic" and predicted Democrats would "walk away" if he rejected the plan. When the Arizonan called Pelosi to complain about the pace of the discussions, the Speaker sharply rebuked him. "We *are* making progress," she sternly corrected. "It is not accurate" to say otherwise.[32]

Sounding wooden and formal, McCain proposed suspending the presidential campaign and convening a bipartisan White House summit instead. Schumer dismissed the idea as "just weird." But the White House signed off on the meeting, and the Speaker reproached Bolten for capitulating to McCain's "political stunt," which could delay the legislation. "That wasn't our doing," he confided, promising that "someday, over a beer, I'll tell you" the whole story.[33]

She also told Paulson to "tell the president to lead [because] I will not allow Congress to look like it's in disarray!" Bush's stubbornness aggravated her. "The president never listened to us on Iraq," she charged. "He never broaches disagreement." Unless Bush embraced the bill Congress formulated, she told the Treasury secretary, "we have wasted our time, and it is an insult to you." Mordantly, Paulson noted, "I'm beyond that point."[34]

Although worried the meeting would delay the first presidential debate, Obama was wary of rejecting the kind of presidential invitation he might soon extend to congressional leaders. "If we didn't go," he rationalized, "it would be a bad precedent."[35] Bush had acknowledged the meeting probably would not be "particularly useful, but I felt obliged to say 'yes,'" he told Obama. "I hope you can come."[36] Obama acquiesced, confident he could handle McCain. "We've got him boxed in," he said self-assuredly. "We have him on the ropes."[37]

The Democratic leaders designated Obama as their lead with the understanding there be no dealmaking at the meeting. Afterward, their message would emphasize the need for Republicans to "get their ducks in a row" as Boehner continued to warn he might not be able to deliver his votes. "I'm trying to manage the Indians," he told Pelosi, who was unforgiving. "I've got a war paint crowd myself!" she reminded him. "I've got two votes right now" for the bill.[38]

"We've got a serious economic crisis," Bush declared to the participants around the enormous table in the Cabinet Room after saluting Pelosi for her collaborative efforts.[39] "I can't tell you how important it is to get something done." He cautioned Democrats against adding controversial provisions that "the markets won't accept. You damn sure don't want to be the people who see it crater." In general, however, he professed flexibility; if Paulson and Bernanke signed off, "we're for it."

"We can argue how got here but we have to solve the problem," Obama began, noting there was "rough agreement in principle." Republicans quickly poured cold water on that assertion. Shelby expressed "deep reservations" about the bailout scheme, producing a letter signed by dozens of conservative economists warning about precipitous action. Boehner and Bachus revived their alternative approaches, drawing sharp rebukes from Frank and Reid. Pelosi reminded the participants her members also had "a million ideas for improving" the "Paulson Plan," but she pledged to "corral them" and insisted the GOP leaders do the same. As the parties parried, Bush became restless. "It's easy for smart guys to sit around," he said, but "if money isn't loosened up, this sucker"—the US economy—"could go down."

"We need to hear from John," Obama finally declared, and all heads turned to the silent McCain, who had proposed the conclave. He stumbled through a rambling statement, thanking Bush for convening the meeting and noting his long record of working "with both sides of the aisle." Puzzled looks flew around the Cabinet Room; he had suspended the presidential campaign for this?

Bush leaned over to the Speaker and whispered, "I *told* you you'd miss me when I'm gone!" "No," Pelosi dryly responded, "I *won't*." McCain concluded by vacuously urging that "concerns must be addressed," and Obama snapped, "That's not an answer!" An exasperated Barney Frank pressed, "I don't know what your proposals are!" Even Bush threw up his hands, admitting, "*I* don't know what the hell they are!"

After the meeting ended, McCain silently edged past the Democrats who huddled in the narrow corridor and then moved into the adjacent Roosevelt Room. Suddenly, the door opened, and a harried Paulson strode into the room. Quickly moving to Pelosi, he fell to one knee and solemnly bowed his head. "Don't blow this thing up, Nancy," he pleaded. Stunned, Pelosi tried to lighten the mood. "Why, Hank," she exclaimed to nervous laughter, "I didn't know you were Catholic!"

Afterward, Paula Nowakowski, Boehner's chief of staff, acknowledged her boss was furious with Paulson for siding with Democrats and Pelosi should "start thinking" about a bill that could pass with only Democratic votes. That was a total nonstarter, I replied. Bush's people were not thrilled with the meeting either, criticizing Boehner's conference as filled with "hardheads" who were using "theatrics . . . to derail" the bill. The meeting had been awful, "chaos . . . typical of

McCain world," allowing others to "outmaneuver him." Bush and Boehner staff admitted "the only person in the room who looked presidential was your guy," Obama.
Bolten was appalled by McCain's performance. "If he had voted 'no' and the economy tanked," Bolten later declared, "*we* would have campaigned against him!"[40]

One fundamental addition to the administration's proposal, Democrats insisted, was that the companies accepting aid fully reimburse taxpayer loans with
interest. Shelby agreed that without repayment, the administration's proposal
was "a blank check."[41] During a drafting session on the provision, Gregg insisted
that any shortfalls by the financial companies be made up from cuts in unrelated domestic spending. "I think we can do that," said Emanuel, the Democratic
negotiator, looking over his shoulder at me for confirmation. As the speaker's
representative, I shook my head no, prompting a heated exchange. Finally, Gregg
exploded, "You're not *listening* to me!" I responded, "Well, Senator, you're not
listening to *me*," as stunned staff and members look on. I suggested he run his
idea for domestic spending cuts past the Speaker. Gregg testily strode off to
pitch the idea to Pelosi, returning a short time later. "Okay, that isn't going to
work," he acknowledged. Blunt quickly intervened, agreeing on the Democratic
repayment provision that ended up with the Treasury making over $110 billion
in profit from the Troubled Assets Relief Program (TARP) loans.[42]

The time-consuming gyrations of congressional negotiations frustrated
Paulson. "It's going slower than I would like," he complained. "People are just
jammering." Delays could produce a meltdown, he feared, and "I don't want to
be Andrew Mellon!" presiding over a depression like Herbert Hoover's despised
Treasury secretary. But Pelosi was irritated by Paulson's obstinance and insensi-
tivity to the Hill's procedures. "It would have been easier," she recalled, "if Paulson had been born with ears."[43]

Meanwhile, Boehner continued to struggle with his members. "I can't put
enough lipstick on it to sell it," he explained. There might be as few as thirty
Republican votes—less than a third of his assigned quota. He could produce
more votes if the Democrats were willing to add a business tax cut, but Paulson
and Pelosi responded coolly. "Don't waste [our] time," she said. Insisting on tax
cuts would mean "all bets are off." Privately, Pelosi told Paulson, "It's disgraceful
the Republicans are not at the table," and the secretary did not disagree.[44]

But the Democratic vote count was also weak. Members were hearing only
negative comments from furious constituents. Reid's office reported receiving
five thousand calls opposing the plan and only twenty in support. Facing weak
Hill backing, the administration's political operatives seized the upper hand in
the negotiations. "It's time to call in the political play," Emanuel told Bolten, who

gratefully responded, "Speaking as a political hack, I say, 'Hallelujah!'" But even if they reached agreement on the policy, Reid warned the Senate could require as many as nine time-consuming votes if Republicans opted for obstruction. That got Pelosi "angry," convinced she would be pressured to accept whatever bill Reid could muscle through. "*I'm* angry at the Senate, too," he responded, but his complex rules might require him to cut deals she might find unsavory. "You can't be a virgin if . . ." he began, but the modest Pelosi waved him off. "You don't have to go any further," she admonished.[45]

"Don't count on the Republicans," Blunt advised Pelosi as the House debate began. The White House's Dan Meyer counted only seventy-five Republicans; the rest, Nowakowski predicted, would "beat their chests" in opposition. As the contentious debate continued, Bush, Vice President Dick Cheney, Paulson, and Bernanke lobbied House members with discouraging results. Boehner asked for more time, but the Speaker turned him down, fearing further Democratic erosion. "We don't have the votes" either, she acknowledged, dispatching Frank to meet with the liberal Hispanic and Black caucuses and the conservative Blue Dogs. Steeling himself for the onslaught of complaints, Frank asked, "When is the Asshole Caucus [meeting], and do I have to address *them?*"[46]

Pelosi ramped up the rhetoric in her floor speech to persuade recalcitrant liberals to support the bailout. "On Wall Street, people are flying high," she charged. "They are making unconscionable amounts of money. They privatize the gain [but] the minute things go tough, they nationalize the risk and the American people have to pick up the tab. Something is very, very wrong with this picture." She castigated Bush for squandering the $5.6 trillion surplus Clinton had bequeathed him, faulting "too little regulation and an 'anything goes' economic policy [that] has taken us to where we are today." But "the party is over," she warned, promising a new Congress and Democratic administration will ensure "nobody needs to worry that we . . . will have to do it again."[47]

Republican supporters also made no bones about their dislike of the legislation. "Frankly, I'm furious," Jerry Lewis (CA) admitted. "The idea of spending taxpayer dollars to prop up risky investments . . . goes against all the principles I have lived by." But there was little choice. "Doing nothing will cause a potential catastrophe."

The toughest selling job fell to Boehner, who privately described the bill as a "shit sandwich" but promised he was "going to eat it anyway." His voice cracking, his cheeks streaked with tears, he acknowledged, "Nobody wants to vote for this, nobody wants to be anywhere around it. I didn't come here to vote for bills like this. But let me tell you this, I believe Congress has to act . . . in the best interest of our country, not what's in the best interest of our party [or] our own reelection." Like most appeals to members that acknowledged electoral risk, his plea received tepid applause.

As the seconds ticked down on the vote clock, it became evident the entreaties had failed. The TARP bill was defeated 205–228, a rare floor loss for Pelosi. Republicans delivered only sixty-five of the hundred votes they had promised, but 40 percent of Democrats also voted no, including fifteen of eighteen members in toss-up races. The defeat was an embarrassment for Bush, who had called all nineteen Republican members of his Texas delegation but persuaded just four to support the bill. One dissenter, Jeb Hensarling, denounced TARP as the first step "on the slippery slope to socialism."

In the cloakrooms, stunned members watched TV screens as the Dow Jones average plummeted 778 points, its largest one-day point loss at that time. Over $1.2 trillion in savings vanished—nearly twice the size of the TARP bailout package. The VIX index of market volatility, the so-called fear index, closed at the highest level in its twenty-eight-year history.

Republicans quickly blamed the Speaker's incendiary speech for alienating their members. Eric Cantor, the highly partisan Virginia conservative and chief deputy whip, castigated her "failure to listen and failure to lead."[48] Hoyer, who often touted his collegiality with Cantor, seethed, "I can't believe the audacity of that SOB!"[49] But other Republicans minimized the impact of her remarks. Pelosi's speech was not "a big issue," Blunt admitted. Denouncing the Republicans' "level of pettiness," Frank paraphrased their argument as "Speaker Pelosi talked badly, so screw the country!"

News commentator (and former congressman) Joe Scarborough blamed the defeat on liberals in the Hispanic and Black caucuses who objected to the absence of mortgage assistance. The Speaker was incensed by the criticism. "I would kick someone in the teeth if they said that," Pelosi said. Some CBC members angrily accused Clyburn of leading them "down the primrose path" by coercing their support while Obama was blamed for "not working the phones" aggressively enough.[50] Overall, the Speaker insisted, her members had "more than lived up to [their] side of the bargain" as she excoriated the "dysfunctional" Republicans who "did not honor their commitment, [and now] we all look bad." She also blamed Bush's lack of influence. "The president has no shtick," she complained to Paulson. "What is going on in the Republican caucus to let the United States suffer this blow?"

Bolten agreed that "the Republicans blew it," but his admission didn't satisfy Pelosi. "If we don't get more votes on your side," the Speaker warned, "we have to have a different conversation." The stakes just went up; without adding a $65 billion stimulus, "there isn't another vote [for the bill] in our caucus." But to her members, she admitted, "We can't have the sun, moon and stars." Even worse, if Bush and Boehner again failed to persuade recalcitrant Republicans, she mused, "we have to pass it with Democratic votes."[51]

The House's failure afforded the Senate the opportunity to do what the Senate instinctively did. Reid quickly added a noncontroversial increase in the FDIC insurance limits and a costly extension of contentious energy tax credits. He called the Speaker to provide confidential advance notice of what was headed back to the House. "I'm not asking your permission," he clarified. "This conversation never happened!"

Boehner was thrilled, predicting the tax extenders would entice "dozens" of Republicans to switch their votes to yes. But the Senate's maneuver caused House Democrats to flare. "Reid screwed us!" Pelosi bitterly complained. "We're being told it's 'our way or no way'" once again, protested Hoyer, describing himself as "a very unhappy camper."[52] Pelosi took out her frustrations on Dodd. "You dole out goodies over there," she tersely said. "We could do it, too, if we gave away tens of millions of dollars!" Dodd blamed his leader. "Reid cared more about the extenders than he did the bailout," he insisted. Furious, she told Bolten she had just "lost some votes because the Senate were asses," adding, "and I don't talk that way."[53]

But Pelosi also blamed her members for defeating the House bill, which gave Reid the leverage to add billions for rural schools, the wool program, tax extenders—"all pork"—to secure votes. "It's awful what the Senate put in, but we enabled them," she acknowledged, chastising the Blue Dogs who would now have to accept billions in tax extenders, an added burden for her since it was "like lifting an anvil to get [our] people to vote for unpaid tax cuts."[54]

Close to midnight on October 1, the Senate approved its TARP bill by a bipartisan 74–25 margin. A last-minute request from Pelosi to "take us a long way home" with disgruntled Democrats by including a $1,000 tax credit for lower-income taxpayers was ignored, and the next morning, Pelosi told Boehner she was hemorrhaging votes. "We're doing a lot better," he promised, although he was still short of a hundred votes despite calls from Bush. "There's no reason to bring it up if it can't pass," she responded. "Call me when you have the votes. I don't finger my members."[55] She also instructed Bolten that "someone needs to drag [Republicans] to the well" to vote yes. "Let me know when you get a hundred. Am I clear?" "You couldn't be clearer," he acknowledged.

There was little to do but accept the Senate's version of the bill. "I don't know there's an alternative," Hoyer said, since sending an amended bill back to the Senate meant long delays and likely the same outcome while the market cratered. One by one, the House leadership team morosely concurred." Two days later, the House passed the Senate bill by a 263–171 vote with Democratic support increasing to 73 percent of the caucus while Republicans again fell short, contributing only ninety-one votes. Compromising with the Republicans "turned out to be the biggest waste of time," Pelosi fumed. "We could have just passed a bill and rammed it down the president's throat. We should have written the bill we wanted on the first night." However, even if the House had passed a House bill, there is little chance it could have succeeded in the Senate, setting up the same dynamic that resulted in the final TARP law.

"You helped with the hard-line liberals," Pelosi credited Obama, but he would have to follow through on foreclosure aid after the election. He agreed to address the housing crisis. The liberals "aren't sending the bill to neverland," he assured. He wouldn't even need a new law because "there is plenty of authorization now."[56]

Passing TARP was a massive legislative achievement, but the public reaction was vociferous and hostile. "We're getting smackerooed," Pelosi complained to Paulson. "The blogs are going nuts" over bailouts for unrepentant Wall Street firms. "Members feel railroaded by what has happened the past few weeks," she said, adding, "I really don't think the administration has an idea of the poisonous atmosphere that's out there." Her members were furious that the president was blaming Democrats for imposing regulations that helped provoke the crisis. "That is pathetic," she insisted to Bolten.[57]

Pelosi relayed her concerns directly to the president when he called to offer thanks. "Hey!" he jauntily greeted the Speaker, who was less cheerful. "There is huge resentment over the bailout," she informed the president. She encouraged him to boost consumer confidence by reconvening the Bretton Woods conference of 1944 that helped stabilize world currencies.[58] "I'm open-minded," he assured her. Another helpful step would be to convince Republicans to tone down their partisan rhetoric, which Bush seconded. "They're getting carried away," he admitted. At least the election momentum seemed to be swinging in her favor. "Things must smell pretty good," he observed. "You sound chipper." When Bolten called to inform her the president was planning a summit on the economy, she was unforgiving. "He should have called for one a lot sooner."[59]

Exhausted, angry, and worried, most members wanted to go home to repair the political damage from the TARP vote, but the bailout season was not over.

Over the summer, Dingell had reported that the impending collapse of the Big
Three auto manufacturers "will turn Michigan into a howling desert." The industry needed a federal loan guarantee of $50 billion by mid-October to prevent
liquidation and the loss of hundreds of thousands of jobs. "We've given money
to Bear Stearns, the railroads," the chairman declared. "Now the auto industry
needs help."[60]

Few industries were less beloved by the Speaker, who believed its obdurate
resistance to efficiency, safety, and emissions improvements explained its withered share of the US auto market. "The industry needs to change," agreed Sen.
Carl Levin (MI), and Dingell seconded that opinion, but now they were "in a
race to change over before they fail." If aid was forthcoming, Dingell pledged,
he would defend the mandate that industry set efficiency at "the highest technically feasible levels. I'm part of the team," he assured Pelosi, "willing to help in
any way" to elect more Democrats. "I won't have the damned Republicans back
running the town."[61]

Even with such concessions, Pelosi confessed she was "not anxious to bail
out the auto companies" because members were reeling with "bailout fatigue"
after TARP. Reid saw "no chance" of passing auto aid. With McCain "dumping
on Democrats" for spending, neither leader was inclined to approach the administration for support. One day before the election, Phil Schiliro, Obama's chief
congressional liaison and a former Waxman staffer, told me that he was unaware
of any commitment by the candidate to the auto manufacturers.[62]

As tense days passed, Dingell reported GM was burning through $1 billion
a month in fixed costs. "If they don't recover," he warned, it would mean "it's
1929 . . . a disaster in the Midwest." Pelosi agreed "the whole situation is scary,"
but she warned Dingell against "throwing money at companies that are on life
support and not going to survive." But she did agree to meet with the auto executives during the first week of November; Dingell assured her he would attend
"skinned or stuffed if necessary."[63]

Pelosi chose this moment of Dingell's maximum vulnerability to mention
that she had changed her mind and would extend the life of the climate committee for another two years with the active support of Jim Sensenbrenner, the Republicans' ranking member, and Boehner. "Hell, no!" Dingell bellowed, but Pelosi
had field advantage on the chair. She pointed out that Markey's knowledgeable
staff provided "a powerful argument for the Select Committee" and wondered "if
you've availed yourself of them." Dingell did not want to utilize Markey's staff.
"We'll provide you with all the staff you need," he assured the Speaker, but she
brushed off the offer. "You have so many issues!" She helpfully ticked them off:

"health, telecommunications, energy." Dingell countered he had produced eight white papers, held twenty-seven hearings, and written an emissions-reducing bill that won support from the auto industry and some environmental groups. But Pelosi's mind was made up, and when the 111th Congress convened, Dingell would face a far more serious challenge than the Select Committee.

The epic battle to pass the TARP occurred under the most adverse political circumstances imaginable, just weeks before a crucial election, with divided government whose parties had been locked in relentless combat for two years. And yet, in just two weeks, leaders with starkly different ideological outlooks, institutional interests, and electoral objectives reached an agreement that averted a national catastrophe.

The commission appointed by Congress in 2009 to investigate the causes of the meltdown would conclude that it "was the result of human action and inaction, not of Mother Nature or computer models gone haywire."[64] Moreover, the collapse had been "avoidable," a conclusion ultimately shared by many at the center of the crisis.

There had simply been too much easy money to be made, and few on Wall Street could exercise any restraint. As the CEO of Citigroup observed, "As long as the music is playing, you've got to get up and dance." The most powerful officials accepted that lax regulation was responsible. "Government let major financial institutions take on too much risky leverage without insisting that they retain enough capital," Bernanke, Paulson, and New York Fed chair (and Obama Treasury secretary) Tim Geithner admitted a decade later. "We should have pushed earlier and harder for ... a stronger and more comprehensive regulatory system ... but during the boom, there wasn't much political appetite for stronger regulation," a statement contradicted by congressional criticism even before the collapse.[65]

Was TARP a unique example of Congress and the presidency putting aside partisan, ideological, and institutional rivalries to avoid economic catastrophe? Was it an intervention to rescue well-connected, affluent interests while largely ignoring taxpayers who paid the price for the companies' recklessness? One fact is indisputable: the damage of the Wall Street collapse continued to grow long after TARP saved the financial houses. Two and a half years after the crisis hit, 4 million families had lost their homes, and an additional 4.5 million were mired in foreclosure proceedings. A decade later, the typical American household's net worth remained nearly 20 percent lower than it was before the crisis, and nearly $11 trillion in household wealth had evaporated.[66]

No factor influenced the government response more than the urgency of the crisis itself, a common feature during periods marking major congressional achievements. The imminent collapse of key banking, investment, and insurance companies compelled joint action because the alternative was simply too dire to contemplate. At the September 18 meeting in Pelosi's office, McConnell had declared, "If it means saving the country's financial system, we can do it," but neither he, Bush, Boehner, nor other members of their party demonstrated comparable concern for the families impacted by the recession. Without that bipartisan alliance, concern for impacted homeowners was brushed aside. It took nearly a decade for homeownership rates to register an increase, and Black ownership, which had reached a historic high in 2004, remained at its lowest level in nearly three decades.[67]

Although Bush pledged investigations by the Securities and Exchange Commission and an expanded Hope Now program to keep people in their homes, there was little time or energy left in his administration for either. Nor did the Obama administration move aggressively enough for many on the Hill on anti-foreclosure initiatives or on holding Wall Street manipulators accountable. Geithner disclaimed responsibility for prosecuting those whose malfeasance had provoked the crisis. He, Paulson, and Bernanke "were not the arbiters of justice," he said. "The scandal was what *was* legal, not so much what was *illegal*."[68]

Obama agreed, blaming the absence of prosecutions "mainly" on the inadequacy of existing criminal statutes.[69] While no Wall Street executives went to prison, the Obama administration did impose significant fines against some of the major firms—Barclay's was fined $2 billion over their mortgage practices and Walmart $1 billion over foreign bribery—although many penalties were subsequently reversed or dramatically reduced by the Trump administration.[70]

TARP saved the economy, but it also provided the kindling that ignited a wildfire of heightened partisanship and distrust of government that has divided Americans and gridlocked political institutions for over a decade. The law supercharged a sense of betrayal especially among the white working class, a belief that the political elite rescued the financial elite from a crisis of its own making with the tax dollars of the largely ignored working and middle classes who bore the brunt of the recession. What emerged from the ashes of the September 2008 meltdown was not only a supercharged Wall Street but also unprecedented income disparity and anti-government fury represented by the Occupy Wall Street movement on the Left and the Tea Party movement on the Right.

CHAPTER 12

"WE HAVE TO LOOK OUT FOR OURSELVES"

The tears shed on election nights are often due to defeat and disappointment. Not so on November 4, 2008, at least not for Democrats. Voters had turned out in massive numbers, an increase of 9 million over 2004 and at 58.2 percent, the highest participation in four decades. The numbers of Black, Asian, and Hispanic voters were unprecedented while the white proportion of the vote—74 percent—was the smallest in history.

As Republican-leaning states like Florida and North Carolina dropped into Obama's column, the breadth of his victory became clear. Although the victorious Democrats were admonished to act in a "sober, low key" manner, it was difficult to restrain the exultation.[1] What had initially seemed an audacious quest by an unknown novice culminated in a massive celebration in Chicago's frigid Grant Park. "You beat a good candidate," Mitch McConnell would tell him. "Sometimes," Obama replied, "it's better to be lucky than good."[2]

At the congressional level, House Democrats held onto the seats they won in 2006 and added another twenty to produce a thirty-nine seat margin that would facilitate enactment of the new president's agenda. Pelosi gave the credit for the huge margin to her candidates, who had run ahead of the presidential ticket in many districts. "Obama needs to get the message," she assertively said the day after the election. "We did well where he lost."[3]

In the Senate, the sweep was even more consequential as Democrats (together with two independents) closed in on a sixty-seat filibuster-proof majority. Two races remained uncalled: in Minnesota, former comedian Al Franken was locked in a close contest with incumbent Norm Coleman, and in Alaska, Mark Begich was slightly ahead of the scandal-tainted Ted Stevens. Reid jokingly attributed the tabulation delays to the fact that "Democrats are dumber voters and they make more ballot mistakes."[4] Begich was soon declared the winner, but the

Minnesota seat would remain in dispute for another seven months. With the possibility of a filibuster-proof Senate, Obama and Democrats were poised to pass sweeping progressive priorities that had been little more than pipedreams for decades.

There was no shortage of Democratic policy ideas: health care, green jobs, employment, stimulus, small business aid, help for the auto industry. Freed from the threat of a presidential veto, expectations for sweeping legislation abounded with jobs and economic revitalization the top priorities. "The voters know the recovery will take a long time," Celinda Lake counseled, "but we need to show we are moving fast." Managing both voter and member expectations would present a challenge.

On Election Day, Emanuel told me Obama envisioned quick approval of a $300 billion stimulus, five times the size of the bill the House had already approved. But Emanuel had a personal issue as well, asking my thoughts on his becoming White House chief of staff. "My father is sitting shiva because I might change jobs," he reported.

"If you're chief of staff," Josh Bolten told him after a TARP meeting in October, "you get to be present at historic moments like this!"[5] I cautioned that, as he well knew, being a staff member "is very different from being a member. You are working for someone else. You're not your own person, and you're not a member anymore." He called back a few days later to tell me he had accepted Obama's offer and would resign from the House.

Pelosi cautioned her colleague about taking the position. "I told him, 'You're on a career path for yourself,'" she reported, one that many anticipated would result in his becoming Speaker. Did he want to give that up to be Obama's staffer? "If things were to go wrong, your head will roll," she advised. "You weren't even *for* him."[6] Others who had worked with Emanuel questioned if his rough-edged style, which included prodigious amounts of obscene language, was compatible with a top administration position. He had once mailed a dead fish to a competitor and had publicized divorce records and debts of one of Pelosi's closest friends during a political battle in the early 1990s.[7]

Chris Van Hollen (MD), celebrating a highly successful chairmanship of the campaign committee, was also looking for broader opportunities. His immediate objective was caucus chair, which would position him generationally as a Pelosi successor; he even considered challenging Clyburn for whip, but Pelosi advised against a challenge. "Wait until there is an opening," she counseled, rather than confront the only minority in either house's upper echelon. Van Hollen agreed after Pelosi appointed him to the "assistant to the Speaker" position vacated by Xavier Becerra, embellishing the ambiguous post with staff money.[8] The caucus chair slot vacated by Emanuel went to John Larson (CT).

The day after the election, the Speaker spoke with Obama. "You did pretty well!" the president-elect declared. "Everybody's walking around with smiles!" Pelosi confirmed. She congratulated him on his "spectacular" speech in Grant Park and said, "I can't wait to hear the Inaugural." How was he coping with the enormity of his achievement? "You just wake up and still feel pretty much same as before," he mused, adding, "it sort of grows on you."[9]

The insularity of the new White House team worried some on the Hill who recalled the Carter and Clinton presidencies, during which many top advisors lacked experience dealing with Congress and the Washington bureaucracy. The president-elect's own familiarity with the capital's political culture was relatively thin, and his staff hierarchy was filled with Chicago loyalists who lacked congressional experience. "The Obama organization is very tight," Reid noted. "We need to figure out how to get him to reach out to *us*. We need to be part of the program."[10] Appointing experienced Hill veterans like Phil Schiliro (congressional relations), Pete Rouse (special assistant), and Emanuel to top slots helped; all had extensive contacts among members and staff.

Obama was "looking forward to plotting and scheming" with the bipartisan leadership. "Meet with me first," she advised, and then Reid, before talking with the Republicans. She shared his belief that "the country must be governed from the middle," she insisted. "We want to work together. The goal is to build consensus" as the parties had over the previous two years on veterans' benefits, CAFE standards, the stimulus, and TARP, despite other disagreements with Bush. "We met the needs of the American people, from right to left," and there was no reason such collaboration couldn't extend under a unified Democratic government.

Hopes for collegiality faded fast, beginning in the Democratic ranks. One day after the election, Waxman informed Dingell it was "time for a change" in the chairmanship of the Energy and Commerce Committee.[11] With the infusion of new members and a host of sensitive issues coming before Commerce, the combative California liberal, who had opted against launching earlier challenges, was unwilling to wait for the octogenarian's retirement.

Few were surprised by Waxman's audacious move, especially after the bitter clashes over the energy and toy safety bills and the Select Committee, but it had enormous institutional and policy ramifications. Replacing Dingell with Waxman would be nothing less than "the shifting of the policy plates of the earth," Eshoo proclaimed.[12]

As with Murtha's challenge two years earlier, virtually no one on Capitol Hill believed that Waxman acted without encouragement from the Speaker. Publicly, she insisted, Waxman's declaration was "not welcome news," but given their forty-year friendship, she could "never oppose him."[13] Emanuel was dismayed, believing the face-off was "a bad idea," but most liberals were fed up with Dingell's bellicose style, industry-friendly policies, and incremental legislating. And the Speaker doubtless did not relish having to do battle with Dingell, who resented her efforts to steer the direction of policy. "Do you want to support the committee system, or do you want to do it yourself?" he had confronted her earlier in the year.[14] "You constantly get into the committees! You micromanage!"[15] It had been a harsh rebuke the Speaker was unlikely to forget or forgive.

Dingell pivoted quickly. "I need and want your help," he insisted, reminding Pelosi he had "raised huge money and a field operation" in Michigan that helped defeat two Republican incumbents. But Pelosi credited Obama's strong performance for the House victories, a claim that conflicted with her assertion that her candidates' strengths, not the president-elect's popularity, had helped the Democrats win their seats.[16]

"Will I wake up on the day of the vote and find you are supporting Henry?" Dingell asked, recalling her last-minute endorsement of Murtha two years earlier.

"People have their ambitions," she evaded. "I never tell people they shouldn't run, although I do point out it is not helpful to put people on the spot" by asking them to choose. "People may have to make decisions between friends," she declared, "but I am not helping Henry, and he is not running at my instigation."

"Are you willing to say that publicly?" Dingell asked.

"I'm noncommittal," Pelosi equivocated. She would "wait and see" how the race evolved, but she assured Dingell, "I don't envision any situation where I would be involved."

That wasn't good enough for Dingell, who believed Pelosi was reneging from support implied by a friendly kiss planted on his cheek months earlier. "That wasn't in the context of a Waxman challenge," she clarified. "I have complimented you, but I have never committed to anyone." She suggested he try to "work out [his] differences" with Waxman, ominously adding, "but I assume he has the votes."

Dingell's temper flared. Waxman was winning because the "committee's powers and prerogative have been diminished by [your] leadership," he charged. Such a challenge was "very destructive at the outset of a new Congress." Pelosi remained unperturbed. "That's when it *always* happens, in a new Congress!" she noted. "People are always coming into this office claiming support for running for something. They have their own careers and timetables [but it] doesn't relate to me." She had other issues to address. "I'm not looking for new problems," she advised. "We need to get organized. I'm telling both of you: 'Go get the votes. You're big boys.' If you have the votes, go for it. It's not my problem at this point."

Dingell leapt at the hint of neutrality. "Can I say you are not involved?" he asked. Pelosi brushed him back. "I'll speak for myself," she advised. Was Waxman empowered "to suggest he is acting on your behalf?" he queried. "At the present time, I am not involved in the race," she said cautiously. She raised a possible compromise reminiscent of the secret Markey-Rahall arrangement. "Why not agree to one more term?" she posited, although she hypothesized Waxman "must think he has the votes now." A day later, Dingell was floating the idea of serving one more term, but Markey was reporting a "decreasing ability to stick with Dingell" among the members.[17]

Frustrated, Dingell suggested, "Let's talk again," and suggested she would be hearing from unions that supported his chairmanship. Indeed, Dingell had put in a call to AFL-CIO president John Sweeney to urge him to pressure Pelosi. But Pelosi had a union card of her own to play. She had just spoken with Ron Gettlefinger, the president of the Auto Workers Union, about a meeting with Reid on the auto bailout. The comment was an unsubtle reminder of her influence on the crucial issue. "I'm happy to have you come to the meeting," she offered Dingell.

Increasingly desperate, Dingell issued a press release quoting a 2005 Pelosi salute to his fifty years in the House, deceptively implying her support in the current contest. The Speaker was "very offended" and clarified with "great sadness" that "a discussion of support was never made," requesting he make no further "representation of my opinion." Dingell's staff called to assure me that the chair had not "intended to confuse" with his statement, although he agreed the language "could be misread" to imply support.[18]

Pelosi instructed her staff to set the chairmanship elections at the earliest possible date before the lobbyists could "weigh in." Appearing before the

Steering and Policy Committee, which would recommend a Commerce chair to the full caucus, Dingell asserted he had been "effective and fair" and reminded his colleagues of his fundraising prowess. But by a narrow 25–22 vote, the committee—heavily stacked with Speaker appointees—recommended Waxman as the new chair.

There was "a lot of emotion in the room" when the caucus took up the dispute.[19] It was payback time for the liberals, and the Speaker's loyalists were fully engaged for the challenger, even Murtha, although Waxman had spoken for Hoyer in the majority leader's race in 2006. Waxman's 137–122 victory ended Dingell's twenty-eight years heading the committee's Democrats.[20] "Seniority is important, but it should not be a grant of property rights to be chairman for three decades or more," said Waxman, who, as a freshman forty-four years earlier helped oust three chairs.[21] Asked what Dingell's ouster meant to the future of the seniority system, Rangel wistfully said, "It has been buried."[22] That was an overstatement, but unquestionably, it was a significant change at a crucial moment for the Commerce Committee and the House.

Later that day, the Speaker confirmed to the new chair she had wanted him to win "more than anything. It was beautiful, wasn't it!" After the vote was announced, she confessed, "I went into a back room and jumped up and down."[23] She had high expectations for Waxman. "Well, now you have it all on your shoulders," Pelosi told him: health care, clean air, climate change, renewable energy, and other high-priority legislation. "I'm on your team," the new chair pledged.

Pelosi moved to patch up ill feelings, adding several Dingell loyalists to Steering and Policy and, after securing Waxman's approval, offering Dingell the title of "chairman emeritus" and maintaining his prized hideaway office in the Capitol. The former chair was hardly mollified. "I don't care about honors," he responded. "I have been stripped of my ability to have significant impact."[24] Still, he declared, as the dean of the House, "I will swear you in as Speaker!" "I will be most honored," replied Pelosi.

Pelosi contemplated other challenges to the seniority system as well, including term limits on chairmanships to allow younger members to rise to leadership roles. Strong opposition arose from the Black and Hispanic caucuses, who believed that absent the seniority system, their members stood limited chances of securing the gavels. Hoyer, who had been sympathetic to term limits, now argued that Dingell's defeat demonstrated there was no need to arbitrarily limit chairmanships, and Pelosi abandoned the idea.[25]

She moved to expand the leadership circle by adding more junior members and greater diversity. Dennis Cardoza promoted himself, advising that "there is no need for any specific portfolio," although he requested a hideaway office in the Capitol. Pelosi appointed him to help build "rapport with the Blue Dogs," whose votes would be crucial in passing the Democratic agenda, but she turned down the hideaway office request.[26]

With many more seats suddenly available on influential committees thanks to the expanded ratios of Democrats in the House, members bombarded the Speaker with requests for appointments to Ways and Means, Appropriations, and Commerce, all of which would consider top-priority legislation. Such appointments came with an expectation of loyalty. She did not countenance members casting "no" votes because of electoral vulnerability, as Emanuel and Hoyer had been suspected of sanctioning. "If you can't take a tough procedural vote on the floor," she advised, "don't expect a committee assignment where you will have tough votes." The changing ratios put reverse pressure on Boehner, who had to remove members from choice assignments. He pleaded for additional seats on Commerce and Financial Services. "Give me one on each," he pleaded, "and we'll call it a day." "Not going to happen," Pelosi responded, although she did offer to hold weekly meetings to discuss the schedules and air grievances, which he rejected.[27]

The Speaker made suggestions for jobs opening in the executive branch. "You may not believe it," she told Emanuel when suggesting Transportation chair Jim Oberstar for that department's secretary. "You're right," Emanuel tersely replied, "I don't." She also discouraged some names being rumored to fill top slots, including several Michiganders who had unsurprisingly aided the auto industry. "You might as well name John Dingell," she remarked.[28] She weighed in emphatically against reappointing CIA director Michael Hayden because of rumors about his sanctioning the use of torture at Baghdad's Abu Ghraib prison.[29] She also disapproved of Obama retaining Bush's defense secretary, Robert Gates, who was so closely identified with the detested Iraq War. "That is not a transformational appointment!" Pelosi reproached. She also disapproved of hiring a lobbyist for a major defense contractor as a violation of an Obama campaign pledge.[30]

With all these moves, as the 111th Congress prepared to convene, Pelosi was restructuring to maximize her power to shape major legislation. Despite unified government and comfortable majorities, she anticipated policy and institutional confrontations with the White House and Senate. Obama remained a largely unknown quantity with minimal legislative experience and no experience dealing with the House. "If we get a weak leader," she told Emanuel, "we [in Congress] will have to lead."[31]

She also was concerned that unless Franken was seated as the sixtieth Democratic senator, Republicans would exploit the filibuster to force the House to make concessions on every major issue. "We're not going to let McCain run the Senate," Emanuel assured her. If the Republicans employed filibusters, Obama would not hesitate to use executive orders to implement his promised "change."

The election appeared to have provided a rare alignment of Democratic power among the House, Senate, and White House, but the Speaker had no intention of allowing anyone else to set the agenda. "God bless Barack Obama and Harry Reid," she said privately, "but we have to look out for ourselves." She asked her friends to "pray for all of the members," adding, "but more for the Democrats." Then she turned to the challenges at hand. "Everybody wants leaders," she noted. "Now we'll find out if they want to be led."[32]

CHAPTER 13

"THE COUNTRY IS FALLING APART!"

With the election over, Pelosi sought to leverage the election results into a major expansion of the stimulus the House had passed in September. "Americans need a recovery package," she told Bolten.[1] But the administration did not agree. "I want to level with you," he responded. "We are not sure the public needs another stimulus" because OMB asserted that infrastructure dollars are spent too slowly to trigger an economic revival. He agreed unemployment aid was stimulative (though he would not say so publicly), but he ruled out extending those benefits on the grounds that doing so discouraged recipients from seeking employment.

Bush continued to assert the free trade agreements his administration had negotiated with Colombia, South Korea, and Panama would boost trade and help revitalize the economy, but the Speaker was noncommittal. "We have different agendas than the White House and Senate," Pelosi observed.[2] The public remained "in a bad mood," and trade agreements, easily stigmatized for sending jobs overseas, were unlikely to improve its temperament. "There's no reason to have a lame duck" if the administration wasn't willing to deal trade for stimulus, she declared.

Reid offered little hope of passing a significant stimulus in the Senate. Reid "says he can't do it," the Speaker reported, "and he isn't happy with us sending him a big, beautiful package" because "our action makes them look bad."[3] But the newly elected Obama also was reluctant about legislating on Bush's watch. "The game plan," Schiliro advised, "was for a minimalist lame duck" so that approval of a major stimulus could serve as an early Obama victory.[4]

Reid proposed the House fashion a slimmed-down package the administration might have trouble refusing—UI, auto aid, and the Colombia trade agreement—but he warned that sending anything else to the Senate was "a waste of time"; in fact, he would have to "jump through hoops" just to schedule this something-for-everyone package. Within hours, however, even that limited bill received a thumbs-down from the administration. "No stimulus!" thundered Paulson, who was "bullshit" over accusations of TARP mismanagement.[5]

With the auto companies still teetering, Pelosi put Barney Frank in charge of writing an aid bill, sidestepping Dingell and Sandy Levin. They were too deferential to the unions whose members, along with the executives, would "have to take a haircut" to get a bill past a filibuster and Bush. Worried the companies would "take the money and burn it," she instructed Frank to write a bill that "puts the taxpayers first."[6] One concept was nonnegotiable: the aid package could "in no way diminish the CAFE standards" imposed by the 2007 law. In years to come, Pelosi's fear proved well justified as the Trump administration attempted to roll back the tough mileage and emission standards, repudiating the link between the taxpayer rescue and the promise of the industry to modernize.

Her anger at the leadership of the auto CEOs remained unabated. "The public thinks we're stupid!" she noted. "These three bozos drive the industry into the ditch and the [Michigan] members enabled them. Now the chickens are coming home to roost, a day of reckoning."[7] At best, she would support three months of assistance—about $25 billion—all of which would have to be repaid as with TARP. She also insisted the Senate act first so House members were not left hanging with another difficult vote.[8] "I will not have the House be where the auto help bill dies," Pelosi vowed. "I can't let the White House say we are ignoring the problem." Obama agreed. The Democratic message had to be "no collapse," he said, linking a bailout to a requirement the companies "get serious about restructuring."[9]

Reid was hopeful McConnell would approve a plan to redirect $25 billion from unexpended TARP funds to the auto industry, although Paulson continued to insist the law did not allow such a reprogramming. But his optimism soon proved misplaced, and Reid reported he was not sure the Senate could pass *any* car aid. "We cannot do nothing," the Speaker responded. Other plans were afoot as well. One senator hinted "the Senate intends to roll" the House by passing a bailout that imposed no modernization or restructuring requirements on the manufacturers. "If you send us that," she warned Reid, "we will send back our plan" loaded with environment and innovation requirements.[10]

Another option involved diverting funds from Section 136 of the 2007 CAFE law intended to subsidize the modernization of auto manufacturing facilities to encourage production of high-technology vehicles. Pelosi saw the proposal as undermining the effort to make US vehicles efficient and competitive and dismissed the idea, warning it was "a nonstarter in the House." "We look like saps if we give away [Section] 136."[11]

Obama wanted no part of the dispute. "Don't get the president-elect dragged into it!" Emanuel instructed. But when a team of economic advisors warned that even $60 billion might not be enough to prevent the companies' collapse, Emanuel was disheartened. "The wheels are coming off," he worried, even before Obama took the oath of office.[12] As crucial days ticked past, Congress and the White House traded accusations about responsibility for the stalemate. "The White House is throwing shit at you and you need to do the same," Emanuel advised Pelosi, who demanded to know what the companies would do with rescue funds. Behind the scenes, Bush's team faulted Congress for being "on vacation" to avoid legislating, an accusation that infuriated Pelosi. The companies, she fumed, "couldn't make a [rescue] plan in a week any more than they could make a fuel-efficient car in a generation."[13]

In their first joint discussion since the election, Pelosi referred to Obama as "Mr. President," but he demurred. "When it's just the three of us," he suggested, "please use 'Barack.'"[14] But Pelosi was a traditionalist, referring to her own colleagues, even in private meetings, as "Madam Chairman" or "the distinguished member from" their state. "No, you are president," Pelosi corrected. "It is 'Mr. President.'"

Reid was going to try to pass a bill authorizing the use of $25 billion from TARP and extending UI, but if that failed, he wanted to instruct Paulson to "make sure the companies don't go bankrupt" by simply transferring the TARP funds.[15] Obama shared the leaders' hesitancy over another bailout but agreed there was little choice. "It's not only good politics," he said, "but it's the right thing to do."

As to their own agenda, they agreed on the top priorities for the new administration: a revised Status of Forces Agreement for Iraq and Afghanistan, climate (still Pelosi's "flagship issue"), and the new stimulus. The president-elect also promised to confer with the key chairs on his signature issue, health reform, leading Pelosi to warn against being manipulated by the Senate Finance chair. "Make sure it is a Democratic plan," she warned, "not just Baucus" off on his own.

Pelosi also highlighted the importance to her members of being proactive on deficit reduction by reinstating Pay As You Go to control deficit spending. "This is a constant fight with the Senate" because of earmarks, she reminded Obama. "I hope *you* don't have a problem with it, so I wanted to say this in front of Harry." Obama jokingly reproached the majority leader. "Harry," he playfully remonstrated, "Nancy says your crew is irresponsible."

Two weeks later, Bush asked for Obama's blessing to release another TARP tranche of $350 million and was "pushing" to secure congressional approval to divert Section 136 money for the auto companies. Pelosi opposed acting only on an auto bailout without including economic assistance to those impacted by the recession. "At least do food stamps" and aid to state and local governments, she urged Bolten. "Wouldn't it be great if the president and Senator Obama stood together" on those issues? "Where we have opportunities, we're looking to do that," he concurred. "It would be good for the markets to see them together."

But the administration remained focused on the auto crisis, and Bolten raised the drastic idea of forcing the companies to first declare bankruptcy, which would facilitate their restructuring. The Speaker balked at the proposal, noting bankruptcy would also allow the employers to cancel collective bargaining agreements, a message she could not deliver to the UAW and the AFL. The heated back-and-forth continued inconclusively until the Speaker decided to cool things down. "How's the president?" she asked the chief of staff. "It's a weird period for us," Bolten admitted. When Bush called later in the day, Pelosi pleaded for support for food stamps and state aid, which enjoyed bipartisan requests from governors. "Can you do just those two?" she asked, adding that an infrastructure jobs plan would be helpful, too. "I know," she admitted. "I'm a broken record."

Bush was now considering the diversion of the Section 136 funds for which he believed there were sixty votes in the Senate, assuming the companies were "viable" entities. "I know the original intent of that program," Bush reasoned, "but if there are no car companies, they can't use those funds" for modernization. But he admitted that after the TARP experience, "the American people don't want to put in a dime from any source" to helping private companies, and Pelosi agreed that "the taxpayers aren't interested in pitching in." Bush sounded like he couldn't wait for January 20 to arrive. "These are ugly times," he said, his voice dripping with ennui, "and I'm sorry we have to go through it." But he was encouraged by a recent meeting with Obama, whom he pronounced a "fine man."[16]

As if there weren't enough expensive items on the docket, legislation was needed to clear the decks on government spending. But the price tag—as much as $500 billion—included hundreds of earmarks that Bush and Obama both opposed. There were several options, including a continuing resolution—with the earmarks—through the end of the fiscal year in September that would allow Congress to focus on the first Obama budget. Many members preferred a

CR that would take them just beyond the end of the Bush administration so the Congress would be able to bump up Democratic priorities once Obama took office. "We look like fools taking Bush's numbers just to get our earmarks," Pelosi responded.

Republicans indicated little interest in being helpful on any of the urgent issues, although Boehner admitted to "getting the right vibes from Obama" about collaboration and open doors. "It's an island mentality," agreed Pelosi. "We all have to get along." There would not be GOP votes, Boehner declared, for any auto plan "unless cars show a path to viability," which probably involved vitiating union contracts.[17] Nor would his members support aiding states hard hit by teacher and first responder costs. "The states spend too much," he protested. Even on freeing up the next $350 billion tranche of TARP money they had voted to authorize, "there aren't five Republican votes," Boehner declared.

The president-elect remained huddled in Chicago with his transition team. As the days went by, there was little communication between the Speaker's office and the Obama team and it seemed it might be weeks before Obama would meet with the House Democrats. "Is talking with Rahm the same as talking with the president," Schiliro asked, "or does the Speaker need a call from the president himself?"[18] Given his own long relationship with the Speaker, Schiliro already knew the answer. A few days later, she would reemphasize the point with Obama himself. "When you make a decision," she said, "I need to hear from *you*, not from Rahm." Reid was similarly mystified by the silence from Chicago. "It wouldn't hurt if Obama met with us," he told Pelosi.

When Obama and Pelosi finally spoke on December 4, it was clear the optimism of the campaign had been tempered by the harsh reality facing them in Washington. "The country is falling apart!" Obama gloomily said. "I think we should move right away on autos and TARP." Reports were circulating that Obama and Bush were commiserating about using TARP funds for the auto companies while Bush still refused aid to beleaguered homeowners. At least negotiations on TARP funds would be easier after the inauguration, when there would be just one president to deal with. "Yeah," the caustic Frank observed, "now, we don't have any."[19]

Dispensing with TARP and autos on Bush's watch would allow Obama to focus on passing a recovery bill. "It sure would be a nice way to start," he mused. Pelosi promised to have one prepared immediately after the holiday break. "It isn't going to be a 1930s public works package," she advised, but it would stress many of her priorities—innovation, broadband coverage, a national electricity grid—within the context of private sector employment. Obama warned about the cost spiraling out of control. "We need to game out what's in it because we're going to have to say no to many people." He hoped there was no "huge divergence between us," although he anticipated problems with the Senate over earmarks. "It's important there is no pork," Pelosi said. "Everything must promote economic growth.[20] "Can we do it fast?" he asked. "The key is to get it right," Pelosi responded. "Your advice is sound," he gushed. "That's why I love you."

The indecision over TARP or Section 136 money to rescue car companies was exasperating Bolten as the companies lurched toward collapse. "At some point," he told Pelosi, "people need to be responsible."[21] Increasingly, the administration was leaning toward taking executive action rather than waiting for Congress to authorize either option. Given Boehner's opposition, Pelosi wasn't even sure that she could find 218 Democratic votes to release the next TARP tranche. "We've given you $700 billion," she noted, "twice the non-defense discretionary budget!" And those votes were based on a promise Bush would "do something on foreclosure forbearance," which still hadn't happened.

Within days, Bush decided a loan from the Section 136 program was the only option "that gets us out of the dilemma we're in" given Paulson's virulent opposition to using TARP funds.[22] Pelosi understood; the mood was "getting very ugly [and so] we have to do something." She would acquiesce "in the interest of compromise" but only if Bush ended efforts to undermine California's strict emissions standard and the bill included strict repayment requirements. Even so, she remained enraged that taxpayers were again compelled to underwrite irresponsible corporate behavior, especially since she suspected the companies were still maneuvering to void their union contracts. "People should be sent to jail!" she seethed.[23]

Responsibility for writing the bill went to Frank's Financial Services Committee, and he soon informed the Speaker the manufacturers needed $25 billion from the 136 fund, far more than the original estimate. "I am taking crap as it is," she declared. Such a request "blows the whole thing up." She instructed Frank to tell the companies she "could not sell" $25 billion and that "the Speaker thinks it's stupid to give it to them." The bill allowing up to $14 billion in loans, conditioned on each recipient submitting a restructuring plan, passed 237–170 with only thirty-two Republicans, mostly from impacted midwestern states, joining with 205 Democrats. But Bolten reported "the situation in [the] Senate is not good" as Republicans railed against the legislation.[24] Shelby denounced the House bill as "a travesty" that would "only delay [the companies'] funeral," and McConnell blamed Bush for agreeing to an approach that "was simply unacceptable to the vast majority of our side."[25] Bob Corker (TN), whose state led the nation in automobile manufacturing, insisted the unions agree to significant wage and pension concessions, including lower salaries for new hires.[26] Miller, who chaired the House Labor Committee, dismissed Corker's proposal as a "horrendous precedent . . . for the rest of labor," and Pelosi concurred. The Corker plan was "dead on arrival . . . a total nonstarter with the House," she insisted. "Our members will never vote for anything that eviscerates the union."[27]

Pelosi was exasperated by the thought that House Democrats would be hung out to dry yet again. "I hate this bill," she seethed to Bolten, who was concerned that if the bill failed, it would "leave the president in a pickle" and require Paulson to reverse himself and use the TARP funds without congressional approval. Reid's effort at cloture fell eight votes short, 52–35, with fiscally conservative Democrats joining a handful of pro-labor liberals like Bernie Sanders (VT) and Russ Feingold (WI) in opposition. Obama was dismayed by his Senate colleagues. "It wasn't handled the right way," he scolded.[28]

"I dread looking at Wall Street tomorrow," Reid said. "It's not going to be a pleasant sight."[29] Emanuel chastised the Bush administration and McConnell for failing to deliver the necessary votes. "The White House and Republicans are incompetent," he brusquely charged. McConnell indifferently shrugged off the criticism. "Very few of us had anything to do with the dilemma [the automakers] have created for themselves," he rationalized. He had made no similar argument against TARP only months earlier, but in that case, the danger was to political allies on Wall Street rather than to union workers in the auto industry.

With congressional action stalled, Bush approved an emergency loan of $13.4 billion from TARP with another $4 billion once the companies initiated restructuring.[30] Failure to intervene, the president said, "could send our suffering economy into a deeper and longer recession. . . . I didn't want history to look back and say, 'Bush could have done something but chose not to do it.'"[31] Most of the conditions included in the moribund House bill were also incorporated into the administration's plan, including the restrictions on executive pay and the requirement the companies sell off their private corporate jets. Eventually, $80 billion of TARP money was redirected to the auto companies, and the government took substantial stock ownership in both GM and Chrysler. Unlike TARP, however, the Congressional Budget Office estimated taxpayers would lose about $14 billion that the auto companies would fail to reimburse the taxpayer.[32]

In the middle of December, Obama and Pelosi spoke about the many legislative initiatives that would require quick action by the new Congress and the coming administration. "Your leadership is a blessing to the nation," Pelosi declared. There would be disagreements down the road, the Speaker accepted, adding, "I don't care. Let's get the policy issues done." She also advised him to be wary of efforts by his former colleagues to manipulate him. "Don't let the senators string you up!" she advised. "It's a heavy lift to get things done around here." Obama understood her frustration with senators. In some ways, he agreed, "the Senate has outlived its purpose."[33] It was time, he said, "to get rid of filibuster rule" that gave the upper house disproportionate negotiating power and marginalized the voices of minorities who were better represented in the House.

That was music to the Speaker's ears, and she made it clear that her commitment to the House came before loyalty to any individual or self-serving institutional rules. "I will walk the plank for you," she promised, "but I will not let legislation die or let the Senate takes hits at it." Despite her large majority, her marginal members would be called on to cast multiple votes that would enhance their vulnerability; she would not have them do so only to see bills fail in the Senate or be transformed by senators' parochial interests.

Obama sought to assure her of his commitment to stand with her and those freshmen. "There will be risks, but we will preserve our majority in 2010," he promised. "No one is more interested" in ensuring it is not like in 1993, when Clinton's mishandling of health care, the budget, and other issues laid the groundwork for the Republican takeover of both houses. The Speaker welcomed his support for her embattled team and indicated she would hold him to it. "When people take risks, you can't walk away," she declared.[34]

For the moment, they relished their mutual triumph. "The Republicans did terrible damage" over the preceding dozen years, "but we'll find common ground to go forward," she optimistically predicted. She urged him to act boldly and follow her lead "leapfrog[ging] over incrementalism and the old ways of thinking." The president-elect described himself as "pretty healthy," fired up and ready to go. "You want to go jogging together?" he offered.[35] They believed themselves on the cusp of a rare historic opportunity: a Democratic president and big congressional majorities. "Everything is terrific!" the Speaker proclaimed, and the youthful president-elect responded, "You're doing a great job!"[36]

The game was on.

CHAPTER 14

"LIKE SWANS GOING ACROSS THE LAKE"

Five days into the new year, Pelosi looked down from her office on the Capitol's West Front as a fleet of black vans bearing the president-elect made its way toward Capitol Hill. Shortly, Obama strode into the speaker's office wearing a beaming smile and with unselfconscious familiarity embraced the Speaker.

As Pelosi motioned for us to sit down, Obama's faced soured. As we watched in disbelief, he began moving the heavy chairs. "*Please*, Mr. President," Pelosi emphatically objected. "It isn't appropriate for you to be moving furniture!" Obama laughed and finished arranging the chairs into a circular configuration.

The first battle of the new Congress was resolving the impasse over the SCHIP bill, which Bush had twice vetoed. Pelosi hoped the senators who had been so "equivocating" under Bush would now be "willing to stand and fight for something!" As soon as the House passed the bill 289–130 in mid-January, she received a call from the president-elect. "That's a huge accomplishment and I'm calling to say, 'thank you,'" Obama declared. "My crush on you gets bigger and bigger!" He would join her in going toe to toe with the minority, whom he believed were "fairly chastened" by the election rout. "And if they're not," he inveighed, "I'll put a stick in their eye and dance on their graves."[1]

To avoid a third Bush veto, the Senate waited until after Obama's inauguration to approve its SCHIP bill, but the bipartisan 66–32 vote masked a contentious disagreement about coverage of immigrant children. "This is a very unfortunate beginning," intoned a "disgusted" Chuck Grassley. "It does not bode well for cooperative work in the coming months." John McCain denounced the bill as "another effort to eliminate, over time, private insurance in America."[2]

In one sense, it seemed, little had changed. House Democrats soon faced a familiar ultimatum from the Senate: accept its version or risk the program lapsing.[3] "Our caucus is not happy," Pelosi told the Obama White House. "Our folks are very disappointed," she reported, with the constant pressure on House negotiators to accept the Senate's limits.[4] "The members are fed up, and they are not here to be taken advantage of."[5] Employing "expedited procedures" to get legislation to the president's desk could not become standard procedure. "Everything else must go to conference" committees in the future, but in this case, she backed off and the House passed the Senate's version 290–135 early in February. While there finally was a signed SCHIP law, the institutional tension between the House and Senate did not seem to have been affected by the election.

The economic situation had continued its slide, and the price tag on the stimulus had ballooned to over ten times the $61 billion bill languishing in the Senate. Even that amount "won't improve things much," Schiliro glumly predicted. The crisis "will keep getting worse."[6] Over 1.2 million jobs had disappeared in the preceding three months; for the first time since World War II, the Treasury was selling bonds at a zero interest rate. To avoid steep losses in the 2010 midterm, it was clear the 111th Congress would have to be unusually productive.

Urgent measures invariably provoke the worst examples of congressional gluttony, and the stimulus was unlikely to be very different. Even though members had already voted for over a trillion dollars in recent spending, there would be enormous pressure to fund the "bleeding-heart agenda" after eight years of Bush austerity.[7] Pelosi called for each stimulus provision to meet three criteria: "timely, targeted, and temporary," in the alliterative messaging style she favored. Other critical initiatives might require executive actions such as reversing Bush's acceleration of offshore oil leasing, but in general, she counseled, crafting permanent policies was the responsibility of her branch of government.

She also urged him to recruit new people for top White House positions. Don't simply embrace the "old-school people who got us where we are," she urged, specifically mentioning Larry Summers and Tim Geithner.[8] "Be visionary. Be transformational!"[9] Later she told me, "If we walk into a meeting at the White House and Larry Summers is there, I am going to be very disappointed." When that exact situation occurred, her dismay was evident.

Obama needed no prodding on how "dire" the economic situation had become. He quoted Nobel laureate Paul Krugman's observation that "this looks an awful lot like the beginning of the second Great Depression," laying the responsibility with Republicans who had "run the economy into the ground." He agreed with Pelosi on the need to undercut McConnell's ability to hold up key legislation through filibuster threats. "McConnell can delay the [stimulus]," he said, "but he can't hold it up." He empathized with her "frustrations with the Senate," observing that Reid was "not aggressive enough." It would fall to the House to "light a fire under the Senate" by passing an expansive bill. That was welcome news, she said, but she warned him that House members would not simply rubber-stamp whatever Reid could pass, which undoubtedly would be loaded with Senate earmarks. "I'm not asking you to walk a plank for the Senate," he assured.[10]

Although several economic advisors embraced a bill of $1.3 trillion, Obama felt that too costly and instead endorsed something in the neighborhood of $800 billion, an amount he believed could be spent "wisely and quickly" to create 2.5 million jobs.[11] He also was sympathetic to a tax credit for new hires, although critics argued it would only reward employers for hires they would have made anyway. Obama's advisors also favored a large personal tax cut, a sore point with many Democrats who believed Bush's cuts had aggravated the deficit with little benefit to lower-income families who paid little or no taxes. "The members are red hot wired for mortgage relief," Pelosi offered, recalling pledges made during the TARP debate.

Pelosi also wanted to replicate the Works Progress Administration's support during the New Deal, which benefited out-of-work artists who produced over a hundred thousand paintings, sculptures, and murals in public buildings, including San Francisco's iconic Coit Tower. For just $50 million, she insisted, hundreds of local museums, theaters, and symphonies—all of which generated jobs from set construction to restaurants—would be preserved. The president's staff grimaced. Arts funding could appear frivolous, like the midnight basketball provision in the 1994 crime bill that had been ridiculed by Republicans. Pelosi was far more concerned that the Senate would turn the bill into "a Christmas tree" by adding earmarks like "parks in Montana," a criticism of Baucus's habit of catering to his parochial interests. "I'll defend the big numbers in a House bill," she promised, but she vowed, but everything "must be economic stabilization, and we need very strong accountability."[12]

When he convened the bipartisan Democratic leadership to promote an "inclusive, transparent" stimulus, Obama warned against slipping into "political gamesmanship coming right out of the box." Instead, "people need to work hard," he directed, and they could not afford to "be puttering around." Members who had worked themselves to exhaustion during the prior six months looked uncertainly around the table and then at the novice president who, he admitted, had not been "in the Senate for much of the last year or two." Pelosi assured him that her members would be diligent. "We want to look like swans going across the lake," she pledged, "serene on top but with frantic paddling" below the surface.[13]

Pelosi hoped to keep the stimulus deficit-neutral by rescinding Bush's upper-income tax cuts, a goal Obama advisors also embraced. "I don't want Obama to think we aren't standing by Paygo," she said.[14] Even though emergency bills rarely were paid for, enunciating the anti-deficit goal was crucial to securing support from conservative Democrats, and she already had heard reports that Hoyer was "play[ing] politics" with the Blue Dogs, "stir[ring] them up" over the bill's cost. Emanuel held a "very positive meeting" with the faction to calm their worries.[15]

Obama was confident he could persuade enough Senate Republicans to support the stimulus to overcome a filibuster so he might begin his term with a bipartisan initiative.[16] Republicans "will provide balance in the package," he believed, and he welcomed their ideas. "There will be times when we are willing to bulldoze you," he told the GOP leaders, "but this is not one."[17]

Obama's optimism about Republican cooperation raised warning flags among those engaged in combat with Republicans for years before his arrival in Washington. Pelosi called pledges of bipartisanship "music to my ears," but recent experience offered little reason for encouragement. "I wouldn't be too hopeful about getting Republican votes," I told Obama during our meeting in the Speaker's office. "We've dealt with these House Republicans. They hate you." Obama nodded, but he said, "You may be right, but I want to try."

It was soon clear the president-elect's optimism about the prospects for bipartisanship was likely to be unwarranted.[18] Congress had to vote to release the next tranche of TARP money, but Republicans who had voted for the law now wanted to leave no fingerprints on spending the money. The approval had squeezed by the Senate 52–42 just five days before Obama's inauguration, with nine Democrats—both liberals and conservatives—voting to block the release and just five Republicans voting in favor.[19] When the House voted the day after Obama's inauguration, just 18 of 174 Republicans voted in favor.[20] Tellingly, both McConnell and Boehner voted against releasing the money they had fought to approve. Obama blamed the GOP opposition on the Bush administration's handling of the bailout and promised to "change the way this plan is implemented."[21]

GOP House leaders also sought to put distance between themselves and the stimulus, fashioning alternative legislation that would rely primarily on tax cuts for businesses.[22] By early February, efforts at bipartisanship in the House would be all but nonexistent, and Pelosi's staff disseminated talking points branding the GOP "the Party of No." Collaborative efforts were no better in the Senate. The level of Republican input accepted would determine if Republicans obstructed the bill, GOP whip John Kyl (AZ) predicted, and he was already dissatisfied with the expedited timetable. "We'd like to be part of the process," McConnell professed, but "the House can't drop a [stimulus] bill on us," and he warned Reid not to bar Republican amendments.[23]

Strong disagreement over providing emergency aid to overwhelmed state and local governments highlighted differences in the approaches of the parties and the two houses of Congress. House members led by Jim Clyburn, the only minority in either party's leadership, demanded that some aid be channeled directly to local communities rather than routing it through the states. Republican governors often failed to allocate aid equitably to minority communities that voted Democratic, he noted. "You tell the White House," Obey lectured his former staff, Rob Nabors, now a White House aide, "our people need to benefit without kissing the governor's ass."[24] Some of the Republicans opposed assisting state and local governments at all, including their own. "Kentucky wants Congress to rescue them from having to make any tough decisions," asserted McConnell. He would support only loans, not grants, and wanted to require states to liquidate their surpluses before turning to Washington for aid.

With the recession deepening, Obama called for a bill to reach his desk by the Presidents' Day recess in mid-February, a breakneck pace for such a massive measure. As the Hill waited for the president's bill, Pelosi invited Obama's chief strategist to brief the Steering and Policy Committee. David Axelrod arrived with grim news. Only 2 percent of Americans thought the economy was in good shape; one-third believed the country was falling into a depression.[25] Ominously, 44 percent expected it would take more than four years before the economy was back on track, a devastating message for House members facing reelection in less than half that time. But voters were offering no blank check to the new administration. Only half of the country favored the government making large new investments. The good news was that 79 percent had confidence in Obama, although no one would bet how long that support would last.

Obama hadn't even raised his hand on the Capitol's West Front before the infighting escalated. Members of the Senate Appropriations Committee were furious at the aged and ailing Byrd and his staff for ignoring their input; Iowa's liberal Tom Harkin was "off the wall" over the administration's parsimonious spending recommendations.[26] Obey was "ticked off" by the president's spending outline and unveiled his own $825 billion bill, well above the president's target, and declared he might not accept any less. The pressure from the members was formidable, and Obama's team of Axelrod, Summers, and Schiliro emerged from a two-hour briefing of Democratic senators, in Reid's words, "beaten to a pulp."[27] The Obama team was surprised by the disgruntlement. "We never meant that our proposal was 'take it or leave it,'" one official told me.

Over a million spectators froze together on the Capitol grounds and filled the Mall to the Washington Monument as Barack Obama took the oath of office as the forty-fourth president. En route to the traditional lunch in the old House chamber, the new president and First Lady walked through the corridors of the Speaker's rooms lined with Pelosi's staff. "We're gonna work you hard!" he told me as he stopped to shake hands. The expectations of House Democrats ensured the feeling was mutual.

Although the margins in Congress were impressive, an incident during the traditional post-Inaugural luncheon in Statuary Hall drove home the frailty of the Democratic hold on power, especially in the Senate. As the speeches began, there was a sudden flurry of activity at one of the tables; police rushed in, startling attendees. The problem was not a threat to the president but the collapse of Ted Kennedy, who had suffered a seizure. It was a sober foreshadowing of how quickly Democrats could lose a supermajority, which could doom the party's agenda in the Senate.[28]

The next day, Obama spoke with the Speaker to commiserate on the economic health of the nation. "It isn't pretty," he observed. "We have to advertise what we're inheriting." Once again, an incoming Democratic administration confronted huge deficits run up by the outgoing Republican president and his party, who now demanded swift reductions in the red ink. Obama pledged to conduct a tough budget review, sparing no sacred cows. "Every program has a sponsor," he acknowledged. "We need to hold the line and cut things that don't work."[29] The frugal rhetoric reminded veteran Democrats of their anguish with Jimmy Carter's parsimoniousness following the Nixon-Ford budgets, which stymied liberal priorities during the 1970s. But the deficit projections left them little choice, he told the Speaker. "The numbers are scary."

Three days after the inauguration, as advisors warned the outlook was becoming "dark, darker, darker yet," the bipartisan leadership reconvened around the Cabinet Room table. They were looking to the administration for guidance, Reid acknowledged, because "I don't know how to do it!"[30] Obama's proposal focused on anti-recessionary spending. "You shouldn't be surprised," he told the Republicans, "because we are Democrats and we are listening to economists who favor more spending than cuts." But he also endorsed $275 billion in new tax cuts favored by Republicans and surprised his own party leaders by agreeing with McConnell to address the "ticking time bomb" of entitlement spending like Social Security and Medicare. Changes to those sacrosanct program, Obama understood, "will make Republicans and Democrats squeal."

Even with those concessions, Republicans offered little encouragement. Boehner objected to the cost while McConnell demanded Democrats propose entitlement changes immediately. They also wanted assurances the bill would be considered under "regular order," allowing unlimited committee and floor amendments. Collaboration meant being treated as equal partners with equal access, declared McConnell. He had been insulted that when he called Emanuel, he had been told the chief of staff was "too busy to talk" to him. "I'm *still* too busy to talk to you!" Emanuel joked to the dour minority leader, who was unamused.

As during the TARP discussions, Cantor insisted on an entirely different approach focused on tax cuts for impacted businesses. The members argued contentiously until an exasperated Obama ended the discussion. "Look, some Republican ideas are not unreasonable, they're in the ballpark, and I want to be respectable," he assured. "But Eric, I won the election," he sharply reminded Cantor, a reprimand that would not be forgotten. "We can't return to the failed theories of the last eight years that got us into this fix in the first place. That's part of what the election in November was all about."[31] He promised to keep spending under control and not allow the bill to include everyone's pet provisions. "If I was doing that," Obama said, "I would put the health care plan into it."

He urged the leaders to set aside their partisan considerations and deal with the crisis. "Republicans and Democrats are all political animals," and he appreciated that conservatives needed to play to their activated base and media megaphones. "I understand that if this effort fails, Democrats will lose seats and I probably will not be reelected." But they needed to rise above electoral calculations. "Do your politics," he conceded, "but when push comes to shove, don't let politics get in the way of the product."[32]

The president soon discerned the Republicans were angling to exploit the crisis for partisan advantage, slowing the process, proposing untenable alternatives, and criticizing Democratic initiatives. Tiring of their "pick[ing] at the balanced package" he had assembled, he agreed to meet with the entire House Republican conference to plead his case. While he was en route, the Republicans voted against supporting any version of the bill, Boehner informed Obama on his arrival. Obama would remember the snub. "I don't want to relitigate it," he advised months later, "but let's not revise history."[33]

House committees held over twenty hours of hearings and markups on the stimulus, and Republicans offered dozens of amendments, most of which were rejected. The confrontational atmosphere in the committees led Pelosi to decide against allowing floor amendments she believed would be designed to wound her vulnerable members rather than secure Republican votes. The closed rule guaranteed negative press, but Pelosi was intractable. "They'll just complain anyway" if their amendments were rejected, she predicted.[34]

Republicans seized on provisions they alleged violated Pelosi's own "3 Ts" criteria. Even the Speaker and the White House questioned Waxman's inclusion of contraception services, which he justified as "completely defensible" because it would save $700 million in health expenses. Cantor also denounced $200 million to restore the dilapidated Tidal Basin on the Mall, four times as much as small businesses would receive. The Blue Dogs were "up in arms" over the abandonment of Paygo, and Pelosi advised Obey to make some minor cuts so they could claim credit for paring down the price tag.[35]

When the House passed the bill on January 28, eleven Democrats broke with the leadership, but there were more than enough votes to pass the $819 billion stimulus 244–188. Republicans stigmatized the bill as overly expensive and laden with spending for special interests, and none voted in favor, which was no surprise to Pelosi.[36] "The Republicans don't share our values," she declared. Hoyer, who prided himself on his camaraderie with the GOP leadership and Cantor in particular, was dismayed by the lockstep opposition from those "who have followed policies that have put us deeply into debt" and bore responsibility for "the weakest economy since the 1930s." For their part, Republicans castigated the majority for securing no GOP votes, contrasting the House's party line votes with "all this talk of bipartisanship in the Senate."[37] Democrats responded they had tried but failed to secure Republican support. "You can't measure bipartisanship by the results of the bill," Pelosi explained, "but by how we try."

But the strong vote concealed a growing frustration in Pelosi's caucus. "House Democrats feel isolated from the president," she warned Schiliro. The president had "no respect for the Democratic caucus," and it was "unfortunate," she told Obama directly, "that you didn't come to the Caucus early."[38] Barely two weeks into the new administration, she worried about the White House. "The members are fed up," she observed. "But they [in the White House] will only betray us once." Senators also felt ignored, as reflected in a letter from Conrad to the new president expressing disappointment there had as yet been no meeting with the caucus.[39]

Relations between the branches were not helped by the rhetoric of some in the administration toward Congress. Like Obama himself, press secretary Robert Gibbs often spoke disparagingly about "Washington" and "Congress," failing to distinguish between Democratic supporters and Republican obstructionists on the Hill. Members of the president's party, who were burning their own political capital to support him, were infuriated by Gibbs's condemnation of the "myopic viewpoint in Washington." Gibbs's time would have better been spent, Hill Democrats argued, promoting a positive message on the stimulus. "They're too busy polishing their halos," Pelosi joked.[40]

She and Hoyer were also "terribly upset" by reports the administration was kowtowing to demands from senators like Arlen Specter (R-PA) who threatened to oppose any changes to the Senate's bill, which would need GOP votes to pass. After the stimulus, she vowed, "This process is over!" Hoyer was in full agreement. "The only way to push back on [the] Senate is by saying 'no.'"[41]

Later the same day, Obama walked into an Oval Office meeting munching on one of the apples he kept in a large bowl on the coffee table. He suggested preconferencing the House and Senate stimulus versions even before the Senate voted. "The White House is willing to put skin in the game," he pledged, reemphasizing his fast-approaching Presidents' Day deadline even if that cost Republican support. "Slowing down is a loss," he warned, "not getting Republican votes is not a loss." Axelrod agreed the real risk was inaction. An encouraging report came from Stan Greenberg's polling that showed a twenty-nine-point lead for Democrats on "handling the economy," and Axelrod noted the stimulus plan enjoyed a 64 percent approval rating. "We have a winning hand," Axelrod assured, "and we should play it."[42]

Durbin had not lost hope for Republican support, though each senator came with a multi-billion-dollar price tag. Specter, a cancer survivor, demanded $6 billion for cancer research, which the National Institutes of Health reported was more than it could spend. These additions pushed the bill's cost to $900 billion, setting off objections from Blue Dogs and Obama, who again insisted "the final package be scrubbed" of anything nonstimulative. But senators, aware of their leverage, defended their additions and called on the House to abandon some of its priorities to keep the overall cost in check.

"Them's fighting words," Pelosi warned.[43] But the senators did not flinch. Only a few days later, Susan Collins and Democrat Ben Nelson demanded $77 billion in cuts from the House bill, a number soon increased to $99 billion.[44] Reid encouraged the House members not to be overly concerned; the goal was to pass the bill in both houses so the differences could be resolved in the conference committee. "We need as little rhetoric as possible," Schiliro advised. "The administration will be there in the end."

But Pelosi was increasingly vocal that Senate concessions to Republicans were "shredding" sections of the House bill affecting education, science, energy, and school construction while producing 17 percent fewer jobs.[45] Her criticism was complicating Reid's efforts to reach the sixty-vote margin, warned Reid's chief of staff, Gary Myrick. Even the normally voluble Obey urged members to "stay silent until the Senate concludes."

On February 9, Snowe, Collins, and Specter joined all Democrats in voting for the bill. But in the call with Pelosi immediately afterward, Reid was fuming. "Those bastards!" he seethed, castigating Republicans for threatening delays. For his part, Obama was pleased; it was "not a perfect bill," he assessed, but "the right size and scope [for] putting Americans back to work."[46] He rejected mutterings that he was letting Republicans "run the show," noting the simple fact that if they peeled off, the bill would die. And the Senate's so-called cuts were really just smaller increases than the House had approved.

Privately, Emanuel assured the leadership that "the House bill is our bill," but Pelosi felt abandoned by the White House. "The President will only tell Congress to 'pass a bill,'" she complained, but the Senate bill created far fewer jobs, which was "all that matters. We lost 600,000 jobs in the country in January, and 500,000 jobs in one day in the Senate," the Speaker declared. The Senate was "throwing us under the wheels" by slashing money in the House bill. And yet, she noted, governors were pressuring her for increased funding for the states. "Why are governors calling me?" she wondered. "We're ineffective!" It was a bitter concession to the reality of the Senate's legislative leverage, but she vowed it would not continue.[47] "I've been 'Mr. Nice Guy,'" but now "those days are over."[48]

When she and Reid huddled with the president and Biden, she offered the time-honored solution of splitting the difference between the bills "to reduce the fighting among ourselves," but Schiliro warned that with that traditional approach, they should "expect a blowup" from senators. "I'll give a very specific outline of what's important," Obama promised, noting, "*I'm* the one with the 78 percent approval rating." His goal was $841 billion, but Reid immediately protested that was too high. "I can't sell 841!" he complained.[49] When the president asked his advisors to crunch the numbers again, Pelosi warned they should not presume the House would embrace whatever level he determined. "Do whatever you want," Pelosi advised his staff, "but the elected representatives will make the [final] decisions."

The pressure was on to resolve the negotiations speedily because Reid's three Republican votes were shaky. Snowe was grumbling she was "getting no attention" despite having broken with the GOP leadership, and Specter, who insisted on $60 billion in cuts that did not touch his additions, told Pelosi he was being excoriated by his fellow Republicans for working with Democrats at all. "I'm apoplectic," Specter bitterly admitted. "It proves that the conservatives say, 'let the country be damned.'" He insisted he would not be intimidated by threats of a primary challenge. "I don't have to be a senator," he said, although to secure his support, Biden promised not to campaign against him in 2010.[50]

The concessions to the Republicans predictably prompted bitter responses from liberals in both houses who felt the bill provided inadequate stimulus. Pelosi consoled her exasperated colleague by saying, "You deserve a special place in Mormon heaven for dealing with Harkin," who wanted large increases added back to the Senate bill. Reid smiled wanly. "I'd take Catholic heaven," he replied. "I'll just let him talk himself out."[51]

Pelosi became animated herself when learning the administration proposed taking money from the child tax credit to pay for school repairs. "Why are we spending money on school construction and not to protect the poorest kids?" she demanded. She insisted she "would not budge on programs for poor people" to pacify "two or three people on the Republican side" who were insensitive to the needs of minorities who were drastically underrepresented in the largely white Senate. "Throughout their careers, senators had no feel for communities of color," she told the president. With remarkable candor, she castigated "senators from lily-white states" who did not understand how race plays into local spending decisions.[52] Obama assured her he shared her exasperation. "If you think I'm not irritated!" he said. "No one is wearier than I am." But "if this gets done," he predicted, "we break the backs of the Republicans. Let's declare victory: we beat back the Republican effort!"

Pelosi made no promises. "You decide what you do," she told Obama, but "I won't support" the bill if it snubbed the House's priorities. The president tried again. "Slow down for a second. I can't say enough about what you've done," he declared. "I love you!" But he had to work with Republicans like Gov. Mark Sanford (R-SC) who "doesn't give a shit" about poor people, quickly rephrasing his remarks to "give a hoot" in deference to the Speaker's disdain for cursing.

Obama also felt obliged to protect the Republicans who "are getting the crap beat out of them" for supporting the bill. Pelosi wasn't impressed, noting they were winning editorial praise for their stance. She had also learned that at the White House's request, Americans United was running ads praising the swing Senate Republicans. Privately, AU director Brad Woodhouse explained the White House was "scared to death" the Senate bill would stall and urged the group to run the ads. Once the bill was passed, he promised, he would condemn the Senate's product.

Obama tried again, enthused at passing an $800 billion stimulus in just one month. "That's an enormous victory," he exulted. Pelosi corrected him, mentioning the lower $789 billion figure demanded by the Republicans. Obama gave up. "Let's get it done," he concluded, pledging to help round up the votes. She made it clear she could deliver her members, counseling, "Don't use your energy on [House] Democrats."

House members remained resistant to acquiescing to the Senate version. When Emanuel extolled provisions in the Senate deal, the Speaker cut him off. "Don't give me the White House talking points," Pelosi reprimanded. Pelosi also castigated the president's budget director, Peter Orszag, for agreeing to Collins's demand to restrict school construction funds to repairs only rather than allow the new construction that could benefit poorer districts. "Collins is empowered by the White House," an annoyed Pelosi told the OMB director, "but this ain't gonna happen!" The Senate limitation presented a "risk to our members," especially minorities, and "you can put it where sun don't shine," a rare vulgarity by the Speaker.[53]

"I know your opinion of the Senate," a contrite Reid explained. But, he explained, "I'm playing cards they give me," sounding every bit like the senator representing Las Vegas casinos.[54] "No matter what I was dealt, [Collins] had a better hand than I had." The rationale didn't salve resentful House members. "It's harder dealing with Senate Democrats than with the Republicans," DeLauro charged. That was a step too far for Reid. "Don't denigrate my Democrats!" he reproached her. He had no choice but to be conciliatory given his thin margin.

Pelosi was now convinced the White House would accept whatever could pass the Senate. "The president is mocking us," she believed. "Your people mowed us down," she said to Obama. "There's a very bad feeling, and the members are furious! The members don't want to pass *any* new bills. They're asking me, 'Why did we give in on all our points?'" The president became impatient, urging the Speaker to face the reality of the situation. "Keep your eyes on the big picture," he insisted. The Republicans "jerk us around. What could we do?" If the bill collapsed, the winners would be McConnell and the Republicans. Once the bill was done, Obama pledged to review how the negotiations were conducted—Pelosi was a big fan of what she termed "after action reviews"—and he predicted, "When we look back, we'll be very positive about this bill."[55] In the meantime, Obama urged, "Declare victory!"

Pelosi knew she had to conceal her disappointments. "We can't inspire confidence if we're tinkling over the bill," she agreed.[56] Obama held a meeting with the reluctant Blue Dogs where he "charmed the pants off all those crotchety buzzards," Cardoza reported.[57] Obama had impressively resisted Blue Dog efforts to demand additional concessions. When one participant suggested awarding a military contract in his district would make his vote easier, Obama rejected the quid pro quo, declaring such decisions "would be based on military necessity, not the parochial interests of a congressional district."

As the vote neared, Obama spoke with the bicameral Democratic leaders on a speakerphone in Pelosi's office, urging them to "work it out in a way that satisfies everyone." Sounding like a high school football coach in the locker room at halftime, Obama prodded the members to "get in the room and figure it out!" with little evident appreciation for how difficult it was to meld the caucuses together. One of the participants hit the mute button on the phone as the president exhorted them further. "This is so disrespectful!" Obey said, and Pelosi unmuted the call. "I know you're very busy, Mr. President," she said, curtly terminating the call.

Finally, on February 13, the House passed the $787 billion America Recovery and Redevelopment Act (ARRA) conference report 246–183 with no Republican support. Later that day, the Senate cleared the measure 60–38 after keeping the vote open for five hours so Sherrod Brown (OH) could return from his mother's funeral.[58] Hopes of securing ten to twenty Republican votes had evaporated under pressure from grassroots conservatives. The three Republican "yes" votes basked in plaudits, but Pelosi's gratitude was measured. "You're getting good press," she told Collins, who complained of being blasphemed as "Benedict Arnold" over her apostasy. House members were the ones who really deserved praise. "We conceded on almost every point," she noted. "This didn't work out our way."

The administration also had some complaints about the final version. Rob Nabors had promised to include $100 million in the president's upcoming budget to compensate for removing the $50 million arts provision. We both knew that budget recommendations were far from an assurance of funding. Encountering Nabors in a Capitol corridor on the day of the vote, he reminded me of his pledge. "Oh, that's OK," I replied. "We kept the arts money in the bill," and as a result, hundreds of museums, concert halls, and theaters stayed open. As Nabors predicted, the tiny appropriation was lambasted by the Republicans.

"Thank you, you did great!" Obama told the Speaker. "I enjoyed working with you."[59] Pelosi downplayed her own enjoyment of the experience, likening it to "the Bataan death march." Still, she credited Obama for having "muscled it through . . . so fast," but she warned the House would not acquiesce in the future. The negotiations "shouldn't have been that hard," Obama agreed, expressing gratitude for the three Republican defections, but Pelosi wasn't feeling grateful. "If you can't [translate] 58 or 59 Democrats into victory" without undercutting the House, she said, "we have a big problem."

Now, she said, it was crucial to hold a first meeting with House Democrats to "reduce the heat" in the caucus. Even more important, he must "take the message to the American people" about the stimulus's benefits. Silence from the White House communications office had left beleaguered House members convinced they had been left alone to "create the drumbeat in their districts."[60] Obama agreed the case for the expensive legislation needed to be made. "If the public doesn't know what the money is for," he advised, "it is a recipe for trouble down the road."[61] He tried to lighten the mood. "I hear you're going to Italy," he joked. "Have some pasta and chocolate!" But Pelosi sharply corrected him. "I'm going to visit the troops in Afghanistan," she explained; the stop in Rome was an ancillary (though frequent) feature of her CODELs. "When I get back," she added, "we'll talk about communications."

ARRA did help those hit hardest by the recession, providing the long-sought extended UI benefits, food stamps, and low-income energy assistance. The $27 billion for energy renewability represented the largest commitment in the nation's history, and $113 million would fund water recycling in the drought-impacted West.[62] In an effort to quell criticism on the Left, pay limits were belatedly imposed on Wall Street executives accepting TARP funds.[63]

But most Americans remained oblivious to the law's benefits. Although nearly 40 percent of ARRA ($288 billion) was spent on tax cuts for low- and middle-income Americans and other tax incentives, taxpayers never received a rebate check or a notice of the savings; instead, the automatic withholding deduction in paychecks was reduced by an average of $15 a week, which drew little notice. One year later, just 12 percent of Americans thought their taxes had been reduced by ARRA, while one-quarter of all voters believed the law had *raised* their taxes. "Virtually nobody believed they got a tax cut," admitted Jared Bernstein, an economist working for Biden.[64]

As it turned out, there were far fewer "shovel-ready" jobs projects than anticipated, and much of the construction money sat idle for months while unemployment ravaged the building trades. Still, overall economic activity began to revive, and by the fourth quarter of 2009, the economy was growing by nearly 4 percent (compared to losses in the first two quarters). By 2010, as the jobs spending began to have an impact, nearly 5 million jobs had been created.

But the promised public messaging effort from the administration never materialized, and in the absence of clear evidence of recovery, many complained the bill had been far too small to have the desired impact. Calls grew for another stimulus later in the year, but proponents seemed clueless about how challenging it had been to pass the bill in February. Republicans remained highly critical of the ARRA with Boehner asserting the law had done little to assist small businesses. Late in October, I wrote a memo to the Speaker challenging the Republican critique and noting that over $13 billion in loans had been made to thirty-three thousand small businesses. In Boehner's own state, thirteen hundred small businesses had received nearly $400 million in loans, notwithstanding the opposition of every Republican House member.[65]

The warnings that the bill was insufficient to stimulate a recovery were borne out over time. Over a decade later Summers acknowledged, "It would have been much better if the Obama administration had been able to legislate a much larger fiscal stimulus in early 2009."[66] As Senate majority leader in 2021, Chuck Schumer characterized ARRA as "too-small a package" that bore responsibility for the politically costly duration of the recovery and its fateful political consequences.[67]

ARRA illustrated the unwarranted optimism of the new president about the prospects for moving beyond partisan wrangling. He believed his resounding election victory would prompt a continuation of the collaboration evidenced during the TARP crisis. But that effort had been about rescuing bankers, the financial houses, the hedge funds and traders; many Republicans were willing to appropriate huge sums for that emergency. When the time came under a

Democratic president to aid those on Main Street who needed nutrition and housing assistance, foreclosure aid, jobs, and unemployment assistance, virtually every Republican who had rallied to aid Wall Street was nowhere to be found.

Pelosi never let Obama forget he had been snookered by the Senate Republicans. "It cost 500,000 jobs to get three Republican votes," she scolded later in the year. Even Obama seemed to recognize that his vision of post-partisan politics did not reflect reality. "The stimulus was an experiment," he told a joint leadership meeting two months later. "I wanted to reach out, but it didn't work [because] Republicans made the strategic decision to oppose."[68]

The stimulus battle also highlighted the resentment of House members over being pressured to accept a lesser Senate bill. Pelosi told Obama of widespread "resistance among members" because they believed Obama and his team were deferential to the Senate, and the obsequiousness to the Senate did not abate. Barely a week after signing ARRA, the president lavished praise on Kennedy and Orrin Hatch (R-UT), the Senate cosponsors of a national service bill. "We have a bill, too!" the Speaker pointedly reminded him.[69]

The stimulus also revealed the ambivalence of the Obama administration to aggressively market its achievements, believing periodic appearance or statement by the president about the benefits of the law would rally public opinion. Several years later, Obama still seemed mystified that Americans did not recognize the beneficial effect of ARRA. "We probably managed this [crisis] better than any large economy on Earth in modern history," he insisted. "The U.S. economy is in a better state after the recession than the American people realize."[70]

Privately, Biden, who was given the task of managing ARRA, admitted he "needed help with the president" in marketing the achievement. "It's a little bit like pushing a rope," Biden confided. "We don't go out and explain why we're doing what we're doing," he agreed. "When we have a good idea, we think it will be self-evident." He praised the laminated pocket cards packed with ARRA facts her staff had produced for members. "This is a significant help to what I'm doing," he told Pelosi, but it did not substitute for a vigorous informational campaign by the White House.[71]

Meanwhile, the Republican message machine was grinding out toxic portrayals of the massive program as "big government, big mess."[72] Within a few weeks of passage, public support for the stimulus plunged by twelve points from its two-thirds peak. It was an oversight, Democrats warned, that could not be allowed to recur when selling the health care initiative. Obama agreed. There would be a massive marketing initiative—"like nothing you've ever seen."[73]

CHAPTER 15

THE FIREHOSE

With the first burst of legislation behind them, Democrats fanned out to their districts, conducting over seven hundred events to boast about their early successes: the stimulus, the Lily Ledbetter equal pay law, and the extended SCHIP program. Obama credited the Hill leaders with doing "a remarkable job" in a short time and insisted "the public has noticed" the new team in Washington. Support for congressional Democrats—53 percent—was the highest in two years.[1] "When we look like we are governing," he said, "our numbers go up." The strategic goal now, Senate whip Chuck Schumer noted, was "to divide the hard right from the rest of the country" by demonstrating how Democrats' legislation benefited most Americans.[2]

In late February, Democrats strategized about how to best convince a skeptical electorate that Washington could be trusted after years of disparagement by members of both parties. Rebuilding that confidence was essential to securing support for their ambitious policies. "Republicans don't care if they are bad at government," the president noted. "It serves their interests." But Democrats needed "to show we are governing responsibly" by "pair[ing] up the ideas of government as a force for good and as an efficient steward of public money." That also meant avoiding "interparty fights that slow things down."[3]

Despite the lack of bipartisan support for ARRA, the president urged the skeptical leaders to remain open to collaboration with Republicans. "If they raise ideas," he counseled, "please, no knee-jerk reactions." While this approach involved "sacrifices," the benefit would be that "we will reduce ourselves as targets for the Republicans and isolate the right wing that just hates government." High-minded appeals to "sacrifice" had limited attraction to ambitious legislators who struggled to secure and keep their seats in the Congress, but Obama sought to set an example with his own potential martyrdom. "I'd be happy to give up my second term to get health care passed," he once told me, and he clearly felt every House and Senate member should be equally prepared to risk defeat. "But, if the Democratic brand is strong," he reassured his colleagues, "we all win."

As much as members wished to move on to high-priority initiatives, the CR from the last Congress was soon expiring, and they still needed to pass a massive omnibus spending bill to avoid a government shutdown.[4] Even though it was presented as a job-creating package, asking members to vote on another costly bill, Pelosi thought, risked stepping on the "afterglow of the stimulus." House members also worried Reid would again add earmarks to secure the 60 votes he needed, allowing conservatives to demagogue Democratic profligacy.[5] That line of attack was probably inevitable, Durbin admitted. "The Republicans allege there are earmarks even if there are none," he noted. "They're terrible," the president admitted.

But Pelosi did not want to hear about Reid's conundrum controlling his members' avariciousness. "Forget Reid!" she told her members. "I've totally lost patience with the Senate process. They have no sense of urgency." She insisted on "an ironclad agreement" that the Senate would move the omnibus swiftly, but Hoyer glumly reminded her, "There *are* no 'ironclad promises' from the Senate."[6] The White House wanted to avoid any protracted battle that would consume time needed for new priorities. "This is last year's business," Schiliro noted. "Let's get it off the books."

The final language of the omnibus confirmed the Democrats' strategy of waiting for the new president to take office instead of agreeing to Bush's lower spending levels. The omnibus was $21 billion above the level Bush had threatened to veto and funded increases in top Democratic priorities like the WIC infant nutrition program and Section 8 low-income housing. Republican priorities suffered. Boehner was furious the bill terminated his pet project allowing students in the District of Columbia to use federal funds to attend parochial schools, something Republicans hoped to expand nationally.

Although House Democrats lined up strongly in support of the omnibus (except for a score of mostly Blue Dogs), the leadership was displeased with their Senate colleagues and the White House. "We're helpless" in the face of the Senate's maneuvering, mourned Rules chair Louise Slaughter (NY). "How are we ever going to pass the Obama agenda?" But even with the inevitable earmarks, Reid was delayed for over two weeks by McConnell's objections. "I told [Obama] he should do us a big favor and stand up to the Senate," Clyburn related but instead, "the White House threw us under the bus" by agreeing to the Senate's additions. Pelosi was dismayed as well, insisting the president "really trampled on us." Miller was one of the House leaders who had had enough. "When the opportunity arises," he counseled, "we need to strike to set the terms for [future] negotiations with the Senate."[7]

Democrats on both sides of Capitol Hill were taken aback by Obama's issuance of a restrictive signing statement when he approved the omnibus. Only two days earlier, he had directed agency heads to ignore such directives issued by Bush and had pledged to avoid such restrictions on bills he signed into law. His objection was based on his reading that Congress had trampled on the president's constitutional authority, a higher standard than Bush's statements that focused on policy disagreements.[8] Even so, within the Congress the statement indicated that the power dynamics between the Hill and the executive branch remained conflicted.

As predicted, Republicans condemned the inclusion of over 8,570 earmarks costing $7.7 billion, pointing to initiatives to improve the employability of former gang members by removing offensive tattoos. Democrats found it hard to take the conservative criticism seriously. "The same people who drove the economy into the ditch are now complaining about the size of the tow truck," cracked Jim McGovern (MA). House Democrats had imposed a one-year ban on earmarks after winning the majority in 2006 and instituted transparency reforms the following year that had significantly reduced the number of earmarks, drawing complaints from lobbyists who had perfected the technique of securing them for their clients.[9] These efforts to impose tighter controls were vigorously opposed by Republicans as well as Democrats. Perhaps the most dramatic defense of the practice involved earmark proponent Don Young (R-AK) holding a knife to the throat of earmark opponent (and future Speaker) John Boehner, warning him against restricting the practice. "Fuck you," a furious Boehner had responded.[10]

Earmarks were also vigorously defended by the Congressional Black Caucus as often the only way to target aid to minority districts ignored by Republican governors. In fact, as Clyburn explained to Obama, two-thirds of all the federal funds benefiting minority districts originated as earmarks.[11] Appropriators also defended the practice as "part of Congress's power of the purse, which all Americans know as essential to the balance of powers between the branches of government," declared Hoyer.[12] He and all of the major Democratic leaders— Pelosi, Reid, Obey, Clyburn—were Appropriations Committee veterans who appreciated the value of earmarks in greasing the legislative wheels.

Even so, the administration pressed for eliminating the practice, which was easily caricatured as wasteful largesse. When Obama denigrated earmarks during the 2008 campaign, an angry Reid had "told him he messed up," and he reiterated the message in February, advising the president against embracing the anti-earmark passion of John McCain. "He's wrong on earmarks," the Senate leader remonstrated. "We're a separate branch of government, and I can't have Washington bureaucrats decide what I get to spend in Nevada!" Without the targeted spending, he predicted, Republican governors "may stiff us" by not approving spending for projects in Democratic areas, and "the losses would be blamed on you."[13] Besides, Patty Murray (WA) noted, appropriators had already agreed to reduce earmarks during the campaign, and it was "unfair to come back to us again" for more cuts.

"This isn't personal with me," Obama assured his former colleagues, but earmarks represented "fat, juicy targets . . . a stereotype of politicians doing their own thing and not the public interest" that much of the public perceived as corrupt. "I don't have any moral qualms about earmarks personally," he assured, admitting he had secured many for Illinois. But they created an easy "story for lazy reporters," and as a result, it would be "a problem if the bill lands on my desk with four thousand earmarks."[14]

Schiliro emphasized the point during one of our weekly Phil-Gary-John/ off-the-record discussions. "I hope we can get an agreement," he said, but Myrick did not mince words. "That's not going to happen," he predicted. He also rejected a proposal by Obey for a limit of forty earmarks on any bill. "That doesn't work in [the] Senate" with a hundred members, any one of whom could initiate delaying tactics if denied funding they wanted. "Reid is not agreeing to *anything*" proposed by the House chair, he predicted. "Senate people think he's nuts."[15]

A few weeks after Obama signed the omnibus, the leaders announced a goal of cutting the number of earmarks by half and requiring sponsors to post their requests publicly and certify they would not benefit personally from the provisions. The new rules would ensure an end to "the 'good old days,'" Obey declared, but none too soon. Within months, senior Democratic appropriators Pete Visclosky (IN) and Murtha were ensnared in controversies for directing millions of dollars to their districts. "I don't know how Jack and Pete operate," Pelosi said.[16] Months later, new appropriations bills contained thousands of earmarks costing billions of dollars, attracting criticism from deficit hawks. Obey suggested blaming the Senate and gave as an example the rejection of a House proposal to require competitive bidding for earmarks benefiting for-profit companies. That seemingly reasonable request drew opposition from the Senate Appropriations chair Dan Inouye (HI) who argued that 95 percent of for-profits were small businesses, most of which could not secure government contracts otherwise.

"The hell with the Senate!" a frustrated Pelosi responded, vowing there would be no agreement if the Senate stood firm. The reforms could "happen nicely or not, it's up to them."[17] "If the Senate wants to stick with a 1970s view of the world, OK," Obey angrily declared. The Speaker advised Obama against obsessing over the issue. "Don't spend your time talking about earmarks," she advised. "I don't care [about them], but the members do," and they should not be blamed for seeking "a little piece [of help] for their district." A much more important issue was providing jobs in members' districts.[18] "If people have jobs," Pelosi argued, "they don't care about earmarks. It's all about jobs." "Fine," Obama agreed. "There's nothing illegitimate about helping your district. But they can be abused." Reforms were inevitable, the Speaker believed, and privately, Reid acknowledged earmarks was probably "not a battle the Senate can win."[19] Even so, Reid angrily confronted Emanuel later in the year, demanding the White House "get off earmarks [and] stop playing up to [Tom] Coburn," an Obama friend "who mucks up the Senate" by objecting to almost any federal spending.[20]

After a year of battling on the issue, the progress was far from notable. The number of earmarks was down by 17 percent, and their cost had dropped by 15 percent; those remaining were subjected to new transparency requirements.[21] But the controversy highlighted the clashes among allies who, for their own institutional reasons, favored different approaches on a sensitive political topic: the House accepted transparency requirements and had less need to employ earmarks as chits given the wide margin Democrats enjoyed, the Senate's overall recalcitrance because of the need to secure votes and the White House's preference for eliminating the practice altogether. Both houses viewed the White House position with institutional skepticism since a complete ban on earmarks empowered the executive branch at the expense of a tradition members needed to build constituent support and raise campaign funds. "You need small things for members to take credit for," John Larson observed.[22]

Meanwhile, the crumbling economy showed little improvement from all the spending approved by Congress. Over 600,000 jobs disappeared in February, the worst statistic in six decades, and unemployment soared to 8.15 percent. In fourteen months, the economy had shed 4.4 million jobs, 2.6 million in the prior six months alone. Republicans, who had remained largely silent as the unraveling began under Bush, now castigated Obama and Democrats as culpable for the "Great Recession."

The tensions took their tolls on relationships among the leaders. "Do you have a problem with me?" Obama asked the Speaker six weeks into his term.[23] "You think I'm green and inexperienced," he said, answering his own query.

Pelosi sidestepped addressing his naiveté and expressed deep displeasure with disparaging comments about her attributed to White House staff. "My members are not happy with an article [in *Newsweek*] that portrays me as your problem," she admitted.

She disapproved of his tendency to emulate Republican critiques of Congress, criticizing "members on both sides of the aisle who don't want to take tough votes." Her members *had* cast multiple problematic votes, she reminded Obama. "What haven't we done" that he has asked, she queried. Sometimes, it seemed, "we make it look too easy in the House" because her margin was big enough to pass bills despite the defection of several dozen members. But reaching 218 on controversial legislation was rarely as easy as it seemed.[24] Obama seemed appropriately chastened. "Fair point," he conceded.

She also mentioned his unfulfilled promise to help distressed homeowners. "Our members are very disappointed," she said, because they had been promised prompt action on foreclosure mitigation in return for voting to release tens of billions of TARP money. "We don't see the White House weighing in," she said, hypothesizing that the delays were related to the long-standing links between administration officials and friends on Wall Street. A few days after registering her concerns with Geithner about the lagging housing market, Obama told the Speaker he would "work with the California finance folks" on housing, but he didn't want to "let Arnold off the hook," he advised, referring to the muscleman actor turned California governor. Weeks later, still awaiting a presidential initiative, Pelosi told Schiliro, "I don't know if people in the White House know how hard hit the American people are." She believed that Geithner retained the "taint of Wall Street" and lacked empathy for impacted homeowners.[25]

Reid was growing increasingly frustrated over Obama's continuing self-confidence that he could persuade Republicans to cooperate with his administration. "They are vicious bastards!" the majority leader insisted.[26] He had similar thoughts about some of his own members, specifically mentioning Kent Conrad (ND), who was "a major problem," and Baucus, who cut deals to benefit Montanans. "Baucus thinks he can [work] with the Republicans," Reid seethed to Obama and Pelosi. "No, he can't!"

Obama got the message from his Hill leadership. "When the three of us are unified," he told them, "there's nothing we can't get done." He deferred to their decades of experience and knowledge of their members that he lacked. "You guys are the experts in procedure, in getting it done," he agreed.[27] And while he would defend certain "principles that are nonnegotiable," he was amendable to "tak[ing] your lead" on timing and strategy.

"What do we end up with at the end of the day, and how do we get there" were the key questions, according to Pelosi. "We can't repeat the stimulus problems" that set House against Senate and enabled the Republicans to "blame us for nonpartnership."[28] Nor could the process be driven by conservative Senate Democrats like Conrad, a formidable player as Budget chair who sanctimoniously portrayed himself as the rare Democrat concerned with red ink. Facing nearly unanimous Republican opposition to the president's initiatives and still short of a sixty-vote majority, a filibuster-proof reconciliation bill might be the only way to pass legislation in the Senate, and that required both houses to approve a budget resolution first.

"We are going to need to use reconciliation," Reid noted, because "the Republicans won't help us" impose cloture. But such a legislative end run empowered Conrad in his role as Budget chair, and moreover, nineteen midwestern senators of both parties had told Reid they objected to using reconciliation to pass climate change.[29]

As spring turned to summer and fall, there was little relief from the slumping economic numbers. When the leaders met with Obama and economic advisors in October, Summers called the situation "dismal." "The stimulus did what it was designed to do by putting the brakes on the disaster," Obama explained, but it was not restoring a vibrant recovery, and public dissatisfaction was escalating. The country remained fixated on jobs as "the number one issue" while Obama and Democrats were focused other priorities like health care and energy, but they could not allow the harsh economic numbers to derail the policy agenda. If Democrats were "distracted by what the Republicans raise," the president warned, "we are playing on their court. If we are on our issues, we will kick their ass."[30]

Even so, there were practical limits. "I thank God for Nancy Pelosi every day," Obama declared. But some of her ideas for additional job creation, like the massive Gallatin Project infrastructure bill, simply lacked the votes. "I understand the sense of urgency," Obama assured.[31] But Reid brushed aside the idea. "There is no chance in hell" the Senate would act on a transportation measure costing $120–140 billion, he warned.[32] The public was not ready for more spending and more deficits. By a two-to-one margin, the public favored giving the current stimulus more time to take effect before approving of a second one. Early in October, Pelosi asked Boehner if he might cooperate on new jobs legislation, but the minority leader just decried "endless" spending. "The deficit is scary," he responded, and was more "the basis for Americans' fears" than the recession.[33]

One idea for addressing deficits was through a commission that would examine all of the factors contributing to the worsening problem: not just spending, but tax policy and sacrosanct entitlements like Social Security and Medicare. The idea had appeal to Obama, who believed it might be easier to pass expensive recovery legislation "if we have [such] a commission paired up with it."[34] But Democratic leaders had reacted harshly to a Gregg-Conrad initiative they feared would empower deficit hawks. Moreover, since Republicans had made clear they would not endorse tax increases, all the pressure would be on spending cuts, an untenable proposition. It was a bad idea, Pelosi argued, to legitimize a process that would almost certainly produce politically unpalatable remedies that reflected poorly on legislators if they rejected the recommendations. "If you want Congress to save money," she told Obama, "ask Congress to do it." She reminded him that they "beat Bush with Social Security" in 2006, and Reid agreed. "Why would *we* raise the entitlements issue?"[35]

But Obama remained adamant about extending a hand to Republicans and did so at a joint leadership meeting in April. "I want to reconcile the parties," he professed. Any bill was "more sustainable with bipartisan support," he acknowledged, citing Democratic cooperation under Bush on SCHIP, No Child Left Behind, and welfare reform. As a "believer in the law of unintended consequences," he preferred to avoid the controversy that accompanied one-party legislation. "I understand how you feel," he told the GOP leaders. "I'm sincere about bipartisanship."[36]

Even the leaders remained open to the possibility of finding bipartisan approach, although they were dubious about the prospects for success from such overtures. Reid welcomed a "more trusting relationship" with Republicans, he said, offering a more open amendment process on the floor that might relieve the tendency to block legislation altogether. And Pelosi, with her massive House majority, reemphasized she was "sincere about bipartisanship," offering to forgo using reconciliation to pass major legislation, if Republicans were cooperative.

But being conciliatory did not mean giving Republicans a veto over the Democratic agenda. "The Republicans are difficult to deal with," Pelosi stated bluntly at the end of April. And a willingness to talk did not mean Democrats would simply capitulate. "The election meant something," Obama insisted. "It's fine to be blunt," he advised the GOP leaders, "but be careful *how* blunt."[37] He cited the "experiment" of the recent stimulus, where his outreach had been snubbed, especially in the House. "I wanted to reach out, but that didn't work," he recalled, because "Republicans made the strategic decision to oppose the bill" to curry favor with their conservative base. He did not want a repetition of that stonewalling during the health care deliberations. In order to proceed, he needed assurances of good faith, that Republicans would not walk away at the last minute. It was fine for Republicans to raise objections, "but it's not OK to sit on your hands and do nothing." When McConnell protested "no one is suggesting we do nothing," Obama pushed back. "If there is no health bill" because of Republican obstructionism, he countered, "it *is* nothing," and that was unacceptable.

Hoyer, who frequently touted his collaboration with Republicans, echoed Obama's impatience. "If no Republicans will be supportive," he advised, "we are left with reconciliation" to circumvent the filibuster. The indifference of the Republicans was demonstrated by Cantor, who chastised Democrats for their "unbridled spending." Rather than reminding Cantor his party had run up enormous debt in the preceding decade, Obama invited the whip to provide a list of wasteful spending, which he promised to "move on a fast track."

This key conversation highlighted the positions each group was staking out in the coming debates. Republicans resented what they perceived as insufficient consultation and remained wary, at best, of the offers of conciliation. Obama, Reid, and Pelosi must have recognized from the ARRA experience there was little likelihood of GOP cooperation. On both sides, leaders recognized their bases were disapproving of conciliatory efforts that were viewed as capitulation, however much voters might decry partisanship. Indeed, opening the possibility of making major concessions on issues like health, Iraq, guns, abortion, immigration, and housing ran the risk of losing liberal votes.

The fall schedule was a firehose of unremitting legislative activity: health care, higher education, financial regulatory reform, food safety, whistleblower protection, the debt limit, Guantánamo, unemployment benefits, hate crimes, and more. There would also be periodic requests for more money for the wars in Iraq and Afghanistan, but Pelosi was warned funding faced tough sledding, especially if Obama did not follow through on promises to bring the war to a close. "We won't pass it," she predicted. "The members won't vote for it."[38]

At the same time, the Speaker had to tamp down the enthusiasm of some of her members to push bills with no likelihood of Senate action. In the early 1990s, the House had voted for a tax on fuel based on its BTU rating promoted by President Clinton, a controversial regressive tax that went nowhere in the Senate, leaving many vulnerable House members with having cast a vote that came back to haunt them in 1994, when many lost their seats.[39] Ever since,

House members lived in fear of being BTU'd again, which increased pressure on the leadership to suppress the liberal base's enthusiastic aspirations that could imperil the vulnerable "majority makers."

She warned the Hispanic caucus, for example, against "pass[ing an immigration] bill if the Senate doesn't move first," fearing Senate inaction would leave members with a controversial vote and no law. And Reid was very dubious about the chances for success. "If the president wants a bill, he needs to push it," he told Pelosi. That seemed unlikely given the continuing recession and the resistance of most labor unions, a key Democratic constituency. Perhaps, Schiliro told Myrick and me in one of our weekly meetings, the White House could do "something administrative" to address the most serious problems facing undocumented residents.[40]

Just months into the new era, a top consultant worried that public sentiment was turning against the Democrats and advised the leaders to prepare for the worst in 2010. There was little sign of improvement in the lives of most Americans, who continued to tighten their belts against a protracted downturn. "Don't sound too optimistic," Jim Gerstein warned. With signs of recovery slim, Democrats had little to offer except that it would be even worse to "go back to the failed policies" under Bush and the Republicans that caused the collapse in the first place. Worried legislators feared prospects for the entire agenda might be dissipating even before they had ventured into the fight on the most complex and politically consequential issue: health care.

CHAPTER 16

SHORT-CIRCUITED

For Pelosi, climate change was the great moral challenge facing the world, one that could not be deferred now that Democrats had power.[1] "Washington is a perishable city," the Speaker would exhort her members. Either they would act boldly, or they would miss the opportunity to save the planet. Pelosi did not intend to fail, at least not for lack of trying.

The core of the climate bill was the cap-and-trade (C&T) system, which had stalled in the Senate in the prior Congress, as well as the renewable electricity standard (RES), which was dropped from the 2007 CAFE law. Proponents rejected the argument that C&T threatened the disruption of the weakened American economy. Instead, they promoted energy modernization as a jobs creator and a "pillar of our economic recovery," especially in regions traditionally dependent on energy production and consumption. Shifting to renewable energy and achieving carbon reduction would admittedly require expensive modifications to manufacturing, transportation, and consumer behavior, but "the cost of *not* proceeding is more expensive than the cost of acting to curb emissions," Pelosi said, quoting Sir Nicholas Stern, a leading British expert. "If we do not have legislation," she insisted, "the United States cannot be taken seriously" as a world leader on energy and climate issues. She enlisted an impressive retinue of validators including Al Gore, energy magnate T. Boone Pickens, Robert Redford, and Vinod Khosla, the multibillionaire proponent of alternate fuel vehicles.[2]

Over a decade earlier, the Kyoto climate conclave had yielded disappointing results. Both large industrial emitters like the United States and emerging economies like China were unwilling to commit to meeting rigorous policies to reduce CO_2 and other global warming gases. Now, with a new Conference of the Parties (COP) convening in Copenhagen in December, climate activists were intent on putting a new law on Obama's desk.

"Once we set mandatory cap-and-trade standards, more countries will participate," Pelosi had insisted in 2007.[3] But the question remained: with Democrats firmly in control in Washington, could the United States set the standard?

Obama had discussed climate issues often during the campaign and vowed to support a major new law. But while Pelosi and climate activists saw the Copenhagen conference as a deadline for enacting legislation, Obama, Reid, and some key House members worried that forcing early votes on climate could jeopardize the willingness of moderates to support the health bill. If Senate Republicans balked on energy as they had on the stimulus, the votes of Democrats from energy-producing states would be decisive. Many of them had opposed the 2007 energy law and liked the climate bill even less, especially given the crippled economy.

"Any bill dealing with energy and climate change will have to be bipartisan to pass," said Senate whip Dick Durbin. One Senate leader, John Kerry (MA), was optimistic he could secure Republicans to offset problematic Democrats like Evan Bayh, an Indiana conservative who dismissed C&T as "unlikely."[4] He was not alone. "It's very difficult in the kind of economic circumstances we have right now," observed Ben Nelson (NE), while Kent Conrad, whose state was about to take off as a major oil producer, told Reid the bill faced "very poor prospects."

In the House, momentum for a bill was revitalized by Waxman's replacement of Dingell as Commerce chair. But even under Waxman's leadership, committee Democrats from energy states—Rick Boucher (VA), Bart Stupak (MI), and Mike Ross (AR)—were wary of signing on to Pelosi's flagship issue. The most conservative chair in the caucus, Agriculture's Collin Peterson, received very negative comments on climate from his rural constituents. Without these Democrats, passing breakthrough climate legislation would be all but impossible. Even so, Pelosi understood the momentum to advance a climate bill would need to come from the House, where she had a favorable chair, a large majority, and the ability to force the bill onto the floor, and she was determined to use her powers as Speaker to do just that, notwithstanding the electoral pain it might cause senators or even some of her own members.

Early in February, energy secretary Steven Chu painted a dire picture of the climate threat for the Democratic issues conference. He described a 30 percent increase in ocean acidity since the beginning of the Industrial Revolution and the massive release of carbon dioxide and methane resulting from the warming of frozen regions.[5] Chu advocated a C&T approach that relied on private sector compacts combined with government regulation. Others, like Rangel, pressed hard for a tax on carbon production, but Pelosi was wary of its crippling impact on key industries. "A carbon tax is easiest to do," she observed, "but it hasn't got a chance" of passage.[6]

There were also serious caucus divisions over reviving the RES. Activists favored an ambitious mandate of deriving 20 to 25 percent of the nation's energy coming from renewable resources by 2020. But southerners including Clyburn argued such a requirement would impose a crushing economic blow to the South, where over half the power was generated by nuclear energy that, while non–carbon-emitting, had costly operational and disposal problems and did not qualify as "renewable." Markey had long criticized nuclear power, but Pelosi professed to being "an agnostic" on the controversial issue. Waxman promised to address Clyburn's concerns on nuclear energy, joking, "I sold Markey out!"[7]

As proponents pressed forward, the opposition quickly threw down ultimatums. Late in March, ten senators representing coal mining and manufacturing states sent Reid a letter rejecting any C&T bill outright. Several House moderates warned that if the Speaker insisted that they first vote on climate, they would be unable to help on health later.[8] Zack Space (D-OH), a frontline freshman, reported the bill was helping Republicans recruit a top opponent for 2010. "I don't want to divide the caucus" by demanding climate come ahead of health, Pelosi said, but the caucus chair feared that was exactly what would happen.[9] "This is a dead dog loser issue," John Larson (CT) declared. "Why are we forced to deal with it?" Others shared his view that moving a climate measure was "a mistake [and] a risk," but "no one wants to deliver the bad news" to Pelosi.[10]

"There's never a good time for energy," the Speaker sighed.[11] She saw the sequencing problem in reverse, believing that her marginal members and the administration would lose their interest in climate after passing health care. Obama had seemed to agree with the Speaker's priority ranking during the campaign. "Energy, we have to deal with today," Obama had insisted during one of his debates with McCain. "Health care is priority number two."

At the White House in late February, Pelosi declared she would give priority to her climate bill. Obama declared his support for highlighting climate, but while he deferred to Congress on the bill's design, many House proponents suspected he favored a Senate approach being formulated by a bipartisan coalition of Kerry, Lindsay Graham (R-SC), and Joe Lieberman.[12] Wary of once again being backed into a corner, the Speaker warned Obama against assuming the Senate would set the parameters for climate legislation. "There is great resistance among the members to taking the Senate bill," she declared.[13]

Obama insisted he wanted climate legislation to pass early, but he was also worried about the Speaker "blowing up" if Reid couldn't pass a bill.[14] Pelosi would not back off her timetable. "We can't get to the anniversary of Earth Day [April 22nd] without a bill," she insisted. "You're preaching to the choir," Obama tried to reassure her. "I'm willing to spend capital" to get a bill done. But as a "realist," he had to admit it would be "very difficult" to pass a bill, and even then, some provisions would face constitutional challenges. Later, Schiliro assured me that the president "is not dropping the ball on energy" and remained "very committed to cap and trade." He had been speaking with Dingell and Boucher and was confident they were amenable to a good bill. But her worries about the administration increased on hearing Obama was open to using C&T revenues to pay for his "Make Work Pay" initiative to boost worker salaries. Doing so would violate their promise to use all C&T revenues to assist those who lost jobs as coal was phased out.[15]

Pelosi reminded the president of the promises to coal states, mentioning the coal miner statuette presented to her father by Sen. Jennings Randolph. "You wouldn't know [him]," she told the president. Still, she promised, "coal will have a place in the energy bill."[16] Obama responded, "The problem isn't coal" but rather progressive Senate Democrats like Debbie Stabenow (MI) and Sherrod Brown (OH), whose states were home to energy-consumptive industries like steel and auto manufacturing. He was annoyed that climate remained for his administration to address because Bush's administration had opposed reform in 2007. "I didn't come here to clean up Dick Cheney's poop," Obama complained. "I have a dog for that."

"It is not an option to do nothing on energy," she warned her chairs in late April. But Waxman was finding it challenging to line up votes, and he suspected Van Hollen was assuring vulnerable freshmen the House might not act without assurances the Senate would also take up the bill. That got the strategy backward, the chair insisted. The Senate was "in shambles" and would only move *if* the House first produced a bill. "There are a lot of nervous new Democratic members," Waxman acknowledged. But hiding from the climate issue would not help them, the party, or the planet. "We need accomplishments for them to run on." Pelosi agreed wholeheartedly, warning that if Democrats tripped and fell on energy, the failure would "lead to trouble for health care" by proving that "special interests can kill" Democrats' legislation, and that would be a victory for the "status quo agents" in Washington.[17]

Markey was heartened by conversations indicating some crucial energy-state members claimed they wanted "to get to 'yes'" on the bill.[18] But the Speaker was increasingly concerned that Obama, on the advice of his staff, might abandon or postpone climate until after the health care bill, and she instructed House drafters to avoid setting overly ambitious goals that could diminish the White House's zeal. Recognizing a 20–25 percent RES by 2020 was probably unattainable, she charged Markey with exploring whether a 15 percent goal could win support, with the additional saving derived from conservation. She was confident that with momentum from a new law, the economics of the marketplace would drive the actual RES percentage higher.

But Markey resisted the 15 percent renewability level, arguing the country was already on track to reach 14 percent by 2020. He also disliked the expanded use of cellulosic plant-based fuels favored by Democrats in agricultural districts. "That's a huge give to farmers," he objected, because it could accelerate deforestation as farmers expanded production of government-supported plants. But Pelosi needed rural allies, especially Peterson, whom she urged join in supporting the legislation. "You should get in on it now," she suggested, "and get what you want."[19]

Pelosi activated her vast network of contributors to pressure recalcitrant members. Utah resident Redford was charged with appealing to Jim Matheson, and early in May, he reported on a conversation with Matheson. "Is he dense?" Redford asked.[20] Pelosi told him Obama had been surprised to learn that Utah's Republican governor, Jon Huntsman, was more supportive than the congressional delegation.

With the vote count very close, the Speaker remained open to additional concessions to members who exerted their leverage. Additional sweeteners were going to be added, including a "cash for clunker" program to encourage the removal of inefficient cars from the roads. "I don't care what *anyone* gets as long as we get [efficiency] standards and renewables," she declared.[21] "I don't need the *best* bill. I just want *a* bill. So what if the refineries get a bigger break? We won't get *anything* if we wait for all the industries" to act first.[22] Redford endorsed the incremental approach. "This is no time to mess around," the actor concurred. "Cap and trade is just the first step."

Waxman was encouraged by a letter from the president of the United Mine Workers, Cecil Roberts, encouraging him to move the compromise forward.[23] Good news also came from Boucher on carbon reduction targets, and several utilities also came on board. Importantly, key Commerce moderates and Dingell had all signed off on 15 percent RES with another 5 percent from efficiency. The coalition of environmental organizations, known in Washington as the Green Groups, was also favorable, as was Gore. But after a "frank discussion" with Waxman, several key Commerce members remained opposed, and the Speaker was losing patience. "Waxman is going to win *without* you," she warned Mike Ross (AR). "This is your time to deal."[24] Hard-edged opponents vowed to slow the committee's action by unveiling five hundred amendments. Wary of concessions that could damage the workability of the program, Pelosi cautioned Waxman to accept only amendments that secured additional votes.

The bill cleared the Commerce Committee by a comfortable margin, 33–25, earning a coveted "bipartisan" label by winning the support of a lone Republican, Mary Bono (CA). But four Democrats—Barrow, Matheson, Melançon, and Ross—voted with the minority, and Boucher and Dingell refused to rule out efforts to weaken the emissions caps on the floor.[25] Even so, the bill seemed a major step forward on climate policy.[26] Obama and most environmentalists were delighted. "We are now one step closer to delivering on the promise of a new clean energy economy," the president declared, while Gene Karpinski, president of the League of Conservation Voters, called the bill "the most important environmental vote this committee has ever taken." Frances Beinecke, the president of the Natural Resources Defense Council, emphasized the bill would aid the broad Democratic constituency by creating "whole new industries, millions of good-paying American jobs, and . . . benefits to low-income families."[27]

Other reformers felt too many concessions had been made, ignoring the fact that even with the changes, the vote had been close. "Some of our environmental friends think that no bill is better than this," she told Gore. Move On leader Wes Boyd's "nose is out of joint" and Sierra Club president Carl Pope was "a bit sour" because of the provisions aiding the coal industry, Gore reported. He promised to help keep the groups "in line" and use a network of two hundred field organizers to build grassroots support.

Even with the victory in Commerce, the bill faced major hurdles in some of the other six committees it needed to clear before reaching the House floor. He had secured concessions on cellulosics, but Peterson remained furious that the bill gave regulatory authority over plant-derived ethanol to the Environmental Protection Agency (EPA), not a popular agency in rural areas. Without more concessions, he threatened, his twenty-six committee Democrats would oppose Waxman's bill.

Rangel was also displeased because it fell to his Ways and Means Committee to raise taxes to pay for much of the C&T measure. The controversies surrounding the climate bill added to his concerns that the health care bill would suffer by forcing an early vote on climate. Worried the Ways and Means members were feeling ignored by all the attention showered on Waxman, Pelosi persuaded Obama to meet with Rangel's members for "a major schmooze" on energy. The president reproached the members who voiced concerns about the impact of doing both climate and health care. "I don't see a lot of energy," he said disapprovingly. "Don't get tired on me! God doesn't give you more than you can bear. You need to do both bills!"[28]

Even with such boosterism, C&T proponents sensed a growing wariness on the administration's part. "We're reading the tea leaves the same way," Gore told Pelosi after speaking with the president. Obama had "said all the right things," but the former vice president remained "unconvinced" of the administration's commitment. "He needs to put the prestige of the presidency on the line," said Gore, who was also annoyed that agriculture secretary Tom Vilsack wanted his agency, not EPA, to play the key role on cellulosics. "I expected more from an ally," Gore said, but Pelosi had no question why Vilsack was indicating discomfort. "He's an employee," she declared dismissively. "He's giving the administration's position."[29] In fact, many believed the president was backtracking, likely influenced by Emanuel, who remained convinced that climate was "poisoning the well" with moderates. "The White House is not a friend on energy," Pelosi told Waxman, knowing the message would be passed along to his former aide Schiliro. "I'll talk to Phil," the chair agreed.[30]

The pieces began to fall into place, with the Agriculture and Commerce Committees narrowing their differences. Although most Republicans ruled out supporting any legislation that included a tax on energy, several moderates were indicating their support.[31] A hostile Blue Dogs letter had been quashed by Hoyer and Cardoza, who pointed out that six of their nine demands had been met. The major significant holdout was Peterson, and Pelosi was clear. "I do not want to go without Collin," she insisted, but she also believed "the farm people are asking for too much."[32] He had gotten "5.5 of the 6 things he wanted," and if he remained opposed, she would give complete authority over plant-based fuel to EPA.

She faced constituent pressures, too, she reminded Peterson. "The San Francisco environmentalists are jumping around" with their own demands, she told him. "I've alienated them [and] read them the riot act."[33] The steel fist was not too hidden within the velvet glove. "If I don't have you," she warned, "I *have* to have them, and you will get nothing. I will win with them or with you, but I prefer you," she told her friend. "I have to have the bill," she declared. "And I *will* have one. I have the votes without you."[34]

Peterson made one more run, protesting that "the agriculture groups don't trust Obama." "I'm ready to retire," Peterson wearily complained, just days from his sixty-fourth birthday. "I've just about had it with the crazy environmental groups."[35] The farm organization complained about "$145 billion going to poor people [in various initiatives] and agriculture gets nothing!" he charged. Not only was the assertion untrue, but it was poorly calculated to appeal to the Speaker's values. It was clear Peterson had run his string with the Speaker as far as he could. Pelosi had given him crucial campaign support against the wishes of many liberals; she had visited the Minnesota State Fair with him, wearing jeans and cowboy boots and munching on a pork chop on a stick, all singularly anomalous Pelosi behaviors. She insisted he could not oppose her bill, especially since she had taken criticism for accommodating his demands.

"Courage and steadfastness," Gore advised, remained the "key factors" in passing the bill. "You are my hero!" Gore gushed, declaring the bill "one of the most important ever." But Pelosi was not yet confident she had 218 votes. Some members, she concluded, were "just scared to vote on anything."[36] Others used the closeness to make demands from their personal wish lists.[37] Bobby Rush (IL), who had denounced Obama as an overeducated Harvard "fool" during a 2000 House primary, insisted on hundreds of millions of dollars for job training for felons and single mothers. Eric Massa (NY), a hard-to-read first-termer, demanded a photo with Obama and arrived at the White House for a Hawaiian luau with books for the president to sign. Luis Gutiérrez (IL) demanded a meeting with the president on immigration reform.

Calls went out to Republicans reminding them of the concessions they had won in the markups. "I don't like pulling [the bill] if I don't have the votes," she told Waxman.[38] "That's why I'm talking to the Republicans." Waxman requested additional time, believing the differences with Peterson "are not insurmountable," but the Speaker was convinced the only way to secure an accurate vote count was to keep the pressure on. "If I didn't go now," she told Gore, "it would be over." Perhaps overconfidently, she told Hoyer, "We're in pretty good shape," despite the many concessions. "We're so close," she urged, "let do it!" Hoyer flashed his toothy grin. "That lady works *so hard!*" he joked.[39]

Gore claimed to have ten thousand activists phoning undecided members at the Speaker's request "because the White House is not working" the bill, he reported. Days before the vote, Obama declared the bill an important milestone and endorsed House passage, but Pelosi considered the effort half-hearted. "You notice the silence coming out of" the White House, she commented.[40] Administration staff pushed back, documenting two dozen members the president had persuaded, but Pelosi dismissed the reports, insisting she had already secured those votes.

When the bill hit the floor on June 26, Pelosi had only two hundred firm "ayes" but remained confident her caucus would not let her down, and she was right, although barely. The American Clean Energy and Security Act slipped through on a razor-thin 219–212 vote. In the end, forty-four Democrats—fully 17 percent of the caucus—opposed the bill, mostly frontline Democrats from energy-producing states and Republican-leaning districts. The Speaker was annoyed that a few liberals, including Dennis Kucinich and Pete Stark, voted against the bill for being too watered down. In a major disappointment, Peterson joined many rural members in opposition. Only eight Republicans, mostly from Democratic-leaning districts, supported the bill. Boehner denounced the rules that allowed no Republican amendments except a doomed complete substitute. In protest, he forced the clerk to read a three-hundred-page amendment added by Democrats that morning.

"I never thought for one minute that we wouldn't win," Pelosi defiantly insisted after the nail-biting vote. "Never."[41] But "it was a heavier lift than it should have been," she told Gore, and she was surprised by the number who had misled the president and her. That, she vowed, was "a big mistake."[42]

The reviews were mixed. Gore was measured in his public comment, acknowledging that the "bill doesn't solve every problem" but insisting its "passage means that we build momentum." The New York Times was largely dismissive, calling the bill "a patchwork of compromises [that] falls far short of what many European governments and environmentalists have said is needed."[43] Several of the green groups, including Greenpeace and Friends of the Earth, were highly critical, evidently unimpressed by the hairbreadth victory. The criticism ran in both directions. Although environmental leaders insisted they had devoted unprecedented time and energy to climate, Pelosi dismissed their efforts. "I could measure on the head of a pin the support we've gotten from the environmental community," Pelosi would bitterly complain. "The groups aren't really committed," Gore bitterly agreed. "They spend only about 1 percent of their budgets on global warming issues. Most is spent on overhead and salaries."

Some House members grumbled anonymously about casting another career-threatening vote for little reason, displeased that Pelosi had placed her personal priority over the political interests of her caucus. Carl Hulse in the New York Times hypothesized that some marginal Democrats who cast a yes vote could suffer defeat like those who lost their seats by supporting Bill Clinton's tax bill in 1994.[44] "We can't let this vote be characterized like that," Pelosi insisted. "We can't let them characterize this as a Pyrrhic victory."

If the bill was to have a future in the Senate, she told Gore, "you have to be very engaged." Within weeks of the narrow House vote, Reid downplayed the chances of passing any climate bill.[45] Even strong proponent Barbara Boxer (CA) questioned the wisdom of forcing her colleagues to vote for a doomed bill. To secure votes from moderate Democrats, Reid warned, he would likely have to agree to an amendment allowing offshore drilling to proceed in the Gulf of Mexico. After Katrina, that was a controversial proposition, but Pelosi indicated she could acquiesce if the environmentally sensitive eastern Gulf was excluded. Hearing about the proposal, one leading environmentalist predicted such a compromise was "going to be tough sledding."[46]

Both Pelosi and Gore felt Obama himself had largely been "missing in action during the climate fight." The day after the vote, Pelosi was unsparing in her comments to the president. "We saw the shock and awe of the carpet-bombing from the other side hitting our people," she said. Her wavering members would need more aggressive presidential engagement when they got to the health care bill.

A battle erupted inside the White House over the president's role going forward.[47] Schiliro, an energy policy veteran from his years with Waxman, advocated for a deeper engagement while agreeing the bill faced a "very tough path" given the narrow House margin.[48] But the Chicago clique feared that "the messiness of congressional horse-trading was destroying Obama's reputation," a curious analysis that naively suggested the president could hover above the congressional dealmaking.[49]

Although Obama praised the House's actions in a speech before the United Nations, the administration clearly feared that the expenditure of time and political capital on climate was undermining the health care effort. "He told me 'time is slipping away'" on health care, Pelosi told Gore, and early in July, Biden confirmed to one environmental leader that health care far ranked above climate as an administration priority. By October, a full three months before the 2010 State of the Union, a White House staffer reported the president's speech would focus on health care and the deficit, not energy.[50] In some ways, even Pelosi could not dispute the need to prioritize. "If health doesn't pass," she told the president, "we're all dead."

Six months after the House's action, a bipartisan congressional delegation traveled to the UN climate conference in Copenhagen with no law on the books. Many European leaders had grown dubious the United States could embrace sweeping legislation. The most significant boost to energy innovation was likely to remain the $27 billion contained in the ARRA stimulus, whose benefits were hailed by US manufacturers attending a congressional breakfast in Copenhagen.

Without ARRA's largely overlooked incentives, they insisted, they would have been incapable of investing in innovative energy technology. Hoyer encouraged them to "let the public know" the benefits of the law since no other messaging effort apparently would do so.[51]

The conversations with other governments were less positive. Obama ruefully noted how resistant many lesser-developed countries were to addressing climate change even with the promise of significant US assistance. "I want to give you money," he told their delegates. "You are making it hard to give you money. Are you crazy? Let me help you!"[52] At one point, Obama, Secretary of State Hillary Clinton, and Pelosi waited with growing impatience in a converted jeans store inside the conference venue for a scheduled conversation with the Chinese delegation. After an hour, they realized the deputy minister had skipped the meeting and instead was addressing the plenary session upstairs.

As Obama prepared to deliver his own remarks at the conference, we stood together behind the stage curtain. Commiserating about the Chinese discourtesy, I told him the level of discussions in Copenhagen seemed significantly below presidential level. "They had to bring you here to do staff work?" I asked. He had not come to Copenhagen "to talk or posture but to act," he assured me. "But man," he added lightheartedly, "this is tougher than dealing with the Congressional Black Caucus!"

When he finally addressed the conference, Obama praised the House's "bold action . . . [in] pursuing comprehensive legislation," pledging "to continue on this course of action no matter what happens in Copenhagen." With more bravado than evidence, he insisted "the United States has made our choice . . . and we will do what we say." In the end, the conference produced only an unenforceable interim agreement, "a pail of water thrown on a raging fire," in the president's own words, and that only after he barged uninvited into a clandestine meeting of the Indians, Chinese, and other large polluters to berate them with what presidential aide Reggie Love called "some real gangster shit."[53]

In April 2010, with no prospect of Senate action, Pelosi confronted energy secretary Chu about the slow spending of ARRA's energy innovation money. "I know you're frustrated," he counseled, but questions had arisen about the solvency of some of the applicants. The embarrassing failure of Solyndra, a green battery company that received over half a billion dollars in federal loan guarantees, would confirm that Chu's caution was warranted.[54] But Pelosi was far past such excuses. "Why don't you have more people working on it?" she demanded, her aggravation spilling out. "For all the bragging of the administration, we had to fight to get" the green jobs provision into the stimulus in the first place. Now, she heard, the administration was considering the diversion of renewable energy money to nuclear plants. "I'm not opposed to nukes," she told Chu, "but not out of green jobs."

Energy and climate policy were supposed to be "the flagship of my speakership," she explained with disappointment. "All I hear around the country is, 'Why isn't it happening?'" She had faced nothing but resistance: to the creation of the Select Committee, to moving the bill in the House, from the Senate and the administration, and in Copenhagen. Despite her own sense of urgency, it appeared, everyone was short-circuiting her effort to address a climate crisis that placed the entire planet in jeopardy. A symbolic end to the climate legislation was delivered in October when West Virginia's governor, Joe Manchin, running to fill Byrd's Senate seat, displayed his virulent opposition to tough carbon control policies by firing a bullet through the proposed climate bill.[55]

CHAPTER 17

"NUMBER ONE AMONG EQUALS"

In late June 2009, Ed Markey boarded a routine flight between his Massachusetts district and Washington. Markey was used to basking in adulation from his liberal constituents, but on this day, a conservative passenger angrily confronted him. "You are a piece of *shit!*" the enraged commuter seethed. "You are *killing* this country. We're going to *get* you!"[1] Markey's encounter was a startling foreshadowing of the conflagration that was engulfing American politics, fueling bitter resentment among allies in the House and Senate and the White House, driving the parties even farther apart and ultimately consuming dozens of Democratic members.

Shortly after the New Year in 2007, freshman senator Barack Obama had confronted the issue that had bedeviled his party for nearly twice as long as he had been alive. Obama embraced "affordable, universal health care for every single American." He called on Americans to "find the will to pass a plan by the end of the next president's first term." Although he had not even announced his candidacy, he fully intended to be that "next president."

Every Democratic president since Franklin Roosevelt had advocated national health care, and each had failed due to the health industry's accusations of "socialized medicine." Not until Lyndon Johnson's presidency were tens of millions of elderly, disabled, and low-income Americans provided affordable coverage through the Medicare and Medicaid programs. But without LBJ's immense congressional majorities, subsequent efforts to expand health care failed, none more spectacularly than under the leadership of First Lady Hillary Clinton during her husband's presidency.

Obama entered office with a lengthy list of policy initiatives, but health care was "number one among equals," the new president declared. "I love both my children, but I love health more."[2] More than 116 million Americans lacked insurance at some point in 2007, and millions more had lost their employer-based coverage due to the recession. By May 2008, nearly 80 percent of Americans endorsed "a major overhaul or fundamental reform of the health insurance system."[3]

In addition, inflation in health care costs posed serious dangers to both the federal budget and the economy. "We can't have health costs rising 8 percent a year," Obama told the joint leadership soon after taking office. The proportion of the economy devoted to health had risen from less than 10 percent in the 1970s to more than 16 percent in 2008, a total of $2.4 trillion.[4] "The single most important act" to alter the nation's "unsustainable fiscal course," OMB's Peter Orszag declared, was to "slow the rise in health care costs."[5]

The Senate presented a challenge for such a complex bill, acknowledged its former majority leader Tom Daschle (SD), whom Obama chose to lead the health care reform battle.[6] Even after the defection of Arlen Specter (PA) to the Democrats on April 28 and the seating of Al Franken (MN) on July 7, Reid had just sixty Democrats, the exact number needed to invoke cloture. But his caucus had a broad ideological range, from the liberal Bernie Sanders (VT) to the conservative Mary Landrieu (LA). "You can lose thirty seats and still pass a bill," Reid would often remind Pelosi. "I can't lose one."

There was another option that would obviate the need to find sixty votes—the budget reconciliation process that only required the votes of a simple majority. But the scope of a reconciliation bill was constrained by limitations added to the Senate's rules by Senator Byrd, and the parliamentarian was given broad authority to dismiss any provision that violated the "Byrd Rule." Key provisions needed in the health care bill, such as protections for people with preexisting conditions, would be excluded from a reconciliation bill by the Senate rule's constraints.

As a result, a truly comprehensive health care bill would have to secure sixty votes to invoke cloture against an all-but-certain Republican filibuster, and that meant every Democrat would have the leverage to extract his or her demands. House members harbored no doubt they would try to do so, and substantial concern focused on the Finance chair, who would write much of the bill. "Make sure it's a *Democratic* plan, not just a *Baucus* plan," Pelosi cautioned the president. "The Senate must do more than complain they can't get sixty votes. I need your commitment to get it done in the Senate."

But Baucus was not Reid's only problem. Ted Kennedy's HELP panel, which shared health care jurisdiction with the Finance Committee, was "a disaster,"

Reid confided, because of Kennedy's serious illness and lengthy absence. "No one is in charge," Reid complained. A suggestion the longtime senator relinquish his chairmanship or even resign his seat to allow a replacement to be appointed had been abruptly rejected.[7] If he could not get the comprehensive bill passed by the fall, Reid warned he would use the more constrained reconciliation process.

Obama acknowledged the Speaker's annoyance. "I understand your frustration with the Senate," he said, musing about the need to reform the filibuster.[8] "I'm not walking the plank for the Senate, and I won't ask *your* people to walk the plank for the Senate." He agreed that "Harry is sometimes not as aggressive as he should be," and they would "need to light a fire under him." The best way to do that, Obama said, was for the House to act first to set a high bar for the Senate to match. "It's all in the sequencing," he said. He looked at his top aides. "We are joined at the hip on this, staff," Obama instructed. But Pelosi was wary of Emanuel's proclivity to cut expedient side deals that irritated liberals. "Isn't Rahm between us?" she teased the president.[9]

Liberals chairing the House's three drafting committees—Waxman at Commerce, Miller at Education and Labor, and Rangel at Ways and Means—agreed to work off the same base bill with each marking up their own section according to the Speaker's deadlines and policy objectives. "If we get too detailed," Miller warned, "all the minor issues can become big issues."[10] They knew that failure to meet the deadlines meant Pelosi would direct the Rules Committee to refashion the committees' product to maximize caucus support on the floor.

Obama's preference remained for "a bipartisan approach," as he told Republicans on April 23. "I don't want to repeat the Charlie Brown football experience we saw on the stimulus," he said, with opponents abandoning an agreement at the last moment. McConnell warned against hasty action. "If you do it unilaterally, without Republican buy-in, is it sustainable?" he asked.[11] Obama agreed the bill "will be more sustainable with bipartisan support." Privately, Emanuel had no illusions about the prospects for such agreement. "The Republicans won't help," he said. "We need reconciliation to protect [us] against them." The threat of a Democratic-only reconciliation bill also helped "keep the doctors at the table and the interest groups in play. It forces them to participate."[12]

Pelosi expressed a preference to avoid reconciliation "unless it is needed," but she also warned the "public doesn't want to hear about fifty-nine votes" not being enough, she told McConnell. "They don't understand [the filibuster], and they're not sympathetic" to it. She was prepared to "play the game" of negotiations, even offering an enormous olive branch to the Republicans by expressing a willingness to negotiate on malpractice award caps, which was anathema to personal injury attorneys who generously supported Democrats. "If we can trade off on other issues, I will take on my own base," she offered.[13] Republicans would have extensive opportunities to shape the legislation in the committees, Reid and Pelosi pledged, but obstruction would not be tolerated. "It is not OK to sit on your hands and do nothing," Obama warned, provoking McConnell to protest, "No one is *suggesting* we do nothing." Obama wouldn't yield ground. "But if there is no bill" because of gridlock, he explained, "it *is* nothing."

Obama's design embraced a model that subsidized and supplemented the existing private insurance model. The approach had been developed by the conservative Heritage Foundation as an alternative to the Clinton plan and had been implemented in Massachusetts by Republican governor Mitt Romney. Many on the Left had long favored a Canadian-style single-payer system or Medicare for All that would dispense with employer plans and private coverage, but such a radical redrafting of the health care system lacked support in either house or among the public. As a result, Pelosi ruled out a single-payer provision, even one that was discretionary at the state level.[14]

Instead, Democrats embraced a "public option" that could save the government $100 billion over ten years and "keep the private sector honest," Xavier Becerra predicted. "I don't see a plan that works without one."[15] Rangel was in full agreement that "there must be a public option" to help provide 40 million new participants coverage and to reduce costs. Three-quarters of Americans supported the public option, and Obama favored including it in the Senate bill, as did Dodd, despite representing the nation's insurance capital.

But the option faced "very strong opposition," Dodd warned, and Reid was "very cautionary" about its prospects in the Senate. Democratic disagreement on this key provision threatened to put the entire initiative in jeopardy. "We need a consensus on the public option," advised Hoyer, responding to grumbling by Blue Dogs and pro-business Democrats. Even a dyed-in-the-wool progressive like Rules chair Louise Slaughter (NY) worried that a public option would be characterized as a precursor to a single-payer system. From the outset, Pelosi was "not sure of the Senate" ever embracing this central feature of the House bill.

Before the health care effort began, members insisted there be a commitment by the administration to a vigorous public relations effort, especially after widespread dissatisfaction with the anemic marketing of the stimulus. Administration spokespeople had offered the excuse "We've only been in office one week" at the time of the stimulus, but weeks had gone by with little promotion, and no such excuse would work with health care. "I'm worried about the messaging," the Speaker told me. "We need to see some life in the White House," she advised

Reid. There was no alternative. "Obama is the only credible, trusted voice we have," consultant Jim Gerstein advised.[16]

Axelrod warned the health care message would be a complicated one. While many legislators emphasized the need to subsidize premiums for those lacking coverage, most voters were more concerned with controlling their rising premiums; premium support smacked of a welfare program. "Moreover, provisions that enthused policy wonks—like electronic medical records—did not resonate. The president's "affordable care for all Americans" plan would "preserve what works and change what doesn't," while safeguarding choice and quality.[17]

A cornerstone of the Democratic message must be "if you like your current health plan, you can stay on it," since the vast majority of those with insurance wanted to maintain their plans and their physicians. In particular, Celinda Lake warned, "You have to reassure seniors" that the popular Medicare program would be unchanged. Endorse anything else, Mark Mellman warned, and "you're headed for disaster." The broader pitch should be about "tell[ing] people five ways this bill will save *your* family money." "Eighty-nine percent are very worried about cost," Axelrod noted. Opposition to the reasonable Democratic bill should be framed as embracing a status quo that left tens of millions of Americans without health coverage and costs rising out of control.

A coalition formed with administration support—Health Care for America Now (HCAN)—had already raised $20 million to build a grassroots lobbying network across the country.[18] Pelosi remained mistrustful. She envisioned a scenario where Obama "signs the bill, his numbers increase, and we are left behind" to take the brunt of any public anger that might arise. "We need to look out for ourselves," she confided to her health team. "The White House is suggesting we are doing nothing," while press critics "want to make us look like bozos." Unlike the stimulus, she vowed, "I'm not getting thrown under the bus by the White House, even if they don't do it purposefully."[19]

"The next ten weeks will be the most significant period of time in American politics in a generation," Obama told the House leadership as they met in the Oval Office in June.[20] The House bill was set for introduction in mid-month, followed by hearings, markups, and hopefully House passage before the August break. The Speaker was optimistic. "Everyone votes for health!" she prophesized. Although she had identified the climate bill as her "flagship," Pelosi was unequivocal on her priorities. "Health is the first among equals," she told the leaders. "That's the way I'd put it," the president agreed.

The Senate was likely to produce a more modest bill. Baucus, who had "spent six months shooting off his mouth" about collaborating with Grassley, was "writing a Republican bill," Reid reported ruefully, "but he has no Republicans." "That wouldn't happen if Teddy [Kennedy] were here," Reid complained.[21] But Reid acknowledged Kennedy was deteriorating and likely unable to return to Washington to vote, let alone maneuver the complex bill through his committee. Reid was not even sure he could secure the sixty votes needed to take up a bill, but if he did, Hoyer's contacts told him, the Senate believed the House and Obama would blink and accept whatever the Senate approved. Obama avoided getting into the dispute. "You handle the sequencing," he deferred. "You know the tempo."

As with climate, the House's Blue Dogs were again raising objections, questioning whether any bill could really succeed in keeping costs under control. Waxman agreed to meet with the dissenters to demonstrate "how far we have come in their direction," he asserted. "People need to join the team!" But as soon as one faction was soothed, another raised concerns. "The Black Caucus thinks the Blue Dogs get whatever they want," complained Rangel, "while the CBC gets nothing!" The Hispanic caucus ruled out limiting coverage to legal immigrants; tax-paying undocumented immigrants should be able to participate, too, a very tough sell to moderates.[22]

Paying for the new program also remained a problem in both houses. "The press is voracious on the issue of payfors," Pelosi noted, and most of the options were predictably unpopular. Members looked to the White House for guidance but found little. "The president can't stand in left field," Miller said. "He needs to make the decisions on payfors."[23] But each suggestion quickly generated opposition. Rangel's suggestion of a $600 billion tax increase enraged Emanuel, who feared voter retribution for raising taxes. He had quietly negotiated a deal with PhRMA, the pharmaceutical industry association, and other health interests to generate over $100 billion in savings in return for which Obama would abandon government negotiation of lower drug costs. The discussions had not been easy, with some of the executives offended by Emanuel's brusque style, but Pelosi wasn't convinced he had pushed hard enough. "It was a little too cute," she said. "That was a small price for their support," she charged. "Someone in the White House sold us short," and now the administration was "covering their butt."[24] The companies defended the deal. "We are doing everything we can to make certain comprehensive reform is enacted this year," insisted Ken Johnson, a PhRMA vice president. "[But] the line in the sand for us was price control."[25]

Another controversial proposal was a tax on the most generous employee health benefits, so-called Cadillac plans typically negotiated by unions. The rationale for the tax was that these plans really represented an alternative form of wages and should be subject to taxation. But unions with Cadillac plans quickly made it clear the proposal was a "time bomb" that could derail a Senate bill. Equally unpopular was paring back reimbursements to hospitals serving a high proportion of indigent patients, which could jeopardize services to low-income constituents.

The challenge of uniting the party rested with the president, and that required his diving into the congressional vortex. "No charm offensive by the president will work on health!" Pelosi warned. Rhetoric aside, she worried Obama's "activities look very hostile" toward the House bill, and perhaps he and his staff understood the challenge ultimately would be squeezing whatever was negotiated through the Senate's cloture keyhole. The Speaker moved swiftly to establish the House's bottom line. "Our members won't vote for anything without a public option," she warned. And unlike the "dysfunctional Senate," the president could count on the House producing a bill by mid-October. Obama promised complete cooperation. "Here's my schtick," he explained. "You and I are plotting together. I will do what needs to be done."[26] Pelosi was encouraged. "You are one million percent correct," she confirmed. He went one step further, promising also to collaborate on a comprehensive immigration bill. "Fine, good, as soon as possible," Pelosi responded. "But July is for health."

The July offensive began with a helpful announcement. The actors who had portrayed "Harry and Louise" in the insurance industry's devastating $20 million attack ads against Clinton's health initiative resurfaced as supporters of the Obama effort. The president urged the leaders to capitalize on the momentum. "This is a defining moment for Democrats and our careers," he said. "There has never been a better time to do what the American people have been waiting for for forty or fifty years. I will not allow it to sink. I will spend capital to get over the hump." Passing health care would establish the trustworthiness of the Democrats to govern. "If we fail, there will be skepticism about the Democratic Party's ability to get anything done," he warned. "We need to keep our foot on the pedal and get the best possible bills off the floors and into conference."[27] Pelosi agreed. "You have to strike when you have the votes. Washington is a city of the perishable."

Reid immediately threw cold water on the effervescent mood. "We're not ready to go to the floor," he insisted. Merging the Finance and HELP versions "is a bitch," the normally reserved Reid declared, despite the welcome collegiality of chairs Dodd (who was standing in for Kennedy) and Baucus, who promised, "We will differ among ourselves but never in public." "It is," Reid declared, "the most difficult legislation I ever have dealt with." Optimistically, Obama thought, some Republicans on the Finance Committee were "quite promising." He had spoken again with Grassley and Snowe, and Dodd was convinced Mike Enzi (WY) "wants to get this done." In the House, there was no hope for cooperation. "The other side is raising opposition and sowing confusion," the president warned, but Miller dismissed the Republican naysayers. "Nobody knows who Eric Cantor or Mike Pence are," he assured. Instead of seeking collaboration, he promised to "step on their necks!"[28]

Obama promised not to endorse one house's version over the other. "I don't want the House griping that the Senate version is not strong enough so nothing gets done," Obama counseled. "In conference, we will have to knock heads. But I don't want an ideological purity test to keep us from getting a bill off floor and to conference." But Obama's pledge of neutrality was questioned when House members learned that White House and Senate members had met with powerful health industry leaders. Pelosi reproached Emanuel for excluding her chairs, particularly Rangel, an unwise decision given the staffer's rocky relationship with the CBC. Emanuel rejected the criticism, professing his deep understanding of how Congress functioned. "I lived my life around this table" in the Speaker's conference room, he indignantly asserted. "No, Rahm," she scolded, "you were here for just six years."[29]

The many complaints of the conservative Blue Dogs presented a challenge to meeting Pelosi's tight schedule, especially in the Commerce Committee, where seven of them held the balance of power. Complaining their demands had been "ignored in the drafts" prepared by Waxman, Mike Ross (AR) insisted the chair accept "a dozen or two dozen changes."[30] Otherwise, he might enlist Republicans to pass them. Ross was also souring on the public option and the requirement that small businesses cover their employees.

Underlying the Blue Dog angst was more than the health care bill. They felt aggrieved by the pressure to support an urgent agenda driven almost exclusively by the liberal base of the party, which was indifferent to the complexities of their swing districts. "Multiple bailouts, cap and trade," Cardoza recited. "Now, health is the final nail in the coffin" of the frontline members. "It can push us over the edge." Baron Hill admitted to being "a little nervous about a new bill," especially after supporting the energy measure.[31] "Cap and trade poisoned the well," agreed Tanner, as some had feared might be the case. A vote on health care before the August recess, he warned, would be "fatal" for Blue Dogs.[32]

"That was an emotional, meaningful meeting," Rangel told Pelosi after the Blue Dogs had vented for several hours. "You can see how shallow other people can be." Ross insisted that no vote be scheduled until two-thirds of the Blue

Dogs were supportive, but Pelosi believed "they are overplaying their hands. They like to show off in front of each other." On Ways and Means, Rangel grew impatient. "The boat is leaving the dock," he said, and the members would have to decide if they were on board or not. Too many still were not; several days later, with eight moderate Democrats on Commerce opposed, the decision was made to delay committee action.[33]

The committees did not represent the only dangers to the bill, of course. Whenever the bill finally came before the House, there were certain to be "floor hijinks" by Republicans aimed at delaying consideration. In a private discussion, Boehner offered to discourage the mischief if Pelosi would agree to more open rules that allowed Republican amendments during floor debates. Pelosi wasn't inclined to empower Republicans who had opposed TARP, climate change, and the stimulus. "Your tactics are designed to prevent the passage of health care," she reprimanded Boehner.[34] Republicans could offer amendments during committee deliberations, but the floor was a different matter.

The certainty of Republican opposition meant that Democrats would have to stick together on both procedural (the previous question, the rule) and substantive votes like the motion to recommit. Hoyer sent a clear message that loyalty was expected regardless of electoral vulnerability because Republicans were "not interested in participating."[35] Securing unity remained a problem in the Senate as well. Democrats were divided on a host of issues—"regional disparities" of medical payments, taxing the Cadillac plans, and a number of prospective payfors. The Democrats on Finance, Reid seethed, were "a bunch of spineless cowards," but he believed that "unless things go crazy," the committee would clear the bill in August. "We have to do it now or never," he insisted. "We might need to stay an extra week, but right now, I feel energized!"

The top Democrats who gathered in the Oval Office on July 13 recognized that the political calendar presented a grim reality.[36] Democrats were facing a challenging environment in 2010, a midterm election with the deficit soaring and unemployment nearing 10 percent. "If we can't deliver on health care, and unemployment is high, the [congressional] re-elect is very, very difficult," Obama unnecessarily observed. "I'll be weakened, and the rest of my agenda will be threatened. The Democratic brand will take a permanent hit." He would "take a deal: one term as president, if we could get health care," he insisted.

It was essential, he insisted, that the leaders "get it done" by August; "no running for cover, no more not taking risks." When George W. Bush was declared victorious in 2000 after winning a disputed victory by 537 votes in Florida, "he walked in like he owned the place," Obama recalled. "We have the biggest majority" in decades, and there could be no rationalizing inaction. The House needed to act despite its "historic distrust" of the Senate. The president insisted he had been "very respectful of the process" in the Senate Finance Committee, but now it was time to "think long-term and take risks, Harry," he told Reid, "you've got to get a schedule. If I need to come over, tell me." Reid pushed back. "I'm just trying to get to conference," he wearily explained.[37]

If success required concessions to conservatives, Obama said, then so be it. His words were "music to my ears," Pelosi declared, expressing confidence she and Reid "can work out our differences." She was worried, however, about leaving a House bill "hanging out there" during the long August recess if the Senate remained deadlocked, which seemed certain. "The ball is in Max's court," Reid asserted, but Baucus wanted to keep talking with the Republicans through the summer. Obama looked sternly at Baucus. If Snowe and Grassley delivered the crucial votes, he would campaign for their reelection, but there could be no lengthy delay chasing their support. "Max, this must be done next week," he insisted. "If things get broken down, our chances decrease."

The president was also focused on conservative resistance in the House. "Don't let the Blue Dogs who didn't vote for energy" get away, he instructed Hoyer. "They have no excuse not to support health care." The major complaint of the Blue Dogs, Hoyer explained, was "voting for things that then don't get done" by the Senate. "The Blue Dogs are just trying to help their own constituents," Pelosi interjected, defending her members. She was willing to make changes to help them, even modifications to the public option.[38]

Obama scheduled individual meetings with Blue Dogs, pointedly reminding Tanner, "You promised you'd be with me on health." To demonstrate the benefits outweighed any hardships in the swing districts, Waxman produced reports demonstrating the local benefits for each Blue Dog. In Mike Ross's Arkansas constituency, 124,000 uninsured residents and 12,500 small businesses would receive premium support under the bill. Hospitals would save $155 million in uncompensated care costs and only 1,064 people out of more than 750,000 would face a tax on their Cadillac insurance plan. Even with this information, however, the committee's Blue Dogs remained "dug in," waiting to see what the Senate produced.

As the August recess neared, Pelosi grew anxious about the "Republican grassfire" growing throughout the country. "It is very different from what we've seen," she told Obama. "They are against government. They carpet-bombed the Capitol on energy to influence our members on health." It reminded her of a Chinese expression: "You shoot the chickens to scare the monkeys." She was concerned whether the members could stand up to the mounting resistance. "There's so much chickenheartedness in this institution," she lamented.[39]

Obama challenged the Speaker's grim outlook. "Maybe you don't read the polls," he told Pelosi. "The Republicans have never been lower," he insisted. The "slash and burn" opposition could not be allowed to prevail. "This is why we got into politics!" predicting, "We will kick the other guy's ass." Pelosi agreed the key was to "stay together" as a party, and back on Capitol Hill, she declared there was no turning back. "If we pass health care," Pelosi insisted, "the Republicans are dead!"[40]

The tensions were not alleviated by the president's confidential outlook. "They might want to build their own virtual fence down the middle of the rotunda," the *New York Times* reported, noting the edginess between the House and Senate.[41] Nor did the presidential pep talk relieve the anxiety of some of his advisors, who increasingly questioned if a comprehensive bill could maneuver its way through the legislative thicket. Fearing the entire effort might collapse, Emanuel quietly began to float a stripped-down bill containing a short list of popular health policy provisions—preexisting conditions, children covered to age twenty-six, preventive care—but deferring the revenue portion.[42] Critics dismissed it as the "Titanic plan," saving women and children first.

Forward progress arrived in mid-July as Education and Labor and Ways and Means passed their bills with nearly unanimous Democratic support.[43] But in the Senate, Baucus balked, blaming the refusal of the Congressional Budget Office (CBO) to ascribe saving to the bill's preventive care provisions that undercut the ability to "bend the cost curve" on health inflation. The savings shortfall put pressure on Baucus's Finance Committee to find other ways to pay for the bill since conservative Democrats would refuse to support any measure that created deficits. Reid was furious. "CBO is the devil in all this," he fumed, and the administration agreed. CBO's obstinacy was "hurting us," Obama said, and Axelrod assured him that "no one is more pissed off" than the administration.[44]

Baucus urged the president to pressure CBO's director, Doug Elmendorf, to change his position on the savings, but OMB's Orszag (himself a former CBO director) warned such intervention "would be very counterproductive."[45] But Pelosi rejected that advice, arguing that failure to intervene meant "the White House is reinforcing Elmendorf's message" and complicating her efforts to win conservative votes. "Unless Elmendorf is turned around, the bill won't pass, and Obama won't sign it," Hoyer warned. "And if the bill doesn't bend the cost curve, *I* won't be for it!" The Speaker declared she was prepared to "proclaim billions in savings" but understood the conservatives would not take her word for it. In

fact, Cardoza warned, the Blue Dogs would insist on even *more* cost containment. "Don't say that publicly!" she sharply warned.[46]

Reid endorsed Pelosi's aggressive schedule. "Declare victory!" he advised,
pledging that Finance would also move a bill before August. That timetable
pleased Obama. "If you had told me a year ago, we'd have three committees,
the AMA, the hospitals, AARP, the nurses, and PhRMA all on board," no one
would have believed it possible, he remarked. And he still believed he would secure Republican support. "Snowe is the most responsible" Republican, Reid declared. "She told me, 'You will get a bill, and I'll help you.'" Obama agreed Snowe
was "a class act, willing to break with her party," but he held little hope for other
Republicans who were "unrelenting and terrible."[47] That meant Reid would need
unanimous Democratic support to move his bill, and that could be a problem.
"Byrd can come and vote," he predicted, but Kennedy's "days are numbered."

Pelosi watched the Senate schedule slip with trepidation. "They have nothing," the Speaker concluded. "There is no guarantee the Senate *ever* does the
bill." The "dog month" of August, when the House would be in recess, would
present "an opportunity for virtual carpet-bombing" by opponents. If she could
"see some pulse of life" in the Senate, she would delay the recess and move ahead
on the floor, even without the Commerce component.[48] But the Senate remained
paralyzed, and she hesitated before committing her members to floor votes. "I'm
no fool," she informed Emanuel. "I am not going to act till I see the whites of
their eyes, but it's more likely I'll see the back of their butts" as they scurried
away. Emanuel smiled; perhaps his famously crass vocabulary was "rubbing off"
on the Speaker, he suggested, but Pelosi wasn't in a wisecracking mood. "This
is going to happen," she told Emanuel, "but the Senate makes it so difficult."[49]
Where was the "ground cover from the White House" she had been promised?
"Where are the signs of life?" She needed presidential engagement to stiffen the
backs of her wavering colleagues. "I love my members," she told Obama, "but
courage is not universally distributed among them," prompting a laugh from
the president.[50]

In hopes of getting Commerce's version to move before the recess, I suggested gathering them with Waxman and the leadership, "and don't let anyone
leave until they reach an agreement." Pelosi favored a smaller group composed
of Emanuel, Hoyer, Blue Dogs, and herself. "That will be a long discussion,"
an irritated Emanuel complained. "It has to be done," Pelosi responded. "I'm
very disappointed the Blue Dogs are not offering solutions." She knew she
would be criticized for bullying the members, but she was resolved. "I don't like

tyranny," Pelosi said, "but I also don't like the risk of waiting." When Waxman hinted he might be willing to delay committee action and continue to negotiate over the break, the Speaker disagreed. "You know what happens, don't you?" if she overruled him. "*Henry* comes off popular and *I* come off as a B-I-T-C-H," she declared, discreetly spelling out the profanity. "That sounds about right," I agreed.[51]

She feared the Blue Dogs were engaged in deception and delay. Running into Ross at a restaurant, she asked, "How are we doing?" His answer was an evasive "Love you!" Pelosi brushed off the pleasantry. "That's not the question!" Emanuel also was working on Ross, puffing up his ego by pointing out concessions made to the Blue Dogs. "A leader knows when they've won," he declared, inviting the congressman to the White House to meet with the president. "*You* won! You've changed the content and character of the legislation." Pelosi was less forgiving of the power play. "The members think we're idiots!" Pelosi fretted. "But I will not let this bill fail because a couple of Blue Dogs can't be peeled off." Perhaps some of them could be persuaded to vote for the bill in Committee but then oppose passage on the floor where she would have votes to spare.

"Tell the president it will happen one way or another," she advised Emanuel. But not before the break. Using the House rules, the Blue Dog strategy had ensured a delay in floor action until September, and proponents were increasingly angry by the conservatives' power play.[52] "Feelings are running raw about seven or eight people denying the House the possibility" of passing legislation that would aid millions of minority Americans, declared an angry Clyburn. "Everyone's frustrated with the Blue Dogs," Hoyer admitted, despite his affinity for them. But there could be "terrible consequences if we push it" prematurely. After Blunt threatened to file seven thousand delaying amendments and some of the Dogs complained Waxman was taking "pot shots" at them, a July 28 markup was cancelled.

As plans were made to reschedule the Commerce markup, a new controversy emerged. A priest began a sit-in outside Pelosi's Cannon Building office protesting the potential coverage of abortion services in health plans subsidized by the bill, and Cardinal Francis George, president of the National Conference of Catholic Bishops, soon demanded a complete and specific ban be included in all policies covered by the bill. Although over a hundred religious leaders held a press conference in support of the bill, abortion suddenly loomed as a barrier to passage with pro-life supporters like Mike Doyle (PA) signaling they had a major problem. "We need an amendment like Hyde but not Hyde," said Pelosi, referring to the long-standing ban on federal funding of abortions. She could support including such a restriction in the bill's expansion of Medicaid, to which Hyde had applied since 1976, but extending it to subsidized private plans was a huge quandary.

Waxman was losing patience with the committee's Blue Dogs. The most conservative—Matheson, Melancon, and Barrow—were "worthless" and Space was "a crybaby," he complained. "I'm telling them, 'Either accept my offer, or give me a counteroffer,'" Waxman said, "but it must end."[53] The Speaker commiserated with the chair. "They are without ideas or imagination," she agreed. The Dogs' counteroffer included lower premium subsidies, state (but no national) exchanges to offer policies, and tighter eligibility for Medicaid. Some of their proposals would increase costs, but the group offered no suggestions for bending the cost curve. For good measure, Ross declared, the public option needed to go.[54] That demand crossed the Speaker's red line. "I respect what you've put on the table, but I do not respect a plan with no public option," she responded. "There will be no bill out of the House or out of conference without a public option."[55]

She advised Waxman to "pull the plug, just take the committee product and go." The delays were affording opponents time to spread a message of doom even in safe districts. Thanks to the negative ads, more than three-quarters of Americans were under the impression their health costs would rise under the proposed law, and even supporters were feeling constituent pressure. "I am getting my ass kicked!" complained Debbie Wasserman-Schultz (FL).[56]

Last-minute negotiations secured the votes of several of the Blue Dogs. They agreed to oppose Republican "poison pill" amendments, and Pelosi credited them publicly for raising "legitimate issues."[57] But the concessions left committee liberals enraged. "I won't vote for anything just to get movement," Jan Schakowsky (IL) bristled. To calm the waters, the Speaker arranged for calls from Obama and respected health experts.[58] "You cannot prevent it from going ahead," Emanuel told his fellow Illinoisan.

But the Senate remained stuck. Reid was promised a Finance markup early in August, but "I have been misled before," he noted, and soon, hopes for a markup or a bipartisan alliance were fraying.[59] Snowe declared her opposition to mandated employer coverage and the public option, and other Republicans were being "beat up" by their colleagues.[60] "You won't like what the Senate passes," Reid warned Pelosi. He also cautioned the Republicans that if their demands were excessive, he would bypass them and pass whatever fit into a reconciliation alternative.[61] That would be "a lost opportunity," Grassley warned, as would offering a "partisan House bill that could not pass the Senate." A glum Reid called Pelosi to give her the bad news. "No markup," he said, "no nothing," not just on health, but on cap and trade and other House bills as well.[62]

Despite that grim report, on July 31 Commerce became the third House committee to approve its component of the America's Affordable Health Choices Act by a 31–28 vote. It was "an historic moment for the House of Representatives and a defining moment for our country," a relieved Waxman proclaimed. Now the three bills could be blended into a unified measure the House would consider in September. But first, House members would face a harrowing August at the hands of a new and vitriolic grassroots conservative movement.

CHAPTER 18

THE SUMMER OF HATE

"Happy birthday, Mr. President!" Pelosi cheerfully said in a call to Obama. "Everyone in my town halls thanks you for being born!" "In Hawaii!" the president joked, mocking critics who insisted he had been born in Kenya. "What's your birthday wish?" the Speaker asked. "Get health care passed," Obama answered without a pause. He had already received one early present. "The House Committees did an unbelievable job," he told her, "and I'm very grateful."

In their districts, however, many members were finding some constituents less appreciative. Ignited by the TARP vote, fanned by the recession, heavy government spending, deficits, the stimulus, and health legislation, and stoked by conservative media misrepresentations and internet hyperbole, a roiling anger had been building. "We knew disruptions were going to happen," Pelosi accepted, but the ferocity was unanticipated.

Angry conservative activists were being bused into public events to challenge Democratic members.[1] Hoyer reported "guerrilla efforts" to shout down speakers who were "afraid of the facts." In the Long Island district of front liner Tim Bishop, opinion against the health care legislation was running five to one. In Colorado and Texas, protestors displayed swastikas; town hall meetings in Lloyd Doggett's district were disrupted by "lunatics."[2] From his very imperiled central Virginia district, freshman Tom Perriello described a brutal five-and-a-half-hour meeting, but he triumphantly insisted, "I am outlasting the critics!" In California's Central Valley, Cardoza reported that "both the left and right are unhappy." In "open carry" states, enraged protestors appeared at public events carrying firearms. "The opposition is vicious," Pelosi conceded. "It frightens people."[3]

Many demonstrators identified themselves as belonging to the nascent Tea Party movement, which had originally burgeoned after discussion of a congressional pay raise. As August wore on, Tea Party disrupters continued to infiltrate events fueled by a memo instructing them to "watch for an opportunity to yell out and challenge the Rep's statements early. The goal is to rattle him."[4] The protestors carried racist placards including, "The Zoo Has an African Lion and the White House Has a Lyin' African!"[5] The movement's leaders included former House majority leader Dick Armey, who once described Medicare as "tyranny . . . a hostile government takeover of all health care."[6] Supporters of the health bill urged wavering members to hold firm. "All the noise is just designed to obscure the facts," Miller confidently reported. "When people hear what's in the bill, they like it."[7] In addition to explaining the bill's details, members shared tricks for calming the angry crowds. Doggett opened each meeting with the national anthem and then received positive responses when he denounced insurance companies.

Members were urged to consider teleconferencing with constituents so as not to create an informational vacuum that would allow the misinformation to metastasize. The Pelosi war room circulated a daily "Mythbuster" broadside to help deflect Republican distortions. Labor organizer Bob Creamer (who was married to Rep. Jan Schakowsky) suggested busing bill supporters into public meetings, although Becerra urged caution. "Don't play on the loonies' turf!" he warned. But the pushback was no match for the well-financed onslaught, and as the recess dragged along, the disruptions caused nerves to fray, and an increase in threats led to a ramp-up in the Speaker's security detail. Pelosi seemed ready for a confrontation. "The tactics need to be addressed head-on," she declared, calling on Obama to "take the gloves off!"[8]

The president was still hoping for a bipartisan bill, but Enzi and Grassley seemed improbable, according to Schiliro, while Snowe was "more reliable."[9] Reid still hoped for a Senate agreement in principle by mid-September, a quick markup in Finance, and floor action. He pledged the Republicans would not obstruct that timetable, which Pelosi welcomed because she believed Senate procrastination had enabled the opposition to flourish. Finally, Baucus declared he would move forward without help from Enzi and Grassley, and Reid promised to take the unusual step of appointing Republican conferees if McConnell refused to name them.

"I think we're in a pretty good place," Obama told the Speaker, adding, "but don't say that publicly!"[10] But Pelosi wanted not only a commitment to move a Senate vehicle but also one that included the public option, which enjoyed a 62 percent approval favorable rating" in a recent poll. There would be "a price to be paid" if he abandoned his support, she warned Obama. "You've mentioned that six times," he impatiently reminded her. "I'm not the sharpest pencil in the box, but I got it!"[11]

The August assault also heightened the importance of an aggressive and well-funded messaging strategy to promote the bill. HCAN, the pro–health care messaging group, held a conference call with a thousand health groups to plan rallies urging supporters to "show up and be bolder," but by mid-August, the number of public meetings had dwindled, especially among the vulnerable freshmen, in the face of withering assaults. The Speaker insisted the president instruct the Democratic National Committee, which had reportedly committed under $1 million for countering the Republican opposition, to underwrite the effort. "The other side is so desperate, and the truth is a casualty," she said quoting Aeschylus. For her part, Pelosi vowed to "beat back the rabble-rousers" on the left and right with their strongest weapon. "You are the best messenger," she told the president. Obama was exuberant. "I can't wait to sign it," he exclaimed, but the Speaker remained wary. "Tell Phil [Schiliro] I am going to say I won't support a deal" that doesn't include a public option, she instructed me.

But even the liberal Dick Durbin was reportedly willing to abandon the public option, leading an angry Pelosi to suspect he was "pimping for the administration," which she suspected was willing to drop the provision to appease the Senate. She turned to Miller, a longtime roommate of the Senate whip. "Tell Durbin his comments are killing us with the grassroots!" she instructed. Durbin explained he wanted "just to get to conference" where the final bill would be crafted. "I'm planning on asking the president, 'How many conference committees have you been on?'" she sarcastically remarked.[12]

Efforts to calm the members were dealt a setback in mid-August. HHS secretary Sebelius and Senator Conrad appeared on the August 16 Sunday talk shows making remarks viewed as detrimental to the House's position. The public option was "not the essential element" of the health bill, according to Sebelius. Conrad went even further. "Look, there are not the votes in the United States Senate for the public option," he said. "There never have been. So, to continue to chase that rabbit, I think, is just a wasted effort."[13]

"No one thinks the secretary acted without instruction," presumably from the White House, the Speaker charged. During the campaign, one White House aide said, Obama was "backed into" supporting the provision, and he continued to believe "it is best for competition." But he had been hesitant to publicly embrace it for fear of provoking problems with the Senate. Now, he described it as "a means to an end, not an end itself." Health policy experts called it "a useful tool" but "not a signal element" in a reform bill.[14] "Everyone who writes on the subject"—he specifically mentioned Jacob Hacker, a progressive Yale economist—had concluded the public option was "no silver bullet" to control costs, and certainly it was not as crucial to expanding coverage as the premium subsidies.

"It's an important element, but I reject the argument that if there is no public option there's no health care reform," Obama insisted. "If we get 35 million additional people covered plus insurance reform, that's a big deal!" He understood "the progressives are angry that private insurance will survive" because they really wanted single-payer "and they're pissed that we aren't doing it. The public option is their substitute." But even without the public option, he reasoned, "we will have done a lot." He did not view his position as "selling out," and he pledged to work with the House Democrats." "I understand the emotions and the politics," he assured, "and you'll be heard. This isn't going to be a giveaway to the insurance companies."[15]

Pelosi's response was measured. "I don't want to be in a fight with the White House," she assured, but her members believed "we cannot have the bill without a public option."[16] If anyone, including Obama, had a "superior plan that cut costs, improved quality and expanded coverage," she declared, she was open to discussing it. Otherwise, "We are not giving up on the public option."

The effect of the president's declarations on the House caucus was stunning. "I'm a dead man walking," Steve Kagen (CO), a second-term physician, declared. Barbara Lee, already of the opinion the House bill was too weak, was furious. In his increasingly competitive Wisconsin district, Dave Obey reported, "We're getting killed by right-wing tactics and by the base on Sebelius's comments [because] our people think they're willing to drop the public option." Jerry Nadler (NY) was more blunt, declaring that "the White House was preparing to sell us out."

Pelosi tried to staunch the bleeding. "The White House position isn't changing," she dubiously assured her colleagues. The administration was trying not to lock Obama into a position that might be rejected by a bipartisan mix of senators. The president reached out as well. "I don't want to spook things," Obama told Schakowsky, assuring her he wasn't abandoning "a robust" public option. "There's plenty of room for fine tuning, so let's just get it done."[17]

Obama refocused the heat on Baucus, who still refused to schedule Finance Committee action. After September 15, the president said, the option for a committee markup was "dead," and he would embrace a scaled-back reconciliation bill. That approach might be needed anyway, admitted one White House source who could only find fifty-eight senators committed to supporting the comprehensive bill. To make matters worse, Conrad reportedly was predicting the Senate bill would specifically *prohibit* a public option.[18]

That was all Pelosi needed to hear. "The bill is not going to pass the House without a public option," she reasserted. While Sebelius's statement was "causing quite a stir," the Speaker aimed her more pointed criticism at the Senate. "If you throw a punch," she declared, "you have to take a punch," and she was preparing to throw a roundhouse at Conrad over his insistence that the public option be replaced with state-approved cooperatives. "They aren't worth a damn!" Dingell declared, and Obama agreed that "co-ops are bogus."[19]

By late August, the Senate seemed hopelessly deadlocked on a big bill, and Myrick was skeptical how much real reform could be shoehorned into a reconciliation bill. "We might be better to have half a loaf" in a standard bill "than use reconciliation" whose provisions could expire in a decade, he suggested.[20] Reid's growing frustration spilled out in a conversation with Pelosi. "Let the Republicans and the cowardly Democrats kill the public option and the employer mandate," he said dejectedly. "I can't get health care done with fifty-nine Democrats," Reid told the Speaker, since Kennedy remained in Massachusetts. It was time "to belly up to the bar," he declared. If Baucus could not produce a bill, a truncated initiative offering a Medicare buy-in for children, a wellness and prevention initiative, and other low-hanging fruit might be the best the Senate could pass.[21]

For House members "rolled repeatedly" by the Senate's sixty-vote requirement, such a prediction was disheartening. "I tell the members that the legislative process will bring us together" on a final product, the Speaker said, but now that seemed doubtful.[22] Obama offered to speak to a House caucus meeting to bolster the members' sagging mood. "Any bill we do will be 90 percent what [progressives] want," he said, challenging the argument that success would be measured solely by whether it included the public option. "If the public option is the only thing we're [still] debating," an exaggeration of the ongoing debate, "it can't be that we've dismissed their views" on other subjects. "But they can't tie my hands," he implored. "We can't win the ideological battle but lose the war."

With the Senate months behind schedule, Kennedy near death, the sixty-vote margin at risk, and the country erupting in angry protest, Obama had his rationalization for abandoning whatever commitment he had ever felt to the public option. The disagreement on the issue between the House and the Senate highlights the structural distinctions between the two houses: activist interests could propel a policy idea in House districts with greater fervency, whereas the nature of state representation and longer terms often took the edge off novel policy ideas in the Senate. In a remarkably short time, the public option had become a progressive talisman in the House, while in the Senate and White House, it was just one option for achieving cost controls. Obama's willingness to back away from the public option often has been confused as a willingness to abandon a broad, comprehensive health care bill in favor of the kind of limited approach Emanuel and others were promoting, but in fact, Obama remained committed to a big bill outside the reconciliation limitations.

The pragmatic Speaker understood the antiseptic analysis that she would have to sell to her members. "This is a 'come to Jesus' moment," she proclaimed.[23] The likelihood of House members securing the design of the bill they wanted was slim. "Even if we do reconciliation, we can only get half the bill," she reasoned. "We still need a separate bill that will require sixty votes," and that meant making concessions to get people like Ben Nelson and perhaps even Olympia Snowe. "Don't lose sight of that." A few days later, the president declared that his primary focus remained controlling costs and ensuring competition; *how* that goal was achieved remained an open question. "I've told the president we can't pass a bill without the public option," Pelosi reassured, but she fudged on Obama's commitment. "The president has said the public option is the best way to keep the insurance industry honest, to increase choice, and to decrease cost," the triumvirate of goals they all had sworn to embrace. "If someone has a better idea how to do that, we will listen," she assured, "but they haven't come up with one" that would cover as many people.

"We will be where we are, for better or worse," Pelosi philosophically said a week later. The members would return with "questions and opinions" fashioned by their harrowing experiences over the break, and the chairmen would "debunk the falsehoods" circulated by the bill's critics. Dingell urged his colleagues not to be discouraged and to stay focused on the larger goal. "Don't let the Republican bastards deter us!" he insisted.[24]

But the summer of hate had a devastating impact, even on bill supporters. Louise Slaughter reported that the mood in her upstate New York district was terrible. "I am not sure I can get reelected" after supporting the bill, "but I'll vote for it." In San Diego, Susan Davis reported, "I'm getting battered!" Even if they managed to pass a bill, much of it would not go into effect before 2013 for planning and budgetary reasons, which meant House members would head into the election without much to show for the health care battle. "Land mines could go off before [the] November" mid-terms, Miller cautioned.[25]

The summer's tumult had also impacted the Senate. Even if Reid managed to bypass a filibuster and take a bill to the floor, Emanuel feared, it likely would be "gerrywritten to put the president on the spot," loaded up with special-interest provisions demanded by senators, creating an unworkable system Obama would fund difficult to reject.[26] The president wanted "a fallback" to be developed along the lines of the earlier "Titanic plan": coverage of children to age twenty-six, major insurance reforms (but not preexisting conditions protections), and closing the co-pay "donut hole" created by Bush's prescription drug law. All the remaining issues could be offered as floor amendments, and the chips would fall as they may. He was optimistic such a limited package could pass the Senate, but I warned that, in the Speaker's mind, universal coverage and the preexisting protection were "the key to the success of the legislation."

"We can't do universal!" he declared, blaming the cloture threshold. The health care battle was "fucking shit," he exploded, and he wanted to be rid of it before it dragged down the president and his administration.[27]

And then, the bottom fell out. Pelosi had held out hope for a miracle to save Kennedy. "I believe in the power of prayer," she explained, but two weeks later, he was gone and the sixty-vote Senate margin was at risk.[28] Democratic governor Deval Patrick would appoint a replacement until a special election in January, but the roiling political environment left uncertain the outcome even in reliably Democratic Massachusetts. Kennedy's vacant seat in the Senate chamber, which he had occupied for forty-eight years, was a stark reminder that in Washington, power was, in Pelosi's words, "perishable." Resolving the impasse on health was now an imperative with a deadline.

CHAPTER 19

"THE MOST IMPORTANT BILL YOU WILL EVER VOTE FOR"

"I'm back for the Second American Revolution," a participant in a Tea Party rally in Kentucky declared. "My weapons this time will be the Constitution, the Internet, and my talk-radio ads."[1] If Democrats were going to outrun that conservative juggernaut and enact health care reform, they had to act swiftly: with the interim appointment of Paul Kirk to fill Kennedy's Senate seat, they were assured a supermajority for only a few months.[2]

Even in the House, however, forward progress faced a formidable obstacle as the abortion controversy gained intensity.[3] Without a strict ban, there were enough pro-life Democrats to doom the legislation; with such a prohibition, pro-choice members would not vote for the bill. The passions dividing the caucus were highlighted when the volatile chair of the Health subcommittee, Pete Stark, dismissed the anti-abortion faction as "brain dead."

Back in Washington after Labor Day, the top Democratic leaders huddled in the Oval Office with Obama, who refused to believe the public would reject the Democratic agenda. "The Republicans are despised," he insisted. "They have nothing to offer." But Pelosi grimly recounted the summer assault against her troops. "They threw the worst at us," Pelosi reported. "And you're still standing!" the president crowed.

The contentious summer had done nothing to diminish Pelosi's ardor for the legislation or for the public option. In fact, abandoning the option would be "a big victory for the insurance industry," which she denounced as "immoral." A Blue Cross executive from California registered his displeasure, but Pelosi defiantly responded, "I stand by my remarks." Others shared her ardor for the option. "It's the only thing to keep the thieving insurance companies honest!" Dingell declared. "They would steal the pennies off a dead man's eyes." But the caucus dissenters remained unconvinced. "I understand you have to run with it," Ross recognized, and some Blue Dogs would support the bill anyway, he noted. "But not me."[4]

The members returned "cold blooded" from the "firestorm," ready for the confrontation. "The best preparation for combat," the Speaker declared, "is combat." Others sought to calm nervousness in the caucus. "The loudest voices at the town halls are not representative" of the broader public, Van Hollen insisted. Miller also favored pressing ahead. "Don't let factions in the caucus make threats," he told her. "If we back down now, every issue will be met with right-wing protests."[5]

They had arrived, she declared, at the "moment of truth," but she was not feeling especially optimistic. She could only find 210 votes for the public option. "If we can't get 218, we have to make an evaluation," she told Hoyer.[6] She knew Obama was not wedded to the provision. He recently had remarked he could live with several versions of the bill that were circulating.

Without "a sliver of hope" of finding GOP support, Emanuel noted, they had to remove all Democratic resistance in the Senate. "We can't continue to dance with Baucus," Emanuel complained. For Reid, the process was becoming interminable. "I've had this conversation before," he told the president. "I hear you, brother," Obama told a disconsolate Reid. "We need to lay the wood to Max daily and tell him 'we will go without you.'" The president believed he had "lit a fire" under Baucus, but Reid countered, "It isn't very hot."[7]

Indeed, Baucus's delays left Reid increasingly thinking he would have no choice but to cobble together a reconciliation measure that would be constrained by "the damn Byrd rule," he fumed. But he was also frustrated at the tepid efforts by the president. "I won't take blows from the White House when they're doing nothing!" he vowed.[8] "They want their fingerprints on nothing." If the Senate stalled, Reid said, "I want the White House to say it was not our fault." Pelosi refused to consider the possibility of failure. "We *must* have [a] major bill," she demanded, even if Reid only sent "a weak bill" to the conference committee. "If we fold under lies, we are doomed."[9]

The third option was Emanuel's "Titanic" alternative, which achieved modest goals but would allow Congress to double back for more. In an Oval Office meeting, one by one, the staff enumerated the numerous roadblocks. "I begged [the president] not to do" the comprehensive bill, Emanuel admitted, and others shared his pessimism.[10] Finally, Obama turned to his congressional liaison. "Well, Mr. President," Schiliro responded, "do you remember Clint Eastwood's line in *Dirty Harry?*" Quizzical looks flew around the room, but Obama was willing to play along. "No, what did he say?" the president asked. "He asked, 'Do I feel lucky?' Well, Mr. President, do *you* feel lucky?" Obama was thoughtful for a moment. "Phil, my name is Barack Hussein Obama," he declared. "I am president of the United States. I am in the Oval Office. I feel lucky *every* day."[11] There would be no truncated bill, the president declared. "This is about whether we're going to get big things done."[12]

I had told Emanuel the Speaker would reject the limited approach he described to me. "If you repeat this idea to anyone," he threatened, "I will never speak to you again." Soon afterwards, we were seated next to each other on a sofa in the Oval Office. "There is concern that some in the White House are encouraging you to take a namby-pamby approach," Pelosi told Obama. Emanuel pivoted to glower at me. We stared at each other for several seconds. "Thanks, John!" he mouthed silently, and I silently (and truthfully) replied, "Not me!"[13]

"Forget the din of the naysayers!" Pelosi told the president. "Your making the bill a priority gives people hope." "What's the best way to go?" Obama asked the Speaker. "Rahm says we only get one bite at the apple, so we need to get to the bottom line." "I can't begin to say how boring it is to say we should do a small bill," she advised. "Let's go for the bill we *need* to do!"[14]

Although Obama pressed to see where she could give on several points, Pelosi was already near her bottom line. "Our bill is nearly perfect," she proclaimed. Obama wasn't so sure. "We need to deal with the Senate politics," he advised. "We don't want to end up with the worst of both worlds [where] you won't be able to pass either version in the other chamber."[15] It was a prescient prediction that would hang over the negotiations for months.

Pelosi urged him to maintain his neutrality. "We'll pass the public option," she noted, "and then we'll go to conference" where other approaches could be considered. That was the preferred course, he agreed, even if it involved "a shitty Senate bill."[16] He also preferred to avoid using reconciliation, which empowered the tightfisted Conrad. "If Levin or Dodd were Budget chair, there would be different situation," he predicted. "But I have to accommodate Conrad." He floated a new idea—breaking the bill into smaller pieces—but Pelosi waved it off. "That approach would not be reconcilable with why you came to office," she replied. "People want something to believe in, something that gives hope, something *different*." Besides, sequential bills would provide multiple opportunities for Senate filibusters.

The Speaker urged him to take the case for a comprehensive bill to the American people before a joint session of Congress. The president quickly agreed, hoping the national address would "stop the feeding frenzy."[17] He received a warm welcome as he arrived in the crowded House chamber on September 9. "They're so excited to see you!" Pelosi excitedly told him on the podium.

"I am not the first president to take up this cause," Obama declared in a carefully scripted line, "but I am determined to be the last." He outlined the core provisions of the bill, repeating the promise that "nothing in our plan requires you to change what [coverage] you have." The misrepresentation would haunt him; the independent PolitiFact labeled the assertion "the lie of the year."[18]

But others were also exaggerating the impact of the bill, and he urged Republicans to stop "making wild claims about a government takeover of health care." Again, he offered to work collaboratively "to address any legitimate concerns," but his speech was rudely interrupted when he insisted that undocumented immigrants would be ineligible under his plan. "You lie!" called out backbencher Joe Wilson (R-SC). A ripple of disbelief swept across the chamber as Biden shook his head and an aghast Pelosi glared at Wilson. The interruption drew immediate bipartisan reproach, and Wilson issued an apology (but also raised substantial contributions in the next few days). Clyburn likened Wilson's unprecedented rudeness to a Black president to "the type of behavior we saw in August," while several others expressed outrage at the "increased racism directed toward the president."[19]

But the speech also raised concerns among Democrats by imposing a cap on the cost. "Whoever advised $900 billion has no idea how to pass a bill," the Speaker told a meeting of White House and Senate negotiators, and she thought she knew. "Maybe you just want to kiss Max Baucus's butt for another month?"[20] The Senate mood was similarly bleak. "Some people are saying this is a disaster and they can't vote for it," Myrick reported. Three days later, thousands of conservative demonstrators flooded onto Capitol Hill to denounce the bill and Obama. Standing on the Capitol's second-floor balcony facing Independence Avenue, looking out to the throng that spilled onto the street, Republican members whipped up the crowd, which responded with vitriolic and often obscene chants. Signs proclaimed "Bury Obama Care with Kennedy," portrayed the president with a Hitler mustache, and denounced the bill as "socialism."

Schiliro assured her Obama would continue to pressure the Senate, although there were a number of Democrats who preferred to stop the entire process. "Don't set us up to pass something nobody wants," Pelosi said defiantly, threatening to "walk away from discussions with you and just pass our own bill." She recalled Obama's touching eulogy at Kennedy's funeral, recounting the senator's exhorting his twelve-year-old son not to give up after losing a leg to cancer. "That's not consistent with us all waiting around for Baucus," she declared. "Every time you hesitate, you lose."

The administration's goal, Schiliro explained, "was to help by creating a balance between the House and Senate," but that only reignited the Speaker's worst fear. "Just because the Senate agonizes is not enough," she explained. She was tired of the Senate and Obama throwing out "surprises" without any consultation. "Any other cow patty in your pocket?" Speaking to Reid, she advised, "You can't have a weak bill," she instructed; the beleaguered Senate leader estimated his best odds of passing any bill were 50–50.[21]

"I'm not spending any more time with the White House people" who treated the House like "imbeciles!" Pelosi told her leadership. There would be no further meetings with presidential staff, she vowed, because they had been deceiving her members while "going down a different path" with the Senate. "I'm just setting out our negotiating position," she assured. "But the package is not worth a damn without the public option."[22]

In late September, the battle was finally joined. "We could go on for the rest of our lives contemplating our navels," the Speaker said. Instead, she outlined a "three-pronged approach" to "get the bill done, explain what is in it, and get the votes internally." She remained confident the "people are eager for the bill," but Hoyer was wary. "Their people are angrier" than Democrats were excited, he warned.[23]

And some Democrats were not all that excited, especially Blue Dogs who complained they had not received sufficient concessions even though every member was provided with a breakdown of savings and benefits that would accrue to his or her specific district from enactment of the legislation.[24] Stephanie Herseth-Sandlin (SD) warned that some of her colleagues were "backing away from the whole framework." Others insisted on larger benefits for their own districts while simultaneously complaining the price tag was too high. Pelosi noted the hypocrisy. "We don't want to look like a bloated House proposal, do we, Stephanie?" Pelosi asked, parroting the cost-consciousness the Blue Dogs frequently employed.[25]

Many of the Blue Dogs simply did not want to be characterized as "Nancy Pelosi's lapdog," Ross admitted. He also resented threats from progressive

groups that insinuated being a pharmacist implied deference to the pharmaceutical industry. "It makes it harder when some of the Democratic caucuses
threaten to run people against us" in primaries, he warned, but Pelosi dismissed
the accusations. The press "loves to get the liberals and the Blue Dogs at twenty
paces" to create fodder for their readers, she advised, but "it isn't relevant" to the
battle at hand.

The Blue Dogs made another run at deleting the public option, against the
advice of Hoyer, who urged them to "keep your powder dry." Only 39 percent
of his constituents supported it, Ross reported, but over 50 percent approved
of the bill if it was dropped. Pelosi again indicated flexibility on the issue. "The
public option was originally a way to keep the plan affordable," she reminded
the deficit-conscious members. Indeed, she had told the president "it must save
money or it isn't worth it."[26] But at the same time, the Blue Dogs needed to be
more sensitive to over two hundred of their colleagues who "want to know why
they can't get what *they* want," which also happened to be the most effective cost-
control measure and enjoyed a 60 percent approval rating. Even so, she assured,
"there's no decision yet on the public option."

For some liberals, coverage for undocumented immigrants remained a core
policy, but sympathetic colleagues argued the question was better suited to the
comprehensive immigration bill they hoped to pass.[27] A failure on health care
due to trying to cover the undocumented would weaken the Democrats enough
that immigration reform would almost certainly die as well. Were they willing to
forgo health insurance for their constituents because the votes did not exist for
undocumented people? "Coverage is more important than symbolism," Obama
advised. Besides, even if the House included undocumented immigrants, the
provision faced impossible odds in the Hispanic-light Senate, Obama insisted.
The president presented the challenge as simple math, but one member privately accused him of "pimping for the Senate."[28]

Indeed, many House members believed that despite pledges of neutrality,
the president had "embraced [the Senate bill] almost obscenely in the middle
of Pennsylvania Avenue," said the Speaker, adding drily, "Of course, *I* don't."[29]
Obama rejected the accusation, insisting he was just as exasperated as they were
by senators like Landrieu, who was "scared of her own shadow." But the bottom line was many House members were wary of putting their votes on the
line knowing the Senate was likely to include provisions they detested like the
Cadillac tax, an idea that "gives our members ants in their pants." Pelosi wanted
to see how key House provisions fared in the Senate. "I can't have my members
go out and vote and then the Senate and White House tinkle over it," she told

Trumka. As the onetime coal miner smiled, she added, "I suppose you said that differently in the mines."[30]

Finance finally acted in mid-October, passing (on a 14–9 bipartisan vote) an $829 billion bill that would leave 25 million Americans still without coverage a decade later.[31] Snowe provided the lone Republican vote but immediately qualified her position. "My vote today is my vote today," she warned. "It doesn't forecast what my vote will be tomorrow," particularly if the cost rose or a public option were added.[32] Even so, Obama praised her "political courage and the seriousness of purpose" in helping defeat a slew of Republican poison pill amendments.

The Senate resistance convinced the Speaker the public option was likely doomed. "At the end of the day, we are likely to get negotiated rates" instead, she conceded, even if that alternative saved less money.[33] It was important not to imbue the provision with mythical properties. "We have to remember," she said, "six months ago, no one had ever heard of the public option" or, as Schiliro suggested rebranding it, the "consumer alternative." Still, she was troubled by a bill that mandated individuals to buy insurance but gave them no option except to purchase it "from people who are messing them up!"[34]

But Obama and many legislators were tired—of the relentless negotiations, breakneck pace, and futile courting of Republicans. We're "in a cesspool," Reid told Pelosi. He encouraged the House to threaten his dissenters. "You could say, 'If the Senate screws around, we will use reconciliation,'" he suggested. "You could accuse the Senate of jerking the House around."[35]

"We feel no rush to come to the floor until we are ready," Pelosi said following the Finance vote. She had already devised her floor strategy: a simple up-or-down vote on the bill with Republicans permitted a substitute that would be vetted by Democrats to assure it contained no "gotcha" provisions. She rationalized the ban on amendments as the best way to insulate her members from having to vote on Republican amendments on abortion or other divisive issues.[36]

Whenever she faced a close floor vote, Pelosi would not rely solely on Clyburn's formal organization; she also reverted to her own vote-counting days in the whip's position. This time, it came up short: only 176 supporters, 42 fewer than needed. After months of discussion, the public option remained the volatile issue. "We're adding 35 million people with subsidized rates," Hoyer declared, "and we could lose the bill over one issue!"

With a close vote imminent, the legislative bazaar was open as members sought to bargain for their votes. Becerra publicly insisted on addressing "the existential issue" of undocumented immigrants, which the Speaker did not appreciate from a member of the leadership. "He threw us under the bus!" she complained. "I will have tire marks on me when I see my family." Privately, she huddled with the ambitious Congressional Hispanic Caucus member and caucus vice chair. "You're my future," she tantalizingly told him. "A lot of hopes are riding on you." If the CHC insisted on "mak[ing] this a big issue," she warned, it would likely "kill health care *and* immigration" by encouraging a Republican motion to recommit—which could not be blocked—on a tough anti-immigrant limitation that could bring down the entire bill. "And if we ain't got a bill, we ain't got nothin'," Pelosi advised. "Let's have no ultimatums."[37]

Other demands flooded in. Zack Space wanted language on diabetes; Dan Maffei (NY) hated the tax on medical devices, a major industry in his district; Debbie Wasserman-Schultz (FL) urged money targeted for breast cancer research; Danny Davis wanted a medical school in Chicago; Tim Ryan wanted a bankrupt Youngstown hospital to qualify for $4 million in higher reimbursements.[38] Not all the demands were related to health care policy. Altmire demanded a pledge of financial campaign support if challenged by a popular US attorney. Jim Costa (CA) and Cardoza wanted millions for irrigation projects, a divisive subject in California.[39] "Don't talk about water," Pelosi admonished. "I need to know you are with us." The best Cardoza would offer her was the ambiguous pledge, "I have never let you down."

Pulled in a dozen directions, the Speaker warned that if her fractious caucus did not unite behind the House product, she might "just take the Senate bill!"—the bill that incorporated little of their hard work. In fact, nothing was more anathema, but she was not above a little gamesmanship of her own. Other senior members also pressed the caucus to unify. "We paid a heavy price for the lack of consensus in the late eighties and nineties," Hoyer recalled.[40]

Jay Inslee (WA), who had lost his seat in the 1994 landslide, urged caucus attendees not to allow fear of electoral consequences to determine their vote. "I was the best damn first-term congressman you ever saw, but when they decided to throw out the Democrats in 1994, none of that mattered," he told his colleagues. "So, just do what you think is right, because if they want to throw you out, it won't matter how you voted." Inslee sat down to indifferent applause. "I've known you for nearly twenty years," I told him, "and that's the most intelligent thing I ever heard you say!" "Thanks!" he replied with his trademark grin.

Although Reid had promised Pelosi "there's not a chance in hell I do a bill without a public option," it became apparent the Senate votes were not there once Lieberman, the prickly independent, announced his unwavering opposition.[41] Many Progressive Caucus members privately admitted there would be no public option. "We only have the choices we have," she said, "and that's probably negotiated prices," as she had anticipated.[42] If the Left rejected that approach, she said with resignation, "then we don't have a bill."

"Let's give Harry a boost," Hoyer suggested, advising the progressives to forgo a fight they could not win, and that could imperil the Senate bill. "Their bill is a huge step forward," the Speaker uncharacteristically agreed. "Why create noise that obscures the many positive issues in the bill? Let's declare victory. We have won!" Pelosi advised the White House to ignore the requests from liberal caucuses demanding more meetings with the president. "Don't waste his time," Pelosi counseled. "The liberals are not operational."[43]

Abortion, not the public option, remained "our biggest issue," Pelosi contended as she canvassed her vast network of cardinals, archbishops, and nuns. "The Church is killing us."[44] One trusted advisor was Washington's former archbishop Theodore Cardinal McCarrick, a savvy political player she asked to speak with wavering Catholic colleagues.[45] Her conversations were less cordial with Cardinal George, whom she described as a "flamboyant nut" who threatened to excommunicate Sen. Bob Casey (PA) if he voted for the bill.[46]

Stupak proposed allowing pro-lifers to vote on an amendment imposing a strict ban on subsidizing abortions so they could double back and support the bill after it lost, but Pelosi rejected the strategy, hypothesizing the amendment could pass with a combination of Republican and pro-life Democrats. The bill would then be saddled with an amendment many liberals could not vote for, "and I couldn't blame them," Pelosi noted. Since Republicans would remain opposed even with the addition of the anti-abortion provision, the bill would fail.

At a meeting with pro-choice members and activists, the unpleasant options were hashed out for several hours. Finally, Pelosi offered her decision. She would not allow the ban the bishops were demanding to be offered, but neither could she guarantee the unfettered coverage the activists demanded. "In the end, this is not an abortion bill," she concluded. "This is a health bill, and I will not allow this issue to kill health care." Ultimately, a modified amendment by Stupak, Ellsworth, and Joe Pitts (R-PA) prohibiting the use of federal funds for abortion services in the public option or the exchanges was allowed in order to secure pro-life Democratic votes. As Pelosi had feared, it passed 240–194, with the votes of all Republicans and 64 Democrats, which left Pelosi "very disappointed at some of those who voted" in favor.[47]

She also had to disappoint liberals by barring an amendment on single-payer that faced an overwhelming defeat. "There are plenty of people on the Left who want to jump off a cliff just to see how high it is," a disgusted Miller noted. The flamboyant Anthony Weiner (NY) claimed he had been promised such a floor vote when he supported the Commerce bill. "You're going to take the hit if the amendment isn't allowed," he warned Pelosi. She turned him down anyway. "Weiner isn't trying to help," Abercrombie told the Speaker. "Your job is to move legislation, not to become Thomas Aquinas in drag."[48]

At the speaker's request, I met with Weiner, whom I had known since his days as Schumer's intern. He flew into a tantrum. Barring his amendment was "a big kick in the teeth," he charged, especially since he claimed to have forgone a race for mayor of New York to fight for the provision. After several minutes of point-less harangue, I said sharply, "Anthony, you are not going to tell your constituents you voted against national health care!"[49] He finally agreed to vote for the bill if he was allowed a floor speech in support of Medicare for All. Afterward, Pelosi praised him as "a tireless and effective advocate for progress on health care."

The final draft also dropped the provision in the Education and Labor bill that permitted states to create their own single-payer system. Kucinich was furious, insisting he had a hundred commitments for his amendment, which was 118 votes short of passage. "I can't believe you'd walk away from a bill that gets us to conference," Pelosi argued, but Kucinich was convinced the House would ulti-mately be forced to accept the Senate's inferior plan. "We won't take that bill," Pelosi flatly promised.

Even as the plans for the House floor were finalized, Baucus announced the Senate vote would be delayed until after Thanksgiving. "The Senate is dys-functional!" the exasperated Speaker declared.[50] Fortunately, other crucial pieces fell into place: AARP, the retirees' advocacy and insurance behemoth, and the American Medical Association both announced their support. The substitute bill filed by the Republicans held little attraction for any Democrats since it covered one-tenth of those included in the Democratic bill and increased the deficit. The plan showed "bad faith on their part," Obama insisted.[51]

The vote was scheduled for Saturday, November 7. When I suggested voting on Monday so members could fulfill their weekend district schedules, Pelosi looked at me incredulously. "Someone could have a heart attack over the weekend," she warned. "Someone could be hit by a bus." Even without a myocardial infarction or wayward bus, she knew she did not yet have 218 votes (although several uncommitted members pledged they would not allow the bill to fail). After hours of reviewing the whip lists, a ritual that ran well after midnight, the yes votes hovered around 215, three votes short. "I have my work cut out for me," she concluded. "It's going to be a real freak show!"[52]

The last push came from Obama, who arrived on vote day to pump up the caucus. "I just came from Walter Reed Army Hospital," the president said, visiting soldiers horribly wounded in Iraq and Afghanistan. "They want no pity. They have no regrets." No one could miss the parallel issues of sacrifice he was discussing. "A year ago, we were all sent to change the country. Today's vote is a test whether we will stop now or push forward. I will spend my political capital to make change." They had already passed historic bills: education, alternative energy, basic research, the Lilly Ledbetter law, tobacco safety, and hate crimes. "If you stopped right now," he observed, "this would be one of the most productive Congresses."

His early hope for bipartisanship had admittedly failed. "Republicans made a tactical decision that saying 'no,' that gumming up the works, was their preferred strategy," he said. "I know you're tired, you've been beat up in your districts, and maybe you're feeling like it's not worth it," he sympathetically said. "But if that [sentiment] wins out, we've failed to seize an extraordinary moment, and what will be remembered will be that we stopped.

"I want all of you back," he assured. "But does *anyone* think we are better off if we don't pass health care? To those of you in the toughest districts, do you really think the Republicans *won't* go after you because you voted against this bill? We have all heard the sad stories, but here it is, time to act," he insisted. "Remember why you got into politics in the first place. The country is at a crossroads. We can go forward or fall back and run with fear. When I sign this, each and every one of you will be able to look back and say, 'This was my finest moment in politics.'"

As the clock neared 11:00 p.m., the vote was called on what Steny Hoyer called "the most important bill you will ever vote for." On the House floor, the mood was excruciatingly tense, and as the votes were tallied, members with tears streaming down their faces wandered on the floor, asking friends to autograph their copy of the bill. When Pelosi crashed down the gavel and announced, "The bill is passed," the floor erupted in deafening cheers, including the Obama campaign chant, "Yes, we can!" The Affordable Health Care for America Act squeaked through on a 220–215 vote, with thirty-nine Democrats voting no and Joseph Cao (LA) the lone Republican in favor.[53] At the White House, Obama rose from his chair, shook hands with his staff, and gave Schiliro a long hug.

"Oh, what a night!" the Speaker exclaimed. Obama phoned to offer congratulations, and an ecstatic Barbra Streisand effused, "Baby doll, you passed health care reform!" Now it was up to Reid. The narrowness of the House vote proved that Pelosi also had few votes to spare, and simply accepting a Senate product was out of the question. The House was "committed to our position," Pelosi told Reid, as she expected the Senate would be to its version. She was drawing "no lines in the sand" about the final bill. "You can only do what you can do," she agreed, promising to "give the Senate as much room as possible. But at the end of the day, we must have health care."[54]

But she was not yet prepared to yield on the public option and excoriated Lieberman, who "thinks he represents the insurance companies of the world!" But "he is one of my sixty," Reid noted, and while he had "told Lieberman to stop talking about the public option," without his vote there was no bill.[55] "I need the public option," she insisted, reiterating the same ultimatum to Obama. "But I need sixty votes!" he protested. "You fight for it!" she demanded. "You're killing me!" the president wearily complained.

Later, when she related this conversation to me, I observed, "You certainly were very clear with him!" Pelosi shrugged. "What do I care?"[56] She had done something no other Speaker had done. Despite a divided caucus, solid Republican opposition, and quarrels with the White House, the Senate, and the Catholic Church, the House had approved a national health care bill.

CHAPTER 20

"LET'S GO FOR IT!"

The deal-cutting in the Senate resumed after the Thanksgiving break with senators demanding additional tweaks as the price for their vote. Those riders were certain to rankle House members, as were the admonitions against altering or dropping any of them in the probable conference agreement with the House.

Pressuring the Senate to act by Christmas, as Reid had promised, was a nervousness about the January 19 special election for Kennedy's Senate seat. A loss would cost Democrats their sixtieth vote, vastly complicating efforts to finalize the health care bill. The race shouldn't have been close; the Democratic nominee, state attorney general Martha Coakley, began with a double-digit lead over state senator Scott Brown, best known for once having posed nude in *Cosmopolitan*. But a rising conservative mood had Democrats increasingly nervous, as did Coakley's disengaged campaign style, highlighted by her inexplicable questioning the value of "standing outside Fenway Park in the cold, shaking hands."[1]

The elongated congressional schedule continued to afford opportunities to organize against the health care bills.[2] Labor remained furious about the Senate's tax on Cadillac plans, which was justified as "one of the [bill's] most important cost-containment measures," by the liberal Center on Budget and Policy Priorities.[3] If the Senate rejected the public option, as seemed likely, Pelosi vowed the House would "never back off fighting" the Senate tax. Early in December, when Emanuel confirmed Lieberman's uncompromising opposition meant the option was dead in the Senate, an enraged DeLauro advocated his recall by Connecticut voters. "Don't over-read or under-read the administration's reaction," Emanuel counseled privately. "We are in a Senate reaction mode."[4]

Although she had criticized Obama's "tin ear" for listening to "academics in the ivory tower" on the Cadillac tax, Pelosi actually had become "agnostic" on the subject.[5] It was up to the unions to "convince me it is a sin against nature," she said. Labor remained defiant, with Trumka predicting its inclusion would mean "a catastrophe" in 2010 for Democrats. In fact, labor insisted even the discussion of the tax helped explain why approval of Democrats on the economy had plummeted. Two-thirds of voters in the Massachusetts special election who opposed the Cadillac tax favored the Republican. "You guys are getting creamed because of the Senate's nonsense," Trumka warned. When Schiliro predicted that opposition to the tax could scuttle the bill, I explained that the Speaker's opinion reflected opposition from labor and the caucus. "If that's the case," he lamented, "we won't get a bill."[6]

But even labor was not united. Anna Burger of the Service Employees International Union sent a letter urging the House to accept the Senate bill despite the Cadillac tax, a benefit few lower-paid SEIU members enjoyed. "Pounding us to pass the Senate bill doesn't help," Pelosi furiously responded. "We barely passed *our* bill!" she reminded Burger. "Why does the Senate get treated so well? Labor opposes the [Cadillac] tax, the Senate passes it, we oppose it, and labor tells us to pass the Senate bill!"[7]

Reid warned he would also have to "make tough deals to pass health care," including on abortion, on which Pelosi warned her hands were tied. Abortion was being used as "a tool for opponents to destroy the bill," Pelosi argued, advising she could "not expand the abortion provision beyond what the House did."[8] In desperation, Reid reached out to Sister Carol Keehan, the president of the Catholic Health Association, a progressive Catholic voice unintimidated by the Church hierarchy. "She doesn't care what the bishops want," he reported.

Both leaders remained frustrated by the president's low profile in the messaging effort. "They haven't taken their message public," Pelosi asserted. He "needs to get off his butt and fight" instead of being "focused on rhetoric."[9] Reid was in full agreement. "Obama never says, 'I support this,'" he complained. "I told Rahm and Messina, 'You haven't helped.'" Concern about the absence of an administration campaign meant "we need our own drumbeat," she told the caucus, although she admitted also being "at my wits' end" about the capability of House members to sell their bill.

Reid finally succeeded in forcing through a cloture vote 60–39 on December 23, and on Christmas Eve, after twenty-five days of consideration, the bill passed by the same margin with no Republican votes. Although Reid declared passage "a victory for the American people," McConnell vowed, "This fight is far from over."

Publicly, like Obama, Pelosi downplayed the differences between the bills. She urged her members to "hold your fire" and to "praise the Senate" bill, which was

"75 percent the same" as the House version, although she understood the remaining differences were substantial.[10] "They have a good bill, but we have a *great* bill," she insisted, but "we have to give the Senate room [because] at the end of the day, we need a bill."[11]

In speaking with her leadership, Pelosi offered a more negative assessment. "All you have to know about the Senate bill," she said, "is that the insurance companies like it."[12] A discussion with Reid in which she identified the non-negotiable House provisions was so blunt that Myrick wondered if she planned "to make Reid the bad guy" for anything objectionable in the final bill. She also reminded Obama that House members would not simply roll over for the Senate version. "He doesn't just need to get sixty votes in the Senate," she noted. "He also needs 218 in the House."[13]

But Reid had to protect senators' provisions to maintain his sixty votes for the conference report. Some of those additions were particularly hard to swallow, like Ben Nelson's $20 billion special treatment of Nebraska's Medicaid expansion. Republicans had a field day denouncing the "Cornhusker Kickback" and accused Nelson of "everything under the sun."[14] But the reality was that "everything has to go through Lieberman and Nelson," Myrick declared. "If they say 'no,' it's no." The House was unlikely to accept that ultimatum, I responded. "Our folks don't want to negotiate twice, once with Reid and your chairs and then again with the dissident Democrats."

It did not take long for the familiar suggestion to bubble up. "Even if only the Senate bill became law, it would be historic," White House staff said, an alternative Pelosi knew was unsellable in her caucus. "Our legacy will not be accomplished by looking anything like Senate bill," she countered. "We can't simply pass the Senate bill if it shafts the middle class. That would be political suicide."[15]

Still, she believed the major differences between the bills were "practical, not philosophical," and therefore could be negotiated. Even the Cadillac tax was, in her mind, "a matter of politics, not policy."[16] But reconciling the two bills would be challenging because each reflected the role its house played: Reid's bill was heavily skewed to the rural states at the expense of larger states, like the Senate itself, while the House version reflected the party's liberal and minority base in the members' smaller districts.

The final design should be built around three A's—"affordability, accountability, accessibility"—a new alliterative goal. The Senate's insurance reforms were "not enough," Pelosi charged, and if the public option was unacceptable, "something strong" was needed as a substitute, perhaps a single national

insurance exchange. Dropping the public option "made me sick," Durbin counseled, but the cold reality was that it "is not going anywhere" in the Senate. "Until I hear what you do" as an alternative, she responded, the House would not
consider deleting it.[17] The disagreements ran in both directions. The Senate
objected to the cost of the House bill and the taxes it raised to pay for the premium subsidies.

Obama emphasized the progress both houses had made. They had "turned
the corner" and were "in the twenty-third mile of a marathon." His only worry
was that the members "are frazzled," a characterization Pelosi sharply disputed.
The only problem, she said, was that the House had "waited for six months
while the Senate contemplated their navel," and now, time was running out.[18]

Now, it seemed, it was the president who was frazzled. "Goddamn it, if we're
spending this much money," he declared, "people ought to be better off." But Pelosi refused to move off her bottom line. "I am not yielding on the public option
until I see strong accountability," she reiterated, not quite an absolute insistence
on the option, but enough to make Obama flare. "I listened to you the *first* time,"
he seethed. "Let's cut through the bullshit! If we can't reach agreement, let's start
discussing reconciliation," a smaller goal he knew the Speaker would strive to
avoid.[19]

Obama's outburst made an impression. On the way back to Capitol Hill, Pelosi
asked if I thought she had pushed him too hard. It was the standard calculus, I
replied. "They assume you have twenty votes in your pocket, so getting to two-
eighteen isn't difficult for you, but sixty is a real problem for Reid," I answered.
"He doesn't like being challenged," she said.

Pelosi's report to her caucus assured members that "the White House is not
trying to get us to take the Senate bill. They are listening to us."[20] Not everyone
agreed. "The White House has surrendered to the Senate," boomed Dingell,
mentioning a "gross" $900 billion ceiling proposed for the program. Hoyer ac-
knowledged he had been surprised when that limit was mentioned. "That was
the first time I heard that number," he said. "That was the first time we *all* heard
it!" Pelosi added as laughs rang out.

The members also backed up Pelosi on defying the Senate's version. "If
there's no public option," Doyle declared, "the bill is a big wet kiss to [the] insurance industry." With no Democrats in Nebraska's three-member House

delegation, they were infuriated by the "Cornhusker" giveaway.[21] John Hall worried his constituents could face thousands of dollars in taxes because of the Cadillac tax. "I can't support the bill with that language or with abortion restrictions," he warned. Still, members recognized they would have to swallow some unpleasant Senate provisions. "There are ten thousand things I'd change," Jim Cooper (TN) noted. "We need to pass this and then we'll spend every year improving it. But first," he reasoned, "we need something to *improve*." Tellingly, Pelosi noted, "if we get one thing" in the negotiations, it should be the national exchange, without which states that refused to set up exchanges could deprive their residents of the ability to participate in the program.

At a White House drafting session just days before the Massachusetts special election, the tension was showing. "We are making history," Obama began, "but [making] history sure is hard."[22] After a disastrous debate performance by Coakley, some feared it might get a lot harder. Hill leaders were joined by the White House health experts for a head-knocking marathon that would include the president (except when he ducked out to attend his daughter's recital). "I can return if necessary," he promised, "because failure is not an option." He pleaded for "empathy" and a willingness to think beyond political self-interest. "Sometimes," he lectured, "politics cuts against sound policy decisions," but "if we can get the basic design, we can tweak and improve it" down the road. He recommitted his administration and himself to a vigorous marketing effort to persuade the public of the benefits of the legislation, "but we have to have a product to market!"

Pelosi made it clear she was prepared to cut big deals, beginning with the national exchange that Miller and other House leaders could accept as a consolation prize for the public option. The president welcomed the concession. "I've learned you shouldn't argue with George Miller!" he joked. But, she warned, "we cannot fix the core organizational principles later." The Senate bill did not work.

There was sharp disagreement on creating an independent cost containment commission that Obama portrayed as the "cheapest ticket out of the problem" of lowering health spending.[23] Pelosi and Waxman objected to a requirement that Congress vote up or down on the commission's proposal, as with plans offered by the military base closure commission, arguing legislators should be able "to pick and choose among the recommendations." As Rangel launched a fulsome attack on the commission, she leaned over to me. "I don't really care that much," she whispered. "I'm just leveraging to get the federal exchange."

Hour after hour, like students cramming for a midterm, the most powerful people in the government methodically reviewed every provision in both versions of the bill. As the meeting was concluding at 1:45 a.m., a sour note from Dodd rattled the collegial spirit. "If Coakley loses, the House probably will need to just take the Senate bill and pass it," he recommended. Few comments could have been less welcome, especially after a day of painstaking horse-trading. "Not a chance!" Pelosi retorted. "That won't happen!" The next morning, she directed her staff to draft an alternative reconciliation strategy. When Cardoza complained that approach would violate "regular order," the Speaker snapped, "Fifty votes *is* 'regular order.'" She brushed aside Blue Dog resistance, telling Reid, "It's none of their business."[24]

Dodd's premonition proved accurate as Brown defeated Coakley, and suddenly, the legislative options were starkly limited. The House could pass the Senate bill unamended and send it to Obama, a total nonstarter. But with the majority down to fifty-nine, there was little chance the Senate could pass either the House bill or any changes the House might make to the Senate version. The last option was scrapping the comprehensive bill and fashioning whatever pieces of the big bill could squeeze through the eye of the reconciliation needle.

"We remain committed to ensuring all Americans can access affordable health care," Reid declared, although how that might happen now was anyone's guess. "I do everything but make love to these senators! How irresponsible it is for senators to do to me what they're doing!"[25] Pelosi sympathized with his plight. "You know, I never counted on Senator Byrd's health being stronger than Ben Nelson's backbone," Pelosi cracked, explaining the Cornhusker provision could not become law.

On the one-year anniversary of Obama's inauguration, Pelosi's freshmen breakfast focused on the new landscape. "If we are going down [the] same road again on health care, we're fucked," Dina Titus (NV) bluntly declared, including Reid, her own senior senator, whom she predicted "certainly won't be back" after the upcoming election.[26] Walt Minnick (ID), who had worked in the Nixon White House, recommended a renewed effort at bipartisanship, but Pelosi brusquely dismissed the front liner's naiveté. "The Republicans don't want to participate," she insisted, so they would have to soldier on alone. "There is plenty that is good in the Senate bill," she counseled the freshmen, but not enough to accept it as the final product.

"How are we doin'?" asked Obama jauntily. The members still "don't want to vote for the Senate bill!" she reported, and Obama admitted to complications on the Senate side as well. Emboldened by Brown's unexpected victory,

McConnell had announced no Republicans would vote for a reconciliation bill, necessitating Reid's keeping his own fractured caucus largely unified behind a pared-down bill lacking many of the provisions that had secured votes for the Senate product. Then he finally got around to the real point of the conversation.

"I would like to be able to say that I would sign the Senate bill," he said, if it was not harmful to do so. Pelosi did not slam the door completely. "Just say the House is moving closer," she suggested. Obama was grateful for the latitude. "Do it fast [because] this can't drag on," he asked. "You're a great partner, and I don't want to give other folks a win."[27]

Afterward, Pelosi painted a grim picture for progressives. The House was boxed in. If the Senate bill was out and a series of smaller bills would face multiple Senate filibusters, it seemed anything beyond the limited reconciliation option was "off the table." Comprehensive health care, it seemed, had eluded Democrats yet again.

Within a few days, however, a bold strategy was hatched. Suppose the House were to pass a reconciliation bill that corrected the most controversial portions of the Senate bill. The Senate could enact that bill with just fifty-one votes, freeing the House to pass the Senate bill knowing its objectionable provisions had been revised. It seemed too good to be true, and it was. Senate parliamentarian Alan Frumin, whose procedural opinion was authoritative, declared that a reconciliation bill amending a bill that had not yet been enacted would be out of order. "So, we must pass the Senate bill first?" Rangel asked incredulously, an action Pelosi described as "nearly impossible unless reconciliation is already in the bank."[28]

Many House members anticipated a double-cross if they followed Frumin's prescription: the House would pass the Senate bill, and the Senate would never pass reconciliation, leaving the flawed Senate version as the final law. "The Senate Democrats," Pelosi said, "are like fifty-nine highly strung violins. . . . Dysfunctional would be a compliment to describe the Senate. That is what they *used* to be." Why couldn't both houses pass reconciliation, just as Republicans had done twenty-two times? she asked Biden, "and *then* we pass the Senate bill."[29] Biden gave her the thumbs up. "It's the only scenario that works," he agreed. But of course, when the Republicans used reconciliation, they were amending existing law.

The procedural morass deepened the frustration in the House. "Obama couldn't have done health care worse," the Speaker seethed. "They never would listen. They gave us no support."[30] But she refused to abandon the comprehensive bill. "If the gate's closed, we'll go over the fence," she insisted. "If the fence is too high, we'll pole vault in. If that doesn't work, we'll use a parachute. We're going to get health care passed."[31] But there was still time to figure out a process. "It ticks me off that we have to deal with it in this manner," she admitted, but "we're not in a big rush."[32]

In their next weekly strategy session, Reid proposed an unconventional idea: what if he could produce a letter with fifty-two senators' signatures promising to pass a reconciliation bill *after* the House passed the Senate version.[33] "What do you think?" the majority leader asked me after Pelosi departed. I laughed disparagingly and shook my head. "I don't think that's very likely, Senator," I responded. House members were reflexively suspicious of Senate promises, and a letter was unlikely to impress them, but I encouraged Reid to gather signatures anyway.

The House mood seemed to justify my skepticism. Caucus chair John Larson spoke for many when he declared he had "no confidence" in Reid. "Our members want us to tell them it's over; we are not supporting [the] Senate bill," Pelosi said, although she feared doing so ensured House Democrats "will be blamed for sinking health care." Miller urged the members to be patient, "talk about this being a work in progress, not a final product," insisting "we *can't* walk away." Hoyer joined the call for calm. "Members are not in panic," he assured, but "they are confused and looking for a simpler product." But Pelosi believed the problem wasn't complexity but that "the president has bought into [the] Senate deal [which meant] we need to look out for ourselves." Miller agreed. "They show no respect for you."[34] Pelosi was besieged from all sides. "I'm getting burned at the stake," she had told Obama and Reid. "It makes Joan of Arc look mild."

Hearing of the House's obstinacy, Myrick proclaimed, "We're done!" to Schiliro and me. Nerves were fraying at an alarming rate. When liberals criticized Emanuel for having "begged" Obama to embrace a scaled-down plan, he dismissed them as "fucking retards," provoking an embarrassing contretemps with the developmentally disabled community.[35] A news report inaccurately stated that the Speaker had requested the president direct her to pass the Senate bill; in actuality, the request had been "*Don't* ask me to pass the Senate bill."[36] The administration was challenged as well. After he addressed Senate Democrats, "things got pretty hot" as Axelrod clashed with senators. Discouraged, Reid asked his staff "to put this [reconciliation] thing together" as a last-ditch effort.

The possibility of an impasse led Obama to take a harder line during his next meeting with the leadership. "It is in the House members' interest that they pass the Senate bill," he insisted.[37] Pelosi was defiant. "That is not happening," she told him, but Obama lost patience. "You keep bringing up that you can't pass the Senate bill!" he challenged Pelosi, but that meant "kicking the can down the road" indefinitely, and time was running out. Something was needed to break the roadblock.

Obama sprang an idea: a bipartisan conference at the Blair House that would expose Republican intractability. Pelosi opined a better use of time would be for the president to urge Reid to "stop confusing the situation" with procedural maneuvers. "No one believes the Senate will act," she explained. "There may *never* be fifty-one votes in the Senate. They don't want to vote for *any* bill." Reid pushed back. "We can credibly give assurances to the House that we will pass reconciliation," he told the Speaker. That wasn't good enough. "What is the *assurance* that the Senate will act?" she pointedly asked, referencing the letter. "I don't have that yet," Reid admitted. Schiliro gloomily observed, "I guess we're stuck."[38]

Just when the bill's proponents needed a boost, one unexpectedly appeared. Anthem Blue Cross announced a premium increase of as much as 39 percent, ten times the rate of inflation, impacting over a million Californians. At the same time, the company was awarding its executives huge pay increases.[39] Double-digit premium increases were soon disclosed in at least eleven more states. Recollections of Wall Street bonuses and golden parachutes flooded the airwaves. "Corporate executives [at Anthem] are thriving, but its policyholders are paying the price," Waxman inveighed. "Health insurers may get richer, but our nation's health will suffer." Anthem's improvident announcement led Schiliro to exult, "We are closer to getting health care passed than at any time in a hundred years!" In retrospect, Pelosi would credit Anthem's ill-timed announcement with convincing Obama not to abandon a sweeping reform bill.[40]

Days before the Blair House conference, Obama told the Speaker that the crucial strategic decisions would follow the conclave. The administration's game plan was to "puncture Republican misinformation" about the Democratic bills. "If we can knock down the Republican talking points," Schiliro predicted, "we win." Obama assured there was no chance he would "get suckered into a three-month negotiation. It will be a lot of fun," he pledged. "Those jamokes don't know what they are talking about." All Democrats needed to do was to "look reasonable." But he also needed to know she would pass the Senate bill before

Reid took up the reconciliation bill. "We'll get back to that," she responded. "If we can't do that," he warned, "then it's the incremental approach," which would mean further compromises "meeting the Republicans halfway."[41]

For the first time, the Speaker appeared to accept the sequencing of the two measures. Perhaps the House *could* pass the Senate bill, she speculated, and Obama could delay signing it until the Senate passed reconciliation. In fact, that was not an option, as Frumin determined the Senate bill must be enacted before the reconciliation bill would be in order in the Senate. But even this admission was risky for the Speaker. "I would get shot at sundown for even suggesting it," she confessed.[42] Even so, the leaders were looking for ways to pass both iterations, and that meant, as Pelosi, Reid, and Emanuel agreed later that day, "we are very close to having a comprehensive health care bill."[43] By refusing to rule out the Senate bill definitively, Pelosi had told Miller all he needed to know. "When she turns for the barn, you know where she's going," he deduced. She had concluded the House "can't be the death of health care."[44]

At a caucus meeting, the leadership insisted there had been major progress in the House's direction. "The president has come to us!" Hoyer declared. Although "we nearly had fisticuffs in the Oval Office" over the Cadillac tax, Pelosi reported, the Senate had agreed to whittle it down by 80 percent and delay its effective date for eight years. "How can you vote 'no' if you get 80 percent of what you want?" she challenged, warning that those who continued to insist on the total elimination of the tax were abetting opponents who favored a small bill or no bill at all. "We didn't get everything we asked for," the Speaker admitted, "but everything in here *is* something we asked for. We are in the red zone; on the one yard line."[45] The message could not have been clearer: do not sabotage this historic opportunity based on procedure or purism.

But she also remained concerned that some in the administration were resigned to a pared-back approach and feared such an alternative could be sprung at the Blair House. "You're pulling your punches," she accused Emanuel. "You'll settle for defeat, and you're not serving the president well." Convinced the chief of staff was "trying to sabotage the bill," she vowed only to speak directly with the president. Reid did not challenge her viewpoint. "You and I know Rahm doesn't want to do a big deal," he confided. The two leaders pledged to stay united against White House proposals that were "so far off the mark," Pelosi said, "I don't know what planet or galaxy they are on."[46]

Others worried too many concessions would be made in an attempt to attract Republican support. "The president needs to be careful not to look too willing to accept Republican ideas," Senator Jay Rockefeller (WV) advised. "If he sits on high and says 'you're both right,' we lost," Schumer bluntly warned, because "the Republicans are only destructive." But Schiliro assured them the administration would hear out the minority but that even acceptable changes would not be adopted "if they don't produce Republican votes."[47] The Speaker agreed to the ground rules with a heavy dose of skepticism. "My demeanor will be respectful," Pelosi promised. "If the Republicans have a good idea, we can accept it, but you know the Republicans will never vote for it."

In a preconference meeting, the president looked the Speaker in the eye. "I want your gut instinct," he asked. Assuming the discussion went as he outlined, "is your instinct to go for it," for the comprehensive bill? He reached for a movie allusion. "I'm Thelma, you're Louise," he said, referencing the 1991 film that ends with the stars driving off a cliff together. "Let's go for it!" Pelosi was in a conciliatory mood. "Do it the way you want it done," she told the president. "We'll get heat either way. Just don't namby-pamby." "I couldn't be prouder," he gushed. "You're a great partner!"[48]

The minimal expectations for the Blair House meetings were foreshadowed in Obama's discussion with Grassley, who once had been considered a potential supporter. The senator "hemmed and hawed" about the changes he wanted, replying "no" each time Obama asked if adoption of one of his suggestions would secure his vote. "If I gave you *everything* you wanted," Obama finally asked, "would you be for health care?" Grassley replied, "Probably not."[49]

Unsurprisingly, the conference only clarified how far apart the parties remained. "We do not agree on the fundamental decision about who should be in charge" of health care, Jon Kyl (AZ) observed. "Let's scrap the bill," Boehner unhelpfully proposed. Even Lamar Alexander (TN), a collaborative Republican, gave no ground. The only clarification to emerge from the meeting was the certainty all Republicans would surely filibuster any House modifications of the Senate bill, ending any chance for that approach. At a press conference afterward, Pelosi dismissed questions about the lack of Republican support. "The bill is bipartisan even if there are no Republican votes," she insisted, "because it includes Republican amendments" adopted in the committees.

One remaining roadblock was the Reid letter, "sign[ed] in blood" by fifty-one senators promising to pass the reconciliation bill.[50] "Now is the moment of truth," Pelosi warned. "If the Senate can't get fifty-one for reconciliation, it's over. Our members are not big on Senate promises." I reiterated the point when Myrick asked again, "What are the chances the House could pass the Senate bill?" "That depends on what it's paired with," I responded. "We need to tie down reconciliation quickly."[51]

Reid also faced challenges with the reconciliation strategy, and he was losing patience. When told Conrad virulently opposed a key provision, the leader angrily spat out, "Let him drop dead." He was focused on structuring the Senate debate to curtail Republican obstructionism, hopefully by convincing the parliamentarian to declare any talkathon filibuster "dilatory" and therefore out of order, but Frumin remained undecided. "He is being terrible," Reid reported. "He's a pain in the ass," Pelosi remarked, suggesting Reid find another parliamentarian.[52]

Another persistent problem—CBO's scoring—was obstructing finalization of the reconciliation plan. "CBO is insufferable!" the president complained. But when the budget numbers finally arrived, Pelosi was ecstatic. The analysts estimated $130 billion in savings during the first ten years and a 1.4 percent reduction in Medicare costs. Savings jumped to $1.2 trillion in the second decade. The favorable scoring led the Speaker to encourage Obama "to use the bully pulpit" more aggressively. "We get too much pulpit and not enough bully," she told Axelrod. The message director again promised a "full mobilization" using Obama's grassroots organization to build support.[53] That was good to hear, DeLauro responded, because even supporters "have absolutely no idea what this bill does." The Speaker did not help clarify the bill's provisions by remarking on March 9 that Congress would have "to pass the bill so you can find out what's in it," an accurate assessment of the unremarkable process of horse-trading that was effectively twisted by the conservative media into a seeming admission that members had no idea what they were voting on.

Reid finally announced that he finally had secured fifty-three signatures agreeing to vote for the reconciliation bill; several more declined to sign but had indicated privately they were on board.[54] But Reid refused to release the letter, so no one knew which senators had committed to do what. "The purpose is to give assurances to the House, and that can be done privately," a Senate staff person claimed.[55] My disquiet was compounded when Myrick declined to provide the Speaker a copy of the signed letter, even in a sealed envelope for archival purposes.[56]

She insisted that Reid appear before her caucus to explain the senators' commitment. I was filled with dread he would be pilloried by the disbelieving House members. In his soft, thin voice, Reid calmly explained he could no longer muster sixty votes to take up either the House bill or a revised version of the Senate bill. He acknowledged the suspicions of House members—he had been one himself in the mid-1980s—but he implored them to trust the word of his signatories that they would pass the reconciliation bill once the Senate bill was enacted. I waited for fireworks, but there was only silence. Reid thanked the members and walked off the stage to polite applause. Dumbfounded, I thought, "Wow, we are *definitely* going to pass health care!"

Even with the assurances, Pelosi still faced resistance on using the reconciliation process. When Kucinich pressed the public option again, Pelosi bluntly told him to "forget it" because of Senate opposition. "I couldn't pass the public option if I made love to every member of the Senate," Reid told Pelosi. Frontline members were also withholding pledges of support, which rankled the Speaker's allies. Miller reminded Herseth-Sandlin that the Speaker had "saved your butt . . . twice!" with campaign aid, but Pelosi seemed philosophical about the resistance.[57] "I break my back every day for people who come here to vote 'no' on health care," she told the president. "How do you not go ballistic?" he asked in amazement. "I think about the one in five children in America in poverty," she said. "That's what I get up and pray for every day. If this bill passes, I could walk out of the Speaker's office and never look back."

The abortion issue loomed as the last barrier, and it needed to be resolved before mushrooming out of control. Already a new concern involving abortion restrictions for community health centers was threatening to blow up the reconciliation bill. Pelosi implored pro-life Democrats to look the other way. "If we go one step further on community health" restrictions, the Speaker warned, "we're gone."[58]

Pro-lifers also had realized that if the House bill died, the Stupak amendment was doomed, leaving only a weaker Senate restriction in place. The bishops ramped up their opposition, and one Catholic Democrat was summoned by his local church leaders for a stern lecture. Obama promised to try again with church leaders, despite an unproductive discussion with the truculent "bad guy," Cardinal George. Bill supporters were counting on Sister Carol and the other activist nuns to entice votes from pro-life members who otherwise favored the bill, but the legislative language proved to be difficult to craft, leading Emanuel to float a new approach. Obama had told the Speaker he was willing to do anything "as long as it is constitutional." What about an executive order to clarify the abortion policy? Pelosi thought that was "perfectly reasonable," although she worried about having "our people tarred and feathered" by the bishops.[59]

Even with the abortion issue potentially resolved, she believed "the [reconciliation] bill is in danger." She counted only 196 hard commitments; even if she counted in the leanings and private assurances, she was still five votes short. "We are really close," Obama insisted. "I'm in a fighting mood! Let's get this damn thing done!" Pelosi was unflappable. "I've been in worse shape," she confided.[60]

The last piece fell into place when the abortion executive order language was cleared with the women's groups and pro-lifers. Alone with the Speaker in her private office, I picked up the phone and called Schiliro. "We're good to go," I relayed. "Hang on," he responded, and a familiar voice said, "Hey!" "Madam Speaker," I said with mock formality, handing the receiver to Pelosi. "The president of the United States." After nearly a century of failure and months of drafting, strategizing, negotiating, and rancor, we were heading to the floor with national health care. And we had the votes.

The House vote on the Senate bill took place close to midnight during an unusual Sunday session. The Republican opposition was scornful. "Look at how this bill was written!" Boehner insisted contemptuously. "Can you say it was done openly? Without backroom deals that were struck behind closed doors? Hell no you can't!" His insinuation of secrecy was preposterous. The unaltered Senate bill that was before the House had been available for nearly three months.

When Pelosi brought her gavel down, the Senate bill narrowly passed 219–212 with thirty-four Democrats—all conservatives or frontline targets—voting no. How many additional votes Pelosi had in her pocket, willing to switch to assure passage, will never be known. "They really didn't want to vote for the Senate bill, but it ended up being a non-issue," Pelosi remarked. "The same with Harry's letter. They never even asked for the signatures!"[61]

As exhilarating as passage of the law was, there had been ugly sides to the day. As Democrats walked from the Cannon Caucus Room to the Capitol in a show of force, hundreds of angry demonstrators grew confrontational, yelling racist taunts and spitting on civil rights icon John Lewis (GA) and other members. "I haven't seen [or] heard anything like this in more than forty years, maybe forty-five," Lewis said, "not since the march from Selma to Montgomery really." Inside the House chamber, emotions had raced out of control as well. When Stupak rose to oppose the Republicans' recommittal motion, a Republican member shouted, "Baby killer!" at the pro-life congressman. Afterward, when anonymous callers threatened to shoot bill supporters, security for the Speaker was ramped up and all members were advised to take increased safety precautions. Obama said the Republicans' angry reaction made them seem "small, like sore losers."

"On to the next thing!" Pelosi cheered when the president invited her to take "a big victory lap" at the White House signing ceremony.[62] "You're a terrific Speaker," the president declared. "I was happier last night than when I was elected president." Pelosi demurred. "I'm not sure I was," she responded, because "we wouldn't be here without it." Two days later, just before the festive signing ceremony, the main Hill negotiators met with Obama and Biden in the Blue Room. Five of the key chairs—Waxman, Baucus, Miller, Harkin, and Dodd—had begun their careers as members of the House class of 1974 pledging to enact national health care.

As the Blue Room meeting was breaking up, the president walked over to me. "Do you remember when you said you'd rather have health care than a second term," I asked as we shook hands. "Now, you can have both." Obama gave a wistful smile. "We'll see," he answered.

Before a large crowd in the East Room, Obama declared the Affordable Care Act a goal "that generations of Americans have fought for and marched for and hungered to see." Although his oratory, as always, was soaring, the triumphant spirit of the day was captured by Biden's aside as he introduced the president. "This," the vice president said faintly, "is a big fucking deal." Afterward, Pelosi told the president, "You were blushing!"[63]

The House then narrowly approved the reconciliation bill 220–211 and waited with trepidation until the Senate fulfilled its part of the bargain two days later in a 56–43 vote on Pelosi's seventieth birthday.[64] "Happy birthday, child, as my mother would say," Biden told the Speaker. "You gave the country a birthday gift." Pelosi was ecstatic. "It is the biggest gift possible," she responded.[65] Durbin claimed to hear the cheering from the House side as it reverberated through Statuary Hall and the Rotunda, down the long Capitol transept, and into the Senate chamber. "The Senate kept its word and made history!" the whip exulted.

Pelosi insisted the signing of their "remarkable achievement" be just as celebratory as the one had been for the Senate bill. Instead, due to the higher education portions of the bill, the ceremony was relegated to the community college in Northern Virginia where Jill Biden was a professor.[66] The New York Times headline the following day blared, "Obama Signs Overhaul of Student Loan Program," and the story barely mentioned the health provisions.

"We feel used," the Speaker told Schiliro. "It's obvious that once you got what you wanted, you didn't care about the rest of the story. I know the president thinks the Senate bill is as good as gold, but without reconciliation, the Senate bill would have been a dead letter." She doubted many on the president's staff (and perhaps the president himself) fully appreciated the "heavy lift" she and her members had been forced to make. "An insane lift," Schiliro acknowledged. "But I never had any doubts," she declared. "I knew the members would find their way."

When she spoke with the president, it was clear her unhappiness had been communicated to him. "What's your problem with me?" he pointedly asked, and the simmering resentment poured out. "You don't respect the House," she charged. At the signing ceremony for the reconciliation bill, he had barely mentioned the House authors. "George Miller is the only reason that bill passed," she insisted. "He crafted the education bill from whole cloth and needs to be recognized."

"George did an outstanding job," Obama agreed, and he promised to send a congratulatory note.[67] But he also reminded her that education secretary Arne Duncan had been involved in developing the bill. Pelosi brushed him off. "What tough vote did *he* take?" she pressed.

Later in the day, however, the tone between the two was decidedly more triumphant. "Are you thrilled?" she asked. Obama was unstinting in his praise. "I am so proud of you," he gushed. "I can't say 'thank you' enough. You and I worked well together. As Joe Biden would say, 'It's a big fucking deal!'"

"Yes," the Speaker responded drily, "as he would say."[68]

CHAPTER 21

THE UNWINNABLE WAR

The exultation of enacting health care reform did not lessen the anguish and frustration over the intractable wars in Iraq and Afghanistan that continued to drain tens of billions of dollars and cost many American lives after nearly a decade of fighting. Ten years after his last visit to Kabul, one veteran recalled an epiphany experienced during that trip. After the stomach-churning corkscrew landing used to frustrate terrorists hoping to destroy a plane filled with dignitaries, he had been hustled onto a helicopter for a quick flight to the Green Zone. Driving in armored vehicles was often unsafe even with protection from soaring concrete Jersey walls. Rockets and other explosives were periodically lobbed inside the zone's perimeter, occasionally with fatal consequences. If you were a member of Congress, you slept in a secure embassy bedroom. Staff was consigned to outdoor rickety metal cabanas protected by sandbags piled up nearly to the roof. Inside, the accommodations were spare. On the door, a sign advised taking cover under the cots in the case of incoming rockets.

"We were six plus years into the fight by then," the traveler observed. "It was pretty clear to me that whatever 'winning' was [going] to look like, we weren't close to it."

Although 93 percent of Americans initially supported intervening in Iraq in 2002, after years of inconclusive fighting and thousands of fatalities, a poll found that nearly seven in ten voters favored bringing the troops home—nearly half within one year.[1] But the conditions Congress had imposed on war funding did not seem to have had any appreciable impact on ending the war or on redeploying US forces.

Congressional efforts in 2007 to tie funding to conditions and timetables for US withdrawal were repeatedly filibustered or vetoed. "That's hardball!" a delighted Charlie Rangel exulted. The hard line was endorsed by Murtha, even though he knew a spending stalemate could trigger base closures and DOD layoffs. "I'm not backing off the conditions" for removing US forces, the former Marine growled.[2] Reid was worried about holding his senators against more funding and suggested looser language on redeployment. Pelosi rejected that idea. "I won't consider it if it doesn't get us what we want," she insisted. "Why should I give the president what *he* wants?"[3] If Bush rejected conditions, she vowed to reject more funding.

On November 14, 2007, the House had passed a bill requiring the withdrawal of forces from Iraq to begin within thirty days and the removal of all US forces of December 15, 2008, except for those needed to protect the US embassy, train the Iraqis, or conduct targeted attacks on terrorists. The bill also extended the ban on torture by any US agency. But such restrictions had no chance in the Senate, and the House was forced to back down yet again.[4] As a result, the legislation that ultimately reached Bush's desk contained $70 billion for Iraq and Afghanistan, more than twice the House's $30 billion, and imposed no restrictions. A disgusted Obey voted against his own committee's bill.

Any significant change in policy would have to await the outcome of the 2008 presidential election, and many Democrats were "very concerned what Hillary Clinton would do on Iraq" if, as seemed likely, she was nominated and elected. Meanwhile, Bush was trying to tie the hands of whoever his successor might be by committing the United States to "very sweeping" obligations to the Iraqis, including counterterrorism training, force protection, and even long-term US bases.[5] He remained upbeat about the prospects for regional pacification, describing recent "mind-blowing" visits to the "very cool" sheikdoms of Abu Dhabi and Dubai and visits with the sheiks, whom he described as "cool guys."[6] He even predicted the "stars are aligned for a peace process" between Israel and her neighbors.[7] Critics did not share his optimism. "Iraq never gets better," Murtha lamented. A month later, Bush requested another $100 billion for the war.

By early spring 2008, criticism was relentless even from pro-military Democrats. The al-Maliki government was riven by factionalism, Skelton declared, and Iraq was at risk of becoming little more than a client state of Iran. "By their own standards, they have failed," observed Hoyer. Such denigration angered Bush, who compared Democrats to Neville Chamberlain, the British prime minister who had advocated appeasement with the Nazis. The insinuation could not have been more offensive to Pelosi. Bush was a "brain-dead, jet-lagged, values-damaged leader," she seethed.[8]

Democrats had been castigating Bush over the use of torture since 2003, demanding investigations and inserting bans in legislation that Bush had vetoed. False entombment, waterboarding, electric shock, sleep deprivation, and humiliating nudity—described as "enhanced interrogation techniques"—subjected the administration to both congressional and international criticism. A report by the FBI released in 2007 documented twenty-six cases of mistreatment held at the Guantánamo Bay prison, including prisoners being in a fetal position on the floor for eighteen hours or more and subjected to extreme temperatures. One detainee was described as a "bearded longhaired [detainee] gagged w/duct tape that had covered much of his head."[9]

Early in the Obama administration, Pelosi again found herself enmeshed in a major controversy with Republicans insisting she had known about the CIA's use of waterboarding but had raised no opposition. Under attack in April 2009, the Speaker adamantly insisted that briefers only had identified the types of torture that *might* be employed but she "was never told they were using those methods."[10] Obama, who had campaigned on a promise to end the abusive treatment, acknowledged his decision came with risks. "If there's a terrorist attack on my watch, I'm responsible," he declared.

While the new president agreed to begin declassifying materials on torture, he rejected calls from Congress for a "truth commission" to investigate allegations of abuse. "I don't want to re-litigate the last eight years," he insisted, promising there would be no "witch hunt" at the CIA. "Monday morning quarterbacking is dangerous," he warned, and could invite "short term political advantage to sneak in" and politicize the issue further.[11] McConnell forcefully rejected any formal inquiry into torture allegations, which he predicted would make the United States "look like a banana republic." But if punishment were to be meted out, he suggested, it should be extended to "those who approved or knew" of torture, an unmistakable reference to the controversy surrounding the Speaker.

Even more controversial than the torture ban was Obama's executive order to close the Guantánamo prison.[12] McConnell didn't think much of that idea either, warning that detainees relocated to mainland prisons were escape risks or targets for breakout conspiracies by extremists. Obama reminded him that "no one has escaped from a [high-security] federal prison," but few members wanted to vote to place known terrorists on the mainland, and the prison remained in operation, with a reduced prisoner population, well past the end of the Obama and Trump administrations.[13]

Obama had also campaigned on reducing the US presence in Afghanistan, and late in January 2009, he told the Speaker he had ordered military leaders to pursue only "minimalist goals" in Afghanistan. He rejected the kind of nation building Bush had initially decried but had been sucked into. "It would be nice if things improved," Obama said, "but that isn't the goal."[14] He vowed there would be no "Vietnam-type escalation on my watch." US forces would do the "bare minimum," ensuring that Afghan-based terrorists could not attack the US homeland.

House Democrats greeted Obama's cautious approach as welcome news. Few were anxious to continue voting tens of billions of dollars every few months, which they preferred to direct to unmet domestic policies. Pelosi warned that she faced a serious challenge managing the "exuberance of my members" who expected expeditious withdrawals from both countries. Securing their votes for war supplementals was going to become much more difficult, and she certainly could expect no help from House Republicans, some of whom were already demanding a select committee to examine the new administration's performance in Afghanistan.

Murtha was no more sanguine about Afghanistan than Iraq and bemoaned having to write yet another multi-billion-dollar supplemental. Moreover, Gates, now Obama's defense secretary, acknowledged there was no possibility of military victory in Afghanistan. The only chance for success, he and Murtha agreed, was through diplomacy, a view shared by Gen. James Jones, the new national security advisor. Those discussions would invariably include numerous warlords, many recently released from prison, who were collaborating with drug lords, the Taliban, and Al-Qaeda.

It came as an unwelcome surprise to war critics when Obama proposed an increase of seventeen thousand US forces in Afghanistan to be supplemented by troops from our hesitant allies. Jordan's King Abdullah told Pelosi the decision would win broad support in the region, but the Speaker was skeptical.[15] Past ramp-ups had yielded no sustained benefits, she insisted. Moreover, with the spring fighting season imminent, a spike in casualties would provoke strong public reactions.

Gates did not dispute Pelosi's grim forecast and had his own doubts about the small surge. Even if the US commitment topped sixty-five thousand troops, nearly double the current level, he admitted that he would "be skeptical" of any positive outcome. In the 1980s, he recalled, the Soviets had a hundred thousand forces in Afghanistan before finally withdrawing in ignominy. Just weeks into the new administration, there was a sense of again being trapped in a foreign quagmire. "If we walk away," she conceded, "the whole thing falls apart."[16]

At least Obama was following through on his promise to withdraw US forces from Iraq. "The president has put us on the path to ending the war," a relieved Pelosi declared. But Murtha was wary that leaving behind thousands of troops to provide force protection, train Iraqi soldiers, and conduct counterterrorism could create targets for deadly attacks. She suggested the administration "sharpen their pencils and take the number down [to a] smaller residual presence."[17]

Obama soon assured that "our combat mission will end" in Iraq by August 2010, with all forces removed by the end of 2011. "Iraq's future is its own responsibility," he declared. There would also be a complete reevaluation of Afghanistan in the fall. "I want to give the generals a chance to secure the ground and get the [August] elections done," he explained. "If we don't see progress, it may lead to a smaller footprint" for the United States. "I support you all the way," she declared, offering to "smooth the way by speaking to other members." A glum Obama admitted privately, "There are no good answers."[18]

Other war critics were less supportive. "The administration has no clue on Afghanistan," Obey complained, denouncing it as a "a miserable mess" and predicting the war would "last eight years" and "destroy the Obama presidency."[19] Most of the terrorist cells and drug running operated out of Pakistan, he pointed out, and he questioned if the new president possessed "the tools to handle" that country. Even so, he said, "We should provide everything [Obama requests] and a bit more" so that if the wars ended in failure, it would be clear that culpability rested with Baghdad and Kabul, not Capitol Hill.

That kind of concern necessitated closer collaboration between the White House and Congress on such a sensitive subject, the Speaker told Denis McDonough of the National Security Council. When another $11 billion supplemental was requested in March, she urged a briefing of the entire Congress on the president's deployment plans, not just the leadership. That was "not what Obama agreed to" before the election, she reminded McDonough. The president needed to spend more time building relationships on the Hill and not assume his top advisors could play that crucial role. "Rahm was in the House for only three terms," she told McDonough, "and the president served for just two years in the Senate" before beginning his campaign for president. "They barely got their feet wet" in dealing with congressional politics. Powerful players in the House were demanding greater accountability. Even military sympathizers like Skelton declared, "I have no idea what the money is being spent for in Afghanistan," while Obey professed "no faith" in al-Maliki or Karzai to address massive corruption or root out terrorists.[20] McDonough got the message and quickly informed the Speaker that the briefing for all members would take place as she had requested.

Several days later, Pelosi huddled privately in her office with Gen. David Petraeus, whose new report on Iraq was grim: ten to fifteen daily attacks on markets, unsecured borders, and threats of "stronger retribution" against Al-Qaeda and Sunnis that prompted waves of destabilizing outmigration. Al-Maliki's stature had grown since his recent election victory, but he remained "very conspiracy minded" toward minorities, including the Kurds and Baathists. To Pelosi's relief, Petraeus did not view these issues as jeopardizing Obama's timetable for withdrawal of US combat forces, although it presented a "major logistical problem."[21]

Afghanistan was a different story. Although Karzai would doubtless win re-election, the situation would "get harder before it gets easier," Petraeus warned. It was proving difficult to dislodge the Taliban, Al-Qaeda, and drug kingpins from the eastern part of the country where they flourished with little worry about the government's efforts to pacify the region. The answer, he recommended, was not to send additional forces who would be perceived as conquerors but rather for civilian agencies to work with the local populations.

In early May, Gen. Charles Jacoby, commander of the multinational forces, told a House CODEL visiting Iraq that most troops would be removed from Iraq by August 2010. That was a political decision, he emphasized, and did not reflect conditions on the ground. "It's a requirement," he admitted, "so we will begin withdrawing."[22] But he warned that "if we pulled *all* of our forces out of Baghdad, we would have big problems" because Al-Qaeda remained "resilient" despite the improvement of the Iraqi forces.

Support for a diminished US presence also came from al-Maliki, who opposed leaving even a small number of forces in Mosul and Baghdad. The remaining pockets of violence "will not affect the stability of Iraq," he predicted, confident upcoming elections would "strengthen democracy and lead to a new Iraq."[23] Pelosi suggested that "the timing for withdrawal needs to be agreed to by Iraq and the United States." "You understand very well," he replied.

But the two leaders disagreed about a recent inspector general's report that concluded al-Maliki's government tolerated what it considered an "acceptable level of corruption." Al-Maliki insisted the problem was well in hand, but Pelosi disagreed, terming the abuse "rampant" and warning it could "ruin reconstruction and lead to a second insurgency."

The Speaker was even less sanguine about the situation in Afghanistan. The country was "a mess," she told US ambassador Louis Susman during a visit to London, recalling Petraeus's prediction that fighting could continue for a decade. Even with conditions on the use of the money and duration of deployments, it would be a "heavy lift" to find the votes in the House for continued war funding. Everyone was tired of the war, terrorism, and tension, she told Prime Minister Gordon Brown. She related a recent conversation with Hosni Mubarak, who after three turbulent decades in office said he simply wanted to "be able to walk down the street unrecognized." "Mr. President," she advised, "being unrecognized is very overrated."[24]

Pelosi returned home to renewed allegations about her knowledge of torture, and she added fuel to the fire by asserting that the CIA lied to Congress on a regular basis. "I was never briefed those tactics were being used," she restated, reminding reporters that Democrats had moved swiftly on winning the majority to impose limitations on the abuse. She recalled that Bush had vetoed those restrictions, asserting they "would take away one of the most valuable tools in the war on terror."[25]

Tired from her long flight, Pelosi's words were unusually harsh. She dismissed Republican and CIA critics as the "scum of the Earth," atypical language coming from the Speaker who blanched at the sharp rhetoric that effortlessly rolled off the tongues of many of her colleagues. "I'm not going to let the irresponsible behavior of the Republicans question my commitment to and record on human rights."[26]

Republicans cheerfully upbraided her. Senior Intelligence Committee Republican Peter Hoekstra (MI) alleged Pelosi had concealed her approval of torture, and Peter King (NY) denounced her as "an enabler" and "an accomplice for failing to disclose criminal activity." Pelosi brushed off the accusations, asserting "torture is my turf" and she knew "it doesn't work and it is wrong." She recalled that even hearing about torture methods in one briefing had revolted her. "I have to get out of this briefing," Pelosi had said. "This is making me sick to my stomach." By contrast, she charged, "Republicans are proud of torture" and were behaving like "cornered animals."[27] In one meeting, Boehner told Obama that critics overlooked the useful military intelligence torture produced, an assertion that was heatedly disputed.

In May, records released by the director of national intelligence indicated that congressional officials had been told in 2002 that torture, including waterboarding, had been used repeatedly on the accused terrorist Abu Zubaydah. But Pelosi continued to insist that the briefing had focused only on torture the Bush administration was "considering using in the future" and that she had been assured any interrogation techniques being contemplated were legal.[28] The CIA director, Leon Panetta, offered her support, noting that the description of torture at the 2002 briefing "may not be accurate." Panetta also lent credence to Pelosi's assertions of CIA suppression of information by revealing that a secret program to assassinate Al-Qaeda leaders had been withheld from Congress by the Bush administration.

Fox News's Brit Hume described the controversy as an "embarrassment" for the Speaker, but friends regarded the attacks as nothing more than pure politics. "Just dismiss the issue," James Carville suggested, "and move on."[29] Suggestions she was in political trouble were rejected by Miller as "ludicrous" and "an attempt by the architects and promoters of torture to try somehow to shift the blame to Democrats."[30] The normally calm Panetta was so infuriated by the Republican assault on the Speaker that he mused former vice president Dick Cheney must be "wishing for an attack" on the United States to justify further military action.[31]

At least with Obama in the White House, there was less resistance to the conditions Democrats placed on the legislation. A June 2010 supplemental included requirements that the defense secretary report to Congress every ninety days about progress in transitioning forces out of Iraq and make assessments of whether the performance of the governments of Afghanistan and Pakistan justified continued US aid.[32] The vote in the House was along partisan lines; 87 percent of Democrats and 3 percent of Republicans voted in favor, reversing the GOP's war support under Bush. In the Senate, the bill passed 91–5 with a few liberals and anti-spending conservatives offering opposition. "I'm tired of the progressives" who could never be satisfied, Pelosi sighed. "They have no strategic bones in their bodies."[33]

Vice President Biden called Pelosi before the vote to thank her for securing the needed votes. Unlike Obama, he had a long-standing friendship with the Speaker and was frequently enlisted to burnish the administration's sometimes frayed relationship with the Hill. "Congratulations, I love you," he told her, acknowledging she had accepted many unpleasant compromises. "I assume where your heart was."[34]

"And my brain!" Pelosi added.

Biden had long shared the skepticism of those who questioned the wisdom of the administration's Afghan policy. At a dinner in Kabul shortly before becoming vice president, he had warned Karzai that Washington's support was in jeopardy unless he curtailed rampant corruption. Karzai not only denied the charge but also testily accused the US military of indifference to the deaths of Afghan civilians. An irate Biden threw down his napkin and stormed out of the room. Returning to Washington, the vice president wrote a report that concluded, "We have no policy."[35]

Months later, he dismissed Obama's contention that escalating the number of forces would alter the outcome of the war. "The idea is you're going to have a united Afghanistan," he asked incredulously, "that we are going to be able to bring [the country] into the 21st century from the 14th century, is a ridiculous assertion." The Speaker remained displeased with the new Obama policy. At the beginning of the administration, she reminded Biden, she had promised to help the administration in every way possible during its first five months. And the five months were up.

In September, there were only "bad and risky options" in Kabul, Obama admitted to Reid and Pelosi, raising "the danger of an open-ended quagmire."[36] The widespread fraud in the Karzai government "makes it difficult to proceed," he acknowledged, but he also adamantly insisted, "I'm not going to let my presidency be consumed" by the war. Pelosi clapped her hands in agreement. No decisions had yet been made about troops or more money, he said. Instead, he would work with Congress to narrow the list of US objectives requiring a continued commitment to Karzai. That was the news Reid wanted to hear. "It's going to be hard to sell [adding] *another* 20,000 troops," the size of the surge favored by most of Obama's advisors other than Biden.

The case for adding forces was emphatically made by the commander on the ground, Gen. Stanley McChrystal, who envisioned a process of nation building that would "likely last many more years, cost hundreds of billions of dollars and entail the deaths of many more American women and men."[37] But the president assured the Speaker he would not order "a single additional troop there" without a complete review. "There won't be any mission creep," he promised. "We won't be bum-rushed . . . no slip and slide into a full-blown posture."

Pelosi advised him to avoid becoming isolated or overly dependent on military advisors. "Get as many hands on the bloody knife as you can, Democrats and Republicans," she recommended, warning the novice president that "the Republicans can pull out on you." Obama recognized the risks. "The right wing is being its usual stupid self," he agreed.[38] Yet while she felt she had given Obama "room to manage the issue," she left a meeting several weeks later feeling "very sad" about the administration's trajectory.

On December 1, declaring "the status quo is unsustainable," Obama announced he would send thirty thousand more troops for an expected duration of eighteen months. "I am convinced that our security is at stake in Afghanistan and Pakistan," he assured. "This danger will only grow if the region slides backward and Al-Qaeda can operate with impunity." Congressional Democrats were stunned.[39] While the president might have "no decent alternatives" at present, Hoyer urged that he explain the precise mission to the American people. Pelosi agreed. The speech had been a "tour de force," but she "didn't hear the clearest mission," which sounded a lot like the preceding seven and a half years.[40] Indeed, Obama's strategy seemed to give the unreliable Karzai yet "another chance to prove he is a reliable partner." The wariness proved warranted. The number of US forces continued to escalate until by early 2010, there were a hundred thousand troops in Afghanistan, a "full-blown posture" Obama had promised to avert.

Pelosi suffered a deep personal loss in February when Jack Murtha died following routine surgery. Murtha's death deprived the Speaker, the caucus, and the anti-war movement of a highly credible critic. In the time-honored spirit of Capitol Hill, the mourning for their colleague was truncated by the aspirations of those seeking to fill his seat on Appropriations. "How offended was I by their timing!" she confided. Others scrambled to assume his mantle of leadership against the war. The mercurial Dennis Kucinich declared he would force a floor vote to require removal of US forces. Anti-war allies warned such a vote doing so would expose their weakness. Early in 2010, Kucinich's motion failed 65–356.

After returning from another Mother's Day trip to Afghanistan in May 2010, Pelosi reported no progress on corruption or improved governance resulting from the surge. "You absolutely cannot go downtown in Kabul or Kandahar," she told Obama. Karzai remained defiant, thrusting a photograph of an impoverished Afghan family into her hands to remind her of the American responsibility. "Forget it," she told him, "we have poor people in the United States, too. The real question is corruption." Obama did not disagree about the shortcomings of the Afghan president. "Karzai is not suddenly going to transform into Abraham Lincoln," he noted. "He's a work in progress."[41]

On a helicopter with the Speaker to Marjah in Helmand Province in 2011, I sat next to the young machine gunner who squinted at the mountains for signs of terrorist threats. Walking across a former poppy field to the madrassa where boys and girls were studying together, surrounded by a phalanx of US troops and contractors, a military escort commented, "If you were here a year ago, you already would have been shot by a Taliban sniper." A request to visit one of the tiny shops ten feet from where our group stood prompted a five-minute conference among our guards. Finally, I was given permission to walk over. "No, thanks," I responded. "If it took that long for you to decide, I'll stay right here."

Another point of tension was McChrystal, who had been a burr under the administration's saddle for months. In the fall of 2009, the feisty commander criticized Biden's caution on Afghanistan, predicting his "shortsighted" counterterrorism strategy would result in "Chaos-istan." The intemperate remark led to a reprimand aboard Air Force One, but in a June 2010 article in *Rolling Stone* magazine, McChrystal struck again, dismissing a mention of the vice president by asking, "Who's that?"[42] The general made light of his remark. "I never know what's going to pop out," he explained.

Biden failed to see the humor. "I'd fire his ass," he told Pelosi. "Fire the bastard!" Reid agreed. "If Obama keeps him, it shows he's weak." The Speaker had warned the president about McChrystal months earlier, but the vice president questioned if Obama had the fortitude to fire the general. Obama hesitated, explaining that McChrystal was "a good man [who] made a mistake," but a second story filled with critical statements left the president no option. Two days later, Obama replaced McChrystal with Petraeus. The change, Pelosi said, was "not optimal but necessary."[43]

Pelosi's characterization could well describe Democrats' conflicted approach to Iraq and Afghanistan in the crucial 2005–10 period, "not optimal but necessary": the issue served as an effective means of unifying a minority but a source of caucus disagreement once in the majority; a point of conflict between the president and the Congress in which Democrats bitterly fought Bush's escalation but then reluctantly acquiesced in Obama's decision to triple the commitment to an Afghan war while praising his withdrawal from Iraq. As seemed always to be the case, the extraction from international military engagements proved infinitely more complex, divisive, uncontrollable and controversial than the decisions to become engaged in the first place.

A decade after the events discussed in this chapter, the *New York Times* published a major report on the Afghan war documenting the mendacity of three US administrations.[44] "Senior U.S. officials failed to tell the truth about the war in Afghanistan throughout the 18-year campaign, making rosy pronouncements they knew to be false and hiding unmistakable evidence the war had become unwinnable," the report found. A report by the latter-day Pecora Commission, whose creation Pelosi had championed, concluded that taxpayers had spent over $132 billion in efforts to rebuild and modernize Afghanistan, more than the cost of rebuilding all of Europe after World War II in current dollars.[45] According to a study by Brown University's Cost of War Project, there was little likelihood of any commercial benefit to the United States in Afghanistan even if taxpayers continued to pour $45 billion a year into the war-ravaged country.[46]

"We invade violent countries to make them peaceful," senior American diplomat James Dobbins has observed, "and we clearly failed in Afghanistan." As with other costly and lengthy military interventions, "We were devoid of a fundamental understanding of Afghanistan—we didn't know what we were doing," acknowledged Douglas Lute, a three-star army general who worked in the Bush and Obama White Houses. In January 2020, the Iraqi legislature voted to request that the United States remove all of its forces from Iraq, and a little more than a year later, President Biden announced the removal of all troops from Afghanistan by August 31. Even before the troops and other Americans departed in a dismal and deadly evacuation for which Biden was vilified, the Taliban overran most of the country, easily overthrowing the isolated and ineffective government in Kabul. After two inconclusive decades, four administrations, ten Congresses, trillions of dollars, and hundreds of thousands of lives, America's longest wars were over.

CHAPTER 22

"KEEP STEERING THE SHIP"

Although high-profile issues like economic recovery, climate policy, and health care dominated much of Congress's time and the attention of the press and the public, a plethora of other pieces of contentious legislation were also piling up for the attention of legislators: deficit reduction, gender discrimination, Wall Street reform. And there were always the unpredictable crises that erupted, distracting both the White House and Capitol Hill from their anticipated schedules. The remainder of the 111th Congress would be filled with all of those complex and unplanned challenges, with the overlay of a difficult midterm election awaiting members at the end of the year.

One month after enactment of the ACA, PBS broadcast *Obama's Deal*, a documentary that many on the Hill felt ignored their role in creating the complex law during the first three-quarters of the program. Pelosi was furious with Emanuel's assertion she had offered "no ideas" when objecting to the Senate's health care bill. "I'm fed up with working with those people in the White House!" Pelosi protested.[1] "This White House is amateur hour!" She would send her concerns to Obama and Biden, she pledged, and "our future relationship will depend on their response."

Minimizing the work of the Congress was particularly galling since members were simultaneously being castigated by the law's opponents. "The atmosphere is like a tinder box," Pelosi told the sergeant at arms. "Any spark can inflame it!"[2] Threats against the Speaker's safety escalated, and the district offices of several members were vandalized.[3] The blowback even reached Sister Carol, who was summoned to the Vatican on allegations of insubordination.[4]

Hoyer reproached Republicans for their inflammatory rhetoric, citing Boehner's comment that freshman Steve Driehaus (OH) was "a dead man" and referencing other GOP leaders who talked about "putting members in the crosshairs" for supporting the health care law. "When leadership does things, it gives license to unstable people," Hoyer warned.[5] For Clyburn, a veteran of the civil rights struggles of the 1960s, the Republicans' refusal to condemn the threats was reminiscent of the indifference shown to the murder of three civil rights activists in 1964. When Cantor objected, citing the anti-war protests against Republicans, Pelosi reminded him that "Code Pink lived on my front porch for a year."

Pelosi suggested passing a resolution admonishing members to "lower the temperature," but Boehner advised doing so would "make it worse." However, Boehner did suggest that Randy Neugebauer (TX) offer an apology after calling Stupak a "baby killer" during the ACA floor debate. "We need a softer touch," he advised. But his new chief of staff complained about Republicans being singled out for using inflamed rhetoric and accused Democrats of "stoking it up [and] inflaming the situation [by] criticizing Bush over the Iraq war."[6]

The heavy spending and deficit concerns of the administration's first year brought together the joint leadership at the White House in February. Obama began with a promise to govern in "a more bipartisan fashion," which depended on Republicans ending their chronic obstructionism in the Senate.[7] "We're in big trouble in the country," Reid told an imperturbable McConnell. "You're holding up over two hundred pieces of legislation the House has sent over, 70 percent of them with more than fifty Republican votes." Unless that deadlock was broken, he warned, Democrats might alter the sixty-vote cloture rule. McConnell coolly dismissed Reid's threat. "It's no different than it's ever been," he responded. "It generally gets worked out and things move along."[8]

Nor was McConnell favorably disposed when Obama quoted him on the need to cut spending. "I can speak for myself," the Republican leader grumbled, launching into a diatribe against Obama's "binge of spending."[9] Boehner concurred, proclaiming all that was needed for a revival of business was to get "regulators off their backs" and lower taxes. "I don't want to be the skunk at the picnic," he assured Obama, by rejecting new spending. "No, *that's* Mitch!" the president said, without drawing a smile from McConnell.[10]

"Everything is on the table," Obama assured, despite "Democratic resistance," a comment not designed to win affection from his own party's leaders around the table. "The bottom line, guys, is I want to work with you. I am aware of the politics. But I am not waiting," raising the threat of executive orders to cut spending, including military and civilian pay and entitlements.[11]

Obama was also dissatisfied with Republicans delaying the confirmation of dozens of his appointees. Sixty-three nominees had waited more than one month for a confirmation vote, ten times as many as at a comparable time for his predecessor. "They are being held hostage," Obama charged. He was all for bipartisanship, but that could not be defined as "just me doing stuff outside the Democratic position," he insisted. "I need a little give on your side." Again, McConnell was unmoved and the issue unresolved. "Bush made the same protest," he noted dismissively. As the Republicans filed out, the president tried again to inject some humor. "I won't insist on you getting photos with me!" he joked, but no one laughed.

For their part, Democrats remained divided over how to pay for a long list of policy initiatives. "The liberals want to pay for nothing," Pelosi sighed, "and the Blue Dogs want to pay for everything." Obey was weary at the constant demands for spending reductions. "I'm ass-tired of people who know nothing about the numbers" making demands, he protested. Hoyer, who cherished his connections to the deficit hawks, agreed. "You can't just say you *want* cuts," Hoyer noted. "The Blue Dogs want cuts everywhere but no impact." Even the perennial target for cuts, foreign aid, was not as easy to reduce as some assumed. "AIPAC will eat our lunch," Obey said of the pro-Israel lobby, noting that Secretary of State Clinton was requesting *increases* in foreign aid. "She must be smoking something illegal," the chair cracked. And to make matters worse, Pelosi still had to muscle tens of billions for the wars through her reluctant caucus. Passing health care, she lamented, "was a day at the beach compared to Afghanistan funding."[12]

The last thing on McConnell's agenda was to help Democrats fashion a bipartisan budget deal, and certainly not one that relied on revising the Bush tax cuts. His offer was a multiyear freeze on domestic spending, including on the pay of federal employees. "My members are pretty enthusiastic about that," he drily declared, knowing Democrats considered such a proposal preposterous.

The approach proposed in 2009 by deficit hawks Judd Gregg (R-NH) and Kent Conrad (D-ND) was still knocking around Washington: a bipartisan panel charged with examining every facet of spending and whose recommendations Congress would be obliged to consider. The proposal had appeal in the senators' tiny, heavily white home states of North Dakota and New Hampshire but was a hard sell among Democratic urban and minority constituencies who feared programs serving their communities would be the prime target. Obey felt similarly about his conservative House colleagues whom he dismissed as "Johnny One Notes" for their relentless emphasis on cutting spending. "I'm tired of kissing the Blue Dogs' butts," he told Pelosi.[13]

In April 2009, Emanuel had told me the administration would not embrace an entitlement commission, a welcome promise as we rallied support for health care. Pelosi had also told the White House "no commission on Social Security" because seniors would be 25 percent or more of the off-year electorate in 2010 when her members would be on the ballot, nearly twice the 2008 level. It was fine "if [Obama] wants to do it in *his* election year," she inveighed, "but not in *ours!*"[14]

By June, however, Obama was flirting with the idea. "I'd be very cautious," Pelosi warned. "We can do some hearings, but I do not like creating a commission." She had little confidence in the administration's assurances Democratic priorities would not be on the chopping block alone. "We are not getting thrown under the bus by the White House," she advised, pledging to "build immunity against what the White House does to us" whether intentionally or not. If the administration insisted on wading into the minefield of spending cuts, she told the president, "Focus on Senate earmarks!" Obama didn't bite. "That's scratching a scab!" he said.[15]

As usual, Biden was dispatched to soothe the Speaker, and he echoed her contempt for the conservative senators. "They're horses' asses," Biden affirmed. "Let's start there."[16] Reluctantly, she approved his writing a letter committing her and Reid to holding a vote on the creation of a deficit panel. Biden expressed anger the pledge had to be in writing. "I'm outraged they won't accept the word of the goddamned Speaker of the House!" he seethed. "But these bastards can't hold us up." Pelosi agreed. "I'm with you," she told him.

But the Senate surprisingly defeated the commission on January 26, 2010, as seven conservative Republicans voted against the plan, including McConnell.[17] His excuse was his concern the panel might recommend raising taxes, but both Democrats and the press lambasted the Kentuckian's hypocrisy. "No single vote could embody the full cynicism and cowardice of our political elite at its worst or explain by itself why problems do not get solved," declared the *Washington Post.* "But here's one that comes close."[18]

A few weeks later, Obama issued Executive Order 13531 creating the National Commission on Fiscal Responsibility and Reform with eighteen members appointed by the congressional leadership and himself.[19] The order set a postelection deadline of December 1, 2010—after the fall elections—for issuance of a report identifying "policies to improve the fiscal situation in the medium term and to achieve fiscal sustainability over the long run." To assure the recommendations would not skew toward tax increases or spending cuts, a bipartisan supermajority—fourteen of the eighteen commissioners—would be required to approve any final recommendations. A stalemate would not block executive action, Obama warned. "We're not waiting for the commission" to attack the deficit, he declared. But the White House itself was sending mixed signals, sometimes criticizing Congress for profligacy while simultaneously promoting new initiatives that burnished the president's reputation. "There's no appetite for spending" unless the president proposed payfors or declared an emergency, Pelosi admonished.[20] "They're triangulating," lamented Hoyer, "we're strangulating."[21]

Prospects for achieving consensus dimmed almost immediately as Republicans insisted the commission rule out any tax increases.[22] The appointments did little to discourage speculation of a likely stalemate.[23] As chairs, Obama named Clinton's former chief of staff Erskine Bowles and Alan Simpson, a retired Senate Republican whose wisecracking personality did little to hide strong conservative views. For months to come, Pelosi would accuse the two tall, lanky chairs of impeding her efforts to pass the administration's recovery proposals by encouraging the Blue Dogs' fervent opposition to deficit spending. "Who sent those two beanpoles to talk to the Blue Dogs?" she demanded. Obama also appointed David Cote, chairman of Honeywell, which had issued a report recommending reductions in Social Security and Medicare benefits for upper-income retirees, a change many Democrats feared would undermine support for the universal programs. "We need to be very careful about Social Security," Pelosi appointee Jan Schakowsky (IL) warned. Even Paul Ryan (WI), a Boehner appointee who strongly embraced entitlement changes, declined to propose such reductions. "I can count," Ryan acknowledged.[24]

Pelosi was confident her priorities would stand up to rigorous scrutiny. "Put everything outside the door," she advised, "and then let it back in selectively." She reminded them Democrats would also insist on the application of Paygo to control spending. "We're in survival mode on the deficit," she agreed. "We may not like the numbers, but the alternative is worse." She also encouraged the commissioners to consider areas that merited *increased* investments like education and health care because they would reduce future costs, but the idea found little receptivity.[25]

"It is a suicide mission," Simpson predicted. "We will get savaged by everyone." His own conservatives resented his ridiculing the supply-side principle that had served as party dogma since the Reagan administration. "No one thinks we'll grow out of the deficit!" he scoffed, although such frankness had not won him plaudits. "The Republicans call me a pro-choice queer-lover who worked with Barney Frank," he laughed. "But you know, George Bush was the biggest spender ever. He never vetoed anything but stem cells!"[26]

Many Democrats doubted a serious recession was the right time to be considering spending cuts at all. Moody's Mark Zandi, who credited Democrats for creating more jobs in six months than Bush had in eight years, advised, "Don't pull back on recovery spending." He endorsed extending UI benefits and mortgage help for 4.3 million Americans at risk of losing their homes, but his advice made little impression on the commission or the Senate, where House bills remained stalled. "It's just pathetic that senators can't get anything done," Pelosi lamented.[27]

Much of the Democrats' core constituency had little interest in deficits and budgets, preferring action on long-delayed progressive issues like the Employment Non-Discrimination Act (ENDA) and ending the Clinton era's "Don't Ask, Don't Tell" (DADT) policy on gays in the military. Those representing frontline districts were less enthusiastic about focusing on such culturally edgy issues. "Members are very nervous," said Hoyer. The Blue Dogs "all think we'll lose the majority" if they pursued such propositions.[28]

DADT repeal seemed likely to happen either by statute or by executive action, especially after Defense officials from the Reagan and Clinton administrations and 132 retired generals and admirals endorsed the change. ENDA was a more complicated matter because it imposed new civil rights standards on millions of private businesses. Moreover, there were divisions even within the LGBTQ alliance over whether the bill's protections should apply to transgender people. Even within the very liberal Education and Labor Committee he chaired, Miller distrusted the optimism of proponents. Worried about stirring up the cultural Right, Hoyer advised that the decision be made whether to move the bills and if so, that the House should act "the sooner the better," before the opposition had time to organize.[29]

Barney Frank, perhaps the most prominent gay House member, argued that since DADT repeal was certain to happen, legislative priority should go to ENDA even if that meant dropping the transgender protections.[30] Shelving ENDA altogether, he warned, would generate "a big reaction" in the gay community. That logic made sense to Pelosi, but DADT repeal proponents claimed enough votes for passage once Gates determined it would have no negative impact on troops, and they wanted their day on the floor.

Reid was uncharacteristically upbeat about ENDA, insisting he had the sixty votes to beat a filibuster. "It's hard to stop," he predicted. But Pelosi remained dubious about subjecting her marginal members to another controversial vote before knowing Reid could pass the bill. It was clear the Republicans were preparing to "make us look bad," circulating amendments linking gay rights to pornography and threatening a divisive vote on transgender coverage.[31]

As the pressure built, Pelosi declared her willingness to schedule both bills "unless someone can show me why we should not." The administration weighed in against a DADT vote, arguing that a defeat would tie Obama's hands on achieving the same goal through an executive order. Frank and Van Hollen agreed it was a "tactical error" to force an unnecessary vote on DADT. "No one wants tough votes," Hoyer said, "and the moderates don't want to vote for *either* bill." Pelosi approved a delay. "Let's keep all the arrows in our quiver," she advised, especially since the Blue Dogs were in a "very bad mood" over the issue.[32]

It did not take long for Reid to sour on ENDA. Instead, he planned to include the DADT repeal in the defense bill despite Gates's entreaties. Not wanting to look like she was following the Senate's lead, Pelosi moved swiftly to include the repeal in the House's Defense bill, and it passed by forty votes. The Senate Armed Services Committee approved the same amendment, but momentum slowed as Reid searched for a sixtieth cloture vote on the floor. His best hope was Collins, who had supported the provision in committee because "the gays and lesbians have her scared to death."[33] But with McCain, the ranking member, fervently opposed, the Republicans blocked the cloture motion, postponing any DADT legislation until after the election.[34] "Congress is increasingly paralyzed by the partisan fury of the midterm elections," the *New York Times* declared in reporting the deadlock that effectively ended any chance of the House taking up the more contentious ENDA bill.[35]

And there were the unpredictable crises that had a way of complicating the legislative schedule. Slightly before 10:00 p.m. on April 20, 2010, forty-one miles off the Louisiana coast, the warning lights on the control panels on the massive oil rig Deepwater Horizon suddenly flashed red. Within moments, a series of explosions rocked the structure and a massive fireball tore into the night sky. Eleven workers were knocked into the sea or incinerated, their remains never found; another seventeen were gravely injured.

Over sixty-two thousand barrels a day of crude oil gushed into the waters of the Gulf of Mexico, dwarfing any previous marine oil spill in US history. With predictions of sixty to ninety days required to contain the leaks, the Gulf Coast, still reeling from Hurricane Katrina, was thrown into panic for good reason. Eventually, nearly five million barrels of crude oil poured into the Gulf, killing millions of fish and shorebirds, fouling miles of beaches and wreaking additional chaos on the coastal economy.

Republicans and local officials sought to compare Obama's response to Bush's record on Katrina, and the White House overreacted, announcing the possible closure of all exploratory drilling in the Gulf, which would have impacted thirty rigs employing ten thousand people.[36] Big oil suddenly looked to be 2010's version of the Wall Street miscreants and the health insurance firms that jacked up premiums. BP did little to dispel the comparisons when it was revealed the company would continue paying dividends to shareholders despite its resistance to providing greater compensation to victims of the spill.

Pelosi seized the opportunity to renew her call for action on the stalled House climate and renewable energy proposals. Obama agreed the disaster presented an opportunity, acknowledging "we keep missing the boat on [a] bold energy agenda."[37] But his immediate focus was on the Gulf, and he demanded that BP create a $20 billion compensation plan for communities impacted by the spill, promised cooperation on congressional inquiries, and vowed to reorganize the Minerals Management Service that oversaw drilling.[38] The initiatives prompted swift criticism from Republicans, including Joe Barton, who apologized to BP's management for the government's "shakedown." Even his own party's leadership criticized his comments, producing rumors his Commerce leadership position was endangered.

Democrats were also dissatisfied with the administration's response. Hoyer questioned the need to suspend drilling on unaffected rigs while Pelosi also felt the crisis exposed Obama's failure to follow through on 2008 promises that "there would be no more offshore drilling." The Speaker also chafed when he rejected her recommendation to appoint the highly respected marine biologist Sylvia Earle to the Gulf Coast investigatory commission. "We'll get a group of white guys," she fumed. "The oldest names! Ancient! Obama would never have been elected if everyone was fixated on white males."[39]

In response to the spill, the House narrowly passed what was described as "the toughest reforms ever to offshore energy drilling" 209–193. Only two Republicans voted for the bill while thirty-nine Democrats, mainly from energy-producing districts, voted no.[40] "I didn't think it would be so tough" to pass, a surprised Speaker admitted afterward. "The members were very impressionable" to industry lobbying.[41] Yet environmentalists described the response as feeble despite the financial penalties and tight regulations, but it didn't matter; oil state Democrats killed the bill in the Senate, leaving some House moderates with yet another difficult vote to explain.

The rocky legislative agenda was not the only source of aggravation by Hill Democrats who grumbled endlessly that the administration was poorly marketing the new health law, contradicting a specific pledge made after the weak marketing of the stimulus.[42] Organizing for America (formerly "Obama for

America"), the Health Care Action Network, and other validators had been charged with building the campaign, and Axelrod had pledged that "the president will be very active." But members became "furious" at what appeared to be a lackadaisical effort especially on Obama's part.[43] There was no evidence of efforts to engage prominent Americans like Colin Powell and Vicki Kennedy to promote the new law. "It's all very slow," one member complained two months after the bill signing. "There is no sense of urgency about selling the Democratic message."[44]

Late in April, I raised the concerns of Hill leaders with Axelrod, and he seemed apologetic. "We are all so caught up in the policy work," I recall him explaining. "Yeah, but you're the *messaging* guy!" I responded. A decade later, he acknowledged his team had been distracted. "We got a little bit too balled up in the details," he reflected. "At times we lost the narrative, but the narrative is really important."[45]

Most Americans not only lacked a clear understanding of the major legislative measures but also felt little benefit from them. The recession seemed unaffected by the recovery efforts, but there were reports that Wall Street moguls were again receiving high salaries and bonuses while the jobs, savings, and homes of average Americans remained precarious. Two weeks from the 2010 election, the Speaker complained there was little evidence of any benefit to House members from any promotional effort.[46]

In her own realm, Capitol Hill, Pelosi remained confident of her ability to crank out the administration's legislation, although she did not welcome the White House's advice on how to do so. "I told them, 'you want results, we'll get it,'" she recalled, "'but don't tell us how to manage the floor!'"[47] One priority was finishing the complex Dodd-Frank legislation tightening the regulation of the "recklessness on Wall Street" that had provoked the economic crisis. "The public wants transparency," Pelosi insisted, an end to the "nationalizing of risk and privatizing of gain at the public's expense." The House had approved its version in mid-2009, losing every Republican and twenty-seven Democrats, mostly Blue Dogs.[48]

Reid had proclaimed himself "happy to work with Republicans," but Dodd's effort to enlist senior committee Republican Bob Corker (TN) had proven futile.[49] "They are opposed to regulatory reform," Reid said. The Speaker agreed.

"The Republicans were not willing to rein in the insurance industry" during the health care debate, and now she doubted "they're willing to rein in the financial services industry." At last, in May, Reid found the votes (including four Republicans) to pass the Senate's version. The Speaker's major hope was that the conference committee could finalize the bill swiftly, before powerful forces could sabotage it. "I've met with Dodd," Obama assured, "and I don't see a problem" finishing the bill by midsummer.

But Dodd did have problems, especially with the unpredictable Russ Feingold, whose opposition was "empowering the Republicans" whom Reid needed to pass the conference report.[50] The changes they demanded were unacceptable to the House's liberal Black caucus without whom Pelosi was short of votes; with too many concessions to liberals, Frank added, he would lose sixty business-oriented New Democrats.

Pelosi sided with her chair against the dilution of the bill demanded by the moderates. "I don't trust banks as much as you do," she told business-friendly Democrats.[51] Obama also weighed in against any effort to weaken the bill. "I did not run for office to be helping out a bunch of fat-cat bankers on Wall Street," he had said in December. "The people on Wall Street still don't get it. They're still puzzled, asking 'Why is it that people are mad at the banks?'"[52]

On June 28, the prognosis for the bill became murkier with the long-anticipated death of Robert Byrd. Myrick reported Reid would have to wait until Byrd's replacement was appointed to be certain of having sixty votes for cloture, a delay that complicated Dodd's effort to keep Republican supporters "locked in." Suggestions they use the time to revisit the conference agreements met with a stern refusal from the Speaker. "I'm telling Barney to stay with what we have," she declared, and to prevent tampering, she put the 2,223-page conference report on the floor just before the Fourth of July break. The vote was 234–192 with only three Republicans in favor. Privately, Pelosi expressed outrage that nineteen Democrats had opposed the bill, accusing them of "looking out for big banks and trading houses."[53] Frank was more upbeat, exhibiting his irreverent sense of humor when a reporter asked if the Republicans' recommittal motion had included an irrelevant reference to pedophilia, a crass tactic often used to embarrass Democrats who procedurally opposed such motions. Citing language from the motion, he cracked, "Well, that depends on what 'end user' means."[54]

Pelosi was deeply worried "some shills for Wall Street" would ramp up opposition to the conference report in the Senate. "The biggest money in the world will go after it over the [Fourth of July] break," she warned, but Reid's hands were tied. "I need Byrd's vote," he explained, "but he's in senator heaven." Pelosi was exasperated by the delays. "There's no reason for us to pass anything," she insisted. "The Senate is not voting for anything!"[55] Yet two weeks later, Reid and Dodd secured their sixty votes and the bill was passed 60–38. Even Elizabeth Warren, the Harvard lawyer and driving force behind reform, declared that "substantively, it turned out very good."

But Pelosi came away with renewed frustration. Once again, the Senate's need for Republican votes had dictated concessions, like removing a $20 billion tax on large banks demanded by Scott Brown.[56] Still, Obama lavished praise on Pelosi for the victory. "Keep knocking things out [of the park]," he told her. "I never take you for granted." She urged him to "give a shout-out" to Frank and other members. "Barney did a great job," the president agreed, "but *you* keep steering the ship!"[57] She was pleased that two years after the TARP turmoil, Congress had delivered a tough rebuff to Wall Street—"the party is over"—an improvement over the "not very salable message" on a bumper sticker a friend made for Frank: "Things would have sucked worse without me."[58]

Other key legislation was proceeding less promisingly, especially in the Senate, where negotiations on the climate bill were proceeding "like Comedy Central," Reid drolly reported. "Build pressure in the districts," she counseled Reid. "There's no reason for us to try to pass anything if the Senate isn't voting for anything!" She pressed for the changes in Rule XXII governing cloture that Reid had threatened but retreated from.

But within the House, many members were losing interest in aggressive legislating, and not just because of the Senate. Constituents "want a reduced emphasis on the government," Miller reported. "They go blank when asked what they think we actually do. Most of their responses are 'spending' and 'deficits.'" Pelosi herself blanched at demands for billions in new spending, asserting, "I have higher priorities before hitting the members with another big new bill."[59] Those attitudes put the top Democrats at odds with activists who continued to insist on promoting their favorite bills.

"Do they have any muscle to get votes?" Pelosi impatiently asked. "Gays, health, nutrition. I'm only interested in people who can deliver votes. I can't run the floor on the basis of outside advocates." She expressed similar frustration with members she had promoted to key committee slots who were proving divisive. "I'm very disappointed," she told Jared Polis (CO), a freshman who received a coveted appointment to Judiciary but then opposed one of her initiatives. "Cooperation is a two-way street." When a chastised Polis agreed to engage in "no more rabble-rousing," Pelosi scolded, "At least know what you are talking about!"[60]

The persistent grousing by the Blue Dogs was another constant irritant. Tanner reported the group was "volatile" and had "hard feelings" about being ignored, although the leadership felt they had devoted many hours to addressing their protestations. "Why don't they go join an independent party?" the Speaker wondered. But even with such second-guessing, she felt the Dogs "aren't the problem" complicating her efforts. It was the delays and division across the Capitol in the Senate that made Democrats "look useless."[61]

And there was still yet another supplemental with $37 billion for Afghanistan and tens of billions more for an emergency in Haiti and the oil-ravaged Gulf Coast. Tougher border enforcement in the Southwest added $600 million more. The Blue Dogs as well as anti-war liberals all shared Obey's vexation about incurring debt for low-priority policies. "I don't give a damn about the war or the Gulf!" Obey proclaimed, convinced the Senate's bill would "help the richest" and bail out the oil companies. Pelosi agreed. The Senate had "test[ed] my patience in the last few months," she admitted. Its priorities were "way out of whack."[62]

Obey had reached his personal breaking point. At a White House picnic, he relayed his concerns about the gloomy 2010 electoral outlook, including his own seat, to an administration aide. "Thank God this isn't 2012!" when Obama would be seeking reelection, the staffer responded. "Well, it is for us!" the incredulous Obey bellowed.[63] Frustrated by the stalemates, exhausted and facing a brutal campaign, Obey told Pelosi he would retire rather than face likely defeat. "The numbers aren't there," he confided. "I hate it, but the only goddamn way to save the seat is with someone without the baggage of incumbency."[64]

The seeming indifference of the White House toward the electoral problems facing House members peaked when, at 7:00 p.m. on a Saturday evening in June, the president called on Congress to provide $50 billion for state and local aid but identified no payfor offset. Members felt the president was grandstanding for weekend press, hoping to gain credit for what Democratic leaders had already agreed to do while ignoring the deficit implications on which he often lectured Congress. An irate Pelosi told Schiliro, "We need to have a truth session. I need *consultation* with Congress, not *notification*. You can't pass anything on your own. You *need* us."[65] Glumly, Schiliro admitted the letter constituted a "breakdown" in communications, but for the Speaker, it "reinforce[d] the members' worst suspicions" about the Obama White House. "We want to help, but you aren't getting the message," she inveighed. "You BTU us every time and it is antagonizing the members."

Still, Congress had to approve the supplemental the Senate cleared on

May 27 by a wide 67–28 margin. Although it contained only modest anti-recessionary provisions, Boehner ruled out Republican support in the House for anything but war funding, a complete nonstarter for Democrats. Obama was finally losing patience with the minority. "They need to be more responsible generally," he concurred.[66] Still, he exuded confidence he could thread the needle and help Democrats survive. "Every bill is a test of my leadership," she reminded him. "We're going to be fine," he insisted.

The House passed its version of the supplemental on July 1 by a 239–182 vote, and as Boehner forecast, all but three Republicans voted "no." But Democrats were stunned to hear Obama might veto the House bill if it became the final product. "They have a hell of a nerve!" Pelosi told Hoyer.[67] While she was forcing her members through another tough vote, the Senate was working just one and a half days that week. Yet five days later, the House, with no hope of passing its more generous version, accepted the Senate bill 308–114. Obey, his domestic initiatives ravaged, voted against his own committee's bill.

The capitulation was significant, as was the Senate's midsummer abandonment of the climate bill. "I had to make a decision," Reid explained. "We don't have the votes." It was, the press reported, "the first major legislative setback" for the Obama administration, and Republicans were delighted to highlight the division within the Democratic ranks. "Reid can hardly blame Republicans when his own party doesn't even support the idea," gloated a spokesman for Alaska's pro-oil senator, Lisa Murkowski.[68] A disappointed Durbin agreed there was no chance of passage, sparking yet another round of stories about the House having been BTU'd. In this case, many believed Pelosi bore culpability for insisting on pressing forward on climate when the chances of Senate action never appeared promising.[69]

In midsummer, Obama made yet another effort to persuade the Republican leadership to cooperate on confirmations and appointments instead of continuing to use their "complete veto power" to "gum up the works," especially in the Senate.[70] "That's not the relationship between how the two branches operate," he lectured, but McConnell blamed the president for naming recess appointees who had been rejected by the Senate.[71] Obama interrupted him to insist he had used the process less than Bush and that some of his appointees had waited eight months for hearings (compared to Bush's average of twenty-four days). McConnell sat by impassively. "You finish [talking] and I'll send you a memo," he dismissively said. "You obviously want to trade statistics." When Obama cited one particular appointment as the basis for the GOP leader "punishing me," McConnell again bristled, "You don't need to represent my position for me."

The bigger problem, Boehner interjected, was that some of the president's legislation "scares people to death. A little clarity would help." The generally unflappable president became exasperated. "Here's some clarity you can take away," he lectured Boehner. The Republicans had sat silently as Bush's tax policies exploded the deficit over the decade. "You can't say you're concerned about the deficit after creating a $700 billion hole that's supposed to be made up magically," Obama charged. As we prepared to leave, an incensed Obama came over to Pelosi and me. "How about those Republicans!" he asked.

Republicans were also obstructing passage of legislation providing health benefits for those sickened by the 9/11 terrorist attacks because of its $7.4 billion price tag. Many suspected the opposition was also due to the assistance going mainly to people in the heavily Democratic New York metropolitan area. "The Republicans are playing politics," reported Whip Jim Clyburn, pointing to the GOP's mischievous effort to bar undocumented victims from qualifying for benefits.

There was a long-shot maneuver that could be used in the House to block crippling amendments: suspension of the rules, a floor procedure that required a two-thirds majority for passage. Weiner and other New Yorkers anxious to move the legislation called suspension "the smart way" to consider the bill. Although Hoyer warned the strategy was "very problematic," Pelosi gave her approval. The bill went down 255–159 with most Republicans opposed.

"It was wrong for the overwhelming majority of Republicans to vote against the bill," a furious New York mayor Mike Bloomberg acknowledged, but he also chastised Pelosi for using suspension, which "made passage so much more difficult." Why hadn't she brought up the bill under normal procedures where a simple majority would have allowed it to pass? The Speaker was incensed by the second-guessing. "I don't tell you how to run New York City," she reprimanded Bloomberg. "Don't tell me how to run the House!" Bloomberg obviously did not understand that under an open rule, Republicans intended to offer amendments that would have made the bill toxic.

"Do you know what a 'motion to recommit' [MTR] is?" she quizzed. Bloomberg admitted he did not. "So, you *don't* know," she angrily reproached, explaining how Republicans used MTRs to raise divisive issues like excluding undocumented people. Bloomberg responded the city would "pay for undocumenteds" even if the bill passed with the restriction, but he missed the Speaker's point. "Our people will not *vote* for a bill that is anti-immigrant," she explained, and the Republicans would have opposed the bill even if their "gotcha" amendment had passed. "I don't like to lose," Pelosi added. Why hadn't he ensured there were hundreds of first responders lobbying on Capitol Hill before the vote? Bloomberg was apologetic. "I could have filled the galleries," he insisted. "Why didn't you?" Pelosi rebuked.[72]

With anti-Muslim violence flaring in New York and Republicans denouncing the bill as "a boondoggle," Schumer announced no Senate action on the measure before the election. "We need a Republican commitment, but we don't have one," Schumer explained. "I have never seen Bloomberg get a Republican vote in the Senate."[73] Even so, Pelosi was not ready to pull the plug, believing House approval would put "great pressure" on the Senate. On September 29, the House passed the $7.4 billion bill by a healthy 268–160 margin.[74] This time, New York first responders and their families packed the public gallery above the chamber.

The Republicans had plenty of controversial votes to use against Democrats in the campaign, but the biggest problem continued to be the stubbornly weak economy. "There's no hope in the hiring halls," unions reported. As Democrats searched for an effective economic message, Hoyer feverishly touted his "Make It in America" (MIIA) plan to encourage the creation of domestic manufacturing. Significant numbers of Americans—including 83 percent of Democrats and 78 percent of independents—favored a national manufacturing strategy, and 58 percent believed that US materials should be required in infrastructure construction. "Every bag of produce should have an American flag on it," Cardoza suggested.[75] "Let's find nationalistic messages in what we've voted for already," Pelosi recommended, contrasting Democratic concern for hard-hit Americans with Republicans' unanimously opposing recovery legislation. But the vague concept found little support at the White House.[76] A few months after the election, Axelrod privately ridiculed Hoyer's initiative as "fake it in America."[77]

But no other election narrative was working either. Mike McCurry detected a "crisis of confidence" among members concerning the leadership's "people versus the powerful interests" frame. "The members won't use it," he warned.[78] The Gulf oil spill, the lagging job creation numbers, the war in Afghanistan, and ethics concerns were all depressing voters who found little to be enthused about in the Democrats' record. "There's too much confusion on the legislation," Steve Ricchetti warned. Even emphasizing legislative successes like health care, which had delivered little thus far, was of questionable value in a weak economy.

Both Pelosi and Reid remained angry the DNC had not produced the $5 million promised their campaign committees. The Senate leadership was "bitching about Obama" and the lack of message coordination, Reid reported.[79] "They're looking at 2012," Pelosi concluded, rather than focusing on the fate of their congressional allies. She questioned whether Obama fully appreciated the implications of a victory by the Republican extremists she battled daily. "The White House and the president have no agenda if we don't win," she reminded Axelrod. "We need air cover from the White House. This is survival. The Republicans will lie. It will be down and dirty."[80]

The midsummer scrambling for money and message—two key components of Pelosi's campaign mantra—illustrated how much time and energy had been consumed on the complexities of legislating at the expense of political positioning. "For the last eighteen months, we've been *governing*," Schiliro noted. "The Republicans have been *campaigning*," and they would only intensify their vitriolic charges over the summer, during the short September session, and up to Election Day. One thing was for certain: political peril lay ahead. "Nothing," Pelosi wearily noted, "resolves itself."[81]

CHAPTER 23

THE UNFINISHED AGENDA

Congress reconvened in September with Democrats ten points behind in the generic race for the House, a devastating gulf that foreshadowed the loss of dozens of seats, and perhaps even majority control. "We need a very strong September," was Pelosi's urgent advice to her colleagues.[1] With the end of the fiscal year fast approaching on September 30, members would have to agree on another mega-billion-dollar continuing resolution to avert a disastrous government shutdown just weeks before Election Day. On other crucial legislation—extension of the expiring Bush tax cuts, 9/11 victims' assistance, and child nutrition among the measures—many House Democrats anticipated renewed pressure to accept the Senate's versions or risk procedural delays that could defer resolution of the issues into a postelection lame duck session or kill them altogether.[2]

Reid had suggested it would be easier to postpone action to a lame duck when his retiring and defeated members might be more inclined to cast controversial votes. It also might be easier to secure votes from Republicans who wanted to see how much their position was improved by the election before entering into negotiations with Democrats. Pelosi reacted negatively, asserting that even the mention of such delay disincentivized members from casting difficult votes during the September work period. "The Senate goes slower than glaciers in retreat," she bemoaned. "The Senate's role is to advise and consent, not to obstruct and veto!"[3] Chuck Schumer agreed the abuse of the filibuster had stymied the Senate's operation. "In January, we will change the sixty-vote rule," he vowed, "or we deserve to hang."[4]

For the moment, however, the Senate retained much of the power to determine whether legislation moved to the finish line. The House's dilemma was illustrated in August, after the House had already recessed. The Senate finally approved a scaled-down aid package for state and local governments that the

House had passed seven months earlier. To avoid further delays, senators sur-
reptitiously suggested Pelosi call her members back from their summer vacations to approve the Senate bill.

"The Senate cracks me up," she said, wondering "who is brave enough to
call me to tell House to come [back] in."[5] Hoyer agreed the suggestion was ludicrous. "Let's amend it and send it back!" he joked. But further procrastination on
the bill would deny long-sought support for hundreds of thousands of teachers,
nurses, and first responders. Pelosi asked Boehner to sign off on moving the
bill by unanimous consent to obviate the need for asking members to return to
Washington for a single vote. "We'll find some way to make it work," Boehner
agreed privately.

But he had misjudged the willingness of his members to be conciliatory,
and Pelosi was compelled to recall members, disrupting family vacations and
campaign schedules. Republicans denounced the bill as a payoff to teacher and
public employee unions, condemning its cost and the Democrats' payfor: closing
tax loopholes that facilitated moving jobs overseas. Only days after agreeing to
consider a unanimous consent approval, Boehner pivoted to oppose the bill as
an unwarranted bailout.[6]

The House members were additionally furious with having to take what they
considered an inferior Senate product after months of delay. But any changes to
the bill would send it back to an indeterminate fate in the Senate, and a post-
ponement could wreak havoc with state and local governments. "The problem is
the Senate doesn't know what it's doing!" Pelosi responded sharply.[7] Nor did she
spare the administration. "The White House has assisted the Senate in shov-
ing legislation down our throats Kevorkian-like," she angrily declared. But once
again, reality undercut the argument of the House, which capitulated, passing
the Senate version 247–161. Only two Republicans voted in favor.

The huge tax cuts enacted in Bush's first term were set to expire on December 31.[8] If Congress failed to approve an extension of all or some of these cuts,
most Americans faced a significant tax increase with the New Year, a fear being
actively exploited by the Tea Party activists. "People don't believe we'll cut taxes
after the election," communications strategist Anita Dunn advised, and since the
extension was all but inevitable anyway, many members wanted to get the credit
before the election.[9]

"All the press cares about is taxes," Pelosi observed.[10] She promised to bring
a bill forward when it was "in best interest of the House." "We should do the middle-
income cut and go" home, advised Miller, a viewpoint shared by 56 percent of

Americans, who felt the tax cuts should expire for households earning over $250,000 per year.[11] Extending the cuts for the richest few percent of taxpayers would "ruin the message" of the "middle-class squeeze" Democrats hoped to exploit during the fall campaign.[12] "Voters are angry because we didn't manage the message well," she told Axelrod. "They want to see us kick the Republicans in the teeth." Instead, the administration's ambivalent marketing of their legislative achievements left her wondering "if the Obama agenda is even recognized."[13]

Myrick was noncommittal about the timing in the Senate, where one Republican would be needed to pass the tax extension, assuming all Democrats remained on board, which the Speaker doubted. "The Senate doesn't know what it's doing," she warned. "We need leadership from the president." Obama also had endorsed extending only the middle-income tax cuts, but she was worried he might pursue fruitless negotiations with Republicans that would delay resolving the issue. "He can't be a little pregnant," she advised. "Either it's a go or a no-go."[14] Van Hollen was in agreement. "The president should say, 'I'll veto the tax bill if it includes an upper-income cut,'" he advised.

Pelosi personally was "agnostic on how to handle the tax cut" and, along with others, was open to allowing the entire Bush package to expire. Doing so would raise taxes but would also cut the deficit by hundreds of billions of dollars, reducing pressure for Congress to slash essential spending.[15] Axelrod insisted the extension for the middle class was essential. "People think we helped the banks, the auto companies," he said. "Now, they're asking, 'Where's *my* bailout?'" If Democrats could not extend the cuts before the election, they would find "the bloody dagger in their backs and have a very bad November."

Another difficult call involved the extension of the child nutrition law, a special interest of First Lady Michelle Obama. The administration was committed to "pull out the stops" to win passage of her only real legislative priority, and that likely meant the House accepting the Senate version, which was much smaller than the House-passed bill and used unexpended food stamp (SNAP) money to finance the child nutrition expansion. It was clear that the popular first lady's interest in campaigning for Democrats in the fall depended on securing her top priority. But Miller and DeLauro, the House's strongest promoters of its significantly more expansive version, insisted "no bill was better than the Senate" measure.[16]

The Speaker was astonished by the pressure to take the Senate bill. "The White House don't know from *nothin'*!" Pelosi vented. "It is amateur hour! They have no understanding of the House at all!"[17] In a conversation with the Speaker, Michelle Obama acknowledged the House bill's advantages but worried that extended debate might result in no bill at all. Her remarks had an unmistakably threatening inflection. "I could be helpful thanks to this crazy platform and my notoriety," she offered. "I want to be on the road [campaigning] *after* signing this important bill," all but declaring a failure to pass the bill meant she would not campaign for House candidates.[18]

It was the wrong approach to take with Pelosi. "People have been working on this issue for decades, even before I got to Congress" in 1987, she reminded the newly arrived first lady. "Members view [the Senate bill] as a missed opportunity" to increase funding. "Anything that passes the Senate by unanimous consent is not a good bill," she explained.[19] "I'd like to see if they can do better," and so would the advocacy groups that supported the House position.

The first lady pushed back. "The groups are not right," she insisted.

Pelosi sought to assure her. "*Something* is going to be done," she pledged. "Nothing is not an alternative. We're problem solvers, not line-in-the-sand people." Would the bill pass "before the session is over?" Obama pressed. "That's not the question," Pelosi corrected. "The issue is the *quality* of what we have for the recipients."

Mrs. Obama responded in personal terms. "This is my life that we're talking about!" she pressed. "I'm going to be effective on this!" Indeed, she admitted, the only reason she was "dallying in the legislative pond is because it is so important."[20]

If she wanted to help, the first lady could promote "collaboration between the House and Senate on bills that [we are told] are 'my way or the highway' by the Senate," Pelosi suggested. "See if you can find more money for nutrition" instead of allowing the SNAP program "to become an ATM" to fund senators' demands. "There will be a bill," Pelosi assured, but she cautioned Mrs. Obama, "Don't try to exploit your position [or] you could become the reason for the bill *not* passing." When the Speaker told Hoyer about the first lady's "condescending" comment about not wanting to "dally in the legislative pond" in the future, he agreed. "She and the president have the attitude that we don't know what we are doing," he bitterly noted, "and if only they were here, it would get done."[21]

Schiliro counseled Miller the additional $1 billion in the House nutrition bill was a nonstarter in the Senate, but he warmed to an additional $450 billion. "But it's a bad deal for the poor," Miller insisted. The administration turned up the pressure with Emanuel weighing in with DeLauro and agriculture secretary Tom Vilsack with Collin Peterson. Unless the House took the Senate bill, another high-ranking administration official warned, there would be "big problems" with the first lady.[22]

The pressure was working with the advocacy groups, which began falling into line behind the Senate measure, but the Black caucus was "in an uproar," Pelosi told Emanuel. The progressive caucus might be behaving "nice nice to the White House," Pelosi told Mrs. Obama, "but they yell at us!" "I'm not happy," the Speaker added, but she cautioned the members not to stir up public controversy.[23] "We'll get slammed if we don't pass it," she concluded. "There's no path to a bill with more money now."

When no response came from the White House for several days, Pelosi asked me to call Schiliro. "Tell him without guarantees of no future stealing from food stamps [SNAP], we can't take up child nutrition." Schiliro could not provide such an assurance. "It's hard to say in the abstract," he told the Speaker. "We could [try to] replace it in a future bill, but it could get blocked." Pelosi didn't like the answer. "If you promised everything, I would still have a problem," she replied, "and you haven't promised anything."[24]

Glumly, Schiliro backed off. "If you can't do it this week, then it needs to be one of the first issues during the lame duck," he advised. "Well, I don't think we can do it now," Pelosi concluded. "I don't have the liberals, let alone the Blue Dogs," she admitted. Reid feigned exasperation as well. "Obama never understood the legislative process," he said. "He wasn't here long enough. And his wife understands it even less!" He was exhausted by some of his own purists. "I'm disappointed in the liberals," he admitted. "You can't make them happy."[25] If he retained his seat and the majority, he vowed, like Schumer, to change the Senate rules to require only fifty-one votes to end a filibuster.

There was some good news on the economy with wages rising, new home sales growing, and the housing inventory at the lowest level in forty-two years. But in August, 473,000 new jobless claims were filed, and 48,000 jobs in state and local government were lost.[26] Even though the Congressional Budget Office, *Time* magazine, and other sources credited ARRA with revitalizing the economy, including in Boehner's own state of Ohio, the GOP leader unsparingly blamed Democrats for the continued economic weakness, ignoring his own party's opposition to the recovery legislation.

The political climate "is very bad for us," the Speaker told the caucus, noting that a growing number of voters believed the country was moving in the wrong direction. To make matters worse, the *New York Times* reported the leadership was preparing a "brutal triage," dropping financial support for faltering candidates to direct assistance to those who still had a hope of winning. Tom Perriello, who had voted reliably with the leadership despite his deeply Republican Virginia district, felt like he'd been "kicked in the stomach."[27] Pelosi dismissed the *Times* story outright. "There is no truth to it," she told the members. "There is no evidence [of such] a decision, no winks, no nods."[28] But the absence of evidence didn't mean no decisions had been made.

With so much grim news, there were few moments of levity as members prepared to recess to campaign full time. One occurred at a caucus meeting on September 29 when Pelosi acknowledged that members were under assault and recalled criticism that had been directed to her a decade earlier when she was managing her first bill on the floor. Dressed smartly and well prepared for the occasion, she handled the job smoothly and was pleased with her performance. Afterward, however, two more experienced hands offered critiques. Barney Frank, who was famous for his sartorial disarray—shirt untucked, tie askew and often stained, shoes scuffed—criticized her choice of wardrobe for the day. Meanwhile, the acerbic Obey advised she could have demonstrated greater tact in responding to critics. "Just what I needed," the Speaker told the caucus. "Fashion advice from Barney Frank and diplomatic advice from Dave Obey!" she recalled, to roars of laughter.

But the light moments were few and far between. Maddeningly, the administration continued to roll out new policy initiatives despite pleas from the Hill. "The president is asking Congress to do popular things without saying how to pay for them," Pelosi complained in mid-October. "He makes us look like we are sitting around doing nothing. I could say that differently," she suggestively teased, "but I won't." Others believed the president had decided the House was a lost cause. "He clearly has made a decision in favor of the Senate," said Miller.[29]

As he spoke around the country, Obama offered sympathy for the Democrats who "took really tough votes," hoping "they would be rewarded." But however messy and frustrating it had been, he insisted, Democrats deserved credit for having "prevented a second Great Depression," not to mention passing health care and Wall Street reform. It might have been "bad politics," he admitted, "but it was the right thing to do."[30] Heading into an election that could decide the control of Congress and their own careers, that was an appeal few members would make to their constituents.

CHAPTER 24

THE "SHELLACKING"

Shortly after the 2008 victory, President-elect Obama conducted a review of the economic and political challenges facing the new administration. David Axelrod recalled walking out of the briefing musing, "We are going to get our asses kicked in the midterms."[1] He and Schiliro warned Hill Democrats that if they headed into the election with the unemployment number north of 9 percent, disaster awaited the party.

Despite the Democrats' efforts since Obama's inauguration, only one in six voters felt they were doing better economically in the summer of 2010. A July *Newsweek* poll found that by a two-to-one margin, voters thought the unpopular TARP law had been unnecessary, and 63 percent saw no benefit from the ARRA stimulus. Two weeks before the election, only 8 percent of voters realized the 2009 stimulus had given them a tax cut at all; far more believed their taxes had *risen*.[2] Far fewer of the promised construction jobs were being filled than anticipated. "Shovel-ready was not as shovel-ready as we expected," Obama later admitted.[3]

Campaign consultants also recommended that members not tout the ACA since few Americans reported feeling any benefits from the law.[4] A frustrated Pelosi argued the administration "blew the selling job," enabling Republicans to characterize the law as laden with "death panels" for seniors and higher taxes for everyone else.

"You couldn't have handled the messaging worse," she reprimanded Axelrod. Now that the election was imminent, unions, the DNC, PhRMA, and progressive groups like Catholics United "want[ed] to aggressively engage" in support of the health law, said Jenn O'Malley of Organizing for America.[5] Americans United sent cupcakes to supporters, generated complaints to Republican offices, and greeted legislators at airports with supportive or displeased supporters.

But these efforts seemed feeble compared to the tens of millions of dollars the Chamber of Commerce and Republicans spent castigating Democrats.

People simply did not believe the legislation Democrats had spent two grueling years passing had made their lives easier, and those displeased with the state of politics were planning to vote Republican by a three-to-one margin. Warnings that Republicans would "go back" to earlier failed policies made little impression. "No one believes us!" confirmed the DCCC's Jenn Crider. Just 31 percent worried Democrats might lose the congressional majority, which made the election "nearly impossible for us," Pelosi conceded. If Democrats claimed success in remedying the crisis Obama had inherited, "people would think we were nuts." Stan Greenberg strongly agreed. "Don't say Democrats did a good job," Stan Greenberg cautioned.[6] "Don't claim you are creating jobs." But if talking about Democratic accomplishments was "not going to move the needle," in Van Hollen's words, Democrats were going to have difficulty finding a workable campaign theme.

One approach was to remind voters of GOP efforts to undermine Social Security and Medicare, popular programs among white, blue-collar workers who detested Obama and with whom Democrats were "falling off a cliff." Geoff Garin stressed this approach would appeal to older, white voters in the South otherwise hostile to Democrats' other priorities. Pelosi agreed that the Republicans had "handed these issues to us on a silver platter," she told her leadership. "We need to smack them in the face with it. People want to see the fight!"[7]

Van Hollen pressed for updating Trout's "differentiation" strategy that had worked so effectively when Democrats were in the minority in 2006. "We need to keep driving the contrast," he proposed. Pelosi was more succinct in her strategizing. "We need to take them down like we took down Bush," the Speaker insisted. "They want to see us kick the Republicans in the teeth." Axelrod agreed on the need to differentiate. "We can't win if the election is a referendum on us," Axelrod cautioned. "We need to keep them in the crosshairs. There's no enthusiasm for the Republicans."[8] Blame their leaders like Boehner, who struck Axelrod as a perfect foil, "the guy in the white belt at the country club screwing his neighbor's wife," completely oblivious to the trauma affecting middle-class Americans.[9]

Part of the challenge was to remind voters that Republicans, not just "Washington in general," were the problem, a distinction Obama often failed to make. "The reason Washington is 'broken' is because the Republicans have held up bills," DeLauro noted. They had "sat on the sidelines, offered no ideas, just hoped for our failure to advance themselves" and the special interests they represented.[10] "Congressional Republicans [are] eager to return to the 'exact same agenda' of failed Bush economic policies that put us in this mess," a March memo from the Speaker's office advised. "This Congress has enacted sixteen cuts for small business [and] voted to close loopholes that ship jobs overseas," but the Republicans had opposed fifteen of the sixteen small business cuts as well as "tax cuts for 98% of Americans" that had dropped tax bills to the lowest rate in sixty years.[11]

"Who's on your side versus standing with Wall Street?" was the key question, Paul Begala insisted. "Too often," Pelosi said, the public "thinks we are in bed with corporate interests," especially when they saw "Wall Street supplying advisors to Obama." But it was also true that many of the House's own economic advisors, former members, and former staff working as lobbyists, while sympathetic to the party's goals, also had ties to the financial services industry.[12]

Obama's inadequate financial support for congressional Democrats remained a sore point. "Everyone is giving their federal money to the White House," the Speaker complained. The president smiled coyly in response. "Are we soaking up all the money?" he teased, looking at Emanuel.[13] But she and Reid were in no lighthearted mood. "You can raise the money, so you need to give us $10 million apiece," she told the president, who declined to give "a hard commitment," promising vaguely to "do as much as I can do." But despite reinforcing the demand through White House political staff like Jim Messina, little help was forthcoming, and the leaders were resentful. "They haven't delivered for us," Reid told Pelosi. "We've never been treated this way!"[14] If control of one or both houses were lost, Pelosi reminded Obama's aides, "the White House and the president have no agenda."[15]

Several conservative Democrats who had opposed Obama's agenda were facing difficult primary challenges that could produce more liberal opponents with diminished chances for holding the seat in November. Parker Griffith (AL) had already changed party affiliations late in 2009, denouncing the ACA as "a major threat to our nation" and insisting the Democratic Party no longer "reflect[s] my core beliefs and values."[16] The president had declined to endorse Georgia's John Barrow, while Clyburn was actively campaigning for his primary opponent. In Arkansas, incumbents Marion Berry and Vic Snyder both faced primary runoffs while the incumbent senator, Blanche Lincoln, barely escaped with a majority. Hawaii's senior senator, Dan Inouye, so detested one of the front-running House aspirants that Pelosi had to remind him, "I need a Democratic Congress, and you don't need a Republican congressman."[17] The Democratic infighting ultimately enabled Republican Charles Djou to win the seat.[18]

Republicans also faced internal challenges, especially from Tea Party–backed conservatives who viewed collaboration with Democrats as "the worst thing you could do."[19] An astonishing nine out of ten Tea Party members viewed Obama as "a socialist," and one-third of Republicans believed he was a Muslim.[20] At one Tea Party event, participants sang a protest song that seemed to foreshadow the rise of Donald Trump a half decade later: "Take it back, take our country back," they sang. "Our way of life is now under attack."[21] Many of these challengers viewed their party leaders as insufficiently confrontational, which fed into growing reports of conflict within the leadership itself. "Eric Cantor's Ambition Raises Concerns, Debate," one headline proclaimed, while another revealed "John Boehner, Eric Cantor in Policy Panel Spat."[22] The sharp-tongued Cantor engaged in a public dispute with GOP Policy Committee chair Thaddeus McCotter (MI) over proposed cuts to the leadership's budget.[23] In the Senate, extreme candidates vying for GOP nominations ran the risk of jeopardizing promising races in Alaska, Indiana, Delaware, and Nevada, which could cost the GOP the Senate majority. In Delaware, outsider Christine O'Donnell, who had admitted having "dabbled into witchcraft," defeated the popular Michael Castle in the Senate primary, extinguishing hopes of capturing Biden's former seat.

Although Messina felt the Democratic base seemed to be firming up in the spring, the dour but accurate Mark Gersh predicted House losses could run as high as forty-one seats, with another twenty vulnerable. "If we only have a four- to five-point lead on Election Day," Gersh warned in July, "we will lose the House." Even Obama was below 50 percent approval, a grim signal to any incumbent's party.[24]

Pelosi accepted the news stoically, although she knew she could lose thirty-five seats. The first step was to "lock down the 218 seats" needed to maintain the majority. Despite denying doing so, as early as April she was planning to "throw some people under the bus" to concentrate financial support where it might be most effective. "We will win as many seats as we have money for," she assured. "My goal is 218. If we get more money, we will win more races."[25] "We'll raise the money," the president promised. "I'll take responsibility for the politics if we lose the House," she volunteered. But the real blame, she insisted, would lie with the Senate for failing to act on the policy initiatives she had sent them. "We did our jobs," she declared. "The Senate didn't."

The Speaker also expressed dissatisfaction to White House officials over the president's seeming indifference to the possible loss of her majority. "The White House is not thinking about how to keep the House" in Democratic hands, a prominent Democratic lobbyist warned, and Pelosi relayed that impression to

Axelrod. "You have a credibility problem with our members," she counseled. "We have people in survival mode. If the White House thinks dissociating from us boosts your numbers . . ." Axelrod cut her off. "The president doesn't care about his numbers," he protested. "He only cares about how we do in November."[26]

But that assurance was undermined when administration officials publicly speculated about a November defeat. Asked on *Meet the Press* whether the House majority was in jeopardy, press secretary Robert Gibbs responded, "There's no doubt there are enough seats in play that could cause Republicans to gain control."[27] Angry Democrats said Gibbs had "gift-wrapped a bludgeon" for the GOP. "The members are not happy," Pelosi said in a jaw-tightening understatement. The remarks were "stupid," she seethed, comparing Obama's top staff to the raucous fraternity boys in the raunchy movie *Animal House*.[28] "The White House is removing all doubt about what they think could happen in November. People are almost disgusted with them."[29]

In particular Pelosi worried that Gibbs's remarks could vastly complicate her fundraising efforts, and indeed, one major contributor called the remark the "dumbest thing in the world."[30] "This doesn't look like a team to me," she observed. "I have known it ever since the recovery plan," when the administration did little to promote the new law. "The administration has thrown us under the bus since the stimulus," she mused. "I'm sorry I cooperated from the beginning!"[31]

She knew such sentiments would be unwelcome by the president, who clearly disliked her criticisms. "He has [the] thinnest skin!" she once remarked. After one testy exchange, Obama had asked someone, "Doesn't she know I'm the president of the United States?" But Axelrod rejected the insinuation the administration was indifferent to the fate of its allies in Congress. "What we did in the last eighteen months has been heroic," Axelrod told me in July. "I'd lie down on railroad tracks for some Democrats," recalling how frequently Obama had observed "how lucky he is that Mrs. Pelosi is there."[32] Obama specifically addressed the rumbling that he was "triangulating" against Hill Democrats like Clinton or indifferent to their electoral fate. "Any notion that I have less than 110 percent interest in . . . every member of [the] caucus coming back," he declared, was untrue. "I've already done a heck of a lot for your members." The complaining was just creating fodder for the nonstop talk shows and tabloids. "Everyone is on edge," he agreed, "so don't watch cable TV, don't read *Roll Call* or *Politico*. Look good, sleep well."

Yet another outburst from the voluble Gibbs disparaged congressional liberals unhappy with Obama for being too moderate. "I hear these people saying he's like George Bush," Gibbs said. "Those people ought to be drug tested! They wouldn't be satisfied if Dennis Kucinich was president."[33] Hill Democrats erupted again. "Either Gibbs was sent out by the White House" to smear her members, Pelosi responded, "or he is a political nincompoop." Emanuel insisted Gibbs's statement was "just stupid," but the damage was done. "Words coming from the White House weigh a ton," Pelosi charged, and Gibbs's "politically inept" words had done "great damage. The White House," Pelosi intoned, "has energized the Republicans."[34]

The growing strain was showing on everyone. At a meeting of Democratic leaders before the August recess, one could not help noting the appreciable graying of Obama's hair as he neared his forty-ninth birthday. "The environment is as difficult as could have been anticipated," he said, and many Democrats seemed to have "slumped shoulders."[35] A setback in November might well be historically inevitable. "We've outperformed for two elections in a row," he observed, "and now, some of our best people are at risk." Other reasons were beyond his control, he insisted, citing criticisms that "Obama can't plug a hole" following the BP blowout or the economic crisis in Greece that led investors to "hit the pause button" about hiring.

"We are really victims of our own success," he observed. It was impossible to "see what we *prevented* from happening" that would have been even worse. Still, he admitted, the administration had fallen short selling its successes like leveraging three dollars for every one the government spent on the recovery. "We can sell that story," Obama assured, "but we haven't because we have been so damn busy with other stuff." Still, he predicted that bungling Republicans would "keep giving us gifts," as when Zack Wamp (TN) predicted his state might consider seceding from the Union. "These guys are nuts," Axelrod affirmed.[36]

But the members needed more than exhortations from Obama. "People feel a sense of indifference by the administration," Larson frankly said at a White House meeting. "Members felt 'Obama is cool and aloof.'" They needed to feel more appreciated for risking their seats to pass his priority legislation. "Members are spoiled," he told the president. "They get lots of attention from Nancy [but] they see you as the leader, and they hope they can depend on the White House." Miller threw out the question members were wondering. "They want to know: will you be campaigner in chief?" he asked. "We can't make it without you."

Biden grew impatient with the grumbling. "You guys are acting like we're losing," he declared. "The members aren't down," Pelosi responded, trying to calm the waters. "The administration has done everything we've asked in our campaigns," she insisted, although that was not at all what she felt from a messaging or financial standpoint.[37]

An effective message remained elusive through the August break. "We don't have a knockout blow," Axelrod admitted. Enthusiasm for the interim frame— "Don't go back!" to Bush's policies—fell flat. "People don't like it," Pelosi reported. "It doesn't electrify, it's not optimistic." Meanwhile, Republicans were unleashing over $20 million in ads in forty districts attacking the slow pace of job creation and the rapid rise in the deficit. Boehner was promising a $50 million national advertising assault and it was clear he would not pay too much attention to accuracy. Pelosi had warned, "We need to slap them down [because] the Republicans will lie," and in fact, the Pulitzer Prize–winning PolitiFact castigated the Republican leader for employing "half-truths" about the state of the economy.[38]

The theme that seemed to have appeal, especially in the economically ravaged Midwest, was economic nationalism and middle-class resentment, both conceptual precursors to Trump's "Make America Great Again" message of 2016. Although the Speaker remained unsold on Hoyer's "Making It in America," insisting "it doesn't move the needle," many members found support for such a theme.[39] In his Wisconsin district, home to the ultraconservative John Birch Society, Steve Kagen's constituents were "still angry because they are paying for mistakes of Wall Street speculators," while seemingly little had been done for themselves. Instead of promoting entitlement cuts and a trade agreement with South Korea, as the administration seemed willing to do, why couldn't Democrats support barring foreign companies from bidding on public works projects? asked AFL-CIO president Richard Trumka.[40]

As the base rained down criticism on the beleaguered Democrats who had taken risks to pass legislation, frustration mounted. "Labor, the environmentalists—they're worthless, they're all incompetent," Pelosi angrily charged. But although the House had promoted the progressive agenda, the loss of the public option, the failure to pass climate legislation, and the ongoing wars sapped Democratic enthusiasm. "The groups haven't gotten everything they *wanted*," the Speaker noted, "but everything they *got*, they got *from* us."[41] Implicit in her remarks was the certainty that if Democrats lost the House, they would get nothing at all; but it wasn't enough.

Hopes had briefly soared in late July with a poll showing a seventeen-point swing toward Democrats among independent voters.[42] By the end of August, however, Democrats had fallen four points behind on the key question of which party should control Congress. "We need a pivot, a game changer from Obama, a 'now, wait a minute' kind of moment," Pelosi said.[43] Members returning from their districts sensed the "momentum is moving in our direction," but they wanted to know "when will Obama put out the message?"

"Tell them the cavalry's on the way," the president assured. "If you think I am going to let knuckleheads like Boehner out-campaign us, you are crazy." But Pelosi was not waiting for the posse from 1600 Pennsylvania Avenue to arrive. "We need to do our *own* message," she instructed. "Anything the president does is additional." She stressed, in her alliterative fashion, the essential "4 M's" of successful campaigns—message, mobilization, money, and management. "There's no point paying for the air game if you don't have the ground game," she said. "You're just having a conversation." Paul Begala was impressed with Pelosi's unflinching combativeness. "If you had been Speaker in 1994," he told her, "there would have been no Speaker Gingrich."[44]

Just before returning to Washington, the Democratic leaders tried to pump up the members. "We're America's Caucus!" the chair, John Larson, exulted, but the bravado had a hollow ring. A few days later, *Politico* reported Democrats were increasingly worried about losing the House. "We are getting our asses pounded by every CEO sitting around a pool," Miller reported. Allies outside Congress were growing worried too, including influential Black ministers who reported the "people are feeling defeated." Pelosi reminded them that House Democrats had voted for everything Obama had wanted, and "if we don't win this, he's no place." But the response remained lukewarm. "They have no information about the benefits of what we've done," she admitted.[45] By the end of August, Democrats had slipped to a ten-point deficit on the generic question of which party voters favored in House races. Even in a strong Democratic state like Connecticut, where the toxic mood put safe seats in jeopardy, the party chair advised both the Speaker and the president to avoid visiting the state.[46]

Republicans were flush with money thanks to the January 20, 2010, Supreme Court ruling in *Citizens United v. Federal Elections Commission*, which freed up hundreds of millions of independent expenditure dollars for campaigns.[47] The Chamber of Commerce alone reportedly was spending $75 million, virtually all for Republicans. Massive ad buys suddenly appeared, even against safe Democrats, intended to force them to spend funds or discourage future statewide races. One conservative group dumped $1.3 million into Bruce Braley's Iowa district even though he was assured reelection, hoping to weaken him for a future statewide race. In Nevada, Reid reported five independent groups were targeting his reelection.[48]

"How are we ever going to regain control with all this outside money if we lose now?" wondered Pelosi. A rout at the state legislative level in 2010 would

mean Republican control of reapportionment, which could handicap the allocation of House seats for a decade. Absent a reversal of *Citizens United,* Tommy
D'Alesandro glumly warned his sister, "Democrats can't win." Indeed, dispirited
funders were already holding back their money. Cardoza, a pipeline to business
contributors, reported that "long-term friends are abandoning the Democrats,"
feeling the party was heading in the wrong direction.

"We have to get money to members," said Pelosi. Van Hollen was preparing to borrow another $5 million to confront negative ads, but the Speaker
also turned to her leadership to make a "full-throttle ask" of donors and divert
$1 million of their own funds to the DCCC. "When I call a member with
$500,000 and ask for 75 [thousand]," she explained, "they ask, 'If it's so impor-
tant, why aren't *they* putting up their own money?'"[49] House Republicans had raised
$3.5 million from their own members compared to just $2.2 million from Democrats. Pelosi knew most members cringed at asking for big contributions. "People
need to be asked for money," she insisted. "If this sounds crude, forgive me."[50]

Early in September, the Speaker was infuriated by a "nasty" *New York Times*
story stating that she was abandoning doomed candidates. "There have been no
such decisions," she protested, "no winks, no nods." But she had initiated such a
process five months earlier, and Van Hollen had acknowledged that "at the end
of the day, the DCCC will look at the races we can win."[51] Several incumbents
already seemed beyond saving. "We have to make tough decisions," said Hoyer.[52]
"We need to be very tough in our triage," agreed Miller, endorsing "whatever is
necessary" to save the majority. Even that might not be enough. Speculation was
rife that even if Democrats clung to a tiny majority, half a dozen conservatives
might follow Griffith and switch parties as occurred in 1994, throwing control
to the Republicans in return for chairmanships or other rewards. Some conservatives were actively dissociating themselves from the party. Jason Altmire
(PA) would probably survive, Pelosi predicted, "but it will make you sick to see
his ad."

With the wind in their sails, Republicans largely abandoned any policy
agenda. Mike Pence, the chair of the House conference, flatly ruled out working
with Obama and Democrats.[53] "This is not a time for compromise," Boehner
agreed, anticipating victory. "We're going to do everything—and I mean *everything*—we can do to kill [Obama's agenda], stop it, slow it down, whatever we
can."[54] His Senate counterpart was similarly inclined. "The single most important thing we want to achieve," McConnell declared, "is for President Obama
to be a one-term president."[55] Only if Obama was prepared to do "a Clintonian
backflip [and] meet us halfway on some of the biggest issues" would it be appropriate for Republicans "to do business with him."

RNC chair Michael Steele undertook a 14,000-mile, six-week national tour in a big red bus festooned with the party's succinct "Fire Pelosi" message, which also filled the windows of GOP offices on Capitol Hill.[56] Ultimately, CNN reported $42 million was spent funding 360 ads and 112 broadcasts impugning the Speaker, often employing unflattering photographs, menacing music, and more than a whiff of misogyny. Inexplicably, CBS News resurrected the Republicans' false accusations about Pelosi's use of military aircraft, prompting the Speaker to press Livingood again to explain that he had advised her to use a military plane.[57] Conservatives hammered the issue relentlessly, although Republican conference chair Adam Putnam (FL) admitted, "We know the plane story isn't true, but it works!"[58]

The *New York Times* also irritated Pelosi by publishing long profiles of Boehner as the putative incoming Speaker and his hard-charging chief of staff, Barry Jackson. *Time* magazine also prepared a story about what would happen if Democrats lost control. The Speaker's mood did not improve when *Newsweek* put John Boehner on its on October 25 cover, something no major national news magazine accorded Pelosi until 2018.

As the campaign wound down, Obama acknowledged the likely outcome. "People are frustrated [and] a lot of folks are hurting out there," he said. "People want to see more progress." He empathized with frustrated voters who could make little sense of "the bickering, the weird rules, the filibuster." Democrats were being "hammered by negative ads every day" but still cast "really tough votes that they knew were bad politics . . . and yet [they] still went ahead and did what was right." While he hoped "such good people will be rewarded" by voters on Election Day, he seemed resigned to facing a Republican majority in January. "I hope that my friends on the other side of the aisle are going to change their minds going forward," he said optimistically. "It's not going to be enough just to play politics. You can't just focus on the next election. You've got to focus on the next generation."

Pelosi knew the president was putting his energies elsewhere. "Clearly, he has made a decision in favor of the Senate," she said, lamenting how difficult it had become even to get a phone call returned from the White House. When Louise Slaughter angrily reported that she had heard Obama say that he could work with Paul Ryan, the likely budget chair if Republicans regained the majority, the Speaker responded, "They've been triangulating since Day 1."[59]

Events at the White House seemed to confirm the desperate mood. On October 1, Emanuel resigned as Obama's chief of staff, and it was clear the Speaker would not miss him. "Rahm hated the House," she declared, because the bills her

Democrats approved went further than Obama or the Senate were prepared to go.[60] She had long doubted his professed negotiating skills and chafed at his self-promotion, especially his taking the lion's share of credit for the 2006 House victory. Nor was she impressed with his temporary successor, Pete Rouse, a highly respected former aide to Daschle. The Speaker would have preferred someone with "significant weight" like former Senate majority leader George Mitchell.

The administration continued to exasperate the Hill by floating new and costly policy initiatives leading up to the election. Over the Labor Day weekend, with no advanced notice to Congress, the White House endorsed $50 billion in small business aid and $100 billion in additional infrastructure. Most members agreed with Cardoza, who recommended "do[ing] as little as possible" in the weeks before the election. "Why would we promote *more* spending?" I asked during a meeting with Schiliro and Myrick. "We look like ineffectual spendthrifts!" Myrick seconded the point. The administration's "idea a day" might be "good for 2012," he advised, "but not for 2010," because it suggested Democrats were contemplating a postelection round of costly spending. Schiliro blamed "a bunch of staff" acting on their own for the release.[61]

Yet a month later, members were surprised when Obama announced a new infrastructure plan funded by an increase in the federal gas tax, as recommended by the bipartisan team of former transportation secretaries Norm Mineta and Samuel Skinner.[62] The endorsement put Democrats in the position just before the election of repudiating their own president or endorsing an unpopular, regressive tax. The president "is trying to be bipartisan," a White House aide explained, but bipartisanship, weeks before Election Day, was the furthest thing from the minds of either party.[63]

There were more disappointments—the Veterans of Foreign Wars withdrew its endorsements of several Democrats, despite Pelosi's initiatives on behalf of veterans. Even so, Pelosi remained publicly upbeat. "I think we are going to win," she counseled. "Don't underestimate our opponents, but don't overestimate them either." Hoyer tried to rally the troops as well. "We're fighting hard," he said, "and we are in striking distance!" "Except for the outside money"—a substantial qualification—many races remained close. Van Hollen reported races "ticking upwards in many places" and donors "raining down money" on the DCCC. "The obituaries are premature," he predicted.[64]

The forced optimism imploded a few days before the election with Gersh predicting losses up to fifty-three of her current 255 seats. Even the typically optimistic Greenberg braced for "a doomsday scenario."[65] As Pelosi realized she would probably lose her majority and her gavel, she sought the advice of close friends about her future. Even if the party miraculously maintained a small majority of five to six seats, Miller questioned if Pelosi should run again for Speaker, an option she admitted she was considering. If the worst happened, Anna Eshoo (CA) doubted she would accept a demotion to minority leader.[66] "Pull a Garbo," her brother Tommy recommended, "and get out!"[67]

Should Pelosi opt not to seek to lead the party in the minority, the likely successor would be Hoyer, who was experienced, polished, and popular. But everyone in Washington believed that Pelosi distrusted Hoyer's ties to lobbying interests and the business community as well as his closeness to the Blue Dogs and some Republicans. Moreover, for all his bonhomie, Hoyer lacked the credibility Pelosi enjoyed with the dominant liberal faction that enabled her to temper its sometimes unrealistic demands.

Many of those who opposed Hoyer's elevation thought Pelosi would be comfortable leaving if the progressive Van Hollen were her successor. But ambitious as he was, Van Hollen was unlikely to challenge Hoyer, his senior Maryland colleague. Moreover, doing so also would entail jumping over Clyburn, the number three on the leadership ladder, provoking furious resentment from the CBC as Emanuel did when he had contemplated challenging Clyburn for whip. "You have to stay," Van Hollen told the Speaker.[68]

Election Day was a blur of activity. Pelosi had spent the previous evening calling nearly a hundred members, mostly those confident of victory. The president offered encouragement, but the conversation had a funereal tone.[69] "It has been one of my great honors and privileges to work with you," he professed. "I couldn't be prouder. You've been magnificent. You're smart, tough, you have a big heart and you did the right thing. You've carried a load as heavy as anyone and taken all the slings and arrows." Pelosi reported the caucus was "at peace on health care, Wall Street reform," and the other legislation they had approved. "Thank you for everything," she said, overlooking the disputes over policy, money, and deference to the Senate. "You're a great president and this has been a great campaign." Even at this late hour, she asserted, she could see a "path to victory."

She had a much more blunt conversation with her close friend Miller. "There's a big decision for me tonight," she confided. She wanted a few days to think it over, but Miller disagreed. "Time is of the essence," he counseled. She should say that all options remained under discussion and that there would be no immediate decision.

The results rolled in quickly and decisively. By the time the dust settled, Democrats had lost sixty-three seats in a historic rout, the largest since 1948.

Their 255–178 majority had been transformed into a 242–193 minority. "It's pretty clear the Obama-Pelosi agenda has been rejected," Boehner exulted. "They want the president to change course [and] change course we will."[70] Boehner declared himself "humbled" by the role awaiting him and promised "we will continue our efforts for small, more accountable government." His chief goal, he pledged, was to "do everything to replace the Affordable Care Act" before it "ruin[ed] the best health care system in the world."

Hoyer predicted, "The Republicans have elected a [House] group that will hang itself" because of the large number of incoming extremists.[71] Shortly after the election, I encountered Boehner walking alone through the Capitol and wished him well. Boehner smiled a tight grin. "In six months, I'll be more popular in your caucus than in my own," he predicted, acknowledging the rowdiness of his new Tea Party members. Indeed, six months later, I asked, "How's that prediction coming along?" The Speaker grimaced. "Not there yet," he responded, adding, "but I'm getting there." After leaving the speakership, Boehner regularly denigrated the extremists who had won the majority and elected him Speaker as "the knucklehead caucus . . . right of right . . . anarchists. They're for nothing."[72]

In 89 percent of Democratic districts, the party's candidates lost vote share compared to 2008. In the shuttered, midwestern industrial centers where white, working-class Democrats had been leaving the party for years, the House delegations shifted from comfortably Democratic to significantly Republican. Typical of the reversal was Phil Hare's defeat in Illinois. Having won without opposition two years earlier, his vote total dropped from 221,000 to under 86,000, losing by 20,000 votes to Bobby Schilling, a pizza shop owner with no political experience. In Virginia, fourteen-term incumbent Rick Boucher, who won 129,000 votes in 2006 and was unopposed in 2008, dropped to just 86,793 and narrowly lost. Even conservatives like Gene Taylor (MI) who had opposed most of the party's legislation were defeated.

The story was less calamitous in the Senate, where miraculously, the tenacious Reid held onto his Nevada seat. Democrats retained a 53–47 majority thanks to losses by the fringe nominees, but any hope of being able to reach sixty votes to break a Republican filibuster on major legislation was gone. With newcomers like Marco Rubio (FL) and Rand Paul (KY), Obama predicted

McConnell would also face difficulties because "the Republicans don't like one another."[73]

Democrats also lost majority control in twenty state legislatures, many of which would now reapportion congressional seats following the 2010 census to benefit the new Republican incumbents. The setback would significantly complicate efforts to win back control of the House through the remainder of Obama's presidency. Most Hill leaders believed their warnings to the White House and DNC about the need to pay greater attention to state legislative races had been largely ignored.

Amazingly, there was little rancor from the defeated members. Indeed, Larson reported, the defeated members were "devastated [because] they feel like they let *us* down!" "We did something great for the American people," declared Earl Pomeroy, one of the senior members to lose. "There's nothing I would have done differently," a sentiment, he assured the Speaker, he heard "over and over again."[74]

> When I sought to console Tom Perriello, he responded, "If the worst thing that every happens to me in my life is that I lost my seat in Congress because I voted to give 30 million people health insurance, I can live with that."

The few notes of bitterness came from veteran legislators like Alan Boyd (FL), who lost, and Mike Capuano (MA), who did not, who blamed the leadership for scheduling so many difficult votes.[75] And it was true that the frontline Democrats who had taken the tough votes on TARP, the stimulus, cap and trade, and health care reform did far worse than their opponents.[76] One Dartmouth study concluded that if more marginal Democrats had voted against the key legislation, the party would have held enough seats to retain the majority in 2010, although the bills would have failed. That was the trade-off Pelosi was unwilling to make. "Would you rather not have passed health care so you could remain as Speaker?" she was asked. "Never," she professed. "Never."[77]

"Peoples' lives are better" because of Pelosi's leadership, Axelrod assured, "and we wouldn't have accomplished all this without her. We were blessed to serve with her, an incredible leader."[78] Still, the Speaker merited some blame for the debacle, according to a longtime admirer, congressional scholar Norm Ornstein, by forcing votes on the "cap and trade" bill and, along with Obama, for "failing to sell the stimulus" more aggressively.[79] Pelosi's staff pushed back on such criticisms, noting that nearly two-thirds of voters identified the slow creation of jobs as their principal reason for voting as they did. "It was not about Nancy Pelosi," the talking points proclaimed.

"How are you holding up?" Obama asked Pelosi, promising to call every defeated Democratic incumbent to praise their "real courage and character." The Speaker agreed it was "a tragedy to lose so many," but she quickly became operational, pivoting to the lame-duck agenda. "I'll bend over backwards with Boehner" to get Michelle's child nutrition package, she promised.

Obama admitted the sweeping defeat was "a shellacking" and took personal responsibility for the loss. "People are not feeling the economic progress," he acknowledged, asserting voters followed emotional appeals, not facts, and did not reject the policies he promoted. "If we had 5 percent unemployment instead of 9 percent," he argued, "the public would be OK with our policy choices." It was tortured logic, to say the least; voters responded to real conditions, not projections of how much worse it could have been.

Although Pelosi spent the morning after the election "sitting shiva" out of concern over members, her organizational side quickly kicked into action.[80] Immediate decisions had to be made about party reorganization, leadership elections, committee reassignments, and the lame-duck agenda. Having decided to run for minority leader, a delicate problem remained to be resolved. With Hoyer slated to resume the job of minority whip, Clyburn, the only Black member in either house's leadership, was out of a job. Quietly, the Speaker suggested Hoyer cede the whip position to Clyburn and use his seniority to claim the powerful ranking member slot on Appropriations. Hoyer rejected the proposal out of hand, insisting he had earned the right to the whip job, which would leave him better positioned for the top position if Pelosi decided to vacate it at some future point. Nor did Hoyer intend to have his profile diminished as he yielded the leader's position to Pelosi. "I'm not going to be a bean counter," he vowed to me. "This isn't going to be a good relationship" if his role was shrunken.[81] Pelosi preserved Clyburn's seat at the leadership table by designating him "assistant leader," a position he held until resuming the majority whip position in 2019.

After a long day, Pelosi commiserated with Miller. "I'm reorganizing the office to promote my work with outside groups, messaging, grassroots, and campuses," the classic role for the out-of-power leader. "This is what I love to do." She blamed the repudiation on the failure to explain clearly what the party had achieved against terrific odds. "Voters don't think we did anything for them," she observed. Her members had spent two years overwhelmed with the economic recovery, Iraq and Afghanistan, financial failures, bankruptcies, unemployment, and deficits—all inherited crises not of their own making. "George Bush laid a dog patty on the floor," she said in an atypically colorful way. "We stepped on it, and now, we carry the stench."[82]

CHAPTER 25

THEIR LAST BOW

The electoral catastrophe necessitated a complete rethinking for the remainder of the 111th Congress. "Forget about trying to pass bills," Jack Trout counseled. Party leaders needed to "shift the battlefield to alter negative perceptions" of the party and become "furious" at Republicans for their intransigence. The president, in particular, needed to "be tough, [to] come out of the blocks hard" in the new Congress. "If Obama wants to be the good cop, Nancy should be the bad cop. (Harry Reid is the undertaker)."[1]

"People are mad!" Axelrod counseled. "They need to believe things will be OK." The election had demonstrated that voters "think Washington is dysfunctional and not concerned with their daily lives." Democrats had to "fight to death" against Republican efforts to cut education or repeal the ACA, he insisted.

The biggest distinction—Trout called it "the defining issue"—between the parties would be the decision on whether to allow the Bush tax cuts to expire on January 1, 2011. If no bill was passed because Democrats refused to extend the upper income cut as Republicans demanded, then everyone's taxes would rise, potentially triggering a double-dip recession.

Obama agreed "the White House has caused problems with its lack of clarity," but a prolonged battle over taxes was not in the president's interest, Axelrod insisted. Sounding very much like "the adult in the room," he said, "the president should say, 'The battle is in 2012, but for now, let's solve problems.'"[2]

Trout was alarmed. "Don't cave on tax cuts!" he pleaded. "You'll be perceived as being rolled." But Axelrod was more worried a partisan battle would make it seem Obama had missed the message of the election. "People believe reasonable people can compromise," he argued, citing public disapproval of McConnell's vow to make Obama a one-term president. "The Republicans have deprived us of bipartisanship and called us 'partisan,'" he said. "It is clear that's their tactic." Trout did not disagree, but once Axelrod left the room, he sternly warned Pelosi, "Don't subordinate House Democrats to Obama."[3]

Pelosi believed her decimated members were prepared "to make the fight" up to their last day in the majority.[4] Committees resumed holding hearings on housing foreclosures and climate change as though the election had not happened. She pressed the soon-to-be-demoted chairs to expand use of social media to "build the narrative" highlighting Republican misdeeds and contemplated enlisting film director Steven Spielberg to help craft the party's new message. Rob Andrews (NJ) was selected to lead the effort to formulate motions to recommit that Democrats would employ in the minority to draw distinctions with Republicans. All members were charged with encouraging support groups outside the Congress to stop criticizing their remaining allies and "get shooting in [the] right direction"—at Republicans.[5]

The lame duck afforded Democrats valuable weeks to enshrine policy that had been stuck before the election when so many members were concerned how their votes would impact their reelection chances. Coming to legislative agreements swiftly was essential, even if that meant, as Hoyer feared, making major concessions to the Senate on bills like the tax cut extension, the child nutrition expansion, and the 9/11 victims' assistance bill, all of which faced very different treatment in the 112th Congress. Not surprisingly, Republicans raised protests about legislating with the votes of so many defeated and retiring members, but their arguments fell on deaf ears.

The Simpson-Bowles report on spending cuts and deficits was due shortly after the election, and many Democrats feared its recommendations might provide momentum for massive spending cuts. Days after the debacle, Becerra warned that his fellow commissioners were "tracking to the right" as many Democrats had anticipated.[6] Republicans had rejected a proposal to require one dollar in tax increases for every two dollars in spending cuts. The incoming majority leader, Eric Cantor, reiterated his opposition to endorsing any tax increases, foisting all of the burden for reducing deficits on cutting programs Democrats were positioned to defend for only a few more weeks. As the division among the commissioners appeared to preclude the bipartisan supermajority required to issue a report, the parsimonious cochairs hinted they would issue their own recommendations anyway. Few expected them to be favorable to Democratic priorities.

Frustrated by reports of the growing impasse within the commission, Obama hinted he might embrace some recommendations even if they received only ten or twelve of the fourteen votes required. The commission was not a "dog-and-pony show," he insisted, but a serious effort to reduce the deficit. When, as expected, the commissioners failed to reach the required consensus to issue formal recommendations, Simpson and Bowles issued their own report calling for changes in payments and benefits under Social Security. They also presumed that the upper income tax cut (UITC) would expire on December 31, helping reduce the deficit by over $1 trillion.[7] But on the very same day Simpson and Bowles issued their proposals, a filibuster-proof group of forty-two Republican senators pledged to kill any extension of Bush's tax cuts that failed to include the highest earners. "Obama should look Boehner in the eye," declared Inslee, "and say, 'You are holding the middle-class tax cut hostage, and we don't negotiate with terrorists!'"[8]

The loss of the House gave Republicans enormous advantages in negotiating on the tax cut extension. If Democrats refused to include the UITC, McConnell could block the remaining extension in the Senate, forcing a $3,000-per-family tax increase on the Democrats' watch. Then, when Republicans took control of the House on January 3, they could reenact all of the tax cuts on a permanent basis knowing Senate Democrats would be hard-pressed to reject the House's bill. That scenario would be the worst of all outcomes for Obama and Reid as they began the 112th Congress: tax increases under Democrats, tax cuts under Republicans. "The Republicans are so irresponsible," Obama insisted. "They would let the house burn down so they could come in and do what they want."[9] That sentiment marked a reversal from the president's more hopeful comment a month earlier, when he said he still hoped for greater cooperation after the election with a "more responsible" Republican party.[10]

The newly emboldened Boehner refused to even meet with Reid to discuss a compromise. When Obama called the joint leadership to the White House for a tax discussion, only the Democrats showed up. "I know it is the instinct of Congress to want to get out," Obama told the press, once again failing to distinguish Democrats who were attending from Republicans who had boycotted the meeting. "But it is not an option to leave without the tax cut getting done."

On the Hill, Democrats were becoming more confrontational. If the Republicans were "ready for a fight," Reid declared, that was fine with him. The one-time lightweight boxer recalled how Jack Dempsey would walk into a bar and challenge all comers. "The sooner the fight was over," he said, "the less chance there was of losing. The longer we play with the Republicans, the longer they will obstruct and we will get hurt more." Clyburn continued Reid's boxing imagery. "People think we're rolling over," the outgoing whip said, condemning the

GOP's disrespect for the president and the Speaker. "It's a big mistake" not to respond, he admonished. "Sexism and racism are taking hold. We know the code words."[11]

The Democratic leaders told the president he was going to have to toughen his stance toward the GOP. "You're daydreaming if you think the Republicans will give us anything the first six months," Schumer warned. "You are a nice guy," he told the president. "I'd be tougher. We can win if we stand firm." Others agreed it would be a mistake to expect any collegiality from McConnell and Boehner. "By your nature, you are bipartisan," said Durbin. "But that's not going to happen." In fact, even appearing cooperative could encourage Republicans to "hold out for a permanent tax cut for all," warned Sen. Patty Murray (WA). House members agreed. "The Republican strategy will be scorched earth," Van Hollen predicted. "They are not willing to deal."

Hoyer was the lone outlier, bemoaning Obama's failure early in 2009 to meet with the minority. "We should try to work with the Republicans," Hoyer insisted, and then criticize them if they failed to respond. He had few illusions about the incoming majority. "The Republicans are totally phony," he said, "but so are the American people," citing a recent *Wall Street Journal* poll showing voters liked cutting spending but not entitlement programs. "There's no concern about the long term," he said.[12] The vice president agreed. "All people care about is whether I get mine," he warned, "so, be careful."

Obama acknowledged he remained a novice at congressional politics. "I was only in the Senate for two years full time, and then two years part time," he admitted. "What's a doable compromise?" He was unambiguous about where he drew the red line—"I won't sign anything with a permanent high-end tax cut," he pledged. But he conceded he was in far from a powerful position. "I'm politically weakened at 47 percent," he agreed, "but in a year, I'll be over 50. I'll get my mojo back. Can I take any bets?" But he was still cautious about getting out too far in front of the Republicans. "I always want to fight, but on our terms," he advised. "I'm not ready to charge up the hill. Let the other side make some mistakes." He tilted his head back in thought. "It's important to make moves that are deliberate and don't divide us," he urged, repeating the dressmaker's admonition. "Measure twice; cut once."

The compromise that emerged was unpalatable to many Democrats: a short-term extension of all Bush's tax cuts, including the UITC, deferring a permanent decision until after the 2012 elections, when Obama would hopefully be reelected and Democrats might regain the House majority. Pelosi noted the House had "chopped off the head right away" by voting to extend only the middle-class cut, but it was obvious the Senate lacked the votes to do the same.

Ultimately, Obama insisted, their future would be measured by the performance of the economy. "If the economy improves" by 2012, Obama predicted, "I'm reelected. Otherwise, I'm packing my bags, and Joe's planning a golfing trip." Pelosi left the meeting wondering if there was a clear presidential game plan beyond the tax cut extension. "He will not discuss anything else" for the lame duck, she told her leadership. To Reid, she said, "Our members don't think Obama cares about any of our stuff."[13]

But it was far from clear how much "stuff" Democrats could pass in the last weeks of their House majority. Members had "reservations about doing too much," Hoyer advised, and they wanted "to stop digging the hole deeper" by creating "irresponsible deficits." Even among the large cohort of Democrats departing in December, some of whom already were contemplating campaigns to regain their seats, "there's not a big appetite" for expensive legislation. Pelosi remained undeterred, proclaiming herself "ready to coat myself with oil to pass the tax bill and unemployment benefits," as well as some other caucus priorities.[14]

The DREAM act granting residency to undocumented young people was an urgent goal for many House liberals, especially Hispanic members, and Pelosi felt an obligation to try to pass the bill. Wary of yet another BTU-like failure, many moderates demanded an assurance the Senate would follow suit. Their caution was warranted. With only two Republican Senate supporters and six Democratic dissenters, Senate approval appeared impossible. But the Republicans, who denounced the program as "a nightmare" and "mass amnesty," were certain to kill the legislation altogether in 2011. The Speaker added a ban on eligibility for health insurance subsidies for the undocumented to secure moderate votes, but even with that concession, forty-six Democrats remained opposed. Pelosi forged ahead anyway, narrowly passing DREAM by a 216–198 margin. The close vote dissipated all hopes in the Senate, where rural Democrats helped defeat a cloture motion.[15] The holdouts were especially infuriating because three Republicans—enough to invoke cloture had Democrats hung together—voted for cloture: Bob Bennett (UT), Richard Lugar (IN), and Lisa Murkowski (AK), recently reelected as a write-in candidate after losing her primary. But there was swift retribution against Bennett and Lugar, both of whom were ousted by more conservative opponents in their next primaries.

The loss of the House also put enormous pressure to resolve LGBTQ issues that were sure to evaporate under the incoming Republican majority. Hoyer advised against forcing moderates to vote to repeal DADT since Obama would likely lift the ban administratively, but Pelosi wanted a vote in the House, in part to honor the sponsor, Patrick Murphy (PA). "If we drop it," she told Reid, "he lost for nothing." On December 15, the House approved the repeal by a seventy-vote margin.

"What do you think if I don't have the vote on DADT?" Reid inquired. Scott Brown, who had endorsed repeal, had ruled out voting for cloture, and Susan Collins was giving "the same squishy answer as always." "Terrible!" was Pelosi's curt response. "Goodbye," Reid said, abruptly hanging up the phone.[16] Two days later, he dared senators to oppose the measure and won a cloture vote with sixty-three votes. The repeal bill passed 65–31, and there was a rare victory celebration in the Capitol Visitors' Center auditorium.

But Reid remained morose about prospects for other House-passed bills. One success was funding for the Pigford-Cobell settlements for minority farmers, which closed "a sad chapter in our history," the secretary of agriculture, Tom Vilsack, declared.[17] But the UI extension, Reid flatly predicted, would "never get done." The DISCLOSE campaign finance bill, creating transparency for donations in response to Citizens United, was "very unlikely," and Michelle Obama's child nutrition initiative would only become law if the House backed down and approved the Senate's version.

Amid the legislative inertia, Pelosi called Biden to commiserate.[18] "You have a PhD in this," he told her. "You know how hard it is to do." She admitted having ambivalence about running for minority leader. "I could have quit the next day" after the election, she said, but the members pushed back. "'You can't leave,' they say," she reported. "'There is no organization without you.'" Ironically, she noted, "the Left is against me" because of the compromises she had accepted to pass legislation, warning the same hostility could turn on Obama.

"The members love you," she confided, "but they think the president threw us under the bus on the recovery. He didn't push hard enough on jobs." She had warned they would face "fire and brimstone" retaliation on ACA, but the president had "downplayed the seriousness of the danger" and not fought back sufficiently. "He got that message," Biden assured her. Indeed, Obama himself had said, "I'm not making any excuse for health care or White House messaging."[19]

"Can you inject some passion into the presidency?" she pleaded. "[Obama's] not emotional. We do need knowledge and judgment, but we also need an emotional piece," she responded, a chronic problem with Democratic leaders. "Mondale and Gore, they had good smarts, but no emotion. People want to see a fight."

"I'm trying, kid," Biden explained. "Lots of people think my passion isn't helpful!" he explained, blaming a "generational" difference between the young White House staff and himself. Obama has "resoluteness and firmness," he agreed, but "he's very cool." Those qualities were fine, Pelosi agreed, adding, "but [congressional] people like a decider" like George W. Bush, someone willing to engage with Congress, extend invitations to White House events, and hang out with members at caucus retreats. "It was all BS," she acknowledged, "but it matters." By contrast, "it wasn't lost on the members that when he was elected, [Obama] didn't call Congress in" for weeks, she reminded Biden. "That's not his instinct," Biden explained.

"He still thinks he's a member of the Senate," Pelosi added, which helped explain the president's preference for cutting deals with the supermajority-run upper chamber. Biden smiled. "The senators think he *dislikes* the Senate, that he's too detached from them!" he countered. "We have to correct the problems" before the 2012 reelect. "The harmony between the White House and Congress needs to be genuine."

Pelosi agreed that improved Hill–White House relations were essential and that Obama needed to understand what motivated House members. "I told him before his inauguration, 'The members love you, but they love *themselves* more.'" Biden smiled. "You got it," he agreed. "If you can't connect to the people you're working with every day, it gets very hard."[20]

Even after the Thanksgiving break, the 9/11 bill remained hung up in Senate filibuster threats. "I've got a bunch of angry people sleeping on couches in their offices!" Reid complained to Pelosi. "Abandoning their families and sleeping on couches! What a bunch of jerks!" Pelosi thought the drama was beneficial. "People need to see who they are," she said. A cloture effort secured just fifty-seven of the sixty votes needed, and this time, Bloomberg pointed the finger of blame squarely at the Senate minority, describing the outcome as "a tragic example of partisan politics trumping patriotism."[21]

In an effort to revive the bill at the end of December, Reid decided to cut the benefits nearly in half and shorten the program from eight years to five. The House had little choice but to accept the Senate's truncated version, even though Pelosi had warned Reid against sending the bill back to the House, which had already recessed for the holidays. Pelosi called Boehner, who was already golfing in Florida, to request a unanimous consent motion that would avoid bringing members back to Washington, since the bill was certain to be approved. "It's hard to imagine we would get it cleared on our side," replied the incoming Speaker, mindful of the extreme turn in his conference. "Some of our characters . . ." he trailed off.[22] Pelosi was compelled to call the House back days before Christmas to pass the bill. Its sponsor, Carolyn Maloney (NY), characterized the legislation as not "everything we wanted."[23]

Republicans were also intent on flexing their muscle on the continuing resolution needed to avert a preholiday government shutdown. The Congress limped through several short-term extensions before the House finally cleared an omnibus spending bill funding the government through the following September. To secure the votes, the members had stuffed the bills with pet projects, and the Speaker warned OMB director Jack Lew against "knocking things out" that would "be seen as all-out war on House Democrats!"[24] As Lew well knew, they were running out of time. "The moon is in [the] seventh house; Jupiter collides with Mars. The sooner Reid has [a vote], the better," she explained. Otherwise, her members might just leave town, and let the Senate stew.

Reid's version of the CR was a $1.1 trillion behemoth laden with over six thousand earmarks costing $8.3 billion, including hundreds of millions for Republicans (forty-eight earmarks alone for McConnell totaling over $100 million).[25] Even with those concessions, Reid was holding onto nine Republican votes by his fingernails. "You know how time collapses around the Senate," he told Pelosi. Despite Obama's veto threats, Biden weighed in to urge acceptance of the Senate's version.[26] Shutting the government over the Senate's earmarks would be "like dying on a small cross," Biden argued. It was far more crucial to lock down the Democratic spending levels on dozens of key programs before the "wacko" Republicans forced additional concessions. Such logic convinced Obama, who reluctantly agreed to sign the bill.

House leaders were furious that the Senate was again positioned to get its way. The House was "being held hostage" to the approaching CR deadline, Hoyer fumed. The Republicans were happy to have the nine-month bill fail since a short-term alternative would allow them to impose massive spending reductions early in January once they took power in the House. Handing them that opportunity would be "absurd," Hoyer argued.[27]

But the Democrats never had the chance to finalize the long-term CR. Two days before the scheduled cloture vote, on the anniversary of the original Boston Tea Party, McConnell ordered the nine Republican supporters to abandon the bill. It was the first victory of the "tea party Congress," the *Christian Science Monitor* declared, even before the new members took their seats.[28] Pulling the bill, Reid condemned the Republican leadership as having "shirked their duty to responsibly fund the government." Pelosi was disgusted. "The Republicans here make Mother Teresa look like Attila the Hun," she bitterly commented. "There are no shared values."[29] Democrats had to settle for a ten-week CR lasting until March 4, preventing a shutdown but leaving much of the federal budget vulnerable to Republican spending cuts early in the new year.[30]

The House also had little choice but to accept the Senate's child nutrition bill to avoid a fatal filibuster. "Well, I can now sleep in my own bed instead of on the couch!" the president joked to the displeased Speaker after the 264–157 passage. "It's ... one more sign people will ... say you were one of the best Speakers!"[31] Pelosi accepted his congratulations before reminding him to replace the $2.2 billion borrowed from the food stamp reserve.

The last major legislation—the tax cut extension—also forced a bitter House capitulation. Pelosi was concerned her members "could get burned" over the upper income extension. "Before I step off the curb, I need to know the plan," the Speaker told the president.[32]

Obama had concluded an across-the-board extension of the cuts was probably the only available option. "We can't play chicken with the economy given where it is right now," he concluded. Pelosi had "no confidence in the administration getting what's good for the economy," but they had few options. The tax extension was "a piece of crap," she bluntly declared, but "we can't let it fail and lead taxes to rise."[33]

Lew was sympathetic. "I hate the upper income cut," he professed. At an evening parley at Biden's home on Observatory Circle, he pledged Obama would veto any bill that extended the Bush cuts for more than two years or that failed to address Democratic priorities. The Speaker wasn't assuaged. "Show some fight!" she advised. "No one knows what you're fighting about!"[34] Biden knew a pragmatic decision would earn no plaudits. "At the end of the day," he told Pelosi, "everyone is going to yell at us."

The final $858 billion bill extended all the cuts until 2012 and included one item Democrats desperately wanted: extension of UI benefits for thirteen months. But it came at a high price: the estate tax—which Republicans had denigrated as "the death tax"—was reinstated after a one-year lapse but with an effective exemption level of $5 million rather than the $3.5 million level in prior law, a huge boon to wealthy taxpayers.[35]

The Senate passed the tax cut by 81–19 and the House by 277–148, although a rebellion by Democrats angry about the UITC and estate tax concessions briefly raised the prospect of defeat.[36] Obama called the bill "an essential economic package" and "a good deal" for taxpayers. "This is progress," he declared, noting that both parties found parts of the bill distasteful, "and that's what [voters] sent us here to achieve." In a powerful symbol of the changing political dynamic in Washington, McConnell attended the White House signing ceremony while Reid and Pelosi declined.

Many Democrats blamed the White House for capitulating to Republicans who were holding hostage 155 million middle-income taxpayers so that

6,600 affluent taxpayers could secure $23 billion in tax benefits.[37] "This bill gives crumbs to the middle class and my constituents!" vented Larson. Pelosi agreed her members were forced "to pay a king's ransom in order to help the middle class."[38] She also was convinced Obama had cut the tax deal with Republicans in return for votes for the new Strategic Arms Reduction Treaty (START) he had negotiated with Russia. Obama dismissed the allegations as "bull," but Pelosi wasn't buying the denial. "If I live to be a thousand," she confided in Reid, "you can't convince me this wasn't all about START." When she vehemently complained to Obama and Biden, she confided, they "thought I was being my usual B-I-T-C-H self."[39]

Even so, she told her staff, "I don't want criticism of the president" over the tax bill. "I will not be a party to anything that diminishes Obama, but he shouldn't do this to us." A dejected Miller advised her to accept the limits of her power. "[You] shouldn't be Ms. Goodwrench," he advised. "[You] shouldn't try to fix everything."[40]

The reality was that following the 2010 rout, House Democrats had little negotiating strength. Refusing to approve Senate bills during the lame duck would only empower John Boehner's Republicans to write significantly worse versions in 2011, if they bothered to write them at all. The best chance of protecting the causes she cared about after yielding the gavel was a strong Democrat in the White House with a veto pen and the ability to issue executive orders if the divided Congress proved incapable of legislating.

The arc of power bent against House Democrats with the adjournment of what Norm Ornstein called "one of the most productive Congresses in history."[41] But on many of the most significant pieces of legislation, the impulse to push the progressive legislation favored by their constituents and the party's activist base, born of the nature of the House itself, had been stymied by Senate conservatives and procedures and a White House that, however sympathetic, would not embrace the House's agenda. With the election of 2010, her influence proved as perishable as Pelosi had always warned was the nature of power in Washington, and the Democratic majority she had fought to win, manage, and maintain passed into history.

CONCLUSION: THE
PERISHABILITY OF POWER

On the morning of November 27, 2010, Nancy Pelosi and I rode in her bullet-proof Chevrolet Suburban from the Capitol to the Cannon Building, where the caucus, still reeling from the loss of the majority, would reelect her and other members of the leadership team for the 112th Congress.

After six years of frenetic activity—as minority leader scrambling to win the majority, as Speaker for four productive years under presidents of both parties and now, heading into the minority once again—many had expected Pelosi to step down. Just before Election Day, she had declared, "Win, I lead; lose, I leave office."[1] Power, she believed, was by its nature perishable, to be used aggressively even at risk of losing it.

As we stood alone in the rising elevator, she remained deep in thought. "I'd prefer not to be doing this," she confessed. "Well," I replied as the door opened on the second floor, "you certainly picked a hell of a time to tell me."

The five-year period covered in this book provides unique opportunities to observe the complexities and nuances of congressional politics, the strategizing that enables a minority to win power, and, just as importantly, the multiple factors that frustrate the ability of political leaders to deliver the results voters—and especially a party's active, ideologically charged base—anticipate, sometimes with disastrous electoral consequences.

The Democratic victory of 2006, as with the Republican resurgence in 2010, illustrates how often congressional victories are not only an endorsement of the successful party but also a reaction to the perceived failures of the opponent. For all the energy devoted to developing and promoting "The New Direction: 6 for '06" or the "Fire Pelosi" frame four years later, voters' dissatisfaction with the seeming inability of the majority to deliver promised results was likely far more consequential. Frustration over Iraq, the perception of widespread corruption among Hill Republicans, and the crumbling economy spelled disaster for the GOP in 2006; the difficulty in revitalizing the crippled economy overwhelmed any positive achievements from the stimulus, health care, or other Democratic accomplishments four years later.

Several important factors complicated the ability of Democrats to succeed in this very unfavorable environment. Certainly, the sharp ideological divide between the parties meant that the burden of legislative success fell solely on one party. As has been the case since the end of Democratic congressional dominance in 1994, a minority focused on its reasonable expectation of returning to power has little motivation to promote the success of the opposition it is aggressively seeking to dislodge. Just as Pelosi saw no value in engaging Bush in a debate over the future of Social Security, neither did Republicans see any benefit in participating in the design of the 2009 stimulus or the health law.

In addition, the relatively close margin between these ideologically segregated parties compounded the challenge of effective legislating. True, Pelosi enjoyed seemingly large majorities in the 2007–10 period, but only because a large number of swing (or frontline) districts had fallen to the Democrats in 2006 and 2008. These moderate members—the so-called Majority Makers—exercised a constraint on the more liberal party faction, much as had the Dixiecrats during an earlier era of Democratic dominance. Without the votes of any Republicans or some of these members in the House and Senate, the dominant progressives lacked the votes to pass most legislation. Making necessary concessions to secure their support, which was crucial in the absence of Republican participation, meant producing legislation that—whether on Iraq withdrawal, punishing Wall Street barons, or including the public option—invariably disappointed the party's liberal base.

In addition, as this book repeatedly demonstrates, the House—its agenda fueled by liberals from safe districts—was repeatedly compelled to accept more modest versions of legislation that could fly through the Senate's sixty-vote keyhole. Capitulating to the Senate's self-imposed supermajoritarian procedures meant abandoning or weakening provisions written by the House's Democrats to reflect minority communities that provided much of base support for the party. Even during the brief interval when there were sixty Senate Democrats (including the independents who caucused with the majority), the necessity of securing the vote of every caucus member, including senators like Kent Conrad, Max Baucus, and Ben Nelson from rural, white, conservative states imposed rigid limits on what Harry Reid could deliver. Presented with the Senate version of legislation—including ARRA, the ACA, the child nutrition bill of 2010, and many others described in this text—the House frequently had little option but to capitulate. This also meant accepting riders and earmarks that senators demanded as the price of their vote, a vexing affront to House Democrats whose only alternative was the failure of legislation they desperately wanted to pass.

During an intraparty battle over a jobs bill in March 2010, Axelrod pressed the House Democrats to accept a weakened Senate version after waiting three months for Reid to deliver. During the health care debate, an exasperated Hoyer, who used the "my way or the highway" imagery to describe the Senate's ultimatums, complained, "The House is becoming irrelevant because we can't make changes to Senate bills."[2] A similar point was offered by John Larson (CT) late in the 110th Congress. "The Senate makes us look irrelevant," the caucus chair observed, an "opinion shared by a large number of our membership."[3]

So long as the Senate continued to protect its cloture rules, there was little arguing with that political math since the defection of a single senator spelled defeat on many of the highest-priority bills. Yet it should also be noted that despite having thirty-eight Democratic votes to spare in the 111th Congress, Pelosi passed major legislation by a razor-thin margin because of the defection of front liners representing Republican-leaning districts and occasional liberal dissidents unwilling to accept the necessary concessions. Indeed, if the House functioned under the same 60 percent rule for considering legislation as does the Senate, Pelosi would likely have faced just as much of an obstacle to success as Reid regularly did.

While an exasperated Reid or Schumer occasionally expressed an intent to alter or dispense with Rule XXII's cloture process for legislative matters, actually doing so was extremely unlikely because it would remove a powerful instrument for managing the Senate and gaining strategic advantage over the House as well as the White House. While the filibuster significantly complicates the majority's legislative maneuvering, it also empowers individual senators to secure concessions, earmarks, and riders and institutionally provides the Senate with the ability to offer ultimatums to the House on the design of legislation. As demonstrated during the productive lame duck in 2010, a process that grants such leverage over the House, the president, and the party's base is unlikely to be weakened or dispensed with even though, as Jim Clyburn often argued, it disadvantages sizable minorities in states where they are powerless to elect sympathetic senators.

A decade later, during her second period as Speaker, Pelosi again articulated the institutional tension that permeates the Capitol. "We in the House think of [the Senate] as [possessing a] sort of a House of Lords attitude," she said early in the Biden administration.[4] "We need equity [but] House members see condescension and a lack of respect for members' intelligence."[5] Pelosi did not dispute that the House acted more aggressively and legislated more expansively than her colleagues across the Capitol, a pattern she attributed to her members returning to their districts weekly and "putting their hands on the hot stove" of public opinion, as compared to the Senate's indecision and inaction. That contrast in a sense of urgency, Hoyer described, complicated the management of the House as well, since "many members refuse to pass good bills because they want to see what the Senate does first since that's what will ultimately pass."[6]

While these tensions between the two houses of Congress affected the design of much of the legislation of this era, the relationship with the executive branch represented another point of institutional confrontation. During the period of divided government, majorities of both parties were frustrated by their inability to overcome vetoes of legislation by presidents of the other party.[7] Nowhere was this more frustrating for Democrats in the 2007–8 time frame than in their inability to impose enforceable timetables and benchmarks on military participation in the wars in Iraq and Afghanistan and or to extend child health programs.

However, even after the election of Barack Obama and the alignment of the executive and legislative branches under unified Democratic control, the interbranch tensions remained on both policy and political strategy. In some cases, as with dissatisfaction with presidential messaging, financial support for campaign organizations, and the use of signing statements to effectively void provisions of bills, the two houses shared a common exasperation. On other occasions, House members decried the administration's seeming preference for the Senate's approach, either out of necessity to advance legislation or because of Obama's greater familiarity with that house of Congress.

Many on the Hill also were perennially frustrated by Obama's persistent belief, despite compelling evidence to the contrary, that Republicans would cooperate in legitimizing Democratic policy goals, an optimism that would similarly aggravate Hill leaders a dozen years later during Biden's early presidency. "I think it took the president too long to fully appreciate" that Republicans were disinterested in reaching compromise, Sen. Bernie Sanders (VT) observed late in Obama's second term. Indeed, that misplaced faith served to give opponents the time to orchestrate popular opposition, often with the help of a friendly conservative media.[8] Obama, like many in Congress, believed policies were more durable when shaped through bipartisan collaboration. As one administration official explained, the president is "not a super partisan person. He's not in it for the fight. He doesn't wake up every day thinking how to defeat Boehner. It's 'how can I get Boehner to agree? How can I have a reasonable conversation with Boehner?'"[9] But in the view of those who had weathered the rise in partisanship more relentlessly than the neophyte president, such hopes persisted too long and allowed opposition to coalesce.

That optimistic attitude was inconsistent with political reality. Obama's understandable self-confidence—shared by many of his top advisors—in his own persuasive power obscured what Frances Lee has documented as the unwillingness of political minorities to grant the majority they are seeking to displace "an implicit 'stamp of approval' for the status-quo allocation of party power."[10] Eventually, Obama himself came to recognize the intractability of the opposition and, under pressure from the Hill, increasingly relied on the use of executive orders to circumvent the congressional roadblocks that threatened to turn his second term into a policy wasteland. "Republicans uniformly resisted our overtures and raised hell over even the most moderate of proposals," he wrote in his postpresidential autobiography, so that "anything we did could be portrayed as partisan, controversial, radical—even illegitimate."[11]

Pelosi's impatience with other leaders' inability to move as decisively as she, even given her factional divisions, was a source of persistent frustration. Often, it seemed, the upper house was intent on playing its role as what a young Woodrow Wilson described as "an undemocratic check to the mass tyranny potentially inherent in the House of Representatives."[12] "We need to take the fight to the Senate," she insisted. "The Senate doesn't know what it's doing. Senators aren't legislators, they're grandstanders. They don't know what's in a bill."[13] She also had little tolerance for those unwilling to trust her judgment in devising the most impactful legislation she believed could still secure the 218 votes that distinguished viable legislation from being "just a conversation." And she had no forbearance for those who withered in the face of approbation from colleagues, the press, or constituents. "When you are in a negotiation, the last place to get weak knees is at the end," she advised.[14] That criticism applied not only to Senate colleagues but also to recalcitrant Blue Dogs, White House officials, and uncompromising purists, those whom Dave Obey angrily dismissed as "posing for holy pictures."

The product she brought to the floor, especially after negotiations with the Senate and the administration, was frequently far from what she or the base desired, but it was, she would explain, the best that could be secured after diligently advocating for something greater. "Some of you are here to make a beautiful pâté," she would tell her frustrated Left after regaining the gavel in 2019, "but [in Congress,] we're making sausage most of the time."[15] While decrying incrementalism as a governing philosophy, Pelosi was relentlessly cold-blooded when negotiating legislative compromises or cutting loose candidates who stood no chance of success. For all the conservative mockery of her as an out-of-touch, culturally extreme San Francisco liberal, Pelosi managed her fractious coalition as a progressively motivated pragmatist, as demonstrated when she persisted in the fight for the public option or against the cost commission so as to secure other concessions like the national health exchange. That unsentimental pragmatism was reflected in her comment following the ACA victory when a reporter inquired about the most crucial political lesson her father had taught her. "Make sure you have the votes," she said without hesitation. When the reporter demurred, observing that the mayor's words were "less than inspiring," Pelosi quickly retorted, "There's plenty of time to be inspiring; get the votes."[16]

Critics have faulted Pelosi for jeopardizing her majority by forcing "BTU" votes in the House on issues that often faced insuperable odds in the Senate and left moderates vulnerable to allegations of excessive liberalism and obeisance to her demands. Even though many front liners voted consistently against the liberal bills (helping explain the narrow margins by which many passed) and like Collin Peterson forced concessions to satisfy their constituencies, the moderates remained vulnerable to accusations tying them to excessive spending, deficit creation, and liberal policy making.

But Pelosi had to balance making concessions to these Majority Makers with demonstrating fealty to her much larger progressive caucus and the party base as well, such as pressing a vote on repealing "Don't Ask Don't Tell," despite requests from moderates, senators, and the Obama administration not to do so. Still, she stopped short of forcing divisive issues like immigration, labor organizing, and ENDA that her vulnerable members complained were certain to leave them "BTU'd" by the Senate. It was a constant balancing act that serves to illustrate the challenges of managing even a thirty-eight-seat majority and not one for which Pelosi apologized. "I have no regrets about anything," she insisted. "Regrets is not what I do."[17]

On October 27, 2010, with the election's grim outcome no longer in doubt, I sent an email to George Miller, for whom I had worked for three decades prior to becoming the Speaker's chief of staff. Musing about the arc of power that seemed to be bending decisively against the Democratic party, I wrote, "Our successes

[have] included the seeds of our own destruction. We have had to do big things, which the US [system] doesn't like, but otherwise, the opportunity was gone for a generation." Had Congress failed to pass the controversial TARP, auto bailout, or the ARRA stimulus bills, "the economy would have collapsed, we would have been in worse economic condition, and the opportunity for doing health care would have been lost." Aware of the electoral risks, the Speaker had "depleted her (and the caucus') political capital to accomplish great things [and] sometimes such achievements contain the seeds of your own destruction—dividing your supporters, providing clear targets, and energizing the opposition. The alternative—doing little but remaining strong—was never an option for her."[18] Considering the Democrats' imminent defeat, I concluded, "This trajectory may have been inevitable." Ultimately, that was not a sacrifice Pelosi lamented even as she believed that, with better messaging, financing, and campaign coordination, it might have been avoidable.

Still, the inability to bring down unemployment faster played a more salient role in the 2010 rout than a vote on, for example, the Waxman-Markey cap-and-trade bill. Indeed, the Tea Party was spawned not by the partisan stimulus, health care, or energy debates of 2009–10. Rather, it was the bipartisan TARP vote in 2008 that seemed to epitomize the sense of middle-class betrayal and government favoritism of the affluent that spurred the movement and its subsequent electoral successes. The effective withdrawal of the Republican Party from the legislative process following Obama's election, even including a refusal to approve the spending of the TARP funds they had already voted to authorize, left Democrats, especially frontline members, exposed to the full wrath of voters who, in a Pelosi-type alliteration, felt deceived, disparaged, and discounted.

An important lesson of this cycle of victory and loss is the indispensable role of effective and constant communication in an era dominated by ideologically driven media and personalized sources of news and opinion. Democrats, with their diverse policy agenda, often leap from legislative victory to the next objective, underplaying the crucial marketing of their achievement. When combined with the stubborn economic conditions that obscured the effective role of ARRA and the rising cost of premiums before the benefits of ACA became apparent, the public was left with the impression that Democrats had failed to deliver on the 2008 promises and unsurprisingly punished them brutally at the polls. Members of Congress and advocacy groups share responsibility for the communications deficit, but there is no substitute for presidential leadership; congressional voices are simply too dispersed and unfamiliar to persuade voters at the national level. These shortcomings during the Obama administration, evident at the time to many congressional Democrats, have been conceded even by the former president.

Congressional critics also faulted Obama for waiting too long to modify his strategies to confront the depths of partisan obstructionism with which they had contended for years before his arrival. "Perhaps we were naïve," Axelrod said in mid-October 2010.[19] The administration, top Obama aide Jim Messina later recognized, gave Republicans too much time to plan their strategy to kill the health care law. "It should've been apparent to us at the time," he agreed a decade later. "We waited too long."[20] That inaction helped create a vacuum filled by conservative critics who effectively exploited the persistence of the recession leading up to the 2010 electoral rout. Moreover, as Obama criticized, his party was ineffective at touting their successes. "One thing we do poorly," Obama later noted, "we win really badly. No one worse at spinning wins than Democrats. Every time we accomplish something big, we piss on it," he said, citing the ACA and Dodd-Frank.[21] Biden shared the same critique. "The Republicans can take loss and turn it into a political victory," he observed, "like saying 'My wife is cheating on me, but she'll have more experience.' The reason we don't win is because we don't go out and say it."[22]

It is always tempting for historians to identify parallels between an earlier period and the contemporary one, and from the perspective of early 2022, the similarities to the 2009–10 period abound: a new president who unifies Democratic control (Obama/Biden), economic hardship provoked by an existential crisis (Wall Street/COVID), a divided Senate struggling to pass legislation approved by the House, a nonparticipatory Republican party necessitating the use of the reconciliation process, frustration on the Democratic Left and rising extremism on the Republican Right, and a potentially uncontrollable cascade into yet another cycle of political turmoil and change.

Yet there are also important differences between the periods. None is more crucial than the far more dramatic narrowness of the Biden-era congressional margins (+4 in the House, a tied Senate) that empowers individual members—especially more moderate lawmakers to the anguish of progressives—in both houses to play outsized roles in determining the design of legislation. One cannot underestimate the challenges during the Bush-Obama periods to reach 218 votes in the House and sixty in the Senate, but contemporary party leaders face a vastly more exasperating situation when there is, quite literally, no margin for error.

The other indisputable difference is that the Republican Party has become significantly more extreme under the enduring influence of Donald Trump and his acolytes in Congress. The two impeachment trials of Trump by the Democratic House, however warranted by the president's actions, and the responses to the January 6, 2021, insurrection at the Capitol inevitably contributed to the unbridgeable gulf between the parties and their supporters. The rapid growth of this partisan divide and the parties' persistent struggles to secure a governing majority meant that the kind of collaboration that occurred between Pelosi, Reid, Boehner, and Paulson during the negotiations over TARP or the Bush stimulus was all but nonexistent months later during the formulation of the Obama stimulus and the health care law; following the 2020 election, as scores of Republicans have embraced unsubstantiated conspiracies and extremist policy viewpoints, the fulcrum of American politics has moved well beyond even the precarious position of 2010.

What has not changed is the historical dynamic: the "arc of power" in which a party secures power by energizing its base and capitalizing on the unpopularity of the party in power. Inevitably, the victorious party—especially in the House because of its two-year terms—must quickly demonstrate legislative proficiency that demands compromises unwelcome by supporters and insufficient for opponents, fueling electoral ambivalence among the disenchanted base while providing a useful target for those disagreeing with the legislative product.

The history recounted in this book admittedly could be discouraging to those who seek quick remedies by selfless politicians or policy breakthroughs that would herald a more efficient and less polarized government. But legislating, as this book describes, is challenging under the best of circumstances due to the factions that exist even within a majority, the design of our national government that allocates power disproportionately, the extreme polarization that discourages collaboration and rewards denigration of opponents, and the susceptibility of many Americans to partisan manipulation by politicians and a complicit media rather than thoughtful political analysis and participation.

Hopefully these accounts also illustrate the dedication and skill of elected officials and their staffs to formulate viable policies and, importantly, their readiness to take risks to achieve what they believe to be important goals. Whether it is President Obama declaring his willingness to lose his reelection, Speaker Pelosi insisting she could unambiguously walk away from her office after passing the ACA, or Rep. Tom Perriello insisting he had no regrets about losing his marginal seat, the accounts in this book indicate that, contrary to public assumptions, there are many women and men in public office motivated not merely by personal aggrandizement but rather by what they believe to be in the best interests of the nation and its residents. The persistent challenges they confront in striving to achieve that goal, their periodic success and frustrating failure, is the story of this book.

Notes

Abbreviations Used in the Text

JALP   John A. Lawrence Papers, Manuscript Division, Library of Congress
LAT   *Los Angeles Times*
NYT   *New York Times*
WP   *Washington Post*
WSJ   *Wall Street Journal*

Introduction

1. Press conference, January 31, 2019.

2. Christine Emba, "Harris and Pelosi Headlined a Night for Women. Almost," *WP*, April 28, 2021.

3. Interview with Chris Wallace on *Fox News Sunday*, July 30, 2017.

Prologue: Discouraged, Disorganized, Defeated

1. Harold Meyerson, "How Nancy Pelosi Took Control," *American Prospect*, June 2, 2004; "Nancy Pelosi Is Ready to Be Voice of the Majority," *NYT*, November 9, 2006.

2. JALP, box 36, file 6, July 12, 2010.

3. More extensive coverage of Pelosi's early life and career can be found in a number of biographies, including Molly Ball, *Pelosi* (New York: Henry Holt, 2020); Susan Page, *Madam Speaker: Nancy Pelosi and the Lessons of Power* (New York: Twelve, 2021); Vincent Bzdek, *Woman of the House: The Rise of Nancy Pelosi* (New York: St. Martin's Griffin, 2008); Marc Sandalow, *Madam Speaker: Nancy Pelosi's Life, Times, and Rise to Power* (Emmaus, PA: Rodale Books, 2008); Ron Peters and Cindy Simon Rosenthal, *Speaker Nancy Pelosi and the New American Politics* (Oxford: Oxford University Press, 2010); Elaine S. Povich, *Nancy Pelosi: A Biography* (Santa Barbara, CA: Greenwood Biographies, 2008); and Nancy Pelosi, *Know Your Power: A Message to America's Daughters* (New York: Anchor, 2009).

4. Dan Balz, "Kirk Elected Democratic Chairman," *WP*, February 2, 1985.

5. Jerry Roberts, "Political Landmark for Nancy Pelosi: She Marks 25 Years in Elected Politics This Week," April 4, 2012, http://blog.sfgate.com/nov05election/2012/04/05/political-landmark-for-nancy-pelosi-she-marks-25-years-in-elected-politics-this-week/.

6. John E. Yang, "House Reprimands, Penalizes Speaker," *WP*, January 22, 1997; Lucy Madison, "Pelosi: My Gingrich Intel Dump Would Be Legal," CBS News, December 5, 2011, https://www.cbsnews.com/news/pelosi-my-gingrich-intel-dump-would-be-legal/. "I know a lot about him," she would tell reporters after his ouster. "One of these days we'll have a conversation about Newt Gingrich." In fact, Pelosi never disclosed any of the classified information beyond that contained in the formal committee report.

7. "Nancy Pelosi Is Ready to Be Voice of the Majority," *NYT*, November 9, 2006.

8. Jennifer Steinhauer, "With the House in the Balance, Pelosi Serves as a Focal Point for Both Parties," *NYT*, October 30, 2006.

9. JALP, Box 36, Folder 8, September 20, 2010

10. Adam Clymer, "Two Competing for Post of Democratic Whip in the House," *NYT*, October 10, 2001.

11. The victory was also something of a belated redemption for San Francisco, whose last candidate for a leadership post, Phil Burton, had been upset by the moderate Jim Wright in 1977 by a single vote.

12. "Democrats Pick Pelosi as House Leader," CNN, November 15, 2004.

13. *Congressional Quarterly*, June 12, 1976, 1634. The agenda included tax incentives for private energy producers, a relaxation of government regulations, a purging of ineligible welfare recipients, tax simplification, and mandatory prison sentencing.

14. Cullinane Active Archive for Entrepreneurs, https://www.cullinaneactivearchive.com/top-tips/how-to-create-a-good-sales-message; Ed Forry, "John Cullinane's Message: Democracy Is in Peril, and We Have to Save It," *Boston Irish Reporter*, June 27, 2018.

15. "House Dems Set Out 'Six Core Values' for Unified 2004 Campaign Message," *The Hill*, September 23, 2004. The New Partnership identified six basic values "to strengthen the middle class" that would shape the party's policies if voters elevated Democrats to the majority: national security, prosperity, fairness, opportunity, community, and accountability. The Partnership promised ten million new jobs, affordable health care for every American, and an end to the spread of nuclear weapons—all long-standing Democratic objectives.

16. "House Dems Set Out 'Six Core Values.'"

17. C-SPAN Archives New Partnership for America's Future, September 22, 2004, https://www.youtube.com/watch?v=1HFMh--S8DQ.

Chapter 1: The New Direction: "6 for '06"

1. JALP, box 31, folder 5, October 13, 2005. Most of the strategists had worked for President Bill Clinton's campaigns or in his White House.

2. JALP, box 31, folder 4, July 27, 2005.

3. William Galston, "Why the 2005 Social Security Initiative Failed, and What It Means for the Future," Brookings Institute, September 21, 2007.

4. Galston, "Why the 2005."

5. JALP, box 36, folder 8, September 6, 2010.

6. House Democrats embraced only an AmeriSave initiative permitting tax-protected private savings in addition to "Social Security's guaranteed benefit." "House Democrats Roll Out Retirement Plan," CNN Finance, July 26, 2005.

7. A similar steadfastness in refusing to buy into a president's legislative demand, and Pelosi's ability to rally her caucus behind her, was also evident in the 2018–19 standoff with President Donald Trump over the funding of a border wall between the United States and Mexico, which led to the longest government shutdown in the country's history. Rachel Bade and John Bresnahan, "'She's Not One to Bluff': How Pelosi Won the Shutdown Battle," *Politico*, January 25, 2019.

8. The team included the Portland-based Weiden+Kennedy communications firm; Cullinane; Lakoff; megadonors like Washington developer Herb Miller, film producer Steve Bing, and higher education entrepreneur John Sperling; technology pioneers Richard Yanowitch and John Kao; communications strategist Doug Hattaway; Doug Sosnick from the Clinton White House; and longtime operatives John O'Hanlon and Michael Perik.

9. Trout's books included *Positioning* (New York: McGraw-Hill, 2001), *Differentiate or Die* (Hoboken, NJ: Wiley, 2008), and *The 22 Immutable Laws of Marketing* (New York: Harper, 1994).

10. "Jack Trout, Who Fought for Consumers' Minds and Money, Dies at 82," *NYT*, June 7, 2017.

11. Naftali Bendavid, *The Thumpin': How Rahm Emanuel and the Democrats Learned to Be Ruthless and Ended the Republican Revolution* (New York: Doubleday, 2007), 14.

12. JALP, box 31, folder 4, August 3, 2005.

13. JALP, box 31, folder 4, August 31, 2005.

14. Cunningham earned the longest prison term in congressional history for accepting over $2 million in bribes.

15. JALP, box 31, folder 7, January 26, 2006; box 31, folder 6, November 1, 2005.

16. JALP, box 31, folder 6, December 13, 2005.

17. Zack Stanton, "The Page Who Took Down the GOP," *Politico*, November 20, 2015.

18. JALP, box 31, folder 12, September 29, 2006.

19. Shimkus also reportedly visited the dorm to instruct the pages to avoid reporters and reproach them for their behavior, leaving many bewildered as to why they were being blamed for Foley's aggressive behavior.

20. Stanton, "Page Who Took Down."

21. "Rep. Bob Ney Pleads Guilty to Bribery," Associated Press, October 13, 2006.

22. "Willfully Ignorant," *Chicago Tribune*, December 12, 2006.

23. "Panel Blasts Hastert in Foley Scandal," *USA Today*, December 8, 2006.

24. "In Partisan Vote, House OKs Ethics Bill by 4 Votes," CNN, May 4, 2006.

25. "Senior Democrat on House Ethics Committee Stepping Down," Associated Press, April 22, 2006.

26. JALP, box 31, folder 9, May 10, 2006.

27. JALP, box 31, folder 9, May 15, 2006.

28. JALP, box 31, folder 10, June 6, 2006.

29. JALP, box 31, folder 10, June 7, 2006.

30. JALP, box 32, folder 4, February 28, 2007. Even so, he was reelected in 2006 and served until being defeated in the 2008 general election. In 2009, Jefferson was convicted of accepting more than $400,000 in bribes and attempting to secure millions more to promote investment in Africa. He spent over five years in federal prison.

31. JALP, box 31, folder 7, June 16, 2006.

32. JALP, box 31, folder 5, October 6, 2005; Proclamation 7924 (September 8, 2005). After Miller introduced a resolution to abrogate Bush's declaration, the president relented.

33. The committee's report blamed "a litany of mistakes, misjudgments, lapses, and absurdities all cascading together, blinding us to what was coming and hobbling any collective effort to respond." Select Bipartisan Committee to Investigate the Preparation for and Response to Hurricane Katrina, *A Failure of Initiative, Final Report of the Select Bipartisan Committee to Investigate the Preparation for and Response to Hurricane Katrina* (Washington, DC: Government Printing Office, February 15, 2006), x.

34. JALP, box 31, folder 4, September 12, 2005.

35. Watson Institute of International and Public Affairs, Brown University, "Costs of War," https://watson.brown.edu/costsofwar/figures/2019/budgetary-costs-post-911-wars-through-fy2020-64-trillion.

36. JALP, box 31, folder 4, September 16, 2005.

37. Don Bailey, a fellow Democrat whom Murtha had defeated in 1982 after reapportionment put them in the same Pennsylvania district, claimed that twenty years earlier, Murtha admitted he did not deserve his Purple Hearts because he only "got a little scratch on the cheek." Howard Kurtz and Shailagh Murray, "Web Site Attacks Critic of War Opponents Question Murtha's Medals," *WP*, January 14, 2006.

38. JALP, box 31, folder 10, June 8, 2006; box 31, folder 6, November 28, 2005.

39. "Pelosi Tells Trump: 'You Have Come Into My Wheelhouse,'" *NYT*, September 26, 2019.

40. JALP, box 31, folder 6, December 14, 2005.

41. JALP, box 31, folder 6, December 7, 2005.

42. JALP, box 31, folder 6, November 1, 2005.

43. Rep. Don Fraser (MN), a leading reformer, had used this phrase in his 1962 House campaign.

44. My own evaluation, I told Pelosi, was that it sounded like a student looking for a "C." Celinda Lake dismissed it as "juvenile." JALP, box 31, folder 5, September 29, 2005.

45. Bendavid, *The Thumpin'*, 143.

46. JALP, box 31, folder 10, June 26, 2006.

47. A copy of the pamphlet can be found at https://www.washingtonpost.com/wp -srv/special/politics/political-rallying-cry/new-direction-for-america.pdf.

48. JALP, box 31, folder 12, October 27, September 27, 2006.

49. JALP, box 31, folder 11, July 12 and 13, 2006.

50. JALP, box 31, folder 12, September 20, October 9, 2006.

51. JALP, box 31, folder 12, October 22, 2006.

Chapter 2: "I Had to Win the House First"

1. JALP, box 32, folder 1, November 2, 2006.

2. The Speaker appointed the chairs of Ethics, Rules, Intelligence, and House Administration as well as joint committees with the Senate.

3. Livingood recommended the mailbox at her San Francisco home be welded shut and closed-circuit cameras installed, which Pelosi vetoed.

4. JALP, box 32, folder 2, December 18, 2006.

5. For a discussion of the battle over seniority in the 1970s, see John A. Lawrence, *The Class of '74 Congress after Watergate and the Roots of Partisanship* (Baltimore: Johns Hopkins University Press, 2018).

6. The senior Democrat on Resources actually was George Miller who had been chairman in 1991–95 but who had voluntarily left in 2001 to become the ranking member of the Education and Workforce Committee.

7. JALP, box 32, folder 1, November 29, 2006.

8. JALP, box 32, folder 2, December 28, 2006.

9. JALP, box 32, folder 2, January 2, 2007.

10. JALP, box 32, folders 2, January 8 and 11, 2007.

11. "Gonzales Said to Have Intervened on Wiretap," *NYT*, April 23, 2009. This allegation may have been the source of Scott Palmer's suggestion of compromising information on a Democrat during the campaign.

12. While technically correct under the rules, Pelosi could have extended Harman's term as she did for John Spratt (SC), who had already served as Budget ranking member for six terms before being appointed chairman in 2006. Several years later, Pelosi acknowledged that in 2006, the Bush administration had alerted her that Harman had been taped in 2005 as part of an investigation into the American Israel Public Affairs Committee (AIPAC). Purportedly, Harman offered to assist pro-Israel lobbyists under investigation for espionage if AIPAC would intervene to pressure Pelosi to appoint her as chair. Pelosi denied that the revelation influenced the decision not to grant Harman the chairmanship but added, "I don't respond to threats." In June 2009, Harman received a letter from the Justice Department advising her that she was "neither a subject nor a target of an ongoing investigation by the Criminal Division." David Herszenhorn, "Pelosi Tells of a Briefing by Officials on Harman," *NYT*, April 22, 2009; JALP, box 34, folder 7, April 20–21, 2009; "Pelosi and Harman Have a Long History," *WP*, April 20, 2009.

13. JALP, box 32, folder 2, December 15, 2006.

14. JALP, box 32, folder 2, December 7, 2006.

15. JALP, box 31, folder 12, October 27, 2006.

16. Prosecutors concluded that Murtha's conversations with the ersatz sheiks were intended to secure needed investment in his hard-pressed Pennsylvania district, and the House Ethics Committee voted against charging Murtha. Former Texas member Chris Bell recalled a charge that Murtha had promoted Allan Mollohan for the chairmanship of the Ethics Committee and then collaborated with the West Virginian to slow down the committee's investigations.

17. Jonathan Weisman, "In Backing Murtha, Pelosi Draws Fire," WP, November 14, 2006.

18. John Fortier, "Hoyer vs. Murtha," The Hill, June 14, 2006.

19. Perry Bacon, "Pelosi's Big Gamble," Time, November 13, 2006.

20. Weisman, "In Backing Murtha."

21. Susan Ferrechio, "Pelosi Sets Up Early Test of Her Clout," NYT, November 15, 2006.

22. Jonathan Weisman, "Pelosi Endorses Murtha as Next Majority Leader," WP, November 13, 2006.

23. Dana Milbank, "Crowning Majority Leader, Democrats Are All Smiles and Bile," WP, November 17, 2006.

24. Jonathan Weisman and Lois Romano, "Democrats Pick Hoyer over Murtha," WP, November 16, 2007.

25. "Hoyer Beats Pelosi's Pick in Race for No. 2 House Post," NYT, November 16, 2006.

26. Howard Fineman, "Pelosi Loses Big on Murtha," Newsweek, November 15, 2006.

27. JALP, box 32, folder 4, February 14, 2007.

28. William Gray (PA) had served as Democratic majority whip in the early 1980s.

29. JALP, box 32, folder 1, November 15, 2006.

30. Use of Air Force planes for travel linked to political appearances or fundraising was prohibited.

31. JALP, box 32, folder 4, February 7, 2007. There were even cases of Hastert authorizing use of a plane for other members when he personally was not on board.

32. Travel schedules were often not released to the press; hotels would be booked under pseudonyms.

33. Jake Tapper, "Pentagon Rejects Speaker Pelosi's Request for Military Aircraft," ABC News, February 7, 2007.

34. JALP, box 32, folder 4, February 7, 2007; box 31, folder 12, December 19, 2006. Wilkie later became secretary of Veterans Affairs under the Trump administration.

35. JALP, box 32, folder 3, January 25, 2007.

36. Hoyer letter to Pelosi, June 10, 2005.

37. Pelosi press conference, October 17, 2019.

38. Susan Ferrechio, "Pelosi: Bush Impeachment 'Off the Table,'" *Congressional Quarterly*, November 8, 2006.

39. Ferrechio, "Pelosi: Bush Impeachment."

40. JALP, box 32, folder 1, November 20, 2006.

41. JALP, box 32, folder 1, November 28, 2006. She even proposed joint hearings with Senate committees, but those never occurred.

42. JALP, box 32, folder 1, November 28, 2006.

43. JALP, box 32, folder 2, December 8, 2006.

44. JALP, box 32, folder 1, November 30, 2006.

Chapter 3: Madam Speaker

1. JALP, box 32, folder 2, December 26, 2006.

2. JALP, box 32, folder 3, January 17, 2007.

3. JALP, box 32, folder 3, January 30, 2007.

4. JALP, box 32, folder 2, December 28, 2006.

5. JALP, box 32, folder 2, January 8, 2007.

6. JALP, box 32, folder 8, June 12, 2007.

7. JALP, box 32, folder 3, January 23, 2007.

8. Paul Kane, "Pelosi and Dingell Rivalry Reflects the Evolution of the Democratic Party," *WP*, February 9, 2019.

9. JALP, box 32, folder 3, January 16, 2007.

10. JALP, box 32, folder 3, January 17, 2007.

11. The select committee employed its subpoena power in 2008 when it voted to compel the Environmental Protection Agency to provide information about fuel and emission rules for automobiles.

12. JALP, box 32, folder 8, June 29, 2007.

13. Kane, "Pelosi and Dingell Rivalry."

14. JALP, box 32, folder 8, June 29, 2007.

15. JALP, box 32, folder 5, March 9, 2007; box 32, folder 3, January 30, 2007.

16. Her appointments included Hilda Solis (CA) and Emanuel Cleaver (MO), well-regarded members of the CHC and CBC, respectively, as well as energy policy experts Jay Inslee (WA) and Earl Blumenauer (OR). The appointments, which included rock guitarist John Hall, "signal change to the younger generation," Pelosi said, embracing a "new, entrepreneurial way to go forward" on climate and energy issues focused on jobs and national security.

17. JALP, box 32, folder 3, January 28, 2007.

18. JALP, box 35, folder 7, January 6, 2010.

19. JALP, box 32, folder 2, December 28, 2006.

20. JALP, box 32, folder 2, December 8 and 11, 2006.

21. JALP, box 32, folder 2, December 8, 2006.

22. Christine Emba, "Harris and Pelosi Headlined a Night for Women. Almost," *WP*, April 28, 2021.

23. Pelosi remarks, Smithsonian Institute Museum of American History, March 7, 2018.

Chapter 4: "Everything Becomes Urgent"

1. JALP, box 32, folder 4, February 22, 2007; box 32, folder 5, February 6, 2007.

2. JALP, box 32, folder 4, March 5, 2007.

3. Andy Kroll, "The Staying Power of Nancy Pelosi," *National Journal*, September 12, 2015.

4. For more on the impact of the Senate's procedures on democratic governance, see Ira Shapiro, *Broken: Can the Senate Save Itself and the Country?* (Lanham, MD: Rowman & Littlefield, 2018); Daniel Wirls, *The Senate: From White Supremacy to Government Gridlock* (Charlottesville: University of Virginia Press, 2021); Adam Jentleson, *Kill Switch: The Rise of the Modern Senate and the Crippling of American* (New York: Liveright, 2021).

5. All 233 Democrats and 82 of 198 Republicans voted for the increase.

6. Just four Democrats voted against the energy bill, all among the most conservative Caucus members: Dan Boren (OK), Nick Lampson (TX), Ed Marshall (GA), and John Barrow (GA).

7. A dozen years later, after she had regained the majority and the speakership in 2019, Pelosi again structured her early agenda to ensure that her first ten bills passed with bipartisan support to undercut charges that a Democratic majority meant extreme policies. "Pelosi, in CT Appearance, Says She's Optimistic on Background Checks," *CT Post*, September 14, 2019.

8. "Democrats Beat 100-Hour Clock," Associated Press, January 19, 2007.

9. Of course, removing the tax cuts in the conference committee would create problems in taking up the conference report, which would be susceptible to a filibuster.

10. JALP, box 32, folder 4, February 13, 2007.

11. JALP, box 32, folder 4, February 27, March 1, 2007.

12. JALP, box 32, folder 4, February 14, 2007.

13. The chief signatories were Ron Wyden (OR) and Jim DeMint (OH). The letter supported developing a plan under which all Americans would have affordable, quality, private health coverage, while protecting current government programs. "We believe the health care system cannot be fixed without providing solutions for everyone. Otherwise, the costs of those without insurance will continue to be shifted to those who do have coverage." Letter available at https://www.wyden.senate.gov/news/press-releases/bipartisan-blueprint-for-health-reformten-senate-leaders-say-lets-fix-health-care-nowsenators-of-both-parties-hope-to-work-with-the-president.

14. JALP, box 32, folder 4, February 14, 2007.

15. JALP, box 32, folder 4, February 16 and 22, 2007.

16. JALP, box 32, folder 4, February 26, 2007. The staff of the Agriculture Committee complained that Obey was only providing half the level of disaster assistance that had been promised. Chet Edwards (TX) was furious that Murtha had rebuked him during a conversation in Pelosi's office. Norm Dicks (WA) fumed at Murtha's presumption in articulating the party's position on Iraq.

17. JALP, box 32, folder 6, April 20, 2007.

18. JALP, box 32, folder 5, March 6, 2007.

19. JALP, box 32, folder 5, March 6 and 13, 2007.

20. Clyburn thought the CBC dissent was "manageable." JALP, box 32, folder 7, May 25, 2007.

21. JALP, box 32, folder 8, June 5, 2007.

22. JALP, box 32, folder 7, May 15, 2007; box 32, folder 5, March 6, 2007.

23. JALP, box 32, folder 6, May 8 and 2, 2007.

24. Pelosi's approval had plummeted from +10 points on Election Day to just +4. JALP, box 32, folder 4, February 22, 2007.

25. JALP, box 32, folder 8, June 7, 2007.

Chapter 5: "The Slowest Ship"

1. JALP, box 32, folder 7, May 16, 2007.

2. JALP, box 32, folder 7, June 8, 2007.

3. JALP, box 32, folder 8, June 13, 2007; box 32, folder 9, June 29, 2007.

4. JALP, box 32, folder 7, May 15, 2007; box 32, folder 8, June 13, 2007.

5. JALP, box 32, folder 8, June 19, 2007; box 32, folder 9, July 2, 2007.

6. JALP, box 32, folder 9, July 2, 2007.

7. JALP, box 32, folder 9, June 29, 2007.

8. JALP, box 32, folder 8, June 15, 2007.

9. JALP, box 32, folder 9, July 6 and 11–12, 2007.

10. JALP, box 32, folder 9, June 26, 2007.

11. JALP, box 32, folder 9, July 17 and 25, 2007.

12. JALP, box 32, folder 8, June 19, 2007.

13. JALP, box 32, folder 8, June 19, 2007.

14. All of the presidential hopefuls—Clinton, Obama, Dodd, Biden—voted against the bill.

15. JALP, box 32, folder 10, July 25, August 4, 2007.

16. Only forty-one moderate and conservative Democrats voted in favor.

17. JALP, box 32, folder 10, August 10, 2007.

18. JALP, box 32, folder 10, August 13 and 10, 2007.

19. Nancy Pelosi, "Bringing the War to an End Is My Highest Priority as Speaker," *Huffington Post*, November 17, 2006.

20. JALP, box 32, folder 10, August 2, 2007.

21. JALP, box 32, folder 11, September 12 and 18, 2007.

22. JALP, box 32, folder 12, October 3 and 1, 2007.

23. JALP, box 32, folder 12, October 22, 2007; box 32, folder 13, October 24, 2007.

24. JALP, box 33, folder 1, December 5, 2007.

25. JALP, box 32, folder 11, September 6, 2007.

26. JALP, box 32, folder 11, September 6, 2007; box 33, folder 1, December 9 and 11, 2007.

27. JALP, box 32, folder 12, October 2, 2007.

28. JALP, box 32, folder 14, November 19, 2007.

29. Nicola Moore, "Omnibusted: The Top 10 Worst Problems with the Omnibus Spending Bill," Heritage Foundation, December 21, 2007.

30. JALP, box 32, folder 14, November 21, 2007.

31. JALP, box 32, folder 14, December 3, 2007.

32. Jonathan Weisman and Paul Kane, "Democrats Blaming Each Other for Failure," WP, December 13, 2007.

33. Paul Krugman, "An Immoral Philosophy," NYT, July 30, 2007.

34. JALP, box 32, folder 11, September 27, 2007. Several days later, Candi Wolfe, the White House director of congressional relations, called to complain about the phone call leaking to the press, especially the portion where the Speaker assured the president she was "praying for you."

35. "Bush Vetoes Children's Health Bill," NYT, October 3, 2007.

36. JALP, box 32, folder 14, November 27 and 28, December 3, 2007.

37. "Democrats Promise Quick Vote on ERDA Override," The Hill, November 2, 2007. The margins were 361–54 in the House and 79–14 in the Senate.

38. "Bush to Veto Pentagon Funds over Iraq Provision," NYT, December 28, 2007. An earlier suit had been blocked in 2005 when the federal courts ruled that Congress had barred private lawsuits against foreign governments.

39. JALP, box 33, folder 2, December 26, 2007.

40. Nathan cited the Barnes v. Klein 759 F.2d 21 (1984) decision in the DC Circuit Court of Appeals to support his argument. Memo of John Sullivan to the Speaker, December 29, 2007; Memo of John Lawrence to the Majority Leader, Whip and others, December 27, 2007.

41. JALP, box 33, folder 2, December 27–28, 2008.

42. Jonathan Wiseman and Paul Kane, "Democrats Blaming Each Other for Failures," WP, December 13, 2007.

43. JALP, box 32, folder 12, October 10, 2007.

44. JALP, box 32, folder 12, October 22, 2007; box 32, folder 10, September 19, 2007.

45. JALP, box 32, folder 12, November 13, 2007.

46. Michelle Cottle, "House Broker," New Republic, June 11, 2008.

Chapter 6: The Economy Wobbles

1. JALP, box 33, folder 2, January 8, 2008.

2. JALP, box 33, folder 2, January 10, 2008.

3. Dan Froomkin, "Bush's Signing Statements: Constitutional Crisis or Empty Rhetoric?" Neiman Watchdog, June 27, 2006, http://www.niemanwatchdog.org/index .cfm?fuseaction=ask_this.view&askthisid=211; for a fuller discussion, see Jeffrey Crouch, Mark Rozell, and Mitchel Sollenberger, *The Unitary Executive Theory: A Danger to Constitutional Government* (Lawrence: University Press of Kansas, 2020).

4. Author's interview with Irvin Nathan, April 6, 2018, Washington, DC.

5. JALP, box 32, folder 13, November 13, 2007. Miers had briefly been Bush's nominee to the Supreme Court seat vacated by Justice Sandra Day O'Connor, but she was widely dismissed as an unprepared Bush crony who lacked gravitas, and she asked Bush to withdraw her nomination.

6. Among the US attorneys removed from office were Carol Lam in Los Angeles, who had secured a corruption conviction against Rep. Randy "Duke" Cunningham (R-CA) and David Iglesias in New Mexico, who ignored requests from Republicans Sen. Pete Domenici and Rep. Heather Wilson, who were demanding he begin inquiries into state Democratic officeholders. Irvin Nathan, "Protecting the House's Institutional Prerogative to Enforce Its Subpoenas," The Constitution Project, 3–4, https://archive.con stitutionproject.org/wp-content/uploads/2017/05/HouseSubpoenas.pdf.

7. Dan Eggen and Paul Kane, "Prosecutors Say They Felt Pressured, Threatened," *WP*, March 7, 2007.

8. Alexander Bolton and Klaus Marre, "House Finds Bolten, Miers in Contempt of Congress," *The Hill*, February 14, 2008.

9. Author interview with Irv Nathan, April 6, 2018. In fact, years later, as Speaker, Boehner would employ the precedent by challenging the Obama administration in the so-called "Fast and Furious" inquiry.

10. JALP, box 33, folder 2, January 14, 2008; Bolton and Marre, "House Finds Bolten, Miers in Contempt."

11. *Committee on the Judiciary, U.S. House of Representatives, v. Harriet Miers et al.*, Civil Action No. 08-0409, July 31, 2008, https://ecf.dcd.uscourts.gov/cgi-bin/show _public_doc?2008cv0409-49.

12. Nathan interview, April 6, 2018.

13. When the documents were turned over to the House, the role of the Bush White House in the USAs' firings was found to have been substantial.

14. JALP, box 32, folder 14, November 22, 2007.

15. National Association of Realtors, "Foreclosure Rates Climb More Slowly," http://www.realtor.org/rmodaily.nsf/pages/News2008022602.

16. JALP, box 33, folder 2, January 8, 2008, December 28, 2007, January 7, 2008.

17. JALP, box 33, folder 2, January 7–8, 2008.

18. JALP, box 33, folder 2, January 17, 2008.

19. JALP, box 33, folder 2, January 17, 2008.

20. JALP, box 33, folder 2, January 17, 2008.

21. JALP, box 33, folder 2, January 17, 2008.

22. JALP, box 33, folder 2, January 17, 2008.

23. JALP, box 33, folder 2, January 17, 2008.

24. JALP, box 33, folder 2, January 18, 2008.

25. JALP, box 33, folder 3, January 23, 2008.

26. JALP, box 33, folder 3, January 23, 2008; box 33, folder 2, January 17 and 18, 2008.

27. JALP, box 33, folder 2, January 17 and 18, 2008.

28. JALP, box 33, folder 3, January 22–23, 2008.

29. JALP, box 33, folder 3, January 23, 2008.

30. JALP, box 33, folder 3, January 23, 2008.

31. JALP, box 33, folder 3, February 5, 2008.

32. JALP, box 33, folder 3, February 5 and 7, 2008.

33. JALP, box 33, folder 3, February 5, 2008.

34. An accusatorial mood endured beyond the handshake. A few days later, Myrick accused House Agriculture chair Collin Peterson of cutting a private deal with the White House that constituted an "end run around the Senate." JALP, box 33, folder 3, February 7, 2008.

35. JALP, box 33, folder 3, February 5, 2008.

36. "Bush Signs Stimulus Bill; Rebate Checks Expected in May," CNN, February 13, 2008.

37. JALP, box 33, folder 3, January 23, 2008.

38. Sara Murray, "Most 2008 Stimulus Checks Were Saved, not Spent," *WSJ*, December 26, 2008.

39. JALP, box 33, folder 3, January 29, 2008.

Chapter 7: "The Flagship"

1. For more detailed discussions of the energy legislation and the machinations within the Commerce Committee during this period, two valuable sources are Henry A. Waxman and Joshua Green, *The Waxman Report: How Congress Really Works* (New York: Twelve, 2009), and Bryan Marshall and Bruce Wolpe, *The Committee: A Study of Policy, Power, Politics and Obama's Historic Legislative Agenda on Capitol Hill* (Ann Arbor: University of Michigan Press, 2018).

2. JALP, box 32, folder 5, March 21, 2007.

3. JALP, box 32, folder 5, March 21, 2007.

4. JALP, box 32, folder 5, March 14, 2007.

5. JALP, box 32, folder 10, July 26, 2007.

6. JALP, box 32, folder 8, June 7, 2007.

7. JALP, box 32, folder 8, June 7, 2007.

8. JALP, box 32, folder 8, June 7, 2007.

9. JALP, box 32, folder 8, June 12, 2007.

10. JALP, box 32, folder 8, June 15 and 19, 2007.

11. JALP, box 32, folder 8, June 11 and 12, 2007.

12. JALP, box 32, folder 8, June 15, 2007; box 32, folder 10, July 31, 2007.

13. JALP, box 32, folder 10, July 31, 2007.

14. JALP, box 32, folder 10, July 26, 2007; box 32, folder 9, July 1, 2007. Pelosi did approve of allowing the government to take royalties in oil instead of cash.

15. JALP, box 32, folder 9, July 26, 2007.

16. JALP, box 32, folder 9, June 26, 27, and 28, 2007.

17. JALP, box 32, folder 9, August 14, 2007.

18. John Broder, "Energy Bill Adopted by House Requires Utilities to Use Renewable Power Sources," *NYT*, August 6, 2007, https://www.nytimes.com/2007/08/05/washington/05energy.html.

19. JALP, box 32, folder 12, October 10, 2007; box 32, folder 11, September 19, 2007.

20. JALP, box 32, folder 12, October 3, 2007.

21. JALP, box 32, folder 13, November 2, 2007.

22. JALP, box 32, folder 12, October 18, 2007.

23. JALP, box 32, folder 13, November 6, 2007; box 32, folder 11, October 18, 2007.

24. JALP, box 32, folder 13, November 6, 2007.

25. JALP, box 32, folder 14, November 16, 2007; box 32, folder 13, November 15, 2007.

26. JALP, box 32, folder 14, November 16, 2007.

27. JALP, box 32, folder 14, November 20, 2007.

28. JALP, box 32, folder 14, November 29, 2007; box 33, folder 1, December 5, 2007.

29. All but seven Democrats, mostly those from energy states, voted no: Alan Boyd (FL), Gene Green (TX), Nick Lampson (TX), Charlie Melançon (LA), Jim Marshall (GA), John Barrow (GA), and Dan Boren (OK). Only fourteen Republicans voted in favor, all from moderate districts.

30. JALP, box 33, folder 1, December 6 and 9, 2007.

31. Republican opponents included John Kyl (AZ), Tom Coburn (OK), Jim Inhofe (OK), Jim DeMint (SC), Orrin Hatch (UT), John Barasso (WY), and Mike Enzi (WY). Obama, McCain, Dodd, Clinton, and Biden were all away on the presidential campaign trail.

32. Robert Hargraves, "Net Zero? More Like Not Zero," *WSJ*, March 7, 2021.

33. Congressional Research Service, "Energy Independence and Security Act of 2007: A Summary of Major Provisions," December 21, 2007.

34. Earth Justice Network, "2007 Energy Bill: Look Before You Leap!" December 13, 2007.

35. John Broder, "House, 314–200, Passes Broad Energy Bill; Bush Plans to Sign It," *NYT*, December 19, 2007.

36. "House, 314–100, Passes Broad Energy Bill; Bush Plans to Sign It," *NYT*, December 19, 2007.

37. JALP, box 33, folder 4, February 12, 2008; box 33, folder 6, April 15 and 17, 2008.

38. JALP, box 33, folder 7, May 4, 2008; box 33, folder 5, March 27, 2008.

39. Brian Darling, "Lieberman-Warner Climate Change Bill," Heritage Foundation, May 6, 2008.

40. JALP, box 33, folder 8, June 11, 2008; box 33, folder 9, June 16, 2008.

41. JALP, box 33, folders 8 and 9, June 11 and 16, 2008.

42. JALP, box 33, folder 8, June 12, 2008.

43. JALP, box 33, folder 9, June 16, 2008.

44. JALP, box 33, folder 9, July 18, 2008.

45. JALP, box 33, folder 9, July 10, 2008. Pete Rouse, an Obama aide, was reportedly sympathetic to releases from the SPR. JALP, box 33, folder 9, August 8, 2008.

46. JALP, box 33, folder 10, September 9, 2008.

47. JALP, box 33, folder 9, July 18, 2008; box 33, folder 10, August 18, 2008.

48. JALP, box 33, folder 10, August 12, 2008.

49. JALP, box 33, folder 10, September 9, 18, and 15, 2008.

50. JALP, box 33, folder 10, August 20, 2008.

51. JALP, box 33, folder 10, August 13 and 19, 2008.

52. JALP, box 33, folder 10, August 20, 2008.

53. Daniel Beard et al., "Green the Capitol Final Report," Office of the Chief Administrative Office, US House of Representatives, June 21, 2007.

54. JALP, box 33, folder 9, June 25, 2008.

55. "Pelosi: Not a Fan of Coal, but I'm a Fan of Coal Miners," *Washington Free Beacon*, January 17, 2019.

56. JALP, box 32, folder 7, May 25, 2007.

57. JALP, box 32, folder 8, June 5, 2007.

58. "Stick a Fork in It: GOP Defunds 'Green the Capitol' Initiative," ABC News, February 28, 2011; JALP, box 37, folder 2, November 29, 2010.

59. "Beard Takes Heat for Greening Capitol," *Politico*, March 5, 2009.

Chapter 8: "You Can't Have It the Way You Want to Have It"

1. Over 96 percent of Republicans voted in favor.

2. Speaker Pelosi press conference, October 17, 2019.

3. JALP, box 31, folder 8, March 1 and 14, 2006.

4. JALP, box 31, folder 10, June 13, 2006.

5. "Democrats' Letter to President Bush," CNN, January 5, 2007, https://www.cnn.com/2007/POLITICS/01/05/dems.letter/index.html.

6. JALP, box 33, folder 10, July 30, 2007.

7. Eric Scheiner, "Pelosi 'Swears' Spirit of Susan B. Anthony Spoke to Her in

White House," CNS News, August 8, 2012, https://www.cnsnews.com/news/article/pelosi-swears-spirit-susan-b-anthony-spoke-her-white-house.

8. JALP, box 32, folder 2, January 11, 2007.

9. JALP, box 32, folder 2, January 5 and 9, 2007; box 32, folder 4, February 13, 2007.

10. JALP, box 32, folder 5, March 6, 2007.

11. JALP, box 32, folder 8, June 8, 2007.

12. JALP, box 32, folder 4, February 6, March 5, 2007.

13. JALP, box 32, folder 4, March 1, 2007.

14. "House Passes Spending Bill with Iraq Deadline," CNN, March 23, 2007. Those calling for a funding cutoff included Earl Blumenauer, Danny Davis (IL), and John Tierney (MA). JALP, box 32, folder 5, March 20, 2007.

15. JALP, box 32, folder 5, March 21 and 13, 2007.

16. *The Hill* hypothesized about such punishment, although there was no evidence it was actually contemplated by the Speaker. JALP, box 32, folder 5, March 21, 2007.

17. JALP, box 32, folder 5, March 10 and 13, 2007.

18. JALP, box 32, folder 6, March 29, 2007.

19. JALP, box 32, folder 5, March 6, 2007; box 32, folder 6, April 16, March 30, 2007.

20. JALP, box 32, folder 6, April 16 and 18, 2007.

21. "Bush Vetoes Bill Tying Iraq Funds to Exit," *NYT*, May 2, 2007.

22. "Iraq: Reject the Toothless Supplemental," Center for American Progress, May 23, 2007.

23. JALP, box 32, folder 9, June 28, 2007.

24. Traveling with Pelosi were Waxman and Lantos, both prominent Jewish members, Rahall (of Lebanese background), and the House's first Muslim member, Keith Ellison (MN).

25. Hassan M. Fattah and Graham Bowley, "Pelosi Meets with Syrian Leader," *NYT*, April 4, 2007.

26. Tom Rogan, "Why Pelosi's Syria Visit Remains Indefensible," *National Review*, March 16, 2015.

27. "Pelosi: My Trip to Syria in 2007 Was Nothing Like the GOP's Iran Letter," *The Hill*, March 11, 2015.

28. JALP, box 32, folder 6, April 18, 2007.

29. JALP, box 32, folder 6, April 18, 2007.

30. JALP, box 32, folder 6, April 19, 2007.

31. White House Press Office, "President Bush Rejects Artificial Deadline, Vetoes Iraq War Supplemental," May 1, 2007, https://georgewbush-whitehouse.archives.gov/news/releases/2007/05/20070501-6.html.

32. "Senate Supports a Pullout Date in Iraq War Bill," *NYT*, March 28, 2007.

33. JALP, box 32, folder 6, May 2, 2007.

34. JALP, box 32, folder 6, May 1, 2007.

35. JALP, box 32, folder 6, May 2, 2007.

36. JALP, box 32, folder 6, May 2, 2007.

37. JALP, box 32, folder 7, May 8, 2007.

38. JALP, box 32, folder 7, May 16, 2007.

39. Congressional Research Service, "FY2007 Supplemental Appropriations for Defense, Foreign Affairs, and Other Purposes," July 2, 2007, https://fas.org/sgp/crs/natsec/RL33900.pdf.

40. JALP, box 32, folder 8, June 8, 2007; box 32, folder 7, May 22, 2007.

41. *Congressional Record*, May 23, 2007, 13734.

42. JALP, box 32, folder 10, July 31, 2007.

43. JALP, box 32, folder 10, August 1 and 14, 2007.

44. JALP, box 32, folder 10, August 23, 2007.

45. JALP, box 32, folder 9, June 27, 2007.

46. JALP, box 32, folder 10, August 16, 2007.

47. JALP, box 32, folder 10, August 23, 2007.

48. JALP, box 32, folder 10, August 21 and 23, 2007.

49. "Maliki Faults Naysayers in U.S., France," *LAT*, August 27, 2007.

50. The Senate vote was 72–25 and the House vote was 341–79; in both cases, large numbers of Democrats joined in to condemn Move On.

51. Administration participants, in addition to the president and vice president, included Defense Secretary Robert Gates, Secretary of State Condoleezza Rice, and National Security Advisor Steven Hadley.

52. JALP, box 32, folder 11, September 11, 2007.

53. JALP, box 32, folder 11, September 11, 2007.

Chapter 9: "The Prospects Don't Look Good"

1. JALP, box 33, folder 5, March 11, 2008.

2. A budget resolution does not require a presidential signature.

3. JALP, box 33, folder 4, February 13, 2008.

4. JALP, box 33, folder 4, February 25 and 13, 2008. The provision involved closing the carried interest loophole.

5. JALP, box 33, folder 5, March 10, 2008.

6. JALP, box 33, folder 5, April 7, 2008.

7. JALP, box 33, folder 5, April 1, 2008; box 33, folder 6, April 10, 2008.

8. JALP, box 33, folder 5, March 10, 2008; box 33, folder 6, April 15 and 28, 2008.

9. JALP, box 33, folder 6, April 14 and 22, 2008.

10. JALP, box 33, folder 5, March 27, 2008.

11. JALP, box 33, folder 5, March 27, 2008; box 33, folder 6, April 22, 2008.

12. JALP, box 33, folder 6, April 9, 2008.

13. JALP, box 33, folder 7, May 1, 2008.

14. JALP, box 33, folder 7, May 8, 2008.

15. JALP, box 33, folder 7, May 7, 2008.

16. JALP, box 33, folder 7, May 24, 2008.

17. JALP, box 33, folder 7, May 16, 2008.

18. "Senator Kennedy Is Hospitalized after a Seizure," *NYT*, May 17, 2008.

19. JALP, box 33, folder 7, May 24, 2008.

20. The vote was 285–132 with Democrats splitting 109–116 against the agreement. https://clerk.house.gov/evs/2007/roll1060.xml.

21. JALP, box 33, folder 8, May 24, 2008.

22. JALP, box 33, folder 8, June 5 and 4, 2008.

23. JALP, box 33, folder 8, June 4, 2008.

24. JALP, box 33, folder 9, June 13, 2008.

25. JALP, box 33, folder 9, June 17, 2008.

26. JALP, box 33, folder 9, June 25, 2008.

27. Democrats registered greater concern (51 percent) than Republicans (39 percent).

28. JALP, box 33, folder 10, September 16, 2008.

29. JALP, box 33, folder 10, September 15, 2008.

30. JALP, box 33, folder 10, September 16, 2008.

Chapter 10: Yes, We Can!

1. JALP, box 33, folder 5, March 10, 2008.

2. JALP, box 32, folder 6, April 25, 2007; box 32, folder 11, September 4, 2007.

3. Obama and Edwards trailed with 33 percent and 14 percent, respectively.

4. JALP, box 33, folder 4, February 12, 2008.

5. JALP, box 33, folder 5, March 28, 2008.

6. JALP, box 33, folder 4, February 29, 2008.

7. JALP, box 33, folder 4, March 3, 2008.

8. JALP, box 33, folder 4, March 5, 2008; box 33, folder 7, May 6, 2008.

9. JALP, box 33, folder 4, March 5, 2008. Former president Jimmy Carter endorsed Pelosi's position that superdelegates should confirm the public's primary and caucus decisions.

10. JALP, box 33, folder 4, March 5, 2008.

11. JALP, box 33, folder 4, March 5, 2008.

12. JALP, box 34, folder 7, April 20, 2009.

13. JALP, box 33, folder 7, April 20, 2009.

14. JALP, box 33, folder 7, May 2, 2008; JALP, box 33, folder 5, March 27, 2008.

15. JALP, box 33, folder 5, March 27, 2008.

16. JALP, box 33, folder 5, March 12, 2008.

17. JALP, box 33, folder 5, March 27, 2008.

18. JALP, box 33, folder 5, March 11, 2008.

19. JALP, box 33, folder 8, May 24, 2008; box 33, folder 6, April 25, 2008.

20. JALP, box 33, folder 5, April 1, 2008.

21. JALP, box 33, folder 5, March 11 and 27, 2008.

22. JALP, box 33, folder 7, May 2 and 7, 2008.

23. JALP, box 33, folder 7, May 2, 2008; box 33, folder 5, March 27, 2008.

24. JALP, box 33, folder 5, March 27, 2008; box 33, folder 6, April 15, 2008.

25. JALP, box 33, folder 5, March 27, 2008; box 33, folder 7, May 7, 2008.

26. JALP, box 33, folder 7, May 8 and 23, 2008.

27. JALP, box 33, folder 7, May 13, 2008; folder 9, June 13, 2008.

28. JALP, box 33, folder 7, May 24, 2008.

29. JALP, box 33, folder 8, June 2, 2008.

30. JALP, box 33, folder 8, June 4, 2008.

31. JALP, box 33, folder 7, May 8, 2008; box 33, folder 8, May 23, 2008.

32. JALP, box 33, folder 9, June 24, 2008.

33. JALP, box 33, folder 8, June 6, 2008.

34. JALP, box 33, folder 10, August 19, 2008. Even being considered publicly by Obama may have hurt Edwards, who was criticized in his district and lost his House seat in 2010.

35. JALP, box 33, folder 10, August 11, 2008.

36. JALP, box 33, folder 10, September 2, 2008.

37. Philip Bump, "Sarah Palin Cost John McCain 2 Million Votes in 2008, According to a Study," *WP*, January 16, 2016.

38. JALP, box 33, folder 10, August 14, 2008.

39. JALP, box 34, folder 2, October 27, 2008.

40. JALP, box 34, folder 2, October 27, 2008.

Chapter 11: The Abyss

1. JALP, box 33, folder 10, September 16 and 18, 2008.

2. Floor statement on Wall Street reform legislation, *Congressional Record*, June 30, 2010.

3. JALP, box 36, folder 6, July 1, 2010; box 36, folder 7, July 22, 2010.

4. JALP, box 33, folder 10, September 17, 2008.

5. "When Did the Financial Crisis Begin?" NPR Marketplace, August 9, 2017, https://www.marketplace.org/2017/08/09/when-did-financial-crisis-begin-many-say -august-7th-2007-france/.

6. JALP, box 33, folder 1, December 18, 2007.

7. JALP, box 33, folder 10, April 14, 2008. The quotation was from Sen. John Kyl (R-AZ).

8. JALP, box 33, folder 3, January 22, 2008; box 32, folder 14, November 18 and 20, 2007.

9. *The Financial Crisis Inquiry Report* (Washington, DC: Government Printing Office, 2011), xvii. Hereafter cited as *FICR*.

10. Henry M. Paulson, Jr., Statement on Comprehensive Approach to Market Developments (September 19, 2008). Pelosi argued for the revival of Glass-Steagall as the crisis played out, but there was little interest in restoring the law. Matt Taibbi, "Obama Defends His Finance Reform Record to *Rolling Stone*: A Response," *Rolling Stone*, November 1, 2012.

11. The firms were Bear Stearns, Goldman Sachs, Merrill Lynch, Morgan Stanley, and Lehman Brothers.

12. Phil Angelides, "Ten Years after the Fall of Bear Stearns, D.C. Is Poised to Cause Another Financial Crisis," *Los Angeles Times*, March 19, 2018.

13. Angelides, "Ten Years after the Fall."

14. JALP, box 33, folder 4, March 5, 2008.

15. JALP, box 33, folder 5, April 3, 2008.

16. JALP, box 33, folder 8, May 24, 2008; box 33, folder 9, July 22, 2008.

17. JALP, box 33, folder 10, September 15, 2008.

18. Ben Bernanke, Timothy Geithner, and Henry Paulson, *Firefighting: The Financial Crisis and Its Lessons* (New York: Penguin, 2019), 61.

19. JALP, box 33, folder 10, September 18, 2008.

20. JALP, box 34, folder 1, September 24, 2008.

21. JALP, box 34, folder 6, March 19, 2009; box 34, folder 1, September 24, 2008.

22. JALP, box 34, folder 1, September 27, 2008; box 33, folder 10, September 14, 2008.

23. JALP, box 33, folder 10, September 14, 2008.

24. JALP, box 33, folder 10, September 18, 2008.

25. JALP, box 33, folder 10, September 19, 2008.

26. JALP, box 36, folder 4, April 12, 2010.

27. JALP, box 33, folder 10, September 19, 20, 22, 2008.

28. JALP, box 34, folder 1, September 29, 2008.

29. JALP, box 34, folder 1, September 24, 2008.

30. JALP, box 34, folder 1, September 23 and 26, 2008.

31. Ed Hornick et al., "McCain, Obama Headed to Washington for Bailout Talks," CNN Politics, September 28, 2008, https://www.cnn.com/2008/POLITICS/09/24/campaign.wrap/index.html.

32. JALP, box 33, folder 10, September 21, 2008; box 34, folder 1, September 24, 2008.

33. JALP, box 34, folder 1, December 5, 2008.

34. JALP, box 34, folder 1, September 25, 2008.

35. JALP, box 34, folder 1, September 24, 2008.

36. Andrew Sorkin, "President Obama Weighs His Economic Legacy," *NYT Magazine*, April 4, 2016.

37. JALP, box 34, folder 1, September 24, 2008.

38. Sorkin, "President Obama Weighs."

39. JALP, box 34, folder 1, September 25, 2008.

40. JALP, box 34, folder 1, September 26, 2008; box 34, folder 2, November 6, 2008.

41. JALP, box 34, folder 10, September 18, 2008.

42. "Bailout Tracker," Pro Publica, February 16, 2021, https://projects.propublica .org/bailout/. Ultimately, the bill included a requirement that, should a shortfall remain after five years, the president would submit a plan to Congress to ensure that the program "does not add to the deficit or national debt."

43. JALP, box 34, folder 1, September 24 and 27, 2008; box 36, folder 1, February 2, 2010.

44. JALP, box 34, folder 1, September 24 and 26, 2008.

45. JALP, box 34, folder 1, September 27 and 29, 2008.

46. JALP, box 34, folder 1, September 29, 2008.

47. The likelihood is strong we will experience this cycle again, as the late historian Arthur Schlesinger Jr. noted, since the Wall Street financial collapse occurred on schedule thirty years after the emergence of the Carter-Reagan deregulation frenzy began. Schlesinger described a mid-1980s "orgy of speculation, and deregulation [that] promoted the casino economy, with its piratical takeovers, leveraged buy-outs, smash-and-grab finance, vulgar consumption, towering debt, and contagious criminality . . . all consequence of a national leadership that . . . systematically sabotaged the laws and agencies designed to protect the public interest." Arthur M. Schlesinger Jr., "The Turn of the Cycle," *New Yorker*, November 16, 1992. Also see his *The Cycles of American History* (Boston: Houghton Mifflin, 1986).

48. Sarah Lueck, Damian Paletta, and Greg Hitt, "Bailout Plan Rejected, Markets Plunge, Forcing New Scramble to Solve Crisis," *WSJ*, September 30, 2008.

49. JALP, box 34, folder 1, September 29, 2008.

50. JALP, box 34, folder 1, September 30, 2008.

51. JALP, box 34, folder 1, September 30, 2008.

52. JALP, box 34, folder 1, September 30, October 1, 2008.

53. JALP, box 34, folder 1, October 2 and 3, 2008.

54. JALP, box 34, folder 1, October 3 and 2, 2008.

55. JALP, box 34, folder 1, October 2, 2008.

56. JALP, box 34, folder 1, October 3, 2008; box 34, folder 2, October 30, 2008.

57. JALP, box 34, folder 1, October 10 and 13, 2008.

58. JALP, box 34, folder 2, October 20, 2008. Bolten was cool to the Bretton Woods idea. "That's kind of hard to do going out the door," he cautioned.

59. JALP, box 34, folder 1, October 10, 2008.

60. JALP, box 33, folder 10, August 20, September 16, 2008.

61. JALP, box 34, folder 2, October 20, 2008.

62. JALP, box 33, folder 10, September 16, 2008; box 34, folder 2, November 3, 2008.

63. JALP, box 34, folder 1, November 3, 2008.

64. JALP, box 34, folder 1, November 3, 2008.

65. Bernanke et al., *Firefighting*, 21, 25, 27, 29.

66. David Leonhardt, "We're Measuring the Economy All Wrong," *NYT*, September 14, 2018.

67. Jonnelle Marte, "'We Haven't Made Any Progress': Black Homeownership Is Stuck near 30-Year Lows," *WP*, July 6, 2018.

68. *Frontline* interview with Steve Inskeep for National Public Radio, April 19, 2019, https://www.npr.org/2019/04/19/715053806/bernanke-geithner-and-paulson-on-lessons-learned-from-2008-financial-crisis.

69. Barack Obama, *A Promised Land* (New York: Crown, 2020), 522.

70. Ben Protess, Robert Gebeloff, and Danielle Ivory, "Trump Administration Spares Corporate Wrongdoers Billions in Penalties," *NYT*, November 4, 2018.

Chapter 12: "We Have to Look Out for Ourselves"

1. JALP, box 34, folder 2, November 3, 2008.

2. JALP, box 36, folder 3, April 4, 2010.

3. JALP, box 34, folder 2, November 7, 2008.

4. JALP, box 34, folder 2, November 14, 2008.

5. JALP, box 34, folder 2, November 6, 2008.

6. JALP, box 35, folder 3, July 17, 2009. The Speaker's warning closely paralleled my own when Emanuel had called me late in 2008 to discuss the offer.

7. JALP, box 34, folder 2, October 31, 2008.

8. JALP, box 34, folder 2, November 7, 2008.

9. JALP, box 34, folder 2, November 5, 2008.

10. JALP, box 34, folder 2, November 5, 2008.

11. JALP, box 34, folder 2, November 5, 2008.

12. Paul Kane, "Pelosi and Dingell Rivalry Reflects the Evolution of the Democratic Party," *WP*, February 9, 2019.

13. JALP, box 34, folder 2, November 5, 2008.

14. Both parties had adopted rules decades earlier noting seniority was just one of several bases for determining chairmanships. Republicans ended reliance on the seniority system when they gained the majority in 1994, relying instead on Speaker appointments as had been the case before the 1910 revolt against Joe Cannon. They also imposed term limits on their chairs. Critics faulted giving the Speaker such unilateral power, complaining it required loyalty to the Speaker and elevated the importance of fundraising in securing the gavel rather than the expertise that came with years of service.

15. JALP, box 33, folder 5, April 2, 2008.

16. JALP, box 34, folder 2, November 5, 2008.

17. JALP, box 34, folder 2, November 7, 2008.

18. JALP, box 34, folder 2, November 12, 2008. Privately, she noted that her respect for Waxman was "unsurpassed."

19. JALP, box 34, folder 3, November 19, 2009.

20. "Waxman Defeats Dingell for Coveted Chairmanship," *National Public Radio*, November 20, 2008.

21. Lawrence, *Class of '74*, 93.

22. "Waxman Dethrones Dingell as Chairman," *Politico*, November 20, 2008.

23. JALP, box 34, folder 3, November 20, 2008.

24. JALP, box 34, folder 3, December 4, 2008.

25. JALP, box 34, folder 3, November 20, 2008.

26. JALP, box 34, folder 4, December 11, 2008.

27. JALP, box 34, folder 3, December 10 and 2, 2008.

28. JALP, box 34, folder 2, November 2 and 6, 2008.

29. Seymour Hersh, "Torture at Abu Ghraib," *New Yorker*, April 30, 2004; JALP, box 34, folder 2, November 14, 2008. Months later, when Obama honorifically referred to the outgoing Hayden (and McConnell) as "honored citizens," Pelosi reproached him. JALP, box 34, folder 8, April 22, 2009.

30. JALP, box 34, folder 5, January 29, 2009.

31. JALP, box 34, folder 3, November 25, 2008.

32. JALP, box 34, folder 3, November 20, 2008; box 34, folder 2, November 3, 2008.

Chapter 13: "The Country Is Falling Apart!"

1. JALP, box 34, folder 2, November 10 and 6, 2008.

2. JALP, box 34, folder 2, November 10, 2008.

3. JALP, box 34, folder 2, November 10, 2008.

4. JALP, box 34, folder 2, November 6–7, 2008.

5. JALP, box 34, folder 2, November 13, 2008.

6. JALP, box 34, folder 2, November 13, 2008.

7. JALP, box 34, folder 2, November 14, 2008.

8. In 1993, House members supported President Clinton's proposed BTU tax on energy only to watch the Senate fail to consider the provision, leaving House members to explain their vote. The aggravating experience gave birth to the new political phrase of "getting BTU'd."

9. JALP, box 34, folder 2, November 20 and 14, 2008.

10. JALP, box 34, folder 2, November 16, 2008; box 34, folder 3, November 17, 2008.

11. JALP, box 34, folder 3, November 20, 2008.

12. JALP, box 34, folder 2, November 16, 2008; box 34, folder 3, November 18–19, 2008.

13. JALP, box 34, folder 3, November 20, 2008.

14. JALP, box 34, folder 3, November 20, 2008.

15. JALP, box 34, folder 2, November 14, 2008.

16. JALP, box 34, folder 3, December 1, 2008.

17. JALP, box 34, folder 3, December 1 and 2, 2008.

18. JALP, box 34, folder 3, December 4 and 2, 2008.

19. JALP, box 34, folder 3, December 2, 2008.

20. JALP, box 34, folder 3, December 4, 2008.

21. JALP, box 34, folder 3, December 5, 2008.

22. JALP, box 34, folder 3, December 5, 2008.

23. JALP, box 34, folder 3, December 8, 2008.

24. JALP, box 34, folder 3, December 6, 2008; box 34, folder 4, December 19, 2008.

25. David M. Herszenhorn and David E. Sanger, "Senate Abandons Automaker Bailout Bid," *NYT*, December 11, 2008.

26. "Tennessee Leads Nation in Auto Manufacturing," *Murfreesboro Post*, July 29, 2013.

27. JALP, box 34, folder 4, December 11, 2008.

28. JALP, box 34, folder 3, December 10, 2008; box 34, folder 4, December 12, 2008.

29. Herszenhorn, "Senate Abandons."

30. JALP, box 34, folder 4, December 19, 2008.

31. Mike Allen and David Rogers, "Bush Announces $17.4 Billion Auto Bailout," *Politico*, December 19, 2008; Andrew Glass, "Bush Bails Out U.S. Automakers," *Politico*, December 19, 2018.

32. Steve Contorno, "Obama Says Automakers Have Paid Back All the Loans It Got from His Admin 'and More,'" PolitiFact, January 22, 2015, https://www.politifact .com/factchecks/2015/jan/22/barack-obama/obama-says-automakers-have-paid -back-all-loans-it-/. Chrysler and GM both filed for bankruptcy in the spring, soon emerging with new owners and partial government ownership that was sold off over the next several years.

33. JALP, box 34, folder 4, December 12, 2008.

34. Contorno, "Obama Says."

35. Contorno, "Obama Says."

36. JALP, box 34, folder 4, December 12, 2008.

Chapter 14: "Like Swans Going across the Lake"

1. JALP, box 34, folder 4, December 24, 2008, January 14, 2009.

2. Robert Pear, "Senate Approves Children's Health Bill," *NYT*, January 29, 2009.

3. Among the problem provisions was a 2,500 percent increase in the tax on small cigars and inflated reimbursement rates for specialty hospitals.

4. Pear, "Senate Approves."

5. JALP, box 34, folder 5, January 31, 2009.

6. JALP, box 34, folder 3, December 5, 2008.

7. JALP, box 34, folder 3, December 1 and 8, 2008.

8. JALP, box 34, folder 4, January 5, 2009. Pelosi was not alone in this evaluation. FDIC chair Sheila Bair accused Geithner of managing the financial rescue to benefit large banks without imposing tough accountability requirements. "He viewed these institutions as entities that needed to be taken care of," Bair said. See her account in *Bull by*

the Horns: Fighting to Save Main Street from Wall Street and Wall Street from Itself (New York: Free Press, 2012).

9. JALP, box 34, folder 3, December 8, 2008.

10. JALP, box 34, folder 5, February 13, 2009.

11. JALP, box 34, folder 4, December 17, 2008.

12. JALP, box 34, folder 4, January 6 and 8, 2009.

13. JALP, box 34, folder 3, December 10, 2008.

14. JALP, box 34, folder 4, December 18 and 19, 2008.

15. JALP, box 34, folder 4, December 19, 2008; *Roll Call*, February 1, 2011.

16. The three senators were likely Susan Collins and Olympia Snowe of Maine, and Arlen Specter of Pennsylvania.

17. JALP, box 34, folder 4, January 5, 2009.

18. See examples of Obama's optimistic and unrequited hope for bipartisanship in his personal history of his presidency. Obama, *A Promised Land*, 255.

19. GovTrack, recorded vote on S. J. Res. 5 (111th), January 15, 2009, https://www.govtrack.us/congress/votes/111-2009/s5.

20. Of 260 Democrats, 242 voted to release the money.

21. David Rogers, "Obama Gets First Major Win with TARP," *Politico*, January 15, 2009.

22. JALP, box 34, folder 4, January 8, 2009.

23. JALP, box 34, folder 4, January 5, 2009.

24. JALP, box 34, folder 4, January 5, 2009.

25. JALP, box 34, folder 4, January 5, 2009.

26. JALP, box 34, folder 4, January 6, 2009.

27. JALP, box 34, folder 4, January 8 and 9, 2009.

28. Even achieving the sixty-vote supermajority still awaited the outcome of Franken's Senate race in Minnesota.

29. JALP, box 34, folder 5, January 21, 2009.

30. JALP, box 34, folder 5, January 23, 2009.

31. "Obama Sternly Takes on His Critics," *NYT*, February 9, 2009.

32. JALP, box 34, folder 5, January 23, 2009.

33. JALP, box 34, folder 7, April 23, 2009.

34. JALP, box 34, folder 5, January 23, 2009.

35. JALP, box 34, folder 5, February 9, 2009.

36. JALP, box 34, folder 5, February 9, 2009.

37. JALP, box 34, folder 5, January 27, 2009.

38. JALP, box 34, folder 5, January 27, February 11, 2009.

39. JALP, box 34, folder 5, January 25 and 27, 2009.

40. JALP, box 34, folder 5, February 2, 2009.

41. JALP, box 34, folder 5, February 9 and 2, 2009.

42. JALP, box 34, folder 5, February 6, 2008.

43. JALP, box 34, folder 5, February 3, 2008.

44. JALP, box 34, folder 5, February 5, 2009.

45. JALP, box 34, folder 5, February 5 and 7, 2009.

46. Ewen MacAskill, "US Senate Passes $838bn Economic Stimulus Plan," *Guardian*, February 10, 2009.

47. MacAskill, "US Senate Passes."

48. JALP, box 34, folder 5, February 9, 2009.

49. JALP, box 34, folder 5, February 3 and 9, 2009.

50. JALP, box 34, folder 5, February 9, 2009.

51. JALP, box 34, folder 5, February 11, 2009.

52. JALP, box 34, folder 5, February 11, 2009.

53. JALP, box 34, folder 5, February 11, 2009.

54. David Rogers, "Senate Passes $787 Billion Stimulus Bill," *Politico*, February 13, 2009.

55. JALP, box 34, folder 5, February 11, 2009.

56. Rogers, "Senate Passes."

57. JALP, box 34, folder 5, February 10, 2009.

58. Kennedy, in worsening health because of brain cancer, missed the vote. His wife called the three Republicans to ensure they would still support the legislation despite his absence, which dropped Democratic support to 58. The Minnesota seat was still vacant while the outcome of the disputed election was being evaluated.

59. JALP, box 34, folder 5, February 19, 2009.

60. JALP, box 34, folder 5, February 11 and 6, 2009.

61. JALP, box 34, folder 4, January 5, 2009.

62. Carolyn Lochhead, "Lack of Support in D.C. Hampers Water Recycling Efforts," *San Francisco Chronicle*, September 7, 2015.

63. "Stimulus Plan Places New Limits on Wall St. Bonuses," *NYT*, February 13, 2009.

64. Sahil Kapur, "The Middle Class Might Not Even Notice If the GOP Cuts Their Taxes," Bloomberg News, December 11, 2017. Summers had worried money sent in a check to taxpayers would be invested or saved rather than spent.

65. JALP, Memo to the Speaker, October 23, 2009.

66. Lawrence Summers, "The Biden Stimulus Is Admirably Ambitious. But It Brings Some Big Risks, Too," *WP*, February 4, 2021.

67. "GOP Blames White House Staff for Lack of COVID-19 Relief Deal," *The Hill*, February 6, 2021.

68. JALP, box 35, folder 4, October 12, 2009; box 34, folder 7, April 23, 2009.

69. JALP, box 34, folder 6, February 25, 2009.

70. Andrew Sorkin, "President Obama Weighs His Economic Legacy," *NYT Magazine*, April 28, 2016.

71. JALP, box 36, folder 1, February 3, 2010.

72. Michael Grunwald, "The Selling of Obama," *Politico*, May/June 2014.

73. JALP, box 37, folder 1, October 22, 2010.

Chapter 15: The Firehose

1. JALP, box 34, folder 6, February 23, 2009.

2. JALP, box 34, folder 6, February 25, 2009.

3. JALP, box 34, folder 6, February 25, 2009.

4. An omnibus combines all the expiring appropriations bills and extends them in one large bill to the end of the fiscal year.

5. JALP, box 34, folder 5, January 31, 2009.

6. JALP, box 34, folder 5, January 31, 2009.

7. JALP, box 34, folder 5, January 31, 2009.

8. Signing Statement for HR 1105, the Omnibus Appropriations Act, 2009 (P.L. 111-8). Obama specifically cited as objectionable a restriction on United Nations peace-keeping missions and a prohibition on paying the salary of any federal employee who obstructed communications between federal employees and members of Congress. A few weeks later, he issued another such restriction on a major parks bill. "Obama Issues Signing Statement with Public Lands Bill," *NYT*, March 30, 2009.

9. JALP, box 32, folder 7, May 16, 2007.

10. Jacqueline Thomsen, "GOP Lawmaker Once Held a Knife to Boehner's Throat," *The Hill*, October 29, 2017; John Boehner, *On the House: A Washington Memoir* (New York: St. Martin's, 2021), 25–26. Remarkably, Boehner later served as best man at Young's wedding.

11. JALP, box 33, folder 5, March 10, 2009.

12. "Pelosi, Hoyer, Obey Announce Earmark Reforms," *Politico*, March 11, 2009.

13. JALP, box 33, folder 5, March 14, 2008; box 34, folder 6, February 25, 2009.

14. JALP, box 34, folder 6, March 3, February 25, 2009.

15. JALP, box 34, folder 6, March 10, 2009.

16. JALP, box 32, folder 7, May 16, 2007; box 34, folder 7, April 2, 2009.

17. JALP, box 35, folder 4, September 23, 2009.

18. JALP, box 34, folder 6, March 11, 2009.

19. JALP, box 34, folder 6, February 25, 2009; box 35, folder 4, September 24, 2009.

20. JALP, box 35, folder 5, November 17, 2009.

21. JALP, box 36, folder 4, April 15, 2010.

22. JALP, box 34, folder 6, February 25, 2009.

23. JALP, box 34, folder 6, March 6, 2009.

24. JALP, box 34, folder 7, April 22, 2009.

25. JALP, box 34, folder 7, April 22, 2009; box 34, folder 8, May 13, 2009; box 35, folder 1, June 3, 2009.

26. JALP, box 34, folder 6, March 11, 2009.

27. JALP, box 34, folder 6, March 11, 2009.

28. JALP, box 34, folder 6, March 11, 2009.

29. JALP, box 34, folder 6, March 10, 2009.

30. JALP, box 35, folder 4, October 6, 2009; box 34, folder 7, April 26, 2009.

31. JALP, box 35, folder 4, October 6, 2009.

32. JALP, box 35, folder 2, July 14, 2009.

33. JALP, box 35, folder 5, November 10, October 21, 2009.

34. JALP, box 35, folder 4, October 6, 2009.

35. JALP, box 34, folder 5, February 10, 2009.

36. JALP, box 34, folder 7, April 23, 2009.

37. JALP, box 34, folder 8, April 29, 2009.

38. JALP, box 35, folder 3, September 8, 2009.

39. Steve Benen, "Getting BTU'd," *Washington Monthly*, May 5, 2011.

40. JALP, box 34, folder 8, May 6 and 19, 2009. In 2012, after Congress failed to act, Obama created the Deferred Action for Childhood Arrivals policy through an executive order. President Donald Trump attempted to end DACA in 2017, but his order was rejected by the Supreme Court in 2020, and the program remains in legal and legislative limbo as of this writing.

Chapter 16: Short-Circuited

1. Katherine Schaeffer, "Single-Party Control in Washington Is Common at the Beginning of a New Presidency, but Tends Not to Last Long," Pew Research Center, February 3, 2021, https://www.pewresearch.org/fact-tank/2021/02/03/single-party-control-in-washington-is-common-at-the-beginning-of-a-new-presidency-but-tends-not-to-last-long.

2. JALP, box 32, folder 7, June 1, 2007; box 35, folder 5, February 4, 2009.

3. JALP, box 32, folder 7, June 1, 2007.

4. Lisa Lerer, "Dems to W.H.: Drop Cap and Trade," *Politico*, December 27, 2009.

5. JALP, box 35, folder 5, February 6, 2009.

6. JALP, box 34, folder 7, March 25, 2009.

7. JALP, box 34, folder 8, April 30, May 4, 2009.

8. JALP, box 34, folder 8, May 26, 2009.

9. JALP, box 34, folder 7, March 31, 2009.

10. JALP, box 35, folder 1, June 3, 2009.

11. JALP, box 34, folder 7, April 22, 2009.

12. Ryan Lizza, "As the World Burns," *New Yorker*, October 11, 2010. This article provides an inside account of the unsuccessful effort to move a climate bill in the Senate. McCain would quickly lose interest in the legislation.

13. JALP, box 34, folder 6, February 25, 2009.

14. JALP, box 34, folder 7, April 22, 2009.

15. JALP, box 34, folder 6, March 12, 2009.

16. JALP, box 34, folder 8, April 28, 2009.

17. JALP, box 34, folder 8, April 30, 2009.

18. Markey reported encouraging conversations with Gene Green (TX), Mike Doyle (PA), and Boucher (VA).

19. JALP, box 34, folder 8, May 4, 2009.

20. JALP, box 34, folder 8, May 6, 2009.

21. JALP, box 34, folder 8, May 6, 2009. Additional incentives included aid to small refiners and a more agriculturally favorable definition of "biomass."

22. JALP, box 34, folder 8, May 4, 2009.

23. JALP, box 34, folder 8, May 12, 2009.

24. JALP, box 34, folder 8, May 20, 2009.

25. George Radonovich (CA) voted against Barton's amendment, while John Shadegg (AZ) and Greg Walden (OR) voted "present."

26. The bill mandated reductions in greenhouse gas emissions of 17 percent below 2005 levels by 2020, rising to 80 percent by 2050 through a combination of increased use of renewables and improved efficiency.

27. "In Landmark Vote, House Committee Approves Climate Bill," *Grist*, May 22, 2009.

28. JALP, box 34, folder 8, May 19, 2009; box 35, folder 1, June 9, 2009. Participants included Earl Pomeroy, Lloyd Doggett, and John Tanner.

29. JALP, box 35, folder 1, June 11, 2009.

30. JALP, box 35, folder 1, June 5 and 9, 2009.

31. JALP, box 35, folder 1, June 9, 2009. The Republicans included Mary Bono, Vern Ehlers (MI), Mike Castle (DE), Tom Petri (WI), Frank LoBiondo (NJ), Todd Platts (IN), and Peter King (NY).

32. JALP, box 35, folder 1, June 22, 2009.

33. JALP, box 35, folder 1, June 23, 2009.

34. JALP, box 35, folder 1, June 22, 2009.

35. JALP, box 35, folder 1, June 22 and 23, 2009. Peterson remained in the House until 2020 and regained his chairmanship in 2019 when Democrats took back control of the House. In December 2019, he was one of just two Democrats to oppose impeaching President Donald Trump, and the other one, Jeff Van Drew (NJ), quickly switched parties.

36. JALP, box 35, folder 1, June 23 and 25, 2009.

37. Moderate opposition came from moderates like Mike Michaud (ME), Tim Holden (PA), and Ron Kind (WI), while liberal concerns were raised by Dennis Kucinich (OH), Rush Holt (NJ), Bob Filner (CA), Lloyd Doggett (TX), and Jim McDermott (WA).

38. JALP, box 35, folder 1, June 22, 2009.

39. JALP, box 35, folder 1, June 17, 2009.

40. JALP, box 35, folder 1, June 25, 2009.

41. Karen Tumulty, "Nancy Pelosi," *Time*, December 16, 2009.

42. JALP, box 35, folder 2, June 30, 2009.

43. John Broder, "House Passes Bill to Address Threat of Climate Change," *NYT*, June 29, 2009.

44. Carl Hulse, "Climate Change Bill May Be Election Issue," *NYT*, June 27, 2009.

45. JALP, box 35, folder 3, July 28, 2009.

46. JALP, box 35, folder 2, June 30, 2009.

47. JALP, box 35, folder 3, June 30, 2009.

48. JALP, box 35, folder 5, November 11, 2009.

49. Lizza, "As the World Burns."

50. JALP, box 35, folder 2, July 1, 2009; box 35, folder 5, October 26, 2009.

51. JALP, box 35, folder 4, September 22, 2009; box 35, folder 8, December 15, 2009.

52. JALP, box 35, folder 8, December 16, 2009.

53. Obama, *Promised Land*, 516.

54. Katie Fehrenbacher, "Why the Solyndra Mistake Is Still Important to Remember," *Fortune*, August 27, 2015.

55. Manchin, who in 2021–22 would undermine many of President Biden's legislative initiatives, ran in 2010 promising to "take on Washington, and this [Obama] administration, to get the federal government off our backs," pledging also to vote to repeal portions of the Affordable Care Act. "Dead Aim," October 9, 2010, https://www.youtube.com /watch?v=xIJORBRpOPM.

Chapter 17: "Number One among Equals"

1. JALP, box 35, folder 1, June 30, 2009.

2. JALP, box 34, folder 8, May 4, 2009; box 34, folder 7, April 22, 2009.

3. "The 2009 Presidential Candidates' Health Reform Proposals: Choices for America," Commonwealth Fund, October 1, 2008.

4. "Kaiser Family Foundation Health Care Costs and Election 2008," October 14, 2008, https://www.kff.org/health-costs/issue-brief/health-care-costs-and-election-2008/.

5. JALP, box 34, folder 6, February 23, 2009.

6. Daschle would soon withdraw from consideration to be HHS secretary due to a tax problem, costing Reid a skilled ally who could have been persuasive with some senators.

7. JALP, box 34, folder 8, May 5, 2009.

8. JALP, box 34, folder 4, December 12, 2008.

9. JALP, box 34, folder 4, January 5, 2009.

10. JALP, box 34, folder 8, April 30, 2009.

11. JALP, box 34, folder 7, April 22–23, 2009.

12. JALP, box 34, folder 7, April 23, 2009.

13. JALP, box 34, folder 7, April 23, 2009.

14. Ryan Grim, "Pelosi: Single-Payer Amendment Breaks Obama's Health Care Promise," Common Dreams, November 5, 2009, https://www.commondreams.org /news/2009/11/05/pelosi-single-payer-amendment-breaks-obamas-health-care-prom ise. Kucinich did win an amendment in Education and Labor that granted states the option of creating a single-payer system.

15. JALP, box 34, folder 8, May 4, 2009.

16. JALP, box 34, folder 8, May 4, 2009; box 35, folder 1, June 4 and 16, 2009.

17. JALP, box 35, folder 1, June 16, 2009; box 34, folder 8, May 19, 2009.

18. The groups included Common Purpose (a coalition of progressive organizations), Unity 09 (composed of Move On, the Sierra Club, and the Center for American Progress), and Americans United and Healthy Communications (which included PhRMA, the American Association of Retired Persons, Families USA, and the American Cancer Society).

19. JALP, box 35, folder 1, June 8 and 4, 2009.

20. JALP, box 35, folder 1, June 4, 2009.

21. JALP, box 35, folder 1, June 16, 2, and 23, 2009.

22. JALP, box 35, folder 1, June 18, 2009.

23. JALP, box 35, folder 1, June 8, 2009.

24. JALP, box 35, folder 2, July 17, 2009.

25. Ryan Grim, "White House Confirms: Deal with Big Pharma Bars Price Negotiation," *HuffPost*, September 7, 2009.

26. JALP, box 35, folder 2, June 30, 2009.

27. JALP, box 35, folder 2, July 2, 2009.

28. JALP, box 35, folder 2, July 2, 2009.

29. JALP, box 35, folder 2, July 9 and 8, 2009.

30. JALP, box 35, folder 2, July 10, 2009.

31. JALP, box 35, folder 2, July 10, 2009.

32. Similar reticence was voiced by the business-oriented New Democrats like Joe Crowley (NY).

33. JALP, box 35, folder 2, July 10 and 12, 2009. The no votes reportedly were Ross, Barrow, Hill, Matheson, Melançon, Gordon, Stupak, and Space.

34. JALP, box 35, folder 2, July 9, 2009.

35. Terry Lierman, Hoyer's chief of staff, confirmed the majority leader pleaded with Blue Dogs to support the bill, but several refused, citing their reelection concerns; many of those who voted no were defeated anyway.

36. JALP, box 35, folder 2, July 13, 2009. The congressional participants included Reid, Baucus, Pelosi, Hoyer, and Rangel.

37. JALP, box 35, folder 2, July 13 and 14, 2009.

38. JALP, box 35, folder 3, July 28, 2009.

39. JALP, box 35, folder 2, July 22, 2009.

40. JALP, box 35, folder 2, July 13 and 14, 2009.

41. Matt Bai, "Taking the Hill," *NYT*, June 2, 2009.

42. JALP, box 35, folder 2, July 16, 2009.

43. The three were Dina Titus (NV), Jared Polis (CO), and Jason Altmire (PA).

44. JALP, box 35, folder 2, July 17, 2009.

45. JALP, box 35, folder 2, July 16, 2009.

46. JALP, box 35, folder 2, July 17, 2009.

47. JALP, box 35, folder 2, July 17, 2009.

48. JALP, box 35, folder 2, July 27 and 23, 2009.

49. JALP, box 35, folder 2, July 27, 2009.

50. JALP, box 35, folder 2, June 30, 2009.

51. JALP, box 35, folder 2, June 30, 2009.

52. JALP, box 35, folder 2, June 30, 2009.

53. JALP, box 35, folder 3, July 28, 2009.

54. For the full list of Blue Dog demands, see *Politico Pulse*, July 28, 2009.

55. JALP, box 35, folder 3, July 28, 2009.

56. JALP, box 35, folder 3, July 29, 2009.

57. Ross, Herseth-Sandlin, and Tanner agreed to support the bill in the Commerce Committee but made no promise about their floor vote.

58. She asked Ted Kennedy's physician and respected health advisor, Larry Horowitz, to lobby Anna Eshoo and arranged an Obama call to Bobby Rush, the Chicago CBC member who had thrashed Obama in a House primary nine years earlier.

59. JALP, box 35, folder 3, July 28, 2009.

60. *Politico Pulse*, July 28, 2009.

61. JALP, box 35, folder 3, July 29, 2009.

62. JALP, box 35, folder 3, July 30, 2009.

Chapter 18: The Summer of Hate

1. JALP, box 35, folder 3, August 4, 2009.

2. JALP, box 35, folder 3, August 4 and 10, 2009.

3. JALP, box 35, folder 3, August 12, 2009.

4. Ben McGrath, "The Movement: The Rise of Tea Party Activism," *New Yorker*, February 1, 2010.

5. "The Obama Presidency in Peril?" *Diverse*, September 15, 2009.

6. "Dick Armey's Claim about Medicare and Social Security Is Only Partially True," PolitiFact, August 24, 2009.

7. JALP, box 35, folder 3, August 12, 2009.

8. JALP, box 35, folder 3, August 5, 2009.

9. JALP, box 35, folder 3, August 5, 2009.

10. JALP, box 35, folder 3, August 5, 2009.

11. JALP, box 35, folder 3, August 5, 2009.

12. JALP, box 35, folder 3, August 10 and 11, 2009.

13. Cary Budoff Brown, "W.H. Backs Away from Public Option," *Politico*, August 16, 2009.

14. JALP, box 35, folder 3, August 7 and 18, 2009.

15. JALP, box 35, folder 3, August 18, 2009.

16. JALP, box 35, folder 3, August 12, 2009.

17. JALP, box 35, folder 3, August 12, 2009.

18. JALP, box 35, folder 3, August 18, 2009.

19. JALP, box 35, folder 3, August 18, 2009.

20. JALP, box 35, folder 3, August 20, 2009.

21. JALP, box 35, folder 3, August 18, 2009.

22. JALP, box 35, folder 3, August 18, 2009.

23. JALP, box 35, folder 3, August 18, 2009.

24. JALP, box 35, folder 3, August 24, 2009.

25. JALP, box 35, folder 3, August 24, 2009; box 35, folder 7, January 4, 2010.

26. JALP, box 35, folder 3, August 24, 2009.

27. JALP, box 35, folder 7, January 4, 2010.

28. JALP, box 35, folder 3, August 10, 2009.

Chapter 19: "The Most Important Bill You Will Ever Vote For"

1. Ben McGrath, "The Movement: The Rise of Tea Party Activism," *New Yorker*, February 1, 2010.

2. Ironically, Kirk had defeated Pelosi for DNC chair in 1985, two years before her election to the House.

3. JALP, box 35, folder 3, August 27, 2009.

4. JALP, box 35, folder 3, September 4, 2009; box 35, folder 4, October 12, 2009.

5. JALP, box 35, folder 3, August 31, 2009; box 35, folder 3, September 4, 2009.

6. JALP, box 35, folder 4, October 16, 2009.

7. JALP, box 35, folder 3, September 8, 2009.

8. JALP, box 35, folder 3, August 18, 2009.

9. JALP, box 35, folder 3, August 3 and 31, 2009.

10. Brian Montropoli, "Emanuel 'Begged' Obama Not to Push Health Care," CBS News, May 10, 2010, https://www.cbsnews.com/news/rahm-emanuel-begged-obama-not-to-push-health-care/.

11. There is a slightly different version of this exchange in Obama's account.

12. Greg Sargent, "Book: Rahm 'Begged' Obama for Days Not to Pursue Ambitious Health Reform," *WP*, May 14, 2010.

13. Wendell Primus, the Speaker's chief health policy expert, may well have primed the Speaker to make this comment at the meeting. A year and a half later, he told a *Washington Post* reporter, "Rahm hates getting called on the carpet and that's what I did. The Speaker was right and Rahm was clearly wrong" in pressing for a reduced bill. "The Speaker's Liberal Brawler," *WP*, June 21, 2010.

14. JALP, box 35, folder 3, September 2, 2009.

15. JALP, box 35, folder 3, September 2, 2009.

16. JALP, box 35, folder 3, September 2, 2009.

17. JALP, box 35, folder 3, September 2, 2009.

18. "Obama's 'You Can Keep It' Promise Is 'Lie of the Year,'" *Tampa Bay Times* / PolitiFact, December 13, 2013. Obama subsequently apologized for the misrepresentation.

19. JALP, box 35, folder 4, September 10, 2009.

20. JALP, box 35, folder 4, September 14, 2009. Cantwell focused on regional disparities and Menendez on immigrant coverage. Ron Wyden (OR) declared he would prepare his own bill, and Jay Rockefeller (WV) reportedly opposed the bill altogether.

21. JALP, box 35, folder 4, September 22, 2009.

22. JALP, box 35, folder 4, September 17, 2009.

23. JALP, box 35, folder 4, September 21, 2009.

24. The breakdowns, which were sent to every House Democrat in March 2010, detailed how many constituents would be entitled to coverage, tax credit, and premium subsidies; how many people with preexisting conditions would become eligible for health insurance; and how many tens—or hundreds—of millions of dollars their local health care providers would save in uncompensated health care costs under the new law.

25. JALP, box 35, folder 4, September 24, 2009.

26. JALP, box 35, folder 4, September 24, 2009.

27. JALP, box 35, folder 4, September 22, 2009.

28. JALP, box 35, folder 5, November 5, 2009; box 35, folder 4, September 28, 2009.

29. JALP, box 35, folder 4, October 14, 2009.

30. JALP, box 35, folder 4, September 29 and 30, 2009.

31. JALP, box 35, folder 4, October 12, 2009.

32. "Senate Finance Committee Approves Sen. Baucus' Health Care Bill," ABC News, October 13, 2009.

33. JALP, box 35, folder 4, October 15, 2009.

34. JALP, box 35, folder 4, October 16, 2009.

35. JALP, box 35, folder 4, October 23, 2009.

36. JALP, box 35, folder 4, November 2 and 5, 2009. The Speaker could have approved a modified closed rule, allowing only certain amendments to be offered, but doing so would invariably anger those whose amendments were disallowed. It was far easier to simply ban all efforts to alter the three-committee bill.

37. JALP, box 35, folder 5, October 23, October 30, November 6, 2009.

38. JALP, box 35, folder 6, December 4, 2009. Fifty other House members sought similar reclassifications for their hospitals. Many other members' requests were included in a memo sent to the Speaker on December 30, 2009.

39. JALP, box 35, folder 4, October 16 and 1, 2009.

40. JALP, box 35, folder 5, October 23, 2009.

41. JALP, box 35, folder 5, October 27, 2009.

42. JALP, box 35, folder 5, October 26, 2009.

43. JALP, box 35, folder 5, October 29 and 27, 2009.

44. JALP, box 35, folder 5, October 30, 2009.

45. McCarrick would later be stripped of his clerical collar by the pope for tolerating child abuse in the church.

46. JALP, box 35, folder 5, October 29, 2009.

47. JALP, box 35, folder 6, November 17, 2009. Plans offered on a government exchange could not cover elective abortion to anyone receiving federal subsidies on their premiums. Women wanting abortion coverage would be required to buy separate abortion coverage using their own money.

48. JALP, box 35, folder 3, September 8, 2009; box 35, folder 5, November 5, 2009.

49. JALP, box 35, folder 3, July 31, 2009.

50. JALP, box 35, folder 5, November 3, 2009.

51. Jonathan Cohn, "What Democrats Can Learn from Obamacare, According to Barack Obama," *HuffPost*, February 21, 2021.

52. JALP, box 35, folder 5, November 5 and 6, 2009.

53. "Final Vote Results for Roll Call 887," http://clerk.house.gov/evs/2009/roll887 .xml.

54. JALP, box 35, folder 5, November 10 and 17, 2009.

55. JALP, box 35, folder 6, November 10, 2009.

56. JALP, box 35, folder 6, November 24, 2009.

Chapter 20: "Let's Go for It!"

1. Eric Randall, "Martha Coakley Can Check 'Shaking Hands at Fenway' Off Her List," *Boston Magazine*, September 19, 2013.

2. JALP, box 35, folder 3, August 18, 2009; box 35, folder 6, December 1, 2009.

3. The liberal Center on Budget and Policy Priorities estimated the Cadillac tax would save $200 billion over ten years.

4. JALP, box 35, folder 7, December 21, 2009; box 35, folder 6, December 15 and 9, 2009.

5. JALP, box 35, folder 7, January 8, 2010.

6. JALP, box 36, folder 1, January 26, 2010.

7. JALP, box 36, folder 1, January 26, 2010.

8. JALP, box 35, folder 7, December 23, 2009.

9. JALP, box 35, folder 7, January 8, 2010.

10. JALP, box 35, folder 7, December 27, 2009. A significant number of complex issues involving the affordability of policies; handling of Medicare, Medicare, and the CHIP program; the Medicare Donut Hole; the bill's effective dates; and eligibility standards separated the two approaches. A useful comparison was produced by the Center

on Budget and Policy Priorities on December 23, 2009, and forwarded to key House and Senate players.

11. JALP, box 35, folder 7, December 27, 2009, January 5, 2010.

12. JALP, box 35, folder 6, December 9, 2009. In addition to the absence of a public option, other objections to the Senate bill included its one-year delay on implementation to 2014 (to save costs), five million fewer people covered, and the failure to close the Part D "donut hole."

13. JALP, box 35, folder 7, January 4, 2010; box 35, folder 7, December 22, 2009.

14. The observation was by Paul Landow, a political scientist at the University of Nebraska. Steve Jordon, "What Was the 'Cornhusker Kickback,' the Deal That Led to Nelson's Crucial ACA Vote?" *Omaha World-Herald*, July 20, 2017.

15. JALP, box 35, folder 7, January 5, 2010.

16. JALP, box 35, folder 7, January 5 and 8, 2010.

17. JALP, box 35, folder 7, January 5, 2010.

18. JALP, box 35, folder 7, January 5 and 12, 2010.

19. JALP, box 35, folder 7, January 5, 2010.

20. JALP, box 35, folder 7, January 7, 2010.

21. JALP, box 35, folder 7, January 7, 2010.

22. JALP, box 35, folder 7, January 13, 2010.

23. JALP, box 35, folder 7, January 13, 2010.

24. JALP, box 36, folder 1, January 26, 2010.

25. JALP, box 35, folder 7, January 19, 2010.

26. JALP, box 35, folder 7, January 20, 2010.

27. JALP, box 35, folder 7, January 20, 2010.

28. JALP, box 36, folder 1, January 25, 2010.

29. JALP, box 36, folder 1, January 21 and 25, February 5, 2010.

30. JALP, box 36, folder 1, January 21, 2010.

31. Patricia Murphy, "Some Dems Want to Dump Nancy Pelosi. Are They Nuts?" *Roll Call*, March 22, 2018.

32. JALP, box 36, folder 1, January 21, 2010.

33. JALP, box 36, folder 1, January 21, 2010.

34. JALP, box 36, folder 1, February 2, 2010.

35. Sargent, "Book: Rahm 'Begged' Obama" reporting on Jonathan Alter, *The Promise* (New York: Simon & Schuster, 2011).

36. JALP, box 36, folder 1, January 22, 2010.

37. JALP, box 36, folder 1, February 4, 2010.

38. JALP, box 36, folder 1, February 10, 9, and 7, 2010.

39. JALP, box 36, folder 1, February 9, 2010.

40. JALP, box 36, folder 3, March 22, 2010.

41. JALP, box 36, folder 2, February 24, 2010; box 36, folder 1, February 17, 2010.

42. JALP, box 36, folder 1, February 17, 2010.

43. Holding the Senate bill at the president's desk was ruled impermissible by Frumin as well; the Senate bill had to be signed into law before the reconciliation bill would be in order.

44. JALP, box 36, folder 1, February 10, 2010.

45. JALP, box 36, folder 2, February 19, 2010.

46. JALP, box 36, folder 1, February 16 and 17, 2010; box 36, folder 2, February 18 and 19, 2010.

47. JALP, box 36, folder 1, February 14, 2010.

48. JALP, box 36, folder 1, February 14, 2010; box 36, folder 3, March 16, 2010.

49. JALP, box 36, folder 2, February 23, 2010.

50. JALP, box 36, folder 3, March 18, 2010.

51. JALP, box 36, folder 2, February 18 and 25, 2010.

52. JALP, box 36, folder 1, January 22, 2010; box 36, folder 2, March 6, 2010.

53. JALP, box 36, folder 3, March 16 and 17, 2010.

54. Those not signing were Cantwell, Lieberman, Bill Nelson, Ben Nelson, Webb, and Lincoln.

55. "Senate Won't Release Letter to Calm Nervous House Members on Reconciliation," *Roll Call*, March 19, 2010.

56. Pelosi claimed to have seen the letter and signatories.

57. JALP, box 36, folder 3, March 16 and 17, 2010.

58. JALP, box 36, folder 2, March 6, 2010.

59. JALP, box 36, folder 3, March 17, 2010.

60. JALP, box 36, folder 3, March 17, 2010.

61. JALP, box 36, folder 3, March 21, 2010.

62. JALP, box 36, folder 3, March 22, 2010.

63. JALP, box 36, folder 3, March 25, 2010.

64. Senators Lincoln, Bill Nelson, and Mark Pryor (AR), all of whom had supported the Senate's bill, voted with all of the Republicans against the reconciliation measure.

65. JALP, box 36, folder 2, March 6, 2010.

66. JALP, box 36, folder 3, March 24, 2010.

67. Pelosi also faulted Obama for having failed to mention Waxman during a signing of the extension of the Ryan White AIDS law. One participant in the event remembered Pelosi impatiently interrupting the president to remind him to recognize Waxman in mid-statement, only to have him turn around and tell her he had not gotten to that part of his presentation yet.

68. JALP, box 36, folder 3, March 31, 2010.

Chapter 21: The Unwinnable War

1. Megan Brenan, "Americans Split on Whether Afghanistan War Was a Mistake," Gallup, July 26, 2021; JALP, box 32, folder 11, October 18, 2007.

2. JALP, box 32, folder 13, November 7 and 8, 2007; box 32, folder 14, November 16, 2007.

3. JALP, box 33, folder 1, December 6, 2007.

4. The sponsors included Democratic senators Carl Levin, Jack Reed, Harry Reid, and Ken Salazar, as well as Republicans George Voinovich, Chuck Hagel, and Olympia Snowe. The second amendment, favored by the anti-war activists, failed overwhelmingly, 24–71.

5. JALP, box 32, folder 13, November 6, 2007; box 33, folder 2, January 14 and 17, 2007.

6. Bush visited Israel, the occupied West Bank, Kuwait, Bahrain, and the United Arab Emirates.

7. JALP, box 33, folder 3, January 22, 2008. Bush wanted Arab governments to pressure the Palestinians to recognize Israel in return for recognition of a Palestinian state to which Palestinian refugees could return. He told Yasser Arafat to acknowledge the right of Israel to exist while also urging Egyptian president Hosni Mubarak to crack down on Muslim Brotherhood extremists. "We want to get some money into Palestinian coffers so they can operate in the West Bank," Bush told members. To help secure their support, he had advised the Saudis against supporting Hamas, which the United States considered a terrorist organization, because such support would significantly diminish the chances for a comprehensive settlement.

8. JALP, box 33, folder 5, April 1, 2008; box 33, folder 7, May 15, 2008.

9. Mark Tran, "FBI Files Detail Guantánamo Torture Tactics," *Guardian*, January 3, 2007.

10. JALP, box 34, folder 7, April 20 and 23, 2009. Her rationale, she explained, was that any inquiry that even hinted of partisan bias would have no value at all.

11. JALP, box 34, folder 7, April 23, 2009.

12. JALP, box 34, folder 4, January 21, 2009.

13. "Why Obama Failed to Close Guantanamo," *PBS News Hour Weekend*, January 14, 2017, https://www.pbs.org/newshour/show/obama-failed-close-guantanamo.

14. JALP, box 34, folder 5, January 27, 2009.

15. JALP, box 34, folder 5, April 22, 2009.

16. JALP, box 34, folder 6, February 23, 2009.

17. JALP, box 34, folder 6, February 27, 2009.

18. JALP, box 34, folder 6, February 27, 2009; box 34, folder 7, March 26–27, 2009.

19. JALP, box 34, folder 8, April 28, 2009.

20. JALP, box 34, folder 6, March 21, 2009; box 34, folder 8, April 28, 2009. The group included Skelton (Armed Services), Murtha (Defense Appropriations), Obey (Appropriations), and Howard Berman (Foreign Affairs).

21. JALP, box 34, folder 8, April 30, 2009.

22. JALP, box 34, folder 8, May 10, 2009.

23. JALP, box 34, folder 8, May 8, 2009.

24. JALP, box 34, folder 8, May 10, 2009.

25. JALP, box 34, folder 8, May 12, 2009.

26. JALP, box 34, folder 8, May 12, 2009.

27. JALP, box 34, folder 8, May 12, 2009.

28. "GOP's Torture Strategy: Pelosi," *Politico*, May 11, 2009.

29. JALP, box 34, folder 8, May 17, 2009.

30. "Pelosi Accuses CIA of Lying in Torture Timeline," *SFGate*, May 15, 2009.

31. JALP, box 35, folder 1, June 13, 2009. That charge went too far for Pelosi. "That's a terrible thing to say," she said.

32. Murtha and Inouye, the Defense Appropriations chairs, poured billions into the bill, exceeding Obama's request for international affairs (+41 percent), the State Department (+17 percent), and international food assistance (+133 percent). Despite a veto warning from Emanuel, the bill also included riders (including nearly $2 billion to address the H1N1 influenza outbreak) that pushed the total cost to $106 billion, 28 percent above Obama's level.

33. JALP, box 35, folder 1, June 16, 2009.

34. JALP, box 35, folder 1, June 13, 2009.

35. Biden interview with *New York Times* editorial board, December 16, 2019, https://www.nytimes.com/interactive/2020/01/17/opinion/joe-biden-nytimes-interview.html.

36. JALP, box 35, folder 3, September 6, 2009.

37. "Stanley McChrystal's Long War," *NYT*, October 19, 2009.

38. JALP, box 35, folder 3, September 29, 2009.

39. JALP, box 35, folder 6, December 2, 2009.

40. JALP, box 35, folder 6, December 1 and 3, 2009.

41. JALP, box 35, folder 6, December 3, 2009.

42. Michael Hastings, "The Runaway General: The Profile That Brought Down McChrystal," *Rolling Stone*, June 22, 2010.

43. JALP, box 35, folder 6, June 22 and 24, 2010.

44. Craig Whitlock, "At War with the Truth," *NYT*, December 9, 2019; see also Craig Whitlock, *The Afghanistan Papers: A Secret History of the War* (New York: Simon & Schuster, 2021).

45. Robert D. Kaplan, "Time to Get Out of Afghanistan," *NYT*, January 1, 2019.

46. "Pentagon Says War in Afghanistan Costs Taxpayers $45 Billion per Year," *PBS News Hour*, February 6, 2018.

Chapter 22: "Keep Steering the Ship"

1. JALP, box 36, folder 4, April 15, 2010; *Obama's Deal*, produced by Michael Kirk, Jim Gilmore, and Mike Wiser, *PBS Frontline*, April 13, 2010, https://www.pbs.org/wgbh/frontline/film/obamasdeal/.

2. JALP, box 36, folder 3, March 26, 2010. Livingood recommended a new, high-security, costly vehicle for the Speaker. Given the press scrutiny and criticism of the use of the air force plane, a high price tag would become a matter of controversy when it invariably leaked to the press. After consulting with the Speaker, I declined Livingood's request.

3. The homes of Louise Slaughter, Tom Perriello, Steve Kagen, and Gabrielle Giffords (AZ) were vandalized. Driehaus's home was picketed. One caller to Pelosi's district office, after mentioning the Speaker's address in San Francisco, warned, "If you vote for health care, don't come back to California because you won't have a place to live." Eggs were thrown at her car as she drove through the city's Marina District, and the security director of a local church was investigated for threatening her life. "Wanted: Dead or Alive" postcards with her picture were circulated. A report from Oregon even mentioned an assassination plot.

4. JALP, box 36, folder 3, April 8, 2010.

5. JALP, box 36, folder 3, March 24, 2010.

6. JALP, box 36, folder 3, March 25, 2010.

7. JALP, box 36, folder 1, February 9, 2010.

8. JALP, box 36, folder 1, February 9, 2010.

9. JALP, box 36, folder 1, February 9, 2010.

10. JALP, box 35, folder 6, November 18, 2009; box 36, folder 1, February 9, 2010.

11. JALP, box 36, folder 6, June 15, 2010.

12. JALP, box 36, folder 4, April 22, April 21, May 4, 2010.

13. JALP, box 35, folder 1, June 9, 2009; box 36, folder 8, May 5, 2010.

14. JALP, box 34, folder 7, April 14 and 17, 2009.

15. JALP, box 35, folder 1, June 4 and 2, 2009.

16. JALP, box 36, folder 1, January 20, 2010.

17. The seven included Robert Bennett (UT), Sam Brownback (KS), Mike Crapo (ID), John Ensign (NV), Kay Bailey Hutchison (TX), James Inhofe (OK), and John McCain (AZ).

18. Fred Hiatt, "McConnell's Cynical Flip," WP, February 1, 2010.

19. Executive Order 13531, National Commission on Fiscal Responsibility and Reform, February 18, 2010, https://www.govinfo.gov/app/details/DCPD-201000104.

20. JALP, box 36, folder 6, June 16, 2010.

21. JALP, box 36, folder 6, June 14 and 29, 2010.

22. JALP, box 34, folder 5, February 17, 2009.

23. Reid appointed his deputy, the liberal Dick Durbin, as well as Baucus and Conrad; McConnell appointed solid conservatives, Gregg, Mike Crapo (ID), and Tom Coburn (OK). Pelosi named her moderate Budget chair, John Spratt (SC), and two solid liberals, Becerra and Schakowsky, while Boehner selected conservative hard-liners Paul Ryan, Dave Camp, and Jeb Henserling. Obama's appointees included corporate leaders; Andy Stern, president of the Service Employees International Union; and economist Alice Rivlin, a former OMB and CBO director.

24. JALP, box 36, folder 6, June 14 and 29, 2010.

25. JALP, box 36, folder 4, April 27, 2010; box 36, folder 6, June 29, 2010.

26. JALP, box 36, folder 4, April 27, 2010.

27. JALP, box 36, folder 6, June 28 and 29, 2010.

28. JALP, box 36, folder 4, April 22, 2010.

29. JALP, box 36, folder 5, May 12, 2010.

30. JALP, box 36, folder 4, April 17, 2010.

31. JALP, box 36, folder 5, May 16 and 12, 2010.

32. JALP, box 36, folder 5, May 17 and 25, 2010.

33. JALP, box 36, folder 8, September 15, 2010.

34. Arkansas's two senators, Blanche Lincoln and Mark Pryor, were the only two Democrats to side with the Republicans. Collins and some other Republicans would not support cloture but remained open to considering the repeal after completion of a DOD study.

35. "Move to End 'Don't Ask, Don't Tell' Stalls in Senate," *NYT*, September 21, 2010.

36. JALP, box 36, folder 5, May 5, 2010.

37. JALP, box 36, folder 5, June 10, 2010.

38. A problem that quickly arose was MMS's dual and conflicting role in managing leases and production safely while also being responsible for maximizing collection of revenues. Eventually, eighteen House and Senate committees held over sixty hearings on drilling technology, damage to the marine environment, wildlife losses, and the cost to coastal communities.

39. JALP, box 36, folder 6, June 14, 2010.

40. "House Approves Oil Spill Reform Bill," Reuters, July 30, 2010.

41. JALP, box 36, folder 7, August 2, 2010.

42. JALP, box 36, folder 7, December 24, 2009. The "branding for the recovery bill wasn't any good," the Speaker had pointedly told the White House team, leaving her members feeling "like they were thrown under the bus." "I'm at my wit's end," she had complained on Christmas Eve 2009. "I don't know if we have the capability."

43. JALP, box 36, folder 4, April 23, 2010; box 36, folder 1, February 3, 2010.

44. JALP, box 36, folder 4, April 13, May 11, 2010.

45. Alexi McCammond, "Biden's High Bar," Axios, November 2, 2020.

46. JALP, box 37, folder 1, October 22, 2010.

47. JALP, box 36, folder 6, May 28, 2010.

48. Among liberals, only Kucinich opposed the bill, arguing (like Bernie Sanders in the Senate) Congress should be breaking up big banks, not regulating them.

49. JALP, box 36, folder 4, April 14, 2010.

50. JALP, box 36, folder 6, June 17, 2010.

51. JALP, box 36, folder 6, June 23, 2010.

52. Andrew Sorkin, "President Obama Weighs His Economic Legacy," *NYT Magazine*, April 28, 2016.

53. The three were Walter Jones (NC), Joseph Cao (LA), and Mike Castle (DE).

54. JALP, box 36, folder 6, June 30, 2010.

55. JALP, box 36, folder 6, June 23 and 29, 2010.

56. In 2012, Warren would return the favor, defeating Brown in the Massachusetts Senate race.

57. JALP, box 36, folder 6, June 29, 2010.

58. Sorkin, "President Obama Weighs."

59. JALP, box 36, folder 7, August 25, 2010; box 36, folder 5, June 10, 2010.

60. JALP, box 36, folder 6, July 12, 2010; box 36, folder 5, May 27, 2010.

61. JALP, box 36, folder 5, May 25, 2010.

62. JALP, box 36, folder 5, June 8, 2010.

63. JALP, box 36, folder 5, June 8, 2010.

64. JALP, box 36, folder 3, April 5, 2010. The seat was won by a Republican anyway.

65. JALP, box 36, folder 6, June 14, 2010.

66. JALP, box 36, folder 3, June 3, 2010.

67. JALP, box 36, folder 6, July 1, 2010.

68. "Senate Abandons Climate Effort, Dealing Blow to President," *NYT*, July 23, 2010.

69. Lisa Lerer, "Dems to W.H.: Drop Cap and Trade," *Politico*, December 27, 2009.

70. JALP, box 36, folder 7, July 26, 2010.

71. McConnell was referring to Obama's appointment of Donald Berwick to run Medicare and Medicaid, despite opposition that included Finance chair Max Baucus.

72. JALP, box 36, folder 7, August 2, 2010.

73. JALP, box 36, folder 8, September 21, 2010.

74. The MTR attempted to repeal portions of the newly enacted health law rather than limit the eligibility of immigrants for benefits. It failed 185–244.

75. JALP, box 36, folder 7, July 29, 2010.

76. JALP, box 36, folder 8, September 15, 2010. Among the legislation enacted in ensuing years were tax cuts and loans for small businesses, an acceleration of the patent process, the training of skilled workers, and the closing of tax loopholes that encouraged outsourcing of jobs overseas. Many of the bills were not novel to the MIIA agenda. Office of the Majority Leader, "Make It in America" Fact Sheet, July 23, 2018, https://www.majorityleader.gov/content/make-it-america.

77. JALP, book 4, January 29, 2010.

78. JALP, box 36, folder 6, June 16, 2010.

79. JALP, box 36, folder 6, July 12, 2010.

80. JALP, box 36, folder 7, July 19, 2010.

81. JALP, box 36, folder 7, July 28, 2010.

Chapter 23: The Unfinished Agenda

1. JALP, box 36, folder 8, August 31, 2010.

2. JALP, box 36, folder 7, August 10, 2010.

3. JALP, box 36, folder 7, July 26, 2010.

4. JALP, box 36, folder 6, June 16, 2010.

5. JALP, box 36, folder 7, August 3, 2010.

6. "House Passes $26 Billion in State Aid," *NYT*, August 10, 2010.

7. JALP, box 36, folder 7, August 10, 2010.

8. The cuts had been designed to expire after a decade so as not to violate reconciliation rules that prohibit legislation to create new debt after the ten-year budget window.

9. JALP, box 36, folder 7, July 27, 2010.

10. JALP, box 36, folder 8, September 14, 2010; box 36, folder 7, August 10, 2010.

11. CBS News, August 26, 2010.

12. "From Obama, the Tax Cut Nobody Heard Of," *NYT*, October 18, 2010.

13. JALP, box 36, folder 7, August 10, 2010.

14. JALP, box 36, folder 7, August 10, 2010.

15. JALP, box 36, folder 7, August 10, 2010.

16. JALP, box 36, folder 7, August 25, 2010.

17. JALP, box 36, folder 7, August 5, 2010.

18. JALP, box 36, folder 8, September 16, 2010.

19. JALP, box 36, folder 8, September 22, 2010.

20. JALP, box 36, folder 8, September 23, 2010.

21. JALP, box 36, folder 8, September 24, 2010.

22. JALP, box 36, folder 8, September 21 and 16, 2010.

23. JALP, box 36, folder 8, September 22 and 21, 2010.

24. JALP, box 36, folder 8, September 27 and 28, 2010.

25. JALP, box 36, folder 8, September 28, 2010.

26. Committee on Ways and Means, Statement of Chairman David Obey, August 10, 2010.

27. "Democrats Plan Political Triage to Retain House," *NYT*, September 4, 2010.

28. JALP, box 36, folder 8, September 7, 2010.

29. JALP, box 36, folder 8, October 14, 2010.

30. *The Daily Show with Jon Stewart*, Comedy Central, October 27, 2010.

Chapter 24: The "Shellacking"

1. "David Axelrod: Democrats Are Walking into Trump's Trap," *Politico*, October 30, 2018, https://www.politico.com/magazine/story/2018/10/30/david-axelrod-2020-democratic-candidates-trump-harris-gillibrand-bernie-castro-patrick-221951.

2. JALP, book 2, October 25, 2010.

3. David Jackson, "Obama Jokes about 'Shovel-Ready Projects,'" *USA Today*, June 13, 2011.

4. JALP, box 36, folder 3, March 24, April 1, 2010.

5. JALP, box 36, folder 7, July 20, August 10, 2010; box 36, folder 3, March 15, 2010.

6. JALP, box 36, folder 6, June 28, 2010; folder 4, April 28, 2010; folder 8, September 16, 2010.

7. JALP, box 36, folder 8, September 7, 2010; box 36, folder 6, June 23, 2010; box 36, folder 7, July 19, 2010.

8. JALP, box 36, folder 7, July 19 and 22, August 10 and 11, 2010.

9. JALP, box 36, folder 6, July 15, 2010.

10. JALP, box 36, folder 4, April 29, 2010.

11. Office of the Speaker, "New Direction for Economic Recovery: Tax Cuts for America," n.d. (2010).

12. JALP, box 36, folder 4, April 13, 2010.

13. JALP, box 34, folder 6, March 11, 2009.

14. Emanuel angrily denied the accusations, noting he was doing his sixth fundraiser for the Senate campaign committee and that the White House had channeled DNC money to the congressional committees. JALP, box 36, folder 2, February 19, 2010; box 35, folder 7, January 5, 2010; box 36, folder 1, January 20, 2010.

15. JALP, box 36, folder 1, January 20, 2010.

16. Josh Kraushaar, "Griffith Faults Pelosi for Switch," *Politico*, December 22, 2009. Griffith lost the Republican nomination for his seat in 2010 anyway, receiving just 33 percent of the vote.

17. JALP, box 36, folder 3, April 1, 2010; box 36, folder 4, April 12, 2010.

18. Djou won with only 36 percent of the vote, supported the initial House health care bill but voted against the final version, and was defeated in his 2010 reelection bid.

19. Ben McGrath, "The Movement: The Rise of Tea Party Activism," *New Yorker*, February 1, 2010. Reformers in earlier periods similarly were contemptuous of their own party leaders, as with the incoming Democrats in 1974.

20. JALP, box 36, folder 7, July 22, 2010.

21. McGrath, "The Movement."

22. Both from *Politico*, June 30, 2010.

23. Jonathan Allen, "John Boehner, Eric Cantor in Policy Panel Spat," *Politico*, July 6, 2010; "McCotter on GOP Policy Committee: Republicans Must Cut First," Fox News, July 8, 2010, https://www.youtube.com/watch?v=0CoIssohu2k; McCotter tweet, July 8, 2010.

24. JALP, box 36, folder 6, July 12, June 15, 2010.

25. JALP, box 36, folder 4, April 13, 2010; box 36, folder 8, September 7, 2010; box 36, folder 6, July 12, 2010.

26. JALP, box 36, folder 4, April 29, 2010.

27. Jonathan Allen, "Gibbs Stokes Dems' Nov. Anxiety," *Politico*, July 11, 2010.

28. Pelosi recalled upbraiding Clinton advisors James Carville and George Stephanopoulos in 1996 after they asserted they saw no point in the Democrats winning the House that year by just two seats, since the thin margin would leave then unable to pass major legislation.

29. JALP, box 36, folder 6, July 12, 2010.

30. Allen, "Gibbs Stokes."

31. JALP, box 36, folder 6, July 1, 2010.

32. JALP, box 36, folder 6, July 14 and 15, 2010.

33. Karoli Kuns, "Where Robert Gibbs Shoots His Own Side in the Foot—Inartfully," Crooks and Liars, August 10, 2010, https://crooksandliars.com/karoli/where-robert-gibbs-whines-and-stomps-his-fe.

34. JALP, box 36, folder 6, July 12, 2010.

35. JALP, box 36, folder 6, July 14, 2010.

36. JALP, box 36, folder 6, July 25, 2010.

37. JALP, box 36, folder 6, July 15, 2010.

38. JALP, box 36, folder 7, August 10 and 23, 2010; Gail Russell Chaddock, "Amid John Boehner Blast at Obama, Hints of How GOP Would Rule," Christian Science Monitor, August 24, 2010, https://www.csmonitor.com/USA/Elections/House/2010/0824/Amid-John-Boehner-blast-at-Obama-hints-of-how-GOP-would-rule.

39. JALP, box 36, folder 8, October 7, 2010.

40. JALP, box 36, folder 8, September 7, 2010; box 36, folder 6, July 15, 2010.

41. JALP, box 36, folder 8, September 16 and 21, 2010.

42. JALP, box 36, folder 7, July 26, 2010. The Republican lead of 52/31 percent had shrunk to a much smaller 43/39 percent advantage. Schumer advised taking another three to five points off the Democratic number to compensate for stronger GOP voting intensity.

43. JALP, box 36, folder 8, August 31, 2010.

44. JALP, box 37, folder 1, October 29 and 12, 2010.

45. JALP, box 36, folder 7, August 27, 2010.

46. JALP, box 36, folder 8, September 27, 2010.

47. SCOTUS Blog, "Citizens United v. Federal Election Commission," January 21, 2010, https://www.scotusblog.com/case-files/cases/citizens-united-v-federal-election-commission/.

48. JALP, box 36, folder 8, September 27 and 28, 2010.

49. JALP, box 36, folder 7, August 23, 2010.

50. JALP, box 36, folder 8, September 14 and 27, 2010).

51. See the earlier remarks about abandoning candidates in chapter 23. JALP, box 36, folder 8, September 3, 2010; box 36, folder 5, April 13, 2010.

52. JALP, box 36, folder 8, August 31, 2010. Among the incumbents, Bart Gordon (TN), Dan Maffei (NY), and Charlie Melançon (LA) were viewed as inevitably losing, and all did.

53. JALP, box 37, folder 1, October 24, 2010.

54. "Boehner: 'Not a Time for Compromise,'" The Hill, October 28, 2010.

55. Andy Barr, "The GOP's No-Compromise Pledge," Politico, October 28, 2010.

56. "Fire Pelosi Bus Tour," *Christian Science Monitor*, September 15, 2010.

57. In her second speakership, beginning in January 2019, Pelosi decided against using the military plane altogether.

58. JALP, box 36, folder 8, October 6, 2010. Rep. Ed Markey cautioned Pelosi about getting into a fight with CBS executive Sean McManus and others because "the CBS brass is against us."

59. JALP, box 37, folder 1, October 13 and 14, 2010.

60. JALP, box 36, folder 8, September 29, 2010.

61. JALP, box 36, folder 8, September 7, 2010.

62. Mineta was a former Democratic House member from California who joined George W. Bush's cabinet. Skinner, who was George H. W. Bush's transportation secretary, also served as his White House chief of staff.

63. JALP, box 36, folder 8, October 6, 2010; box 37, folder 1, October 11, 2010.

64. JALP, box 37, folder 1, October 20 and 26, 2010.

65. JALP, box 37, folder 1, October 29, 2010.

66. JALP, box 37, folder 1, October 14, 2010. In the late 1940s and early 1950s, Sam Rayburn (TX) and Joe Martin (MA) traded the speakership twice between 1946 and 1954, and both remained in office after losing the gavel. Tom Foley did not face the decision in 1994 since he had been defeated in his own reelection campaign. Newt Gingrich (who was deposed by his own party) and Dennis Hastert both resigned from the House soon after leaving the speakership.

67. JALP, box 37, folder 1, October 31, 2010.

68. JALP, box 37, folder 1, October 30, 2010.

69. JALP, box 37, folder 1, November 2, 2010.

70. "US Midterm Election Results Herald New Political Era as Republicans Take House," *Guardian*, November 3, 2010.

71. JALP, box 37, folder 1, November 5, 2010.

72. "Former House Speaker John Boehner Calls Hard Right Conservatives 'Knucklehead Caucus,'" *Dayton Daily News*, July 26, 2017. See Boehner, *On the House*.

73. JALP, box 37, folder 1, November 3, 2010.

74. JALP, box 36, folder 1, November 2, 2010.

75. Capuano survived, although he would lose his seat to a progressive primary challenge in 2018.

76. Brendan Nyhan, "The Effects of Health Care Reform in 2010 and Beyond," *HuffPost*, March 8, 2012.

77. JALP, box 37, folder 1, October 11, 2010.

78. JALP, box 37, folder 1, November 3, 2010.

79. Greg Sargent, "Minority Leader Nancy Pelosi Will Play Rough with GOP," *WP*, November 7, 2010.

80. JALP, box 37, folder 1, November 4, 2010.

81. JALP, box 37, folder 3, December 20, 2010.

82. JALP, box 37, folder 1, November 3, 2010.

Chapter 25: Their Last Bow

1. JALP, box 37, folder 2, November 16, 2010; Jack Trout email to author, November 10, 2010.

2. JALP, box 37, folder 2, November 15 and 16, 2010.

3. JALP, box 37, folder 2, December 1, 2010.

4. JALP, box 37, folder 1, November 5, 2010; box 37, folder 2, November 9, 2010.

5. JALP, box 37, folder 2, November 9, December 16, 2010.

6. JALP, box 36, folder 7, August 3, 2010.

7. Richard Kogan, "What Was Actually in Bowles-Simpson—and How Can We Compare It with Other Plans?" Center on Budget and Policy Priorities, October 2, 2012.

8. JALP, box 37, folder 2, November 18, 2010.

9. JALP, box 37, folder 2, November 15, 2010.

10. Peter Baker, "The Education of a President," *NYT*, October 17, 2010.

11. JALP, box 37, folder 2, November 18, 2010.

12. JALP, box 37, folder 2, November 18, 2010.

13. JALP, box 37, folder 3, December 9, 2010.

14. JALP, box 37, folder 2, November 15, 2010.

15. "House Passes 'Dream Act' Immigration Bill," Reuters, December 8, 2010. Democratic "no" votes in the Senate included including Baucus, Kay Hagan (NC), Ben Nelson (NB), Mark Pryor (AR), and Jon Tester (MT).

16. JALP, box 37, folder 2, December 3, 2010; box 37, folder 3, December 16, 2010.

17. Stewart Doan, "Senate Approves Funding for Pigford and Cobell Settlements," *Agri-Pulse*, November 22, 2010. Congressional leaders had promised district court judge James Robinson that the payment would be approved following a ruling in favor of the farmers.

18. JALP, box 37, folder 2, November 19, 2010.

19. JALP, box 37, folder 2, November 18, 2010.

20. JALP, box 37, folder 2, November 19, 2010.

21. "9/11 Responders Bill Defeated by Senate GOP Filibuster," CNN Politics, December 10, 2010, http://www.cnn.com/2010/POLITICS/12/09/senate.9.11.responders /index.html.

22. JALP, box 37, folder 3, December 20 and 22, 2010.

23. "Senate Passes 9/11 Health Bill as Republicans Back Down," *NYT*, December 22, 2010.

24. JALP, box 37, folder 2, December 3, 2010.

25. David Rogers, "Dems Concede Budget Fight to GOP," *Politico*, December 16, 2010.

26. JALP, box 37, folder 3, December 15, 2010; box 37, folder 2, November 22, 2010.

27. JALP, box 37, folder 3, December 16, 2010.

28. Patrick Jonsson, "Collapse of the Omnibus Spending Bill: Rise of the 'Tea Party Congress'?" *Christian Science Monitor*, December 17, 2010.

29. Humberto Sanchez, "Congress Sends Another Continuing Resolution to Obama," *Government Executive*, December 21, 2010; JALP, box 34, folder 3, December 16, 2010.

30. The House vote was 193–165 and the Senate 79–16.

31. "Obama Signs Child Nutrition Bill," CNN Politics, December 13, 2010, http://www.cnn.com/2010/POLITICS/12/13/child.nutrition/index.html; JALP, box 37, folder 2, December 2, 2010.

32. JALP, box 36, folder 8, September 3, 2010.

33. JALP, box 37, folder 2, December 3, 2010; box 37, folder 3, December 16, 2010.

34. JALP, box 37, folder 2, December 3, 2010.

35. The inheritance tax had actually expired a year earlier. Two dozen moderate Democrats sent the Speaker a note endorsing the higher limits.

36. The final House vote was 139 Democrats and 138 Republicans in favor and 112 Democrats and 36 Republicans opposed, an unusually bipartisan division on a major bill.

37. Gail Chaddock, "House Passes Bipartisan Tax Cut Deal, First of Obama Administration," *Christian Science Monitor*, December 17, 2010.

38. JALP, box 37, folder 2, December 6, 2010.

39. JALP, box 37, folder 2, December 3, 2010; box 37, folder 3, December 13, 2010.

40. JALP, box 37, folder 3, December 10, 2010.

41. Norman Ornstein, "Actually, It's Quite a Productive Congress," *Dallas Morning News*, February 12, 2010.

Conclusion: The Perishability of Power

1. JALP, box 37, folder 1, October 28, 2010.

2. JALP, box 36, folder 2, March 1, 2010.

3. JALP, box 37, folder 2, December 6, 2010.

4. Pelosi press conference, February 4, 2021. Woodrow Wilson, as a young political scientist, had used the same frame for the Senate: "an American House of Lords." John Morton Blum, *Woodrow Wilson and the Politics of Morality* (Boston: Little, Brown, 1956), 18.

5. JALP, box 36, folder 6, June 14, 2010.

6. JALP, box 36, folder 2, March 2, 2010.

7. Office of the House Historian, "Presidential Vetoes," https://history.house.gov/Institution/Presidential-Vetoes/Presidential-Vetoes/.

8. Amy Chozickoct, "A Likely Debate Highlight: Democrats' Distance from Obama," *NYT*, October 11, 2015.

9. David Corn, *Showdown: The Inside Story of How Obama Fought Back against Boehner, Cantor, and the Tea Party* (New York: McGraw-Hill, 2012), 11.

10. Frances Lee, *Insecure Majorities: Congress and the Perpetual Campaign* (Chicago: University of Chicago Press, 2016), 50. See chapter 3 in particular.

11. Obama, *Promised Land*, 595.

12. Blum, *Woodrow Wilson*, 18.

13. JALP, box 36, folder 7, August 10, 2010.

14. "Hopes Dim for More Stimulus as Democrats Block Narrow G.O.P. Plan," *NYT*, September 12, 2020.

15. Heather Caygle and Sarah Ferris, "'Do Not Tweet': Pelosi Scolds Progressives in Closed-Door Meeting," *Politico*, July 10, 2019.

16. JALP, box 36, folder 3, March 25, 2010.

17. Caygle and Ferris, "Do Not Tweet."

18. JALP, book 2, email to Rep. George Miller, October 27, 2010.

19. Peter Baker, "The Education of a President," *NYT Magazine*, October 17, 2010.

20. Sahil Kapur, "Democrats Fear Health Care 2009 Déjà Vu as Biden-GOP Infrastructure Talks Drag," NBC News, June 3, 2021.

21. JALP, box 40, folder 1, December 30, 2012.

22. JALP, box 40, folder 2, January 1, 2013

Bibliographical Guide to the John A. Lawrence Papers

The John A. Lawrence Papers (JALP) are located at the Manuscript Division of the Library of Congress (Jefferson Building). By arrangement between the author and the LOC, these records are sealed, not to be opened without written permission of the author, until May 2026.

Lawrence Papers

Box 31

Folder 4	July 22–September 16, 2005
Folder 5	September 17–October 31, 2005
Folder 6	November 1–December 16, 2005
Folder 7	December 17, 2005–February 14, 2006
Folder 8	February 27–April 12, 2006
Folder 9	April 12–May 22, 2006
Folder 10	May 22–July 7, 2006
Folder 11	July 7–September 18, 2006
Folder 12	September 19–October 30, 2006

Box 32

Folder 1	October 30–December 7, 2006
Folder 2	December 7, 2006–January 20, 2007
Folder 3	January 12–February 6, 2007
Folder 4	February 6–March 6, 2007
Folder 5	March 6–28, 2007
Folder 6	March 29–May 8, 2007
Folder 7	May 9–June 4, 2007
Folder 8	June 4–22, 2007
Folder 9	June 25–July 23, 2007
Folder 10	July 23–August 27, 2007
Folder 11	August 27–September 27, 2007
Folder 12	September 27–October 23, 2007

Folder 13	October 23–November 15, 2007
Folder 14	November 15–December 5, 2007

Box 33

Folder 1	December 5–26, 2007
Folder 2	December 26, 2007–January 18, 2008
Folder 3	January 21–February 12, 2008
Folder 4	February 12–March 5, 2008
Folder 5	March 10–April 9, 2008
Folder 6	April 9–29, 2008
Folder 7	April 29–May 25, 2008
Folder 8	May 27–June 13, 2008
Folder 9	June 13–August 10, 2008
Folder 10	August 11–September 23, 2008

Box 34

Folder 1	September 23–October 13, 2008
Folder 2	October 14–November 16, 2008
Folder 3	November 17–December 20, 2008
Folder 4	December 21, 2008–January 15, 2009
Folder 5	January 16–February 18, 2009
Folder 6	February 20–March 23, 2009
Folder 7	March 23–April 27, 2009
Folder 8	April 27–June 1, 2009

Box 35

Folder 1	June 1–30, 2007
Folder 2	June 30–July 27, 2009
Folder 3	July 27, 2009–September 9, 2009
Folder 4	September 10–October 19, 2009
Folder 5	October 20–November 17, 2009
Folder 6	November 17–December 15, 2009
Folder 7	December 15, 2009–January 20, 2010

Box 36

Folder 1	January 20–February 18, 2010
Folder 2	February 18–March 13, 2010
Folder 3	March 13–April 8, 2010
Folder 4	April 11–May 12, 2010
Folder 5	May 12–June 11, 2010

Folder 6	June 13–July 15, 2010
Folder 7	July 19–August 30, 2010
Folder 8	August 30–October 8, 2010

Box 37

Folder 1	October 11–November 5, 2010
Folder 2	November 15–December 8, 2010
Folder 3	December 8, 2010–January 18, 2011

Additional notes are available in boxes and files for the period between January 2010 and January 2013.

The JALP include the handwritten pads of notes catalogued above as well as other materials including memos, clippings, printed materials (such as legislative pocket cards and talking points), and electronic files (noted in this book as "JALP book").

Selected Bibliography

Alter, Jonathan. *The Promise: President Obama, Year One*. New York: Simon & Schuster, 2011.

Angelides, Phil. "Ten Years After the Fall of Bear Stearns, D.C. Is Poised to Cause Another Financial Crisis." *Los Angeles Times*, March 19, 2018.

Bair, Sheila. *Bull by the Horns: Fighting to Save Main Street from Wall Street and Wall Street from Itself*. New York: Free Press, 2012.

Baker, Peter. "The Education of a President." *New York Times Magazine*, October 17, 2010.

Ball, Molly. *Pelosi*. New York: Henry Holt, 2020.

Beard, Daniel. "Green the Capitol Final Report." Office of the Chief Administrative Office, US House of Representatives. Washington, DC: Government Printing Office, June 21, 2007.

Bendavid, Naftali. *The Thumpin': How Rahm Emanuel and the Democrats Learned to Be Ruthless and Ended the Republican Revolution*. New York: Doubleday, 2007.

Benen, Steve. "Getting BTU'd." *Washington Monthly*, May 5, 2011.

Bernanke, Ben S., Timothy F. Geithner, and Henry M. Paulson. *Firefighting: The Financial Crisis and Its Lessons*. New York: Penguin, 2019.

Boehner, John. *On the House: A Washington Memoir*. New York: St. Martin's, 2021.

Bzdek, Vincent. *Woman of the House: The Rise of Nancy Pelosi*. New York: St. Martin's Griffin, 2008.

Cohn, Jonathan. "What Democrats Can Learn from Obamacare, According to Barack Obama." HuffPost, February 21, 2021.

Congressional Research Service. "Energy Independence and Security Act of 2007: A Summary of Major Provisions." December 21, 2007.

———. "House Office of Congressional Ethics: History, Authority, and Procedures." March 28, 2019.

Corn, David. "The Myth of the Obama Cave-In." *Mother Jones*, November 26, 2012.

———. *Showdown: The Inside Story of How Obama Fought Back against Boehner, Cantor, and the Tea Party*. New York: McGraw, 2012.

Dickson, Caitlin. "Will the $1.2 Trillion Earmark-Packed Bill Pass before Saturday?" *Atlantic*, December 15, 2010.

Firestone, David. "Don't Tell Anyone, but the Stimulus Worked." *New York Times*, September 15, 2012.

Grunwald, Michael. "The Selling of Obama." *Politico*, May/June 2014.

Hastings, Michael. "The Runaway General: The Profile That Brought Down McChrystal." *Rolling Stone*, June 22, 2010.

Kane, Paul. "Pelosi and Dingell Rivalry Reflects the Evolution of the Democratic Party." *Washington Post*, February 9, 2019.

Kogan, Richard. "What Was Actually in Bowles-Simpson—and How Can We Compare It with Other Plans?" Center on Budget and Policy Priorities, October 2, 2012.

Lawrence, John A. *The Class of '74 Congress after Watergate and the Roots of Partisanship.* Baltimore, MD: Johns Hopkins University Press, 2018.

———. "When America Stared into the Abyss." *Atlantic*, January 7, 2019.

Lee, Frances E. *Insecure Majorities: Congress and the Perpetual Campaign.* Chicago: University of Chicago Press, 2016.

Lizza, Ryan. "As the World Burns." *New Yorker*, October 11, 2010.

Marshall, Bryan W., and Bruce C. Wolpe. *The Committee: A Study of Policy, Power, and Politics and Obama's Historic of Legislative Agenda on Capitol Hill.* Ann Arbor: University of Michigan Press, 2018.

McGrath, Ben. "The Movement: The Rise of Tea Party Activism." *New Yorker*, February 1, 2010.

Meyerson, Harold. "How Nancy Pelosi Took Control." *American Prospect*, June 2004.

Obama, Barack. *A Promised Land.* New York: Crown, 2020.

Page, Susan. *Madam Speaker: Nancy Pelosi and the Lessons of Power.* New York: Twelve, 2021.

Pelosi, Nancy. *Know Your Power: A Message to America's Daughters.* New York: Anchor, 2009.

Pelosi Official Press Releases by year, https://pelosi.house.gov/news/press-releases -by-year/2009.

Peters, Ron M., and Cindy Simon Rosenthal. *Speaker Nancy Pelosi and the New American Politics.* Oxford: Oxford University Press, 2010.

Povich, Elaine S. *Nancy Pelosi: A Biography.* Santa Barbara, CA: Greenwood Biographies, 2008.

Sandalow, Marc. *Madam Speaker: Nancy Pelosi's Life, Times, and Rise to Power.* Emmaus, PA: Rodale Books, 2008.

Sorkin, Andrew. "President Obama Weighs His Economic Legacy." *New York Times Magazine*, April 4, 2016.

Taibbi, Matt. "Obama Defends His Finance Reform Record to Rolling Stone: A Response." *Rolling Stone*, November 1, 2012.

Waxman, Henry A., and Joshua Green. *The Waxman Report: How Congress Really Works.* New York: Twelve, 2009.

Wertheimer, Fred. Interview for the John W. Gardner Legacy Oral History Project, on
   HLOG 2007, Stanford Historical Society (April 17, 2018), https://searchworks-lb
   .stanford.edu/view/yp355sk9633.
Whitlock, Craig. "At War with the Truth." *New York Times*, December 9, 2019.
Zelizer, Julian. *Burning Down the House: Newt Gingrich, the Fall of a Speaker, and the Rise
   of the New Republican Party.* New York: Penguin, 2020.

Index

Abercrombie, Neil, 77
abortion controversy, 40, 198, 207–208,
    329n20, 330n47
Abramoff, Jack, 2
Affordable Care Act (ACA), 225, 261, 273,
    277. *See also* health care bill
Affordable Health Care for America Act,
    209–210
Afghan war
    cost of, 34–35, 44, 163, 227–228
    New York Times report on, 237
    public opinion of, 227, 230
    US policy in, 235–238, 250
Alexander, Lamar, 221
Altmire, Jason, 269
American Clean Energy and Security Act, 173
American International Group (AIG), 95, 109
American Recovery and Redevelopment Act
    (ARRA)
    benefits of, 152–154, 174–175
    communications with the public about, 152
    criticism of, 153–154, 261
    energy innovation money, 175
Andrews, Rob, 278
Andrews, Tom, 76
Anthem Blue Cross, 219
Armey, Dick, 193
arts, government support of, 141, 152
Assad, Bashar al-, 78–79
Authorization for Use of Military Force
    (AUMF), 72–73
auto industry, bailout of, 120–121, 127,
    132–134, 137
Axelrod, David
    2010 congressional elections and, 265,
    266, 267
    on House Democrats, 278, 289

    on Pelosi's leadership, 274
    on Republicans, 277–278
    stimulus bill and, 143, 144, 147
    tax cut bill and, 257

Bachus, Spencer, 111, 112, 114, 160
Baker, James, 76
Baldwin, Tammy, 15, 43
Barrow, John, 170, 190, 263
Barton, Joe, 26, 246
Baucus, Max, 288
    criticism of, 58, 141
    health care bill and, 181, 183, 186, 187,
    200
    immigration bill and, 342n15
    on Paygo rules, 88
    tax cuts initiatives, 34, 89
Bayh, Evan, 33, 46, 166
Beard, Dan, 70–71
Becerra, Xavier, 31, 125, 180, 205, 278
Begala, Paul, 263, 268
Bernanke, Ben, 89, 109, 111, 116, 121
Bernstein, Jared, 153
Berry, Marion, 40, 263
Biden, Joe, 73
    9/11 victims' assistance bill and,
    284
    2010 congressional elections and,
    264, 266
    Afghan policy and, 234, 238
    health care bill and, 174, 226
    Pelosi and, 234, 242, 282–283, 286
    stimulus bill and, 148, 154
    tax extension bill and, 285
    White House staff and, 282–283
Blinder, Alan, 110
Bloomberg, Mike, 252–253

Blue Dogs
  climate bill and, 70, 171
  criticism of, 92
  fiscal conservatism of, 88, 91, 241
  health care bill and, 182, 184–185, 186,
    188–189, 190, 200, 203–204
  Obama and, 129, 151, 186
  stimulus package and, 57, 116, 142, 146, 147
Blunt, Roy, 20, 115, 117, 189
Boehner, John
  9/11 victims' assistance bill and, 283
  2010 congressional elections and, 264,
    267, 268, 270, 273
  Bolten and Miers inquiry and, 51
  financial crisis and, 112, 115, 116–117
  on food stamp eligibility, 54
  health care bill and, 224
  job legislation and, 161
  position on earmarks, 157
  stimulus bill and, 55, 58, 135, 136, 142, 153
  tax cuts proposals, 53, 279
Bolten, Josh, 82, 92
  auto crisis and, 134
  contempt of Congress, 51
  on McCain, 115
  Pelosi and, 113, 117, 118, 119, 131, 134
  stimulus bill negotiations and, 136–137
Boucher, Rick, 62, 166, 168, 169, 170, 273
Bowles, Erskine, 243
Boxer, Barbara, 68, 174
Boyd, Alan, 91, 274, 309n29
Brown, Scott, 211, 249, 282
Brown, Sherrod, 151, 168
Burger, Anna, 212
Burton, John, 34
Bush, George W.
  appointments of US attorneys, 50
  auto industry bailout, 134, 137
  ban on stem cell research, 33
  Colombia trade deal, 95
  economic plan, 53–54
  financial crisis and, 109, 111–114, 116
  fiscal policy, 32, 34–35
  foreign policy, 1, 6, 21, 72, 73, 333n6
  health care policy, 10, 52
  Hurricane Katrina and, 5–6
  immigration policy, 34, 36
  inquiry into torture allegations, 229

  Iraq policy, 50, 73, 74–75, 78, 81, 228
  "New Way Forward" surge, 75, 80
  Pelosi and, 46, 47
  tax policy, 23, 141, 142, 252, 256, 278, 279
  veto powers, 46–48, 65, 81
Byrd, Robert, 89–90, 143, 178, 248

Cadillac tax, 211–212, 213, 215
Cantor, Eric, 117, 145, 146, 163, 184, 264, 278
cap-and-trade (C&T) system, 165, 166–168,
  170, 171
"carbon neutral" goal legislation, 64
Cardoza, Dennis
  2010 congressional elections, 269, 271
  on Blue Dogs, 94
  climate bill and, 171
  health care bill and, 184, 187, 188, 192, 216
  on nationalistic message, 253
Carville, James, 1, 234, 339n28
"cash for clunker" program, 169
Cheney, Dick, 30, 97, 116, 234
child nutrition bill, 257, 258, 259, 284–285
Chrysler, 137, 319n32
Chu, Steven, 166, 175–176
*Citizens United v. Federal Elections
  Commission*, 268–269
climate bill
  environmentalist groups and, 171–172
  House debates, 166, 170
  Senate debates, 165, 167–168, 249, 251
Clinton, Bill, 97, 99, 163, 173, 183, 265, 318n8
Clinton, Hillary, 73
  2008 presidential nomination campaign,
    96, 98, 100, 101–102, 103, 105
  Copenhagen Climate Change
    Conference, 175
  Pelosi and, 100
  position on Iraq, 96, 100
  promotion of universal health care, 177
  on sexism, 105
Clyburn, Jim
  9/11 bill and, 252
  2010 congressional election, 272, 275
  attitude to Republicans, 240, 279
  Blue Dogs and, 189
  House leadership and, 20, 125
  on nuclear power, 167
  Obama and, 156, 157, 263

stimulus bill and, 90, 109, 143
TARP bill and, 117
tax cut bill and, 279–280
on troops withdrawal from Iraq, 81
Code Pink demonstrators, 72
Collins, Susan, 33, 148, 150, 151, 282, 336n34
Colombia trade agreement, 90, 95
Congressional Budget Office (CBO), 187, 222, 335n23
Conrad, Kent, 33, 88, 147, 160, 161, 166, 241, 288, 335n23
continuing resolutions (CRs), 23, 33–34, 44–45, 284
Conyers, John, 11, 42, 52
Copenhagen Climate Change Conference, 174–175, 176
Corker, Bob, 136–137, 247
Corporate Average Fuel Economy (CAFE) bill
    aid to auto industry, 132
    bipartisan support of, 60, 62–65
    renewable electricity standards, 67, 165
    Senate debates on, 63, 64, 65–66
Cox, Christopher, 95, 109
Crocker, Ryan, 83, 84
Cullinane, John, xvii, 299n8

D'Alesandro, Tommy, 269
Daschle, Tom, 178, 325n6
Davis, Artur, 89
Deepwater Horizon disaster, 245–246
DeLauro, Rosa, 4, 68, 262
DeLay, Tom, xviii, 2, 20
Democratic Congressional Campaign Committee (DCCC), 2, 12, 263, 269, 271
Democratic National Committee (DNC), 98–99, 253, 261, 274
    chairman of, 2, 82
Democratic Party
    6 for '06 agenda, 8, 10, 12–13, 23–24, 33, 41, 48
    2004 election, xvii–xviii
    2006 election, xviii, 2–3, 12, 287–288
    2008 presidential nomination, 96, 98, 105
    2010 elections, 185, 269, 272–273, 274
    A New Direction for America, 8–10, 23
    disagreements within, 35–36, 40
    financial crisis and, 113–114, 115

legislative priorities, 44, 124, 155, 244, 293
    Obama and, 263, 274, 294
    public opinion of, 13, 41, 48, 91, 255, 259–260, 270
    Republicans and, 42, 48, 278, 280, 284
Dingell, John
    auto industry aid, 120–121, 132
    CAFE bill debate, 65, 66–67
    criticism of, 11, 67
    energy bill, 62, 69
    Markey and, 26
    Pelosi and, 25, 27, 66, 126–127, 129
Dodd, Christopher, 108–109, 118, 180, 184, 248
Dodd-Frank Wall Street Reform, 247–249
"Don't Ask, Don't Tell" (DADT) policy, 244–245, 281–282
Doyle, Mike, 15, 189
DREAM Act, 281
Driehaus, Steve, 239, 335n3
Duncan, Arne, 226
Durbin, Dick
    appointment to National Commission on Fiscal Responsibility, 335n23
    climate issues and, 166
    health care bill and, 194
    Iraq policy and, 74, 97
    on Republicans, 156, 280
    stimulus bill and, 147

earmarks practice, 38–39, 45, 157–159
Edwards, Chet, 64, 105, 305n16
Elmendorf, Doug, 187
Emanuel, Rahm
    2010 congressional elections, 266
    auto industry bailout and, 133, 137
    CAFE bill debate, 62, 66, 133
    Clintons and, 102
    Democratic policy and, 8, 35
    health care bill and, 179, 182, 184, 188, 189, 197, 200–201, 218, 328n13
    on Iraq War, 75–76
    negotiations with PhRMA, 182
    Pelosi and, 129, 263, 339n14
    political career, 2, 19, 124, 125, 270
    Reyes' appointment and, 16
    stimulus bill and, 115, 142, 148
    Waxman's declaration and, 126

Employment Non-Discrimination Act
    (ENDA), 43–44, 244–245, 292
Energy and Commerce Committee, 125,
    127–128
energy policy, 60, 62, 69, 174–175, 246,
    304n6
Energy Policy and Conservation Act, 60
Enzi, Mike, 184, 309n31
Eshoo, Anna, 25, 126, 272, 327n58

Feingold, Russ, 33, 78, 137, 248
financial crisis of 2008
    appropriation of foreclosed property, 109
    bailout schemes, 109, 111, 114, 117, 119–120
    Bush administration and, 108, 109–110
    causes of, 108, 109, 117, 121, 316n47
    Congressional debates on, 110–112
    economic advisors on, 109–110
    "Paulson Plan," 114
    recovery measures, 52–58, 94–95, 131–132,
        141–143, 153, 161, 261, 336n42
    Wall Street failure, 95, 108–109
Foley, Mark, 3
Foreign Intelligence Service Act (FISA),
    41–42
Frank, Barney
    auto industry bailout bill, 136
    DADT repeal and, 244–245
    Employment Non-Discrimination Act
        and, 43
    financial crisis and, 108–109, 111, 114, 116,
        132
    health care bill and, 8
    Pelosi and, 18, 260
    tax cut bill and, 58
Franken, Al, 123, 130, 178
Frumin, Alan, 217, 222

Gates, Robert, 79, 129, 230, 312n51
Geithner, Tim, 121, 122, 140, 160, 319n8
General Motors (GM), 120, 137, 319n32
George, Cardinal Francis, 189
Gersh, Mark, 264, 271
Gerstein, Jim, 164, 181
Gettlefinger, Ron, 62, 127
Gibbs, Robert, 147, 265–266
Gingrich, Newt, xiv, xvii, 14, 341n66
Glass-Steagall Act, 109, 315n10

Gonzales, Alberto, 3, 4, 16, 51
Gore, Al, xiii, 60, 63, 102
    climate policy and, 165, 169, 170, 171, 172,
        173–174
    Clintons and, 103
Goss, Porter, 16
Grassley, Chuck, 139, 181, 184, 186, 190–191, 221
Greenberg, Stan, 1, 147, 262
Gregg, Judd, 111, 115, 241, 335n23
Gregg-Conrad initiative, 162
Guantánamo Bay prison, 229

Hacker, Jacob, 195
Hagel, Chuck, 35, 77, 333n4
Hall, John, 11, 215, 303n16
Harkin, Tom, 143
Harman, Jane, 16, 301n12
Hastert, Dennis, 3–4, 5, 20, 22, 302n31,
    341n66
Hatch, Orrin, 46, 154, 309n31
Hayden, Michael, 129, 318n29
health care bill
    abortion issue, 189–190, 207–208, 215,
        223–224
    amendments, 207, 223, 329n36
    Blue Dogs and, 182, 184–185, 186, 188–
        189, 190, 326n35
    Cadillac plans, 182–183, 185, 186, 211–212,
        213, 215, 220
    church leaders and, 223
    cost of, 202, 214, 215
    Democrats' position on, 182–183
    drafting of, 179, 208
    Finance committee vote on, 205
    House debate on, 191, 197, 206, 240
    House vote on, 206, 209–210, 224
    issue of undocumented immigrants, 182,
        205–206
    Medicaid expansion, 190
    opposition to, 181, 192–193, 202
    Pelosi and, 183
    promotion of, 180, 183–184, 194, 209
    public opinion about, 194–196, 204, 205,
        213–214, 223
    reconciliation vs. comprehensive version,
        215–218, 220, 221, 222, 225
    Republicans' position on, 180–181, 184,
        185, 188, 190

Senate debate on, 181–182, 186, 188, 196, 201–203, 205, 211, 213, 214
Senate vote on, 198, 208, 212
signing ceremony, 224–225
vote for reconciliation bill, 222–223
See also Affordable Care Act (ACA)
Herseth-Sandlin, Stephanie, 203, 223, 327n57
"Honest Leadership-Open Government" (HLOG) bill, 32, 39
House of Representatives
 ban on smoking in, 27
 bipartisanship efforts, 142–143
 Black caucus, 116, 117, 128, 157, 182
 committee appointments, 14–16, 129
 debates of financial crisis, 91, 93, 115–117
 diversity of appointed officials, 27
 Hispanic caucus, 116, 117, 128, 164, 182
 opposition to earmarks, 157, 158
 restriction on bundling campaign contributions, 39
 revisions of rules of, 14, 15
 Senate's relationships with, 87, 196–197
 seniority system, 14, 128, 275, 317n14
 White House and, 51–52, 87, 147, 249
House Select Committee on Climate Change, 61
Hoyer, Steny
 2010 congressional elections, 267, 269, 271
 Blue Dogs and, 70, 142
 as caucus chair, 17, 18–19
 climate bill and, 70, 171
 committee appointments and, 129, 275
 funding requests, 20–21
 health care bill and, 180, 182, 187, 209–210, 220, 289
 "Make It in America" (MIIA) plan, 253
 Pelosi and, 11, 192
 position on earmarks, 157
 on Republicans, 163, 239–240, 279
 TARP bill and, 117, 118–119
Hulse, Carl, 173
Human Rights Coalition (HRC), 43
Hurricane Katrina, 5, 6, 22, 47, 174, 300n33

Ickes, Harold, Jr., 99, 100
Iglesias, David, 51, 307n6
immigration bill, 164, 172, 342n15

Inconvenient Truth, An (film), 63
inheritance tax, 343n35
Inouye, Daniel, 66, 158, 263, 334n32
Inslee, Jay, 206, 303n16
Iraq
 sectarian violence in, 74
 transformation of the US mission in, 79
Iraq Study Group, 75, 76
Iraq War
 causes of, 7
 congressional debates on, 6, 77–78, 81–82, 84–86, 93–94
 cost of, 34–35, 47, 163, 228
 diplomatic initiatives to end, 73–74, 76
 opposition to, 31, 72, 73, 76–77, 83
 Pelosi and, 6
 protests against, 7
 Republicans and, 75
 Responsible Redeployment from Iraq Act, 83
 US troops withdrawal from, 76, 77, 78, 80, 81, 84, 228, 232, 234, 238

Jackson, Barry, 270
Jefferson, Bill, 4–5, 11, 300n30
Johnson, Jim, 105

Kagen, Steve, 195, 267, 335n3
Kantor, Mickey, 98
Karzai, Hamid, 231, 232, 234, 236
Keehan, Carol, 212
Kennedy, Ted, 78, 91–92
 endorsement of Obama, 97
 HELP panel, 178–179
 illness, 144, 179, 182, 188, 198, 321n58
Kerry, John, xviii, 102, 109, 166, 167
Khosla, Vinod, 165
King, Peter, 233
Kirk, Paul, 199, 328n2
K Street Project, 39
Kucinich, Dennis, 76, 173, 208, 223, 236, 266, 324n37, 326n14, 336n48
Kyl, John, 143, 221, 309n31

Lake, Celinda, 48, 124, 181
Lakoff, George, 8, 299n8
Landrieu, Mary, 33, 178
Lantos, Tom, 76, 311n24

Larson, John
  2010 congressional elections and, 266,
    274
  bill on removal of US forces from Iraq, 78
  cap-and-trade bill and, 167, 266, 268
  as caucus chair, 125
  on Reid, 218
  on Senate, 289
  tax cut bill and, 286
Lehman Brothers, 108
Levin, Carl, 63, 85, 120, 333n4
Levin, Sandy, 132
Lew, Jack, 283
Lewis, John, 5, 224
Lieberman, Joe, 33, 68, 167, 332n54
Lincoln, Blanche, 33, 332n54, 332n64,
    336n34
Livingood, Wilson "Bill," 14, 270, 334n2
Low-Income Home Energy Assistance
    Program (LIHEAP), 44
Lugar, Richard, 281

Maffei, Dan, 206, 340n52
Majority Makers, 288, 292
Maliki, Nouri al-
  corruption of, 84, 231
  efforts at national reconciliation, 73
  political weakness of, 83, 85
  sectarian violence under, 74
Maloney, Carolyn, 15, 105, 283
Manchin, Joe, 68, 104, 176, 325n55
Markey, Ed, 14, 127, 167, 168–169, 177, 341n58
Markey-Rahall arrangement, 127
Mark Foley scandal, 3
Massa, Eric, 172
Matheson, Jim, 64, 169, 170, 190
Matzzie, Tom, 31, 80
McCain, John
  criticism of earmarks, 158
  financial crisis of 2008 and, 95, 109, 113,
    114–115
  presidential nomination, 106
  on SCHIP bill, 139
  vote on commission on Social Security
    commission, 335n17
McCarrick, Theodore, Cardinal, 207,
    330n45

McChrystal, Stanley, 235, 237
McConnell, Mitch, 29
  9/11 victims' assistance bill and, 36, 40, 284
  2010 congressional elections, 269
  auto industry and, 132, 136, 137
  CAFE bill and, 65
  continuing resolutions and, 34
  Democrats and, 54, 163
  health care bill and, 179
  "Honest Leadership and Open
    Government" bill and, 39
  inquiry into torture allegations and, 229
  Iraq War and, 75, 81
  Obama and, 251, 269, 274, 337n71
  position on earmarks, 45
  procedural delays, 57
  stimulus bill and, 122, 123, 140–141, 142,
    143, 145, 151
  tax cut bill and, 279, 285
McCurry, Mike, 13, 253
McDermott, Jim, 77, 324n37
McDonough, Denis, 231
McGovern, Jim, 157
Medicaid program, 177, 337n71
Medicare, 162, 177, 193, 337n71
Melançon, Charlie, 170, 190, 309n29, 340n52
Mellman, Mark, 181
Messina, Jim, 263, 264, 294
Meyer, Dan, 48, 95, 116
Miers, Harriet, 51, 307n5
Miller, George, xiii, xvii, 97, 157
  2010 congressional elections, 266, 268, 269
  auto industry bailout and, 137
  health care bill and, 182, 184, 226
  Pelosi and, 37, 98, 272, 275, 286
Miller, Lorraine, 27
Mineta, Norm, 271, 341n62
Minnick, Walt, 216
Mollohan, Alan, 4, 302n16
motion to recommit, 252
Move On movement, 31, 76, 82, 83, 85
Murkowski, Lisa, 251, 281
Murphy, Patrick, 282
Murtha, Jack
  2008 presidential nomination and, 102
  Afghan War and, 230
  death of, 236

Pelosi and, 17–19
position on earmarks, 158
US troops withdrawal from Iraq and,
83–84
Waxman's declaration and, 126, 128
Myrick, Gary, 31, 308n34
health care bill and, 218
Iraq war and, 45, 77
stimulus bill and, 148, 158, 164, 271
tax cut bill and, 257

Nabors, Rob, 143, 152
Nathan, Irvin, 47, 51
National Commission on Fiscal
Responsibility and Reform, 242, 243,
335n23
Nelson, Ben, 148, 166, 288, 332n54, 342n15
New Direction for America initiative, 8–10,
23–24
New Partnership for America's Future, xvii,
298n15
Ney, Bob, 2
9/11 victims assistance bill, 252–253, 278,
283–284
Nowakowski, Paula, 114, 116

Obama, Barack
2010 congressional election and, 263, 265,
268, 270
Afghan policy, 229–230, 235–236
auto industry and, 134–136
on bankers, 248
bipartisanship of, 107, 125, 142, 145, 154–
156, 160, 162–163, 179, 240, 290–291
Blair House conference, 219
Blue Dogs and, 129, 151, 186, 250
climate policy, 166, 167–168, 171
congressional politics and, 52, 157, 179,
280
Copenhagen Climate Change
Conference address, 174–175
Deepwater Horizon disaster and, 246
economic policy, 261, 281
energy agenda, 246
executive orders, 242, 291
financial crisis of 2008 and, 113, 114, 115
on George W. Bush, 185

health care bill, 177, 180, 183–184, 186,
193–194, 197, 200–202, 204, 209–210,
214, 215, 219, 221, 223–225
House Democrats and, 101, 146–147, 196,
226, 260, 265–266, 290
Iraq policy, 97, 230–231
Pelosi and, 52, 103–104, 123, 125–126, 133,
135, 138, 139, 144, 152, 154, 159–161, 192,
210, 259, 261, 265, 295, 332n67
presidential election, 96, 99, 101, 103,
104–105, 106, 113, 123–125
security detail, 97
stimulus package, 133, 141–142, 145, 148
tax cuts, 141–142, 145, 279, 285
view of public opinion, 195, 196, 197
Obama, Michelle, 257, 258
Obama administration
cost of policies of, 330n10, 331n12
criticism of, 125, 159, 163, 164
DACA policy of, 323n40
deficit spending, 133–134
earmarks practice, 157–158, 159
economic policy, 122, 124, 135, 160, 161–
162, 261–262
fiscal policy, 134, 141, 143–144
health care reform, 180–181
LGBTQ policy, 281
marketing strategies, 154, 246, 336n42
military spending, 163
omnibus bill, 156–157, 158, 322n8
Obama's Deal broadcast, 239
Obey, David, 39, 44, 82, 143
on Columbia agreement, 90
health care bill and, 195
legislative priorities, 250
on Obama administration, 106–107, 231
on "obstructionism" of the White House, 88
opposition to abortion, 40
spending cuts and, 241
support of earmarks, 157, 158, 159
Occupy Wall Street movement, 122
offshore drilling, 174, 246
109th United States Congress
6 for '06 agenda, 24
ethics enforcement, 25
legislative priorities, 24
threatened filibusters, 23–24

110th United States Congress
  abortion issue, 40
  bipartisan compromises, 94
  budget confrontation, 44–45
  domestic surveillance bill, 41–42
  ethics enforcement, 39
  immigration reform, 35, 36
  legislative agenda, 31–32, 33, 36–38, 39, 41,
    46, 47, 50
  transparency reform, 32–33, 39
111th United States Congress
  committee appointments, 128–129
  legislative agenda, 239, 289
  productivity of, 140, 286
112th United States Congress, 279, 287
Ornstein, Norm, 274, 286
Orszag, Peter, 150, 178, 187

"Pain in the Gas" anti-leasing campaign, 69
Palin, Sarah, 69, 106
Paulson, Henry
  financial crisis of 2008 and, 108, 109,
    110–111, 112, 114, 115, 116, 121
  on housing legislation, 110
  Pelosi and, 55, 92, 108
  recovery package debate, 52, 53, 55–57,
    58–59
  on stimulus measures, 55, 132
Pay As You Go (Paygo) rule, 8, 21, 32
Pelosi, Nancy
  6 for '06 agenda, 21
  2008 Democratic presidential nomi-
    nation and, 97–98, 99–100, 101, 102
  2010 congressional elections, 263, 264–
    265, 266, 267–268, 269, 270, 271–272
  Afghan War and, 231, 232–233
  aid to auto industry and, 61, 132–136
  on banks, 248
  Baucus and, 89
  Biden and, 234, 242, 282–283, 286
  on bipartisanship, 21
  Bloomberg and, 252–253
  on Blue Dogs, 188
  on Boehner, 107
  Bush and, 1–2, 46, 47
  child nutrition bill and, 259, 285
  climate policy and, 60, 166, 167, 168–169,
    172, 173, 175–176
  Commerce Committee chairman election
    and, 128
  on cooperation with Republicans, 162–
    163, 163, 179–180
  critics of, 11, 79, 82, 192, 233, 270
  DADT bill and, 244–245, 281–282
  on deficit spending, 133, 242, 243
  Dingell and, 66, 68
  Dodd-Frank bill and, 248–249
  on Emanuel, 270–271
  ENDA bill and, 43–44, 244–245
  endorsement of Murtha, 18–19
  energy reform and, 60–62, 68, 175–176
  ethics reform and, 4
  financial crisis of 2008 and, 108, 110, 112,
    113, 114
  foreign trips, 78–79, 152, 236, 311n24
  governing style, 18, 29–30, 46, 130, 295
  "Green the Capitol" (GTC) initiative,
    70, 71
  health care bill and, 180–197, 199–202, 207,
    212–214, 217–218, 220–221, 222–225
  on Hillary Clinton, 100
  House official appointments, 16, 27, 129,
    140, 303n16
  immigration reform, 35, 164
  on impeachment of Bush, 21
  on institutional tension in Congress,
    289–290
  Iraq War and, 42, 76–77, 78, 79–82, 85, 86
  Jefferson corruption case and, 5
  leadership style, 8, 22, 48–49, 278, 291–
    292, 299n7
  legislative agenda, 88–90, 92, 135, 161, 249,
    255, 304n7
  Mark Foley scandal and, 3
  Michelle Obama and, 258
  use of military plane, 270, 341n57
  Miller and, 272, 275
  Murtha and, 17
  New Republic profile of, 49
  9/11 victims' assistance bill and, 283
  Obama and, 52, 103–104, 123, 125–126,
    133, 135, 138, 139, 144, 152, 154, 159–161,
    192, 210, 259, 261, 265, 295, 332n67
  partisan politics, 102–103
  personality of, xiii, xvii, 16, 29–30, 37, 52,
    70, 106, 287, 291–292

political career of, xiv, xv, xv–xvii, 12–13, 23, 328n2
position on earmarks, 158–159
Rahall and, 15
on Reid, 156
security protocol, 14, 19–20
Senate and, 92, 179, 256, 291
on seniority system, 128
stimulus bill and, 56–59, 91, 124–125, 131–132, 135, 139, 140–141, 149–150, 152
TARP bill and, 116–119
torture controversy and, 233–234
use of military plane, 270, 341n57
US-Mexico border wall and, 299n7
value of loyalty, 18, 138
Wednesday breakfasts, 22
White House and, 52, 54–55, 74, 160, 239, 247, 250, 253–254, 257–258, 264–265
Pence, Mike, 184, 269
Perriello, Tom, 192, 259, 274, 296, 335n3
Peterson, Collin
American Clean Energy and Security Act and, 173
child nutrition bill, 258
climate bill and, 166, 170, 171–172
Pelosi and, 169, 171–172
Petraeus, David, 81, 84–85, 86, 232
PhRMA (Pharmaceutical Research and Manufacturers of America), 182
Pickens, T. Boone, 165
Pigford-Cobell settlements for minority farmers, 282
Plouffe, David, 101
pocket vetoes, 47–48
Pope, Carl, 64, 170
Putnam, Adam, 20, 270

Rahall, Nick Joe, 14–15, 67, 70, 311n24
Randolph, Jennings, 70, 168
Rangel, Charlie, 46, 215, 217
on Afghan War, 228
climate bill and, 170
health care bill and, 182, 185
Jefferson corruption scandal and, 5
tax cut debate and, 34
real estate market crisis, 42–43
Redford, Robert, 63, 165, 169

Reid, Harry, 335n23
2008 presidential election and, 33
2010 congressional election, 263, 268, 273
auto industry and, 132, 137
Bill Clinton and, 99
CAFE bill debate, 65, 67
cap-and-trade bill and, 167, 174, 251
Dodd-Frank bill and, 247–248
on ENDA, 244, 245
financial crisis of 2008 and, 111–112, 113, 115–116
health care bill and, 178–179, 182, 185, 186, 187, 188, 190–191, 197, 200, 207, 211, 212, 213, 216, 222
Hurricane Katrina reconstruction and, 47
immigration bill and, 35, 164
Iraq War and, 74–75, 80, 81, 82, 86, 333n4
neutrality of, 102–103
9/11 victims' assistance bill and, 283, 284
Obama and, 69, 104–105, 125, 157–158, 160
Pelosi and, 45, 46, 88, 130
position on earmarks, 45, 157, 158, 159
as Senate leader, 32, 46, 57, 156, 288, 289
stimulus bill and, 53–54, 57, 89, 92, 131–132, 133, 141, 144, 149, 150, 161
tax cut bill and, 279, 285
renewable electricity standards, 165, 167
Republican Party
2010 Congressional elections, 264, 272–273
bipartisanship efforts and, 142–143
climate bill and, 166, 172
culture of, 2
delays of confirmation of presidential appointees, 240–241
Democrats and, 277–278, 284
extremist turn, 295
financial crisis and, 113, 115, 116
health care bill and, 180–181, 184–188, 190
Iraq War and, 75
obstruction of legislation, 252, 254
stimulus bill and, 135, 145–146, 147, 150, 153
tax cut extension and, 278, 279, 343n36
"Restoring the American Dream," 42
Reuther, Alan, 26, 63
Ricchetti, Steve, 253
Rice, Condoleezza, 76, 79, 84, 312n51
Roberts, Cecil, 169, 170
Roemer, Tim, 98

Romney, Mitt, 180
Roosevelt, Franklin, 177
Ross, Mike, 166, 170, 184, 186, 189, 190
Rouse, Pete, 125, 271
Rove, Karl, 5, 50
Rush, Bobby, 172, 327n58
Ryan, Paul, 243, 270, 335n23
Ryan White Comprehensive AIDS
    Resources Emergency Act, 332n67

Samuel, Bill, 63
Sanders, Bernie, 33, 137, 178, 290, 336n48
Sarbanes, John, 18, 68
Scarborough, Joe, 117
Schakowsky, Jan, 8, 190, 243, 335n23
Schiliro, Phil
    health care bill and, 200–201, 218, 221,
        225–226
    Pelosi and, 146, 250
    stimulus bill and, 131, 135, 144, 148, 156,
        160, 271
SCHIP bill (Children's Health Insurance
    Program), 46, 139–140, 155, 162
Schumer, Chuck, 113, 340n42
    9/11 first responders bill and, 253
    health care bill and, 221
    Obama and, 97, 280
    on Senate Rule XXII, 289
    stimulus bill and, 153, 155
    tax cut debate and, 34
Schwarzenegger, Arnold, 69, 160
Sebelius, Kathy, 105, 194
Select Committee on Energy Independence
    and Global Warming, 25–27
Sensenbrenner, Jim, 120
Shelby, Richard, 114, 115, 136
Shimkus, John, 3
Shinseki, John, 73
Simpson, Alan, 243
Simpson-Bowles report, 278–279
Sinai, Alan, 108
Skelton, Ike, 48, 73
Skinner, Samuel, 271, 341n62
Slaughter, Louise, 156, 180, 197, 270, 335n3
Sloan, Melanie, 17
Snowe, Olympia, 33, 148, 149, 190, 333n4
    health care bill and, 184, 186, 188
Social Security, 145, 162, 242, 243, 262, 288

Sosnick, Doug, 41, 299n8
Space, Zack, 68, 167, 190, 206
Specter, Arlen, 22, 33, 147, 149, 178
spending cuts debates, 241, 243–244
Spratt, John, 78, 301n12, 335n23
Stabenow, Debbie, 63, 67, 168
Stark, Pete, 173, 198
Steele, Michael, 270
Stern, Andy, 31, 335n23
stimulus bill
    bipartisanship approach to, 146
    Blue Dogs and, 142, 146, 147
    House debate of, 54–57, 91, 93, 146
    marketing of, 246, 336n42
    Obama administration and, 124, 135,
        141–142, 148–149
    Pelosi and, 56–57, 59, 89, 131–132, 135, 139,
        140, 149–150, 152
    Republicans and, 140–141, 142, 143, 145,
        146, 147, 151
    Senate debate, 140–141, 147–149, 150, 154
Strategic Arms Reduction Treaty
    (START), 286
Stupak, Bart, 166, 240
Summers, Larry, 140, 144, 153, 161
supplemental appropriations for 2010 fiscal
    year, 250–251
Sutton, Betty, 15
Sweeney, John, 41, 59, 127

Tanner, John, 91
tax policies, 141–142, 163, 256–257, 278,
    285–286, 318n8, 337n76, 343n35
Tea Party, 122, 192–193, 199, 264, 293
Trade Adjustment Assistance (TAA)
    Program, 44, 53
Transportation Security Administration
    (TSA), 40–41
Troubled Assets Relief Program (TARP)
    auto industry bailout and, 136
    bipartisan support of, 118–119, 121–122, 125
    congressional debate on, 116–117, 141,
        142, 145
    public opinion on, 119, 261
    Treasury profit from, 115
    vote on, 118–119, 293
Trout, Jack, 2, 262, 277, 278
Trumka, Richard, 62, 212, 267

Trump, Donald
auto industry regulations, 132
economic policy, 122
influence of, 295
"Make America Great Again" message, 267
rise to power, 264
2006 Congressional elections, xviii, 1, 2–3, 12, 287, 288
2008 presidential election, 96, 99, 101, 103, 104–105, 106, 113, 123–125
2010 Congressional elections
ads spending, 270
Democrats' strategy in, 262, 264, 265–267, 268
House seats, 272–273
Republican strategy in, 262–263, 264, 267, 268, 269, 340n42

unemployment insurance, 93, 131, 133
unemployment rate, 88–89, 93, 95, 159, 259, 275, 293
upper income tax cut (UITC)
negotiation of extension of, 279, 280, 285
vote on, 343n36
US attorneys (USAs), firing of, 50–51
US Congress
conditions to war appropriations, 75
debate of financial crisis, 110–112, 121
institutional tensions, 289–290
legislative process, 288–289
partisan divide, 294–295
US House of Representatives
ban on smoking in, 27
bipartisanship efforts, 142–143
Black caucus, 116, 117, 128, 157, 182
diversity of appointed officials, 27
Hispanic caucus, 116, 117, 128, 164, 182
revisions of rules of, 14–15
Senate's relationships with, 87, 196–197
seniority system, 14, 128, 275, 317n14
White House and, 51–52, 87, 147, 249
US Senate
bipartisanship efforts and, 142–143
child nutrition bill debate, 284–285
climate bill debate, 165, 167–168, 171–173

defeat of Social Security commission, 242
disagreements between House and, 196–197
filibusters, 87–88, 93, 138
financial crisis of 2008 and, 55, 112–114
health care bill debate, 178, 181–182, 186, 188
ineffectiveness of, 255, 294
position on earmarks, 158–159
Republican obstructionism, 240
rules and procedures, 288, 289
SCHIP bill and, 139–140

Van Hollen, Chris, 82, 269, 271
on Democrats' campaign strategy, 262
political career of, 124–125, 272
on Republicans, 279
Veterans of Foreign Wars, 271
Vilsack, Tom, 171, 258, 282

Wagner, Carl, 103
Warner, John, 68, 82, 84
Wasserman-Schultz, Debbie, 190, 206
Waxman, Henry
AIDS law and, 332n67
climate bill and, 168, 169–170, 172
Energy and Commerce Committee leadership, 125–126, 128
health care bill and, 184, 189, 190, 191, 215
on Markey, 167
support of clean air legislation, 26, 62
Waxman-Markey cap-and-trade bill, 293
Weiner, Anthony, 208
Weinstein, Harvey, 102
Wilkie, Robert, 20
Wilson, Joe, 202
Wolfson, Howard, 42
Women, Infants and Children (WIC) nutrition program, 44
Wounded Warriors program, 28

Yanowitch, Richard, 299n8
Young, Don, 157

Zandi, Mark, 244